Competition Policy in the EU

Competition Policy in the EU

Fifty Years on from the Treaty of Rome

Edited by
Xavier Vives

OXFORD
UNIVERSITY PRESS

OXFORD
UNIVERSITY PRESS

Great Clarendon Street, Oxford OX2 6DP

Oxford University Press is a department of the University of Oxford.
It furthers the University's objective of excellence in research, scholarship,
and education by publishing worldwide in

Oxford New York

Auckland Cape Town Dar es Salaam Hong Kong Karachi
Kuala Lumpur Madrid Melbourne Mexico City Nairobi
New Delhi Shanghai Taipei Toronto

With offices in

Argentina Austria Brazil Chile Czech Republic France Greece
Guatemala Hungary Italy Japan Poland Portugal Singapore
South Korea Switzerland Thailand Turkey Ukraine Vietnam

Oxford is a registered trade mark of Oxford University Press
in the UK and in certain other countries

Published in the United States
by Oxford University Press Inc., New York

© Oxford University Press 2009

British Library Cataloguing in Publication Data
Data available

Library of Congress Cataloging in Publication Data
Data available

Typeset by SPI Publisher Services, Pondicherry, India
Printed in Great Britain
on acid-free paper by
the MPG Books Group, Bodmin and King's Lynn

ISBN 978-0-19-956635-8

1 3 5 7 9 10 8 6 4 2

Preface

This book is the product of a conference organized by the Public–Private Sector Research Center of IESE Business School on November 19–20, 2007, in commemoration of the 50 years of the Treaty of Rome and of the 50 years of IESE. The aim of the conference was to take stock of and to look ahead at the development and implementation of competition policy in the European Union. I hope that the book contributes to advance our knowledge on the application of economics to competition policy, to a better design of law and of institutions, and to transatlantic convergence (inasmuch as this is efficient).

The encouragement and support of the dean of IESE, Jordi Canals, has been crucial for the successful completion of the project. The support of the Abertis Chair of Regulation, Competition, and Public Policy and of the Departament d'Economia i Finances and Departament d'Innovació, Universitats i Empresa of the Generalitat de Catalunya (Government of Catalonia) is gratefully acknowledged.

I would also like to thank Commissioner Neelie Kroes for opening the conference, former Commissioners Mario Monti and Karel van Miert for presenting closing remarks, and all the discussants and panel participants: Peter Alexiadis, Arnoud Boot, Rachel Brandenburger, Carles Esteva-Mosso, John Fingleton, Ian Forrester, Vivek Ghosal, Richard Gilbert, Chris Giles, Enrique González-Díaz, William Kolasky, Kai-Uwe Kühn, Massimo Merola, Patrick Rey, Paul Seabright, John Swift, Nils-Henrik von der Fehr, Mike Waterson, and Wouter Wils. Sofia Anisimova, Coloma Casaus, Salvador Estapé, Albert Farré-Escofet, and Lidia Pradas provided efficient support to the project at different stages.

The Public-Private Sector Research Center was established in 2001. Its mission is to foster cooperation between the private sector and public administration through research and education. The main objectives of the Center are to promote high quality scientific research and about the the business sector and public administration and to consolidate a group of international research excellence in the following fields: regulation and competition, innovation, and regional economics and industrial policy.

The sponsors of the Center are: Accenture, Ajuntament de Barcelona, Caixa Manresa, Cambra de Comerç de Barcelona, Consell de l'Audiovisual de Catalunya, Departament d'Economia i Finances i Departament d'Innovació, Universitats i Empresa of the Generalitat de Catalunya, Diputació de Barcelona, Endesa, Fundació Agbar, Garrigues, Mediapro, Microsoft sanofi-aventis, and VidaCaixa.

Public-Private Sector Research Center

Contents

Contents

Contents

List of Figures

List of Tables

Abbreviations

AA	Anti-trust Authorities
ABA	American Bar Association
ACE	Association for Competition Economics
AEA	American Economic Association
ATP	Airline Tariff Publishers
B2B	business-to-business
BGH	Bundesgerichtshof [Federal Supreme Court]
CAR	cumulative abnormal return
CCE	Chief Competition Economist
CCP	Centre for Competition Policy
CD	collective dominance
CE	coordinated effects
CECED	Conseil Européen de la Construction d'appareils Domestiques [European Committee of Domestic Equipment Manufacturers]
CEMFI	Center for Monetary and Financial Studies
CEPR	Center for Economic Policy Research
CET	Chief Economist's Team
CFI	Court of First Instance
CMLR	Common Market Law Report
CRD	Capital Requirements Directive
DG Comp	Directorate-General for Competition
DG	Directorate-General
DGCCRF	Direction générale de la concurrence, de la consommation et de la répression des fraudes [General Directorate for Fair Trading, Consumer Affairs and Fraud Control]
DoJ	Department of Justice
DOT	Department of Transportation
DT	dominance test
DTI	Department of Trade and Industry

EAGCP	Economic Advisory Group on Competition Policy
EARIE	European Association for Research in Industrial Economics
EC	European Communities
ECJ	European Court of Justice
ECM	electronic communications' market
ECMR	European Community Merger Regulation
ECN	European competition network
ECPR	efficient component-pricing rule
ECR	European Court Reports
ECT	European Commission Treaty
EEA	European Economic Association
EMU	Economic and Monetary Union
ERG	European Regulators Group
ERGEG	European Regulators Group for Electricity and Gas
EU	European Union
EUI	European University Institute
FDC	fully distributed cost
FEEM	Fondazione Eni Enrico Mattei
FSAP	Financial Services Action Plan
FTC	Federal Trade Commission
HHI	Herfindahl-Hirschman Index
HM	horizontal merger
HMSO	Her Majesty's Stationery Office
ICN	International Competition Network
IDEI	Institut d'Économie Industrielle
IERP	Institute for Energy Research and Policy
IESE	Instituto de Estudios Superiores de la Empresa Business School, Universidad de Navarra
IO	Industrial Organization
IPTV	television over Internet Provider
LLU	local loop unbundling
LOLR	lender of last resort
LRIC	long-run incremental cost
M&A	merger(s) and acquisition(s)
MIF	Multilateral Interchange Fee
MPSE	Midi-Pyrénées School of Economics at the Université des Sciences Sociales, Toulouse

Abbreviations

MTF	Merger Task Force
NBER	National Bureau of Economic Research
NGN	next generation network
NHM	non-horizontal merger
NRA	National Regulatory Authority
NTA	New Transatlantic Agenda
OECD	Organisation for Economic Co-operation and Development
OEM	original equipment manufacturer
OFT	Office of Fair Trading
OLG	Oberlandesgericht [Higher Regional Court]
R&D&I	Research, Development, and Innovation
RPM	retail price maintenance
S&Ls	savings and loan associations
SAAP	state aid action plan
SCP	Structure–Conduct–Performance
SEPA	Single Euro Payments Area
SIEC	significant impediment to effective competition
SLC	substantial lessening of competition
SMP	significant market power
SP–SP	Public–Private Sector Research Center, IESE Business School, Universidad de Navarra
USO	Universal Service Obligation
VoIP	voice over Internet Provider

Country abbreviations

A	Austria
Aus	Australia
B	Belgium
Can	Canada
D	Germany
DK	Denmark
E	Spain
EL	Greece
F	France
FIN	Finland
I	Italy

Ice	Iceland
IRL	Ireland
Jap	Japan
Kor	Republic of Korea
L	Luxembourg
Mex	Mexico
NL	Netherlands
Nze	New Zealand
P	Portugal
S	Sweden
Swi	Switzerland
UK	United Kingdom
USA	United States of America

List of Contributors

Matthew Bennett *Director of Economics, Office of Fair Trading, London*

Elena Carletti *Professor of Economics, European University Institute, Florence*

Richard Green *Director of the Institute for Energy Research and Policy, University of Birmingham*

Jordi Gual *Professor of Economics, IESE Business School, Universidad de Navarra and Chief Economist, Research Department "la Caixa"*

Martin Hellwig *Director, Max Planck Institute for Research on Collective Goods, Bonn, and Member of the Law and Economics Faculty, Universität Bonn*

Sandra Jódar-Rosell *Economist, Research Department, "la Caixa"*

William E. Kovacic *Commissioner of the US Federal Trade Commission*

Philip Lowe *Director-General of the Directorate-General for Competition at the European Commission*

Bruce Lyons *Professor of Economics, ESCR Centre for Competition Policy, University of East Anglia*

Massimo Motta *Professor of Economics, Università di Bologna*

A. Jorge Padilla *European Chief Executive Officer of LECG*

David Spector *Professor of Economics, Centre National de la Recherche Scientifique and Paris School of Economics*

John Vickers *Professor of Political Economy, Warden, All Souls College, University of Oxford*

Xavier Vives *Professor of Economics and Finance, Director of the Public-Private Sector Research Center, IESE Business School, Universidad de Navarra*

1

Introduction: Competition Policy in Europe

Xavier Vives[1]

1.1. The Treaty of Rome

Fifty years ago, in 1957, the Treaty of Rome established the foundations of competition policy in Europe; prior to that there were different national traditions with different objectives (in Germany and in the UK, for example) or no policies whatsoever, such as in southern Europe. In contrast, the United States established a competition policy tradition at the end of the nineteenth century with the Sherman Act. Many things have happened since then. For one thing, antitrust objectives have converged (mostly) on both sides of the Atlantic into economic efficiency and consumer welfare. The United States has lead the way. In Europe, the market integration mandate still looms large (and sometimes enters into conflict with the economic efficiency objective). However, the self-proclaimed mission statement of the Directorate-General for Competition of the European Commission has changed from an emphasis on market integration in the 1990s to one of making 'markets operate as efficiently as possible'. In any case, today there is consensus that competition is the driving force for economic efficiency and for the welfare of society.

Competitive markets, or competitive pressure in imperfectly competitive markets, are seen as crucial determinants of the welfare of citizens. This is not, however, assumed naively, on the basis of a premise that there are no frictions in markets and that laissez-faire will always deliver optimal results. The role of competition is instead understood after years of accumulated learning concerning the functioning of imperfect markets. Indeed one of the main driving forces of transatlantic convergence has been the application of economic reasoning grounded in the analysis of industrial organization using 'game theory' and empirical methods as a fundamental toolbox. The evolution in analysis has been from the Structure–Conduct–Performance paradigm to the application of game theoretical tools and sophisticated empirical methods, recognizing also the 'Chicago' critique of the naive market power hypotheses. The result has been a common framework of analysis which has proved a very powerful convergence force because it increases the transparency of the assumptions made in the analysis and the procedures employed to reach conclusions. It can be checked by independent observers and can be falsified.

Competition policy is about the welfare of citizens. This is why competition policy is so important and so central on both sides of the Atlantic (and increasingly in the emerging economies)—the more so in Europe where competition has been seen with suspicion from different quarters, and the lack of competition in some industries may be behind the relative lower dynamism of Europe in terms of innovation (for example, in the adoption of information technology). The connection with the Lisbon Agenda should be obvious. If vigorous competition is the key to innovation, then competition policy should be at the centre stage in the European Union.

In the fifty years after the Treaty of Rome:

- merger control was introduced (in 1989) and reformed (in 2004);
- case law has established Articles 81 and 82 as fundamental tools to control and to prevent anticompetitive behaviour;
- state aid control has consolidated and evolved towards a more economic approach; and
- the authority of the European Commission and the judicial review of the Court of First Instance and the European Court of Justice have been firmly established.

Much has been learned in the United States and the European Union—in both cases some of it with the help of judicial review. In what follows, I outline the topics and contributions which reflect the main areas of interest of this book.

1.2. An Overview and Summary of the Contributions

Philip Lowe opens the volume by reviewing the experience of the European Commission in the design of competition policy institutions. In so doing, he presents an overview of the topics that are covered in the book with an emphasis on organizational and process issues. Indeed, any competition policy enforcement system consists of rules and the administrative structures and processes to implement those rules. The rules relate to the areas of antitrust, merger control, and state aid control.

The set of underlying questions is long and important. To start with, what should be the objective of intervention? Consumer welfare is one answer. When this is understood in the long-term sense it should be in agreement with economic efficiency. However, if understood in a short-term sense it may diverge from the total surplus criterion. For example, when it comes to state aid, considerations other than economic efficiency may come to play, as we will see.

Lowe's contribution addresses the goals of competition policy enforcement in order to achieve predictable, efficient, and fair treatment. Concerning the role of economics, he states that 'the long-term legitimacy of any competition enforcement system rests on the economic story which it tells in each case'. How to balance form-based rules with effect-based analysis? What is the role of guidelines in the different competition policy fields? What has to be the role of private enforcement in the European Union? How to use resources efficiently for optimal competition policy enforcement? How to attract talent to the competition policy authority? How to communicate effectively the results of the intervention? These are some of the questions that the Director-ate-General for Competition at the European Commission has confronted with several modernization packages. Some of them have been a response to judicial overturns of EC decisions and include new checks and balances on decisions and the establishment of the office of the Chief Competition Economist. These reforms pose the deeper institutional design issue of the optimal arrangement for instruction, decision, and judicial review. In the European Union, instruction and decision is in the hands of the European Commission with possible appeal to the Community Courts (CFI and ECJ).

Matthew Bennett and Jorge Padilla provide an overview of the structure, goals, and implementation of Article 81 of the Treaty of the European Union in assessing horizontal and vertical agreements. They also draw a parallel with the debate on the implementation of Article 82 (discussed by John Vickers). Article 81(1), broadly, prohibits agreements and concerted practices that have as their object or effect to restrict competition. Article 81(3) allows exceptions, under certain conditions, if the agreements are justified on efficiency grounds. The implementation of Article 81 involves several stages. First, hardcore practices such as price fixing, output restrictions, or market sharing (covered in the chapter by Massimo Motta) are presumed to restrict competition and per se illegal. There is agreement that such practices have such high anticompetitive potential, with the object of restricting competition, that there is no need to demonstrate their effects on the market. To this some hardcore vertical restrictions are added—resale price maintenance, exclusive territories, and some forms of selective distribution. However, economic theory does not support a per se prohibition of those practices, even though they restrict intra-brand competition, given their efficiency enhancing potential. Second, agreements of minor importance are presumed legal. Third, other agreements are assessed to check whether they have an anticompetitive object or effect. To analyse the potential effect of a restriction of competition, it is fundamental to assess the degree of market power of the parties involved in the agreement. The Guidelines on Article 81(3) state that the degree of market power required for an Article 81 infringement is less than the one required for a finding of dominance under Article 82. This seems at odds with the fact that vertical agreements have important potential efficiency benefits. Fourth, Article 81(3) provides a block exemption for certain agreements that are capable to restrict competition (like R&D cooperation or horizontal specialization agreements) if the combined market share of the parties is below some thresholds (around 20–25 per cent of the market). For vertical restraints, the safe harbour is 30 per cent of the upstream market. Finally, for the other agreements that are capable of restricting competition (by object or effect), a balancing test must be performed according to Article 81(3). The conditions for exemption are that it contributes to efficiency, allows a fair share to consumers, is indispensable, and does not eliminate competition. With respect to the last issue, the Guidelines of Article 81(3) state that the protection of rivalry is given priority over potentially pro-competitive gains. The idea is that short-term gains may be overwhelmed by long-term losses when rivalry is significantly hurt.

The authors review specific non-hardcore horizontal and vertical agreements. Article 81 identifies two instruments to reach the goal to enhance consumer welfare and an efficient allocation of resources—the protection of competition and single market integration. The authors doubt that the instruments are compatible with the stated goal. The tension of market integration and consumer welfare objectives has manifested itself in the use of Article 81 towards vertical restraints that affect cross-border trade (as the Glaxo case demonstrates). The authors finally debate whether the competitive assessment of agreements under Article 81 is conducted under a structured rule of reason or under a quasi per se rule. They think that the requirement (from the fourth condition in Article 81(3)) to look at the impact on the competitive process indicates that the second option is the right characterization (since even if an agreement can be shown to have a positive impact on consumer welfare it will be deemed de facto illegal if it substantially reduces competition). The quasi per se rule will result in more false convictions while the structured rule of reason will result in more false acquittals, but, according to the authors, the second is to be preferred since the Commission can control false acquittals applying the first three requirements in Article 81(3). The authors think that a structured rule of reason is also the way to advance in the implementation of Article 82 and that the disparities in the implementation of Articles 81 and 82 should be eliminated.

John Vickers looks at exclusionary abuse of dominance according to Article 82. This article prohibits abuse of a dominant position and mentions explicitly instances of abuse such as imposing unfair trading conditions, limiting production, discrimination, and restrictive contracts. The point of departure is the realization that European competition law and policy towards mergers and anticompetitive agreements has become more based on economic principles over time (particularly in the last decade) and the question now is whether the same will happen with abuse of dominance. Dominance analysis must come first, basically to screen out cases, but if there is abuse analysis (harm to competition and consumers) then it should integrate the dominance analysis.

In terms of safe-harbour thresholds, Vickers argues for a high share of a properly defined market of the sort: dominance is more likely to happen above 50 per cent than below and unlikely below 40 per cent. The author poses the problem of distinguishing good (competition on the merits) from bad (anticompetitive) exclusion, and surveys economic theory relevant to assess exclusionary abuse. Three possible guiding principles to deal with the problem are: whether there is profit sacrifice, whether the practice excludes an as-efficient competitor, and whether there is consumer harm. Pricing below cost implies a profit sacrifice, may exclude an equally efficient competitor, and may end up hurting consumers if the policy increases the market power of the firm in the long term. This is why below-cost pricing is considered a necessary condition for a finding of predatory pricing, but it is far from sufficient since there are normal business justifications for the practice and there is debate over the relevant cost concept, the role of intent, and whether a separate proof of recoupment should be required. Vickers analyses the *Wanadoo* case (2007 judgment by the CFI dismissing the appeal by *France Télécom* against the 2003 finding of predatory pricing by the European Commission) and claims that it is defensible to do away with showing probable recoupment as long as dominance is established with a stringent standard, price is below variable/avoidable cost, and below-cost pricing is in the dominated market. The CFI, in a controversial statement, dismissed the allegations of Wanadoo of economies of scale and learning effects to justify below-cost pricing precisely because predatory pricing may be necessary to induce them.

The author reviews the theory on partial exclusion to exploit rivals, divide-and-rule exclusion, and leverage and maintenance of market power. The 'post-Chicago' economic analysis has proved the coherence of theories of anticompetitive exclusion. The conclusion is that a necessary condition for a finding of abuse is to have a theory of harm to competition consistent with the facts. Two other main cases of abuse are analysed: *British Airways* (*BA*) on rebates and *Microsoft*. The appeal of *BA* against the 2003 judgment of the CFI upholding the 1999 Commission's finding of a bonus scheme abuse was dismissed by the ECJ in 2007. In the United States, the case against BA was dismissed. The key of the European case was the weight given to the properties of the discount scheme and their 'very noticeable effect at the margin'. According to the author, the analysis used in the case was seriously incomplete in terms of economic effects. Finally, the author looks at refusal to supply and the tying in the *Microsoft* case, found to have abused its dominant position in client PC operating systems by the European Commission in 2004. The refusal to supply refers to interoperability information for rivals in group server operating systems; the tying refers to Media Player and the Windows operating system. The CFI agreed with the decision of the EC in 2007. This case has striking parallels with the *IBM* case of the early 1980s. In the *Microsoft US* case, the Court upheld the finding that Microsoft had attempted to protect its Windows operating system monopoly but not of extending it to browsers. The tying of Internet Explorer with Windows was remanded for a structured rule of reason assessment. In the European case, the CFI found that the four-pronged test for exceptional circumstances for refusal to supply intellectual property (IP) to be abusive were met in the *Microsoft* case (according to the analysis of the European Commission and on the assumption favourable to Microsoft that interoperability information was protected by IP rights). That is, interoperability information was indispensable for rivals to compete, there was a risk of competitive exclusion, the refusal to supply would limit techno-logical development for which there is potential demand, and there is no objective justification. On this last issue, the CFI considered that Microsoft had failed to show that its incentives to innovate would be impaired by the disclosure of interoperability information. With regard to harm to the consumer, the CFI made the extraordinary statement that Microsoft had impaired the effective competitive structure of the workgroup server operating system market by 'acquiring a significant share on that market'.

The questions for the future are what is now the principle that limits the obligation of a dominant firm to supply rivals with access to important inputs (including IP)? And, if so, at what price? With respect to the Media Player, the CFI agreed also with the European Commission that Microsoft had bundled without objective justification. Microsoft had offered an unbundled version, but at the same price as the bundled one, according to the (ineffectual) remedy proposed by the European Commission. This points at the need to regulate prices to have an effective remedy.

In summary, the ball to reform European competition policy with regard to Article 82 is in the hands of the European Commission since the recent CFI judgments on Wanadoo, British Airways, or Microsoft neither compels nor pre-cludes the European Commission so to do. The author argues for guidelines to apply Article 82 similar in nature to the recent non-horizontal merger guidelines: consumer-oriented and not competitor-oriented (focusing on anticompetitive foreclosure), recognizing the scope for efficiencies, and spelling out the concrete mechanisms of harm to competition and the key facts to check. The European Commission finally issued a guidance paper on its enforcement priorities in applying Article 82 to exclusionary conduct by dominant firms in December 2008.

Massimo Motta looks at the economics of collusion and reviews the EU experience in fighting cartels, including standards of proof of infringement and enforcement policy. Motta starts by reviewing the economic theory of collusion, the situation where firms sustain prices above a competitive bench-mark. For economists, both tacit and overt agreements may support a collusive outcome. Collusion is a dynamic phenomenon where firms refrain to deviate from an agreement to sustain high prices for fear of being detected and conse-quently suffering retaliation. This punishment must be credible to be an effect-ive deterrent. However, firms may sustain many different collusive outcomes and face the problem to coordinate on one of them. This can be accomplished with explicit coordination lacking a focal point of action. The factors that facilitate collusion are examined—among them, the role of the exchange of information in helping detect deviations. This is particularly the case of the exchange of individual price and quantity data. The exchange of plans on prices and production may help coordination. Those are particularly suspicious when price announcements do not represent a commitment to consumers.[2] Some other highlighted facilitating practices are meeting competition clauses, resale price maintenance, and some spatial pricing policies. As stated before, in the European Union, cartels are dealt with through Article 81. In Article 81(1) both agreements and concerted practices that restrict competition are prohibited. Price fixing, restricting production, and market sharing are explicitly mentioned. For those agreements like cartels that have as their object to restrict competition it is not necessary for the competition authority to investigate their effects. Cartels are almost per se prohibited (the 'almost' comes from some exemptions given in particular cases such as 'crisis cartels'). The problem is how to infer collusion from market data, since parallel behaviour may be the outcome of competitive markets. This is why, after the ECJ decision on the *Wood Pulp* case, parallel behaviour cannot be proof of 'concertation', 'unless concertation constitutes the only possible plausible explanation for such conduct'. To prove this is quite difficult (but was done in the *Dyestuffs* case). The ECJ also stated that the Treaty 'does not deprive economic operators of the right to adapt themselves intelligently to the existing and anticipated conduct of their competitors'. This may be construed as allowing tacit collusion as long as no evidence of explicit coordination exists (the reopened and pending *Soda-Ash* case may clarify whether this is the case). The standard of proof for a cartel infringement therefore depends in general on hard documentary evidence (which on the other hand preserves legal certainty). The analysis of market data is a complement to such evidence as well as the control of facilitating practices. For example, in the *UK Tractor* case, the information exchange (detailed at firm level) in place was considered an Article 81 infringement even though there was no evidence of coordination.

The European Union can impose fines of at most 10 per cent of annual worldwide turnover of the infringing firm. The author provides evidence of the toughening of the anti-cartel policy in the European Union in regard to fines (that tend to be reduced but confirmed by the Community Courts). The European Union introduced leniency policy in 1996 (in the United States it was introduced in 1978), according to which firms that collaborate with the antitrust authority get total or partial immunity. In 2002, the policy was revised and the first firm reporting a cartel was given complete immunity. There is a debate over the effectiveness of such policies and the author provides evidence that in most recent EU cartel cases the leniency programme played an important role. However, leniency has not managed to free resources to fight collusion since there is no evidence of a downward trend in the average length of cartel investigations.[3] This is problematic since a leniency programme helps to uncover existing cartels (and for this it is important that firms may apply for lenience once the investigation has started) but may lower the ex ante cost of joining or forming a cartel. This tendency may be counteracted by an increase in fines (as the European Commission has done). Deterrence may be further increased with private actions to recover damages and by the personal liability of executives (in the United States, prison for a cartel offender is a distinct possibility). In the European Union, given the difficulty of introducing criminal penalties in this area, administrative fines for convicted executives could be considered. The author concludes that, by and large, EU cartel policy is in line with the learning from economics.

Bruce Lyons assesses merger control in the European Union. He starts by reviewing the history of competition economics and its interaction with the legal approach. The Treaty of Rome made no provision for merger control and the European Commission had to rely on the current Articles 81 and 82 (originally 85 and 86) to control mergers. In 1989, the European Community Merger Regulation (ECMR) was established. Lyons distinguishes between a phase of consolidation of merger control between 1989 and 2002 and a phase of reform between 2003 and 2007. A Merger Task Force was set up within the Directorate-General for Competition (then known as DG IV) to work within a tight timetable for decisions to be made in Phase I (scrutiny) and Phase II (investigation) of a merger procedure. A decision was made by the College of Commissioners based on the work of the case team in charge of both Phases I and II. The Directorate-General for Competition was (and is) therefore investigator, prosecutor, and jury. The decision can be appealed to the CFI (with further recourse for matters of law to the ECJ). This is in contrast with the US adversarial procedure where the Courts intervene earlier, with fact-finding capacity, on the proposals of the Department of Justice (DoJ) or the Federal Trade Commission (FTC). In the European Union, the role of the Courts is of judicial review of the European Commission's decision.

One advantage of the EU system is that reasoned decisions are published. In terms of substantive issues an important feature of the ECMR is the concern with market integration. The ECMR wants to consider mergers of Community dimension and combines absolute size threshold and sufficient sales of the undertakings of their main market (more than one-third of the turnover). The substantive test was one of 'creating or strengthening a dominant position'. This encouraged a formalistic approach based on market share and was in contrast with the 'substantial lessening of competition' test in the United States (which is currently interpreted as whether the merger will create or enhance market power, or facilitate its exercise). The EU test had the potential problem that substantial market power could remain even if no dominance was found. This meant that the European Commission could have had the temptation to rely excessively on the concept of collective dominance to fill the gap. In 2004, the test was replaced by the 'significant impediment to effective competition' (SIEC) test, very close to the US approach. This reform, together with the dismantling of the Merger Task Force, the introduction of more checks and balances in the decision procedure (for example, a 'devil's advocate' panel as internal critique in handling a case), and the establishment of the Chief Competition Economist with a support team, was in part triggered by a series of setbacks of the Commission decisions by the CFI (namely, *Airtours/FC*, *Schneider/Legrand*, *Tetra Laval/Sidel*, and the criticism in *GE/Honeywell*).

Merger analysis considers three main categories of harm: two types of horizontal harm (unilateral effects and coordinated effects) and non-horizontal effects. Unilateral effects refer to the exercise of market power when there is no coordination of the firms' strategies. These effects imply that a merger of firms producing substitute products that does not create synergies will result in raised prices. There is a settled oligopoly pricing theory which provides robust models (like the Cournot and Bertrand ones) on which to base predictions of the effect of the merger with the help of econometric estimates and simulations.[4] The latter can go from back-of-the-envelope analysis to a full-blown simulation. In any case, the estimation or calibration of demand elasticities and cross-elasticities is crucial. The European Commission has started to use some full-blown simulation models that go beyond the simple market-share analysis. The treatment of efficiencies has gone from a potential efficiency offence (in the early days of the ECMR where efficiency was viewed as a way to reinforce dominance) to an efficiency defence formally accepted in the reform of 2004. However, it still remains to be seen how far it can go in justifying a merger.

Coordinated effects refer to the dynamic sustainability of collusion (before it went under the heading of 'collective dominance'). The basic theory is reviewed in Motta's contribution and the emphasis here is on how a merger may influence the conditions that facilitate collusion (for example, by reallocating capacities and products among the firms or by changing the transparency in the market). It must be stated, however, that the repeated game model is silent on how coordination is achieved in the plethora of possible outcomes. The result is that 'coordinated effects' analysis is much more tentative than the 'unilateral effects' one. The CFI endorsed in its judgment on Airtours, in criticizing the decision of the Commission, the basic elements from the theory for collusion to be an issue (transparency, credibility of retaliation, and competitor and consumer response). In the *Sony/BMG* case, the CFI in 2006 annulled the clearance decision of the European Commission because of problems in the analysis of transparency and retaliation.

Finally, the analysis of non-horizontal mergers has proved the trickiest. Non-horizontal mergers have important potential efficiency benefits (since they typically bring together complementary products) but often the European

Commission has implicitly worried about damage to competitors. The result has been severe criticisms to the EC decisions by the CFI in the *Tetra Laval/Sidel* and *GE/Honeywell* cases. Guidelines on non-horizontal mergers are now out and they outline the steps according to which foreclosure analysis has to be performed (in terms of showing ability, incentive, and anticompetitive effects). It remains to be seen whether efficiencies will be seen as an integral part of the analysis or just a final balancing check.[5] Lyons analyses also the trends in EC intervention and finds that, over time, more mergers are being remedied than prohibited, and that Phase I resolutions gain at the expense of Phase II. The 2001 increase in prohibitions sees a substantial reversal. The author also reviews the effectiveness of remedies and possible improvements such as not dismissing behavioural remedies in some well-specified cases and caring about potential collusion between buyers and sellers of divested assets. The speed of agreement (for example, in remedies) has also improved, although this fact must be carefully interpreted. Finally, some event stock market studies have tried to make out possible type I and type II errors in the EC decisions. A result, to be interpreted with care, given the nature of the studies, is that many more errors tend to be made in Phase I. In summary, merger control in the European Union seems to be in a path which is consistent with the learning from economics and has shown flexibility to correct mistakes and make improvements.

David Spector analyses state aid control in the European Union, which has been in place since before the Treaty of Rome. This is in stark contrast with the United States, where the competition authorities have no jurisdiction over state aid. State aid is a complex subject since it encompasses many fields in economics ranging from international trade and oligopolistic competition, to political and public economics, to economic geography. State aid control must address both market and government failures. State aid control can be justified on paternalistic grounds (the internal effect on countries) as well as on non-paternalistic ones (cross-country externalities). The first type of reasons include helping governments resist interest groups and lobbies and providing an external commitment device that alleviates dynamic inefficiencies such as soft budget constraints, rent-seeking behaviour, or short horizons for decisions. EU state aid control may play a filter role to allow some needed flexibility in aid while limiting wasteful aid. The European Commission, however, is increasingly reluctant to play this scapegoat role. The justifications of state aid control based on cross-country externalities fit better the EU rhetoric since, at least in principle, they could only be dealt with on a European-wide basis. Those justifications range from preventing wasteful subsidy races and cross-country rent-shifting to the impact of aid on market structure and competition. However, subsidy competition may be efficient if the deadweight cost of taxation is low and the external benefit varies substantially across locations. On the other hand, it may seem paradoxical that in the European Union 'inefficient' competition across states is prevented while there is no coordination on corporate taxation (in contrast to the United States where there is a federal corporate tax and no control on subsidy competition across states). With respect to rent-shifting incentives using strategic trade policy it must be pointed out that even if the aid reduces foreign firms' rents it may also increase the benefits to foreign consumers with an ambiguous total effect. Finally, the aid may help the predatory behaviour of national firms or end up being pro-competitive. State aid can correct market failures associated with externalities and public goods (for example, in R&D), informational asymmetries in capital markets, and, in some circumstances, it may create competition. State aid may also be a means to achieve 'personalized' corporate taxes. Clearly, all these potentially positive effects of correcting market failures have to be balanced against the possibly larger effects of government failure. The author points out the limits of economic analysis and the lack of clear-cut prescriptions in this domain. For example, should market power be considered a necessary condition of the identification of cross-border externalities? Is the bias towards R&D aid warranted? How to measure the impact of aid to R&D? What is a desirable welfare standard for state aid control?

The author discusses the difficulties of implementing a set standard given measurement problems. The current overhaul of state aid control emphasizes a more economic approach and concentrates on a small set of well-defined market failures. Distortion of competition and affectation of trade among Member States, according to the letter of Article 87(1) of the Treaty, are necessary conditions for prohibition of state aid. What is the standard of proof for the EC for a case to meet the two criteria has been established in a series of cases, seemingly in a tightening direction. Fluctuating assessment criteria according to case law are interpreted as reflecting underlying uncertainty over the mechanism by which state aid causes harm. The commonly held view that the disregard of the European Commission for competition distortion and trade affectation criteria reflects a paternalistic tendency must be qualified since the definition of distortion of competition depends on the 'theory of harm'. Spector concludes his chapter with the provocative question of whether the present, more-refined economic approach will be the Trojan horse of paternalism. In principle, one could expect that a more 'economics' approach would provide more attention to the specifics of competition distortion and trade affectation but those seem no longer to be necessary conditions for a prohibition. Both in the state aid action plan and in the R&D&I framework of the European Union, state aid is viewed as appropriate when it is a remedy to a market failure and when it causes the least possible distortion to competition. It could well happen that state aid is prohibited because it does not address a market failure despite the fact that it does not distort competition.

Martin Hellwig discusses the relationship between sector-specific regulation and competition policy in network industries. Those are industries, such as electricity, gas, telecommunications, or transportation that involve an important element of natural monopoly arising out of the fixed investment in a network infrastructure. Network industries have undergone a change of structure from regulated vertically integrated monopolies to the introduction of competition in the segments deemed not to be natural monopolies. This has posed the question of the boundaries between regulation and competition policy and whether regulation should be transitory or permanent. The movement has gone together with privatization of the industry and regulatory reform. Regulation is to stay in the natural monopoly segments and it has to promote also competition in downstream markets as well as competition between networks when feasible. One main trade-off is that facilitating access to bottlenecks reduces the incentives to build infrastructures to bypass the bottleneck. A big question is the consistency between competition policy and sector regulation. This is particularly important for activities which are subject to both. At the national level, sector-specific regulation has precluded in practice the application of competition law in the past (in the United States this is the case after the Trinko decision by the Supreme Court). But the European Commission (and national competition authorities) can intervene when a contradiction between national regulation and the competition provisions in the European Union Treaty are found. This has been the case in recent decisions by the European Commission imposing fines on Deutsche Telekom and Telefónica because of a price squeeze despite the fact that both companies were complying with the requirements of the national sector regulator.

Hellwig surveys the pros and cons of using competition policy versus sector regulation. He points out that competition policy is not well placed to mandate price and quality of access because it occurs *ex post* and is of a piecemeal nature. This is the reason why competition policy has trouble dealing with excessive pricing issues (despite the prohibition in Article 82 of the Treaty in contrast with the US approach). He advocates for a systemic approach to access regulation that can deal with the problem of attribution of common fixed costs. A problem with sector-specific regulation is that it is more likely to be captured. He compares naive and sophisticated approaches to drawing the line between sector-regulation and competition policy. An example of the naive approach would be in the energy sector, where regulation is confined to the networks. An example of the sophisticated approach would be the telecommunications sector, where markets are defined and regulation applies in those markets where competition is not effective. Hellwig highlights the problems that plague the sophisticated approach and wonders whether it would not be better to fall back into a 'naive' approach. Among the problems are that the market definition does not coincide with the usual competition policy definition, which is narrower, despite the fact that systemic effects are not taken into account. In short, the coexistence of sector regulation and competition policy poses important challenges, among them the very definition of some crucial terms such as the limits of a market and costs standards, the consistency of treatment in the same industry, and the institutional design of regulators and judicial review. He advocates the role of the ECJ as the ultimate source of all jurisdiction on the legal norms common to competition policy and sector regulation.

Jordi Gual and Sandra Jódar-Rosell look at the past performance and prospects of regulation in the telecommunications sector. The authors review the EU regulatory frameworks of 1998 and 2003. Behind the 1998 framework are the objectives to increase competition and integrate the market in a strategy of 'host country rules within limits', which involves harmonization with Member State application of regulations. The concern was to protect nascent competition given the legacy of vertically integrated multiproduct national monopolies by ensuring efficient entry abolishing exclusive rights and encouraging tariff rebalancing (for example, in voice), minimizing the risk of market tipping (with mandatory interconnection between networks and decreasing switching costs), and preventing the abuse of dominant position by incumbents. The idea is to regulate *ex ante* prices of firms with significant market power (SMP). For example, with the unbundling of the local loop, firms with SMP have to provide access at a regulated price. Member States had a lot of leeway on many aspects—like granting licences, the way to compute costs of interconnection (on which to base regulated prices), and line of business restrictions. The results of the 1998 framework have been mixed, with improvements in efficiency of the incumbents but less success on broadband penetration and introducing competition in conventional telephony. An interesting effect is that investment increases and prices decrease when privatization is combined with introducing competition. In general, the establishment of a National Regulatory Agency (NRA) has had positive effects and there is a lot of variation on results among countries.

Faced with increased convergence of technologies in digital networks, the European Commission proposed in 2003 a new package with an increased role for competition policy and *ex post* measures. Now NRAs are required to define relevant markets where operators with SMP can be found and where *ex ante* regulation can be applied. The idea is that when in a market effective competition develops then the regulation is withdrawn. However, the European Commission retains veto power on the decisions of NRAs on market definition and designating SMP operators. At the same time, measures to increase regulatory harmonization and limit the discretion of Member States are proposed. Typically, NRAs have redefined markets to narrow them to mimic the technology predominant in each country. In summary, regulatory reform has brought rate rebalancing and potentially efficient entry, minimized the risks of market tipping, and modernized price regulation. A potential risk of the new framework is the extension of mandatory access to the deployment of new generation networks because of the regulatory uncertainty it creates on investment incentives.

Elena Carletti and Xavier Vives deal with regulation and competition policy in the banking sector. The banking sector had long been exempted from the application of competition policy because of a claimed potential trade-off between competition and stability. In the chapter the authors review the academic literature on this issue and describe the design of competition policy in Europe and its application in the European Union in the last two decades. The banking sector, and the financial sector more generally, is one of the most regulated sectors of the economy because of its potential fragility and systemic risk, and the need to protect consumers who have limited information. The analysis of competition in banking is complex. Banking is a multiproduct business and competition is imperfect, with many frictions and barriers to entry which may generate rents. In retail banking switching costs for customers are very important, and reputation and branch networks act as entry barriers. In corporate banking established relationships and asymmetric information are frictions that explain why the market for small and medium-sized firms remains local. Electronic banking pushes in the direction of contestability, but it is also subject to exogenous and endogenous switching costs. In other segments of banking, like wholesale and investment banking, competition is at the international level and may be fierce. The authors present the debate about how much of a trade-off there is between competition and stability to conclude that once a certain threshold is reached an increase in the level of competition will tend to increase risk-taking incentives and the probability of bank failure. The question remains open as to what degree of market power should be allowed in banking and therefore whether the application of competition policy should be modulated because of the stability concern. The chapter documents how banking is no longer an exception in the enforcement of competition policy rules in the European Union. The European Commission has by now examined cases in all areas of antitrust and has adopted important, landmark decisions. It has opposed anticompetitive mergers as well as forms of cooperation in pricing schemes and in credit card systems, and stated that regulatory measures cannot justify the granting of state aid to financial institutions if they entail distortions of competition. The authors highlight the conflicts between the European Commission and Member States in regard to merger policy and state aids and the role of the European Commission in fostering cross-border mergers. The efforts of the European Commission at market integration are also explained and the main results of the enquiries that the European Commission conducted in the financial sector described.

Still, much remains to be done in terms of academic research and of the role that the European Commission can play in fostering competition in banking in Europe. The authors conclude that competition policy in banking should centre on the sources of market power and use a refined economic analysis that takes into account the complexities of the sector, and they warn against potential conflicts between market integration and competition objectives.

Richard Green surveys the regulation and competition policy of energy utilities. He starts by looking at the obstacles to introducing competition in the sector: the fact that the network is a natural monopoly, and at economies of scale in transmission, storage, and distribution, and the presence of long-term contracts. A review of the early moves to 'liberalize' in the UK and Norway, and of the EU directives is provided. The directives were the first instrument of the European Commission to introduce competition in the sector given the progress made by the pioneers in liberalizing the energy sector. The second instrument was the application of competition policy, since once the liberalization process is started the energy sector is no longer off bounds for antitrust. The European Commission has intervened on agreements between firms relating to clauses of gas contracts prohibiting resale and destination clauses, on long-term contracts for interconnectors, and on non-compete clauses. The European Commission has also been active on merger control, blocking the EDP–GDP merger, on the grounds that the companies were perceived to be the main potential competitors of each other in the affected relevant market (Portugal). The decision was upheld by the CFI. Other mergers have been approved with divestitures or the auction of virtual power plants (for example, Veba and Viag to form E.ON, and the operations of EdF and EnBW, and of E.ON and MOL).

It is worth noticing that the merger of E.ON and Ruhrgas escaped EU scrutiny and was cleared by the German government against the opinion of German competition authorities. The European Commission has been active also in removing potential obstacles to cross-border mergers as the battle over Endesa by Gas Natural, E.ON, and Enel shows. Finally, the merger by Enel and Endesa and the divestment of Enel's Spanish assets in favour of E.ON was cleared by the European Commission. The author goes on to assess the impact of liberalization showing that there is still a wide variation among European Union countries. A more recent tool that the European Commission has used is a sector inquiry on the gas and electricity industries where several concerns of lack of competition and market integration have been expressed. This inquiry has led to open investigations of suspected abuse of dominant position and to the formulation of a legislative package proposing: the full ownership unbundling of transmission systems or setting an independent system operator; the strengthening of national regulators; and the formation of an EU agency of energy regulators. To this, a third country clause preventing foreign firms to control transmission unless there is reciprocity has been added. One immediate outcome of the European Commission initiatives has been the proposal by E.ON to unbundle its network (against the position of the German government).

Bill Kovacic closes the volume with some reflections on whether competition policy in the European Union and the United States are converging or diverging. Kovacic is of the view that the big picture is a convergent one. The issue is of some importance given the increasing interdependency between jurisdictions, where the more restrictive one sets the standard—the process of enforcement which entails costs to firms—and the development of new competition policy systems in the world, where the European Union model based in civil law is becoming the standard. Despite this, many innovations in antitrust policy, such as the treatment of cartels and horizontal mergers, come from the United States. Furthermore, some degree of experimentation in antitrust enforcement is to be welcome. What is needed is to have a flexible enough system so that superior norms and procedures end up being adopted.

The US and the EU competition policy systems have the same overall objective, which is consumer welfare. On substance, there is agreement on the treatment of cartels and horizontal mergers. On the control of state intervention in the economy, there is no divergence of principle, but the European Union has a stronger platform to challenge state aids restraints. On abuse of dominance, there is no equivalent in the United States of the excessive pricing ban in Article 82, and the interpretations of Article 82 by the CFI and the ECJ have created 'a wider zone of liability for dominant firms than the decisions of the US courts under Section 2 of the Sherman Act'. The question is whether there will be convergence on an effect-based standard on abuse of dominance cases. On vertical restraints, there has been convergence over the years, but there still remain differences with the European Union relying more on per se prohibitions (for example, on resale price maintenance). On non-horizontal mergers, in the European Union there is more scope for intervention—that has been used—but recent CFI decisions (*Tetra Laval* and *GE/Honeywell*) put a high bar on the European Commission for a prohibition.

The main transatlantic convergence forces are the use of economics (and industrial organization tools in particular), as economic analysis assumes an increasing importance in the investigations of the European Commission, and the role of judicial review. Although the timing of judicial intervention is not the same in both jurisdictions, with earlier intervention in the US system providing a more direct disciplining effect on the US authorities, recent decisions of the CFI make clear that judicial review in the European Union is critical. Another important centripetal force are the consultation procedures established between the jurisdictions at the level of intergovernmental, transgovernmental, and transnational contacts. The forces of divergence are the role of private litigation, and the raising of liability standards by US courts to compensate the potential excesses of private claims; the adversarial US procedure versus the administrative EU procedure; and the more prevalent use of the 'revolving door' for public servants in the United States. To this it may be added that EU authorities may perceive the economy in Europe to be more rigid than that in the United States and therefore be more sceptical about the self-correcting nature of markets. An intriguing hypothesis is whether the European Union and the United States will converge on abuse of dominance if private claims take hold in the European Union. Kovacic ends by suggesting concepts and means to deliver convergence on superior norms.

1.3. Concluding Remarks

The chapters in this book present an overview of where we currently stand regarding competition policy in the European Union. There has been a significant amount of scholarship and research in this area in recent years. The trends towards putting efficiency and consumer surplus as central objectives of competition policy, and using economic tools to assess the effects of agreements and practices, are consolidating. This is in agreement with US practice and is set to become the international standard also for emerging economies. By now there is broad transatlantic consensus on the treatment of cartels and horizontal mergers where well-established economic models are used. Nevertheless, abuse of dominance and non-horizontal mergers still show important discrepancies. Indeed, in the European Union, the use of economics has advanced effectively in the application of Article 81 decisions (regarding cartels, in particular), and in mergers, while in the application of Article 82, reform is pending. The recent guidelines provided on non-horizontal mergers may provide a good example for Article 82 decisions. The implementation of Article 82 illustrates the tension between the legal certainty that a form-based approach provides and the desirability of an effects-based approach. The challenge is how to make operational an effects-based approach while preserving legal predictability. To think in terms of a pure effects-based approach may be risky if it does away with dominance screens and even naive, given that it is very difficult to ascertain the impact of practices on consumer welfare. This is precisely why the level of rivalry or strength of competition has been taken as the main indicator of efficiency. It would make sense in this respect to think in terms of a structured rule of reason for the application of Article 82 where the protection of competition is an instrument and, in any case, homogenize the market power thresholds in the application of Articles 81 and 82.[10]

Form-based elements, like the treatment of some information-sharing practices in Article 81, seem to be an indispensable component of the implementation of Articles 81 and 82. The leeway that the European Commission gets from the CFI on the implementation of Article 82 is large. A major challenge is to be found in the analysis of exclusionary behaviour on solid economic principles. At the same time it may be considered whether the EU distinction of exploitative abuse is appropriate and whether it would not be better instead to attack the underlying market structure or practices which are at the source of the competition problem.

The box of tools employed to analyse horizontal mergers (unilateral and coordinated effects analysis) is well established and the guidelines on non-horizontal mergers have made a step forward. However, there is still the pending issue of how efficiencies will be considered in practice. Those are central in non-horizontal mergers but also crucial in horizontal mergers, in particular when the merger may have an impact on innovation incentives. The bias of the competition authorities towards analysing the short-term effects of mergers is understandable but worrisome. Economic analysis still has to offer practical recommendations in this respect. The European Commission possibly has tried to put more weight on the long-term consequences of mergers than the United States, perhaps implicitly thinking that the EU economy is more rigid and that market forces have less scope to correct monopoly abuses.[6] The European Commission has reformed its merger-control procedure in the right direction with the revised substantive test, publication of merger guidelines, more checks and balances, and introducing the Chief Competition Economist. The question is whether it has gone far enough, in particular in terms of checks and balances and in separating instruction and decision.[7] More, in general, the issue is whether the implementation of competition policy in the European Union has found the right balance between instruction, decision, and judicial review.

With regard to state aid, a tension is perceived between a competition approach (according to which aid to firms with no market power or not generating cross-border externalities should be allowed) and a more encompassing approach (where aid not targeted in general to remedy a market failure should be forbidden). It is still early to see the precise implications of the 'more economic approach' of the European Union to state aid. Consistency with general competition policy would seem to favour the competition approach. A topic not directly addressed in the volume, but related to the present discussion, is the interaction between competition and industrial policy. Tensions may arise, for example, in dealing with mergers which may increase the international competitiveness of firms but increase market power of the merged entities, and with industrial, R&D, or regional state aid that distorts competition.[8]

The interaction of regulation and competition policy is evolving as technological developments impinge on network and other regulated industries and as we learn from experience. The general idea is that in an industry in which there is a natural monopoly element regulation is there to stay—as long as this bottleneck is not superseded by technology, in which case competition policy should take over. In the energy sector, the natural monopoly component is not challenged for now while in telecommunications arguably it is. The difficult question is how to approach the regulation of sectors in which the bottlenecks can be potentially bypassed (as in telecommunications). Competition policy is not well placed to set the terms of access to the bottleneck, as well as dealing with excessive pricing issues despite the formal prohibition in Article 82, while regulation to mitigate market power is difficult to implement—and intrusive. An important challenge remains here (not least how to regulate a bottleneck while maintaining investment incentives to upgrade it on the one hand and/ or to bypass it on the other, or, more in general, how to improve the complementarity between competition policy and regulation). Another challenge is how to avoid opportunistic behaviour by national regulators and firms profiting from the fragmentation of regulation in network industries in the European Union. The tension between antitrust in Brussels and national regulators needs to be resolved with regulatory harmonization and tighter coordination of national regulators. Another instance of this tension are the artificial obstacles that cross-border mergers encounter (with cases in the banking and energy sectors). In this respect, one issue that probably will have to be reviewed is the neutrality of the Treaty in relation to public and private ownership. Public ownership causes obvious distortions in regulated sectors, among other issues, since the state is on both sides (regulator and regulated).[9] In the banking sector, the increased application of competition policy still has to be tested against the stability concern, and the sophistication of economic analysis enhanced. In regulated sectors, the inquiries of the European Commission (in energy and financial services, for example) have raised a number of competition issues and proved useful in targeting cases of potential anticompetitive abuse.

Finally, the potential tension between market integration and competition objectives, although increasingly solved in favour of the latter, is still present. For example, it manifests itself in the suspicion with which price discrimination across countries is viewed and the typical lack of scrutiny of cross-border mergers for multimarket contact.

In short, the story of the fifty years of competition policy in Europe is the story of a success, showing resiliency and capacity of self-reform. Competition policy has become central in the European Union, with the authority of the European Commission firmly established and with an increasingly international leadership role. A challenge for the European Commission will be how to attract and retain human capital. In the immediate future, we will have to see the effects of private litigation in the European Union as well as a more decentralized enforcement of competition policy in national courts. In fifty years' time the role of the European Commission will most probably be quite different in general but we can conjecture with some confidence that the role of competition policy will not have diminished in Europe. A possible change in such a time frame is the evolution of the institutional frame for competition policy implementation and judicial review. Here is where the creation of an independent competition policy agency in the European Union (say, along the lines of the US FTC) may be discussed. Meanwhile, for economics and economists the challenge is to deliver operational tools which translate the accumulated knowledge into guidelines and practical advice.

Notes

[1] I am grateful to Giulio Federico for his helpful comments.

[2] See Kühn and Vives (1995) for a comprehensive treatment of the theory and practice of competition policy on information exchange and Vives (2006) for a summary and update.

[3] In July 2008, the European Union unveiled a fast-track settlement procedure with reduction in fines in exchange for admitting guilt.

[4] See e.g. Tirole (1988) and Vives (1999).

[5] Economic Advisory Group on Competition Policy (2006): report prepared for the Directorate Competition, Brussels.

[6] For an analysis of the differences in approach between the European Union and the United States in the GE–Honeywell case, see Vives and Staffiero (2009).

[7] See the discussion in my 15 Dec. 2005 *Financial Times* article: 'Brussels has not gone far enough in its merger reforms'.

[8] See Vives (2008) for an overview of those issues.

[9] Another source of potential tension is the allocation of jurisdiction between the European Union and national competition authorities. For a description of some of the tensions between national regulators and EU competition policy, see my 15 Sept. and 20 Dec. 2006 *Financial Times* articles: 'Barriers need to be lifted for an integrated market' and 'European competition policy needs urgent reform'.

[10] The guidance paper on exclusionary abuse issued by the European Commission in December 2008 outlines an effects-based approach for the application of Article 82.

2

The Design of Competition Policy Institutions for the Twenty-first Century: The Experience of the European Commission and the Directorate-General for Competition

Philip Lowe[1]

2.1. Introduction

For the purposes of this chapter I will rely on a wide understanding of 'competition policy institution' as referring to a public competition policy and enforcement system taken as a whole. All competition policy and enforcement systems consist of essentially two components: the legal instruments ('rules') governing both substance, competences, and procedure and the administrative structures and processes through which the legal instruments are implemented. Each of these is necessary for the success of the system as a whole. Good rules remain a dead letter if there is no efficiently run organization with the processes to implement them. Conversely, an efficiently managed authority cannot compensate for fundamental flaws in the rules which it is to implement.

The analysis and design of these components are also interdependent. The management of the processes within the organization has to be adapted to the rules which it has to apply. And the rules must be shaped in a way that they can be implemented within the real world constraints to which the organization is subject—such as limited resources.

Academic attention focuses mainly on the legal instruments and not so much on the organizational side. One reason for this is probably that competition policy and enforcement are still mainly subjects for lawyers. Another reason could be that it is not easy for outsiders to obtain detailed and comprehensive information about the interior workings of a competition authority. Finally, it is perhaps assumed that the management of a competition authority does not pose any different challenge from the management of other public or private institutions with a comparable mission and size.

Perhaps as a result of my initial business management education and subsequent further 'déformation professionnelle', I find organizational and process issues of considerable interest and will in this chapter focus more on this second aspect of European competition policy and enforcement experience of the last years.

Before starting, I need to make a preliminary point that will be obvious to many, but which is none the less important. The competition authority in the European Union is not the Directorate-General for Competition, but the European Commission. The European Commission is a collegiate institution composed of twenty-seven Commissioners from the twenty-seven Member States of the European Union. It is this College of Commissioners that, on a proposal of the Commissioner for Competition, adopts final decisions in individual competition cases as well as on policy documents such as guidelines and notices and legislative proposals to the Council. On the basis of a delegation of powers from the College (so-called 'empowerment'), the Commissioner for Competition can herself directly adopt certain preparatory or intermediary acts such as a Statement of Objections, as well as final decisions in less-important cases, such as a merger dealt with under 'simplified' procedure. The decisions taken by the College and the Commissioner are prepared and implemented by one of the departments of the Commission: in the case of competition, the Directorate General for Competition, which currently has around 800 staff.

I do not intend in the remaining sections of this chapter to give further attention to the classical institutional issue of the degree of independence of a competition authority, and in particular of the Commission as a competition authority. However, some remarks on our general approach to this question may be useful.

The European Commission finds itself in a substantially different position to a national authority. In the first place, its institutional independence should not be in question. As reflected in the EU treaties, its independence from national and political interests is fundamental to its mission of promoting the 'common interest' of the European Union as a whole.

Secondly, the Commission has delegated fully its powers to investigate a case, and manage the due process, to DG Competition. The Commissioner for Competition is in addition empowered to take decisions on cases and problems which raise no significant policy issue. These arrangements offer a solid guarantee of the integrity and impartiality of investigations and their conclusions, while reserving all key decisions on cases and policy for the college of Commissioners as a whole.

Thirdly, a competition certainly needs to be independent and impartial. But it should not be isolated or uninformed. It needs to be fully aware of the market and the regulatory environment around competition law enforcement. And it needs to be in a position to influence legislators and regulators, particularly when competition problems can be better addressed by new or amended regulation. This only underlines the advantage for EU competition policy of having the work of the Competition Commissioner and DG Competition fully embedded within the Commission. Finally, it is worth underlining again that the Commission as an institution, and not just DG Competition, retains the role of Europe's competition authority.

2.2. How to Design a Modern Competition Policy and Enforcement System

Independently of whether we speak about merger control, antitrust, or state aid control, a competition authority should ideally intervene at the right time, on the right markets, in relation to the right problems and with the correct remedies. At the same time, its intervention should be predictable, correct, and have a measurable positive impact.

In the real world, however, external constraints—resulting from limited resources and the institutional context—often disrupt this ideal. No competition authority has the resources to deal with all possible cases: some form of prioritization is necessary. Moreover, there are inevitable trade-offs—for example, there may be a need to resolve a competition problem in a given market quickly to bring some form of anticompetitive conduct to an end. But there is obviously a parallel pressure to achieve correct (no error) outcomes in each and every case. Similarly, hard and fast per se rules provide a higher degree of predictability of outcomes, but can lead to more type 1 or type 2 errors when compared to effects-based rules. Against this background what should a modern competition try to achieve? I see several basic requirements.

(1) Policy, rules, and individual enforcement actions must be based on *sound law, economics, and market knowledge*. Legally, enforcement must be—and be seen to be—subject to the rule of law, due process requirements, and effective judicial control. As to economics, the long-term legitimacy of any competition enforcement system rests on the economic story which it tells in each case. Any competition enforcer should be able to explain why and how its enforcement actions contribute to the wider public interest, and in particular to consumer welfare, whether in the short or longer term. As regards market knowledge, the authority must have effective investigative powers to gather relevant data that set priorities and focus its use of its legal instruments accordingly.

(2) The enforcement system must be designed in a way that guarantees *coherence and predictability for business*: coherence ensures equal treatment.

Predictability allows firms to plan for compliance. To achieve this, *ex ante* rules and individual enforcement decisions should be based on a common methodology, clear and publicized enforcement objectives, and an in-depth knowledge of how markets function. Again, there is a certain trade-off between predictability and the need to deal with each case on its merits. Based on empirical evidence, some structures or conducts have almost always produced outcomes which are harmful to competition and to consumers. As a result, it may be possible to establish some clear *ex ante* rules which offer a high level of predictability. However, where past evidence is mixed, the most that can be done to provide a degree of predictability is to indicate what assessment methodology will be used. Usually, an effective enforcement system will be based on a mix of *ex ante* (per se) rules and an analytical framework for a case-by-case effects-based analysis.

(3) The system should allow the competition authority to *concentrate its limited resources on specific priorities*. The authority must be able to determine those priorities on the basis of the expected direct and indirect effects of its action. The system should make it possible to concentrate resources on the potentially most harmful conducts and on precedent-setting cases. This depends crucially on knowledge of markets and the capacity to focus on key issues without the need for repetitive in-depth investigations on individual cases.

Notification thresholds, block exemptions, *de minimis* rules, and graduated decision-making procedures *must allow the authority to deal quickly*, and with limited resources, *with unimportant and simple cases*, or not to deal with certain cases at all.

(4) As to the length of investigation procedures, any effective competition system must enable a public agency to take *decisions in a timeframe which is relevant to the problem it is supposed to remedy*. Being well informed on market developments before cases arise is again important here. Precedents must also be set at a moment when they still have the intended wider policy impact. This means that procedural rules and internal best practices should ensure timely investigation and rapid internal decision making.

(5) Last, but certainly not least, enforcement must always go hand in hand with an *effective communication of its benefits, for consumers, taxpayers and for business*. Public intervention cannot depend on some abstract rule or unsubstantiated theory of problems, but must explain why and how it contributes to the wider public interest.

2.3. Modernization of the Legal Instruments

Although the fundamentals of competition law set out in the Treaty of Rome have essentially remained the same for more than fifty years, the legal instruments implementing them have been continually reassessed and amended.

2.3.1. *Antitrust*

Substantive antitrust rules have been progressively reviewed in order to reflect developments in economic thinking, reduce the regulatory burden on companies, and improve the speed and efficiency of enforcement. In addition to legislative rules, the Commission has adopted various non-regulatory documents such as notices and guidelines, explaining in more detail the policy of the Commission on a number of issues and interpreting legislative antitrust rules.

Between 1999 and 2004 a set of Block Exemption Regulations and Guidelines was adopted to reflect a more economic and less regulatory approach to competition policy. Relating to agreements concerning supply and distribution, research and development, specialization, and licensing of technology, they have simplified the rules and reduced the regulatory burden, especially for companies lacking market power. While they represented a move away from form-based rules, the combination of block exemptions and explanatory guidance seems to have provided a good balance between predictability and economic accuracy. In particular, the focus on the issue of market power has led to a more effective control of agreements made by companies with significant market power.

The 2001 *de minimis* Notice defined when agreements do not appreciably restrict competition under the European Commission Treaty. It thereby reduced the compliance burden for companies, especially smaller companies, and at the same time allowed the Commission to concentrate on more-problematic agreements.

Focusing on more-significant distortions of competition must go hand in hand with the ability to impose effective sanctions. The Guidelines on the method of setting fines, adopted by the Commission first in 1998 in order to enhance transparency as to its fining policy, were revised in 2006 with a view to increasing the deterrent effect of fines.

Similarly, as cartels are clearly the most harmful impediment to the competitive process, it was inevitable that the rules facilitating their detection had to be improved. The Commission's leniency policy has played an important role in uncovering and punishing secret cartels. The first Notice on immunity from fines and reduction of fines in cartel cases was adopted in 1996. Subsequent reforms in 2002 and 2006 created greater incentives for companies to blow the whistle, provided more guidance to applicants, and increased the transparency of the procedure.

On 1 May 2004, a new enforcement system for Articles 81 and 82 EC entered into force, abolishing the notification system and empowering national competition authorities and courts to participate fully in the application of Articles 81 and 82 EC. It also introduced new and more effective ways of addressing competition problems, such as the possibility for the Commission to make commitments binding on undertakings, when such commitments meet the concerns expressed by the Commission in antitrust proceedings. Regulation 1/2003 also gave the Commission wider investigative powers by expanding its inspection rights.

As a complement to Regulation 1/2003, the Commission adopted the 'modernization package' consisting of a new Regulation on details of its antitrust procedures and six Notices aimed at providing guidance on a range of issues. The Network Notice established the main pillars of cooperation between the Commission and the competition authorities of the Member States within the European competition network (ECN) and set out the principles for sharing casework. The Notice on cooperation with national courts clarified the procedural context in which national judges operate. The Notice on complaints gave explanations on the Commission's assessment of complaints in the antitrust field and the procedures applicable. The Notice on guidance letters provided details on when and how the Commission will give guidance to undertakings in writing where a genuinely novel question concerning Article 81 or 82 EC arises. The Notice on effect on trade explains the application of this jurisdictional criterion determining the reach of Articles 81 and 82 EC, and establishes presumptions when the criterion is not met. Finally, the Guidelines on Article 81(3) EC facilitate the application of Article 81(3) EC by national competition authorities and national courts, and at the same time allow companies to assess the legality of their agreements.

In parallel, the Commission increased the transparency of competition procedures and expressed its commitment to due process and the parties' rights of defence. In 2001, it strengthened the role of the Hearing Officer by attaching it directly to the Commissioner for Competition and by making their report available to the parties and publishing it in the Official Journal of the European Union. In 2005, it revised its rules for access to the Commission's files by parties involved in its merger and antitrust cases by updating its previous notice from 1997. The revised Notice also increased procedural efficiency by confirming that access to the file can be granted electronically or on paper.

Recently the Commission introduced a form of direct settlements for cartels through which companies that acknowledge their responsibility in a cartel infringement benefit from a shorter administrative procedure and receive a reduction in the amount of fines. This opened up the prospect of more rapid prosecution of cartels and a more effective use of scarce enforcement resources. Similarly, the Commission has published guidance on its enforcement priorities in applying EC Treaty rules on abuse of a dominant market position to abusive exclusionary conduct by dominant undertakings. The guidance paper sets out an economic and effects-based approach to exclusionary conduct.

Evaluating procedural and substantive rules is, and should be, a permanent task. For example, facilitating private enforcement would help ensure that those damaged by infringements of European Commission competition law can exercise their right to compensation, as well as adding to overall sanctions and deterrence, as a complement to public enforcement. As a follow-up to its White Paper of 2008 on compensating consumer and business victims of breaches of the competition rules, the Commission is currently considering possible further steps.

2.3.2. Merger control

The Merger Regulation, first adopted in 1989, created a one-stop shop where companies apply for regulatory clearance for mergers and acquisitions above certain worldwide and European turnover thresholds. The recast Merger Regulation, adopted in 2004, introduced some flexibility into the investigation timeframes, while retaining a much-praised degree of predictability. It reinforced the 'one-stop shop' concept, and clarified the substantive test so that the Commission now has the power to investigate all types of harmful scenarios in a merger, from dominance by a single firm to coordinated and non-coordinated effects in oligopolistic markets.

The 2004 Regulation also introduced a new streamlined referral system in order to put in place a more rational corrective mechanism of case allocation between the Commission and Member States. It ensured that the authority or authorities best placed to carry out a particular merger investigation should deal with the case. Amendments to the referral system have been complemented by a new Notice on the principles, criteria, and methodology upon which referral decisions should be based. A revised Notice on a simplified procedure was adopted in 2005, further reducing regulatory burden on undertakings for certain concentrations that rarely, if ever, raise competition concerns.

Furthermore, a set of best practices was adopted on the conduct of merger investigations to provide guidance for interested parties on the day-to-day conduct of European Commission merger control proceedings. These best practices were designed to streamline and make more transparent the investigation and decision-making process, ranging from issues of economic indicators to rights of the defence.

The 2004 Merger Regulation was complemented by Guidelines on the assessment of horizontal mergers. These Guidelines set out the analytical approach the Commission takes in assessing the likely competitive impact of mergers and reflect the re-wording of the substantive test for the competitive assessment of mergers in the 2004 Merger Regulation. The objective was to provide guidance to companies and the legal community alike as to which mergers may be challenged.

The Guidelines explain the circumstances in which the Commission may identify competition concerns, but also provide clear quantitative indications as to when the Commission is unlikely to intervene—for example, when a merger results in market concentration levels below certain specified levels. They also set out the factors that may mitigate an initial concern that a merger is likely to harm competition and the conditions under which efficiency gains resulting from the merger will be taken into account.

In addition, with the aim of providing guidance to undertakings, a 2001 Notice on remedies sets out the general principles applicable to remedies acceptable to the Commission in merger proceedings. The Notice describes the main types of commitments that have been accepted by the Commission, the specific requirements which proposals of commitments need to fulfil in both phases of the procedure, and the main requirements for the implementation of commitments.

Similarly, a 2005 Notice provides guidance on the interpretation of the notion of ancillary restraints—that is, restrictions directly related and necessary to concentrations. In order to provide legal certainty to the undertakings concerned, the Notice explains the Commission's practice and sets out principles for assessing whether and to what extent the most common types of agreements are deemed to be ancillary restraints.

The assessment of all proposed merger transactions must be based on sound economic theory and analysis and high-quality investigative techniques. As part of these efforts, in 2007, the Commission adopted Guidelines for the assessment of mergers between companies that are in a so-called vertical or conglomerate relationship. The Guidelines provide examples, based on established economic principles, of where vertical and conglomerate mergers may significantly impede effective competition in the markets concerned, but also provide 'safe harbours', in terms of market share and concentration levels below which competition concerns are unlikely to be identified.

In order to further improve the transparency, predictability, and consistency of the Commission's policy and to ensure that it is based on a sound economic framework, a revised Remedies Notice, published in 2008, adapted the 2001 Notice in the light of an extensive study undertaken by the Commission into the implementation and effectiveness of remedies, recent judgments of the European Courts, and the 2004 Merger Regulation.

2.3.3. *State aid control*

Following reforms of legal and interpretative instruments in the field of antitrust and mergers, the Commission engaged in the first comprehensive modernization of both substantive and procedural rules in the area of state aid control. The state aid action plan (SAAP), launched in 2005, aims at an increased efficiency of state aid control. It is based on four guiding principles:

(i) less and better-targeted state aid (ii) a refined economic approach (iii) more effective procedures, better enforcement, higher predictability, and enhanced transparency, and (iv) shared responsibility between the Commission and Member States.

Since 2005, a number of legislative and interpretative instruments have been adopted that reflect the new approach to state aid policy. The 2005 package on Services of General Economic Interest provides legal certainty with regard to compensatory measures, while ensuring transparency in order to avoid over-compensation and cross-subsidization. It reduces 'red tape' by exempting from the notification obligation compensations below a certain threshold.

The 2005 Guidelines on regional aid specify rules for the selection of regions that are eligible for regional aid, provide more flexibility for Member States to decide when and how they want to support regional development, and contain a number of other changes to clarify and simplify the previous rules.

The 2005 Communication on short-term export-credit insurance focuses on the question of whether there is a market failure that can be remedied by state aid, taking into account recent developments on the market for export credit insurance.

New Guidelines on risk capital, adopted in 2006, help stakeholders to determine when state aid in support of risk capital investment in SMEs is compatible with state aid rules. It sets out different types of assessments the Commission makes on the basis of the economic impact of state aid.

The new *de minimis* Regulation of 2006 exempts a greater number of small subsidies from the obligation to be cleared by the Commission in advance. The 2006 state aid framework for Research, Development, and Innovation helps Member States to target R&D&I state aid on the best projects, on the basis of economic analysis, thereby minimizing distortions of competition and trade and maximizing public spending efficiency.

A General Block Exemption Regulation was adopted in 2008. On the one hand, this simplifies and consolidates into a single text five existing block exemptions—for aid to SMEs, research and development aid in favour of SMEs, aid for employment, training aid, and regional aid. On the other hand, the new Regulation also allows the block exemption of three new types of aid—environmental aid, aid in the form of risk capital, and exempting R&D aid also in favour of large enterprises. The regulation facilitates proper compliance with state aid rules while minimizing bureaucracy for both Member States and the Commission.

Additional reform steps taken recently include—among others—Guidelines on environmental aid, a new Notice on state aid in the form of guarantees, a revised Notice on cooperation with national courts, and a Notice on the recovery of illegal or incompatible aid. In the Autumn of 2008, the Commission has responded rapidly, decisively but flexibly to the financial and economic crisis through, *inter alia*, the adoption of guidance on the application of state aid rules to measures taken in relation to financial institutions, in particular decapitalizations, and the adoption of a temporary framework for state aid measures to support access to finance.

This comprehensive review of the substantive rules will be accompanied by improvements in the way the Commission deals with the state aid notification procedures. Procedural reforms should aim at shortening procedures, improving transparency, ensuring that state aid is duly notified or recovered if implemented illegally, and improving administrative efficiency, among others, by allowing an easier collection of relevant sectoral information.

2.4. Resource and Change Management Inside Directorate-General Competition

In parallel to the reforms of the legal instruments, over the last years, DG Competition has changed its mission, internal structures, and processes to align it more closely with the requirements of a modern framework for competition policy.

2.4.1. *Past culture and traditions*

For the years up to around 2000, the mission of DG Competition was essentially defined as 'promoting competition, thereby promoting an efficient allocation of resources'. Enforcement was necessarily reactive, as it was driven largely by notifications and complaints. This was also reflected in the internal structures and processes of the DG. Work was focused on the development of the various legal instruments, with lower priority given to economic analysis and market knowledge. With the exception of the Merger Task Force, resources were mostly allocated on a unit-by-unit basis within each directorate, often resulting in ring fencing of staff within the boundaries of both the legal instrument and the market sector concerned. There were very few examples of a case-handler in the telecoms antitrust unit working on either a telecoms merger case, or a media antitrust case.

In addition, there was limited priority-setting or planning of cases and other initiatives. Negative priorities—Drucker's 'posteriorities'—were almost non-existent. Without positive and negative priorities, it was difficult to deploy resources effectively. This led to some very lengthy anti-trust and state aid investigations which stretched out well after the moment at which the final decision on the case would have had most impact.

DG Competition also had a reputation for a rather inward-looking culture vis-à-vis the rest of the Commission and national competition authorities. Although a high value was placed on professionalism, intellectual rigour, and integrity, there was at least a perceived tendency towards a monopoly of the truth in external relationships. The DG rarely involved itself in an analysis of competition issues in the work of other Commission departments.

Around 2002, there were signs that the platform on which DG Competition was operating needed to be stabilized. A series of merger prohibitions were reversed by the CFI for inadequate legal reasoning and economic analysis by the Commission and for procedural errors. Outside criticism targeted the DG's formalistic approach, as well as the lack of transparency and long delays in state aid control.

2.4.2. Change management

There are a number of general success parameters that are key to managing change effectively in an organization such as DG Competition.

Most importantly, there is the need to establish objectives. The role, mission, and core values of the organization need to be clearly defined. Competition authorities should not shy away from regularly reassessing their role as a public institution and from redefining their mission in light of changes to the environment. Debate about the mission also helps to devise a clear strategy. Multi-annual forward-looking strategic planning is essential to the success of the organization and the system as a whole. The strategy, in turn, should translate into operational objectives together with planning and monitoring of results to be achieved. Strategic goals have to be broken down into operational objectives that can be planned in advance, monitored during their execution, and evaluated afterwards.

Secondly, the organizational structure should target resources towards these objectives. Such structure should reflect the core values of the organization and help mobilize resources to achieve the objectives.

Thirdly, the organization needs people with the right skills and experience. The biggest asset of a competition-policy institution is its staff. An efficient management and development of people is fundamental.

Fourthly, an organizational culture must be created which promotes values crucial to the success of the organization such as ethical standards, integrity, intellectual rigour, objectivity, public- and client-service culture, and results-orientation.

Finally, within every organizational structure there is a need to establish the right processes which help make things happen. These can include, for example, decision-making procedures, 'liturgies' of meetings, or IT systems.

2.4.3. Defining objectives

If competition policy is to make a significant contribution to a policy of sustainable economic growth, a narrow law enforcement and instrument-based approach which focuses only on the preservation of existing competition is not sufficient.

Competition policy must therefore act on a number of fronts at the same time. First, it must enforce competition law whenever there are harmful effects on Europe's citizens or businesses. But, second, it must also ensure that the regulatory environment fosters competitive markets. It needs to screen proposed and existing legislation. Thirdly, it must help shape global economic governance through promoting the convergence of substantive competition rules, strengthening cooperation with other jurisdictions, and promoting a shift of emphasis from trade regulation to competition regulation in the WTO. Finally, it must develop a competition culture in the society in which it operates. This is in itself one of the principal elements which can guarantee the competitiveness of an economy in the longer term. Ultimately, competition policy must make markets work better for consumer and businesses in Europe.

Competition-policy institutions must also make clear, in economic terms, whose interest they are there to protect. In the Commission's view, the ultimate objective of its intervention in the area of antitrust and merger control should be the promotion of consumer welfare. Under European Union antitrust and merger control the aim is to ensure that consumers are not harmed by anticompetitive agreements, exclusionary and exploitative conduct by one or more dominant undertakings, or by mergers that significantly impede effective competition. A good example is the Commission's 2007 prohibition decision in the *Ryanair/Aer Lingus* merger case, which prevented a reduction in choice and, most likely, higher prices for more than 14 million EU passengers using one of the thirty-five routes operated by both parties.

However, a consumer-welfare standard cannot be transposed directly to the world of state aid. In fact, beyond any justification it may have in terms of allocative efficiency, state aid can be justified on the basis of non-economic grounds such as reducing social disparities which consumer welfare does not measure. Whether the rationale for state aid is efficiency or equity, the correct welfare standard for state aid policy—expressed in economic terms—would seem to be the social welfare of the European Union, which is equivalent to the notion of common interest found in Article 87(3) EC.

The concept of consumer welfare should also be interpreted dynamically in the sense of the effects of any structure or conduct on price, choice, quality, and innovation in the short and long terms. Sometimes these effects are immediate and measurable. However, often the effects are difficult to quantify and the only way to protect consumer welfare in the longer term is by safeguarding the process or dynamic of competition on the markets. In this sense, there is convergence between the German and Anglo-Saxon antitrust traditions.

Most theories of harm do not require sophisticated econometric or simulation modelling. Usually the economic 'story' behind a case is simple to explain and simple to test against the evidence drawn from a market investigation. It is also sometimes impossible to carry out in-depth analysis within the confines of the legal deadlines of a merger investigation. However, in some cases, detailed econometric tests have been applied with success.

Following the legislative and policy changes described above, the Commission now uses an 'effects-based approach' both in merger control and in antitrust, which focuses on the actual and likely effects on consumer welfare. This means that a framework is needed to establish a theory of consumer harm, and this framework should also come up with hypotheses which can be tested. For example, in the *Oracle/PeopleSoft* merger case in 2004, we examined with econometrics the extent to which Oracle's bidding behaviour was affected by the specific identity of the rival bidders in the final rounds of a given bidding contest.

In line with the state aid Action Plan, the Commission is also moving towards a more economic approach in state aid policy. Assessing the compatibility of state aid is fundamentally about balancing the negative effects of aid on competition and trade with its positive effects in terms of the 'common interest'. However, economic analysis in state aid cases is more challenging than in antitrust and mergers: first, it is not just concerned with competition between firms, but also with negative effects of an aid on trade within the EU Single Market or location decisions, and, secondly, equity considerations (jobs, benefits for the environment) need to be balanced against efficiency considerations.

The objective of making markets work better requires, in the first place, carefully selected priority sectors. DG Comp's action therefore focuses on sectors that are key for the functioning of the internal market and for the Lisbon agenda for growth and jobs. For example, public monopolies established to provide telecommunications, post, energy, and transport services have not always proved efficient and able to satisfy consumers' needs in the best possible way. Gradually opening up these markets to competition and making sure that they remain open not only allows consumers to benefit from new, cheaper, and more efficient services but also reduces significant input costs for companies. The Commission's antitrust decisions against *Deutsche Telekom* and *Wanadoo* in 2003, against *Telefónica* in 2007, and its ongoing investigations following the sector inquiry into the gas and electricity sector are but a few examples of this focus.

The more harmful anticompetitive practices for the European economy and consumers are the greater the need there is for competition policy to intervene. As cartels are clearly the most harmful restrictions of competition, high priority is given to the prevention and deterrence of cartels, as evidenced by the imposition of fines in excess of €3.3 billion in 2007 and €2.2 billion in 2008. Similarly, abuses of dominant position with a clear negative effect on consumer welfare must remain in the spotlight of enforcement. Finally, erecting barriers to market entry through special or exclusive rights, granting distortive state aid, or restricting takeovers of national companies often result in serious restrictions of the competitive process and therefore also warrant priority.

There may also be alternative ways of remedying a market failure. Proper priority setting should be based on a 'competition obstacle' approach. This approach is based on identifying the main competition problems in a sector and subsequently selecting the most effective instrument(s) to tackle those problems. These instruments may be (i) competition enforcement by the Commission, by national competition authorities, or by both; (ii) the adoption, modification, or abolition of legislation at the Community level, at the national level, or at both levels; (iii) action by a sectoral regulator; (iv) self-regulation by the industry; or (v) a combination of these. The way the Commission has been challenging unjustified public obstacles to takeovers—for example in the *E.On/Endesa* case, jointly through its competition and internal market rules, is a good example of this 'competition obstacle' approach.

2.5. Reforming the Structures

2.5.1. *Two major reorganizations of DG Comp in 2003 and 2007*

Against this background of the progressive reorientation of EU competition policy, there have been two major reorganizations of the structure of DG Comp, complemented by a number of other incremental changes in between.

In 2003/4 we created for the first time a matrix structure by integrating Merger Units with antitrust units in directorates dedicated to enforcement action in key sectors of the EU economy such as energy, telecoms, transport, financial services, and information technology. The 2007 reorganization went one step further and integrated state aid units with antitrust and merger teams in five 'market and cases' directorates.

The advantages of this more sectoral organization are evident. It pools and increases market knowledge so that investigations are more informed and effective. It allows for more flexible use of staff across the policy instruments (antitrust, mergers, state aids) and helps spread best practices. It establishes closer links between competition policy and other EU sectoral policies and allows for more effective competition advocacy. It also makes sector enquiries easier to organize and run. Finally, it helps the dialogue with other DGs within the Commission and with national competition authorities and national regulators both within and outside the European Union.

On the other hand, there are areas where market knowledge is not as important as instrument knowledge and where therefore an instrument-based organization is more effective. The Cartel Directorate, created in 2005 and specifically dedicated to the enforcement and development of competition policy in relation to cartels, remains instrument based. This structure brings economies of scale and consolidates the Commission's cartel expertise in one directorate. Similarly, the content and procedures of horizontal state aid work, such as regional aid or aid for R&D&I, are more difficult to integrate into sectoral directorates and warrant an instrument-based directorate.

2.5.2. Creation of a Chief Competition Economist function

In line with the objective of strengthening the economic assessment of cases and new policy initiatives, a Chief Competition Economist function was created in 2003. The Chief Competition Economist reports directly to the Director General and is assisted by a team of more than twenty PhD economists. First, she provides guidance on the economic methodology in competition investigations. Secondly, she also gives guidance in individual competition cases from their early stages. Thirdly, she provides detailed guidance in key competition cases involving complex economic issues, in particular those requiring sophisticated quantitative analysis. Fourthly, she contributes to the development of general policy instruments.

In addition, the creation of the Chief Competition Economist function has contributed to the wider dissemination of economic expertise in DG Comp. She acts as a focus for economic debate within DG Comp, in liaison with other Commission services and in association with the academic world. Members of her team organize training sessions on economic issues and give advice on studies of a general economic nature, as well as on market monitoring.

2.5.3. Project-based allocation of resources

Setting priorities has no meaning unless priorities determine the use of scarce staff resources. Resources need to be flexibly allocated to cases or other projects. But the Commission's administrative structure (Directorate-General composed of directorates which are themselves composed of units) can create rigidities. So it has become standard practice in DG Comp to allow for 'décloisonnement' of staff to be assigned to any priority project with a 'case manager', reporting directly to a Director, who may come from any unit within a directorate. In addition, case teams can be created by bringing together staff from different directorates but who are skilled in antitrust merger or state aid investigations. It is also becoming general practice to assign to a case team a secretary who is specialized in the type of investigation concerned (mergers, antitrust, or state aids) who is given overall responsibility for the case's administrative aspects of the case.

So, project-based resource allocation is used both within a Directorate (each member of the Cartel Directorate can work for different case-managers under the single authority of a Director) and across Directorates (a member of a merger unit can work with colleagues from a merger unit from another Directorate within the 'Merger Network'). This project-based approach is applied not only for casework, but also for policy projects requiring the participation of staff having different sector- or instrument-specific expertise.

The advantages of the project-based allocation of resources became particularly visible in the past months when the need for a rapid reaction to the crisis necessitated the creation of a large number of new case teams assessing state aid notifications, consisting of staff with state aid and/or financial sector expertise.

2.6. Reforming the Processes

2.6.1. *Introducing a two-stage procedure in antitrust*

Following the entry into force of Regulation 1/2003 and as a part of the efforts to streamline and increase the efficiency of the working methods in the field of antitrust, in 2005 we introduced a two-stage procedure. The goal of this procedure is to allow the Commission to discriminate quickly and effectively between those few cases that deserve an in-depth investigation and to which resources should be allocated and the other cases that are not a priority and that should be closed as soon as possible and with the least use of resources. The procedure is also designed properly to plan investigations in order to achieve results within specific target deadlines. As a result, all antitrust cases now start with a first-phase investigation of usually no more than four months, after which a decision is taken as to whether or not a theory of harm has been identified and whether these are reasons to regard the case as a priority for the Commission. If the case is considered a priority, in principle, a Commission decision to initiate proceedings is adopted and an in-depth investigation is carried out.

The theory of harm on which an eventual investigation is based must be robust and there must be prima facie, facts-based indications of the alleged infringement. This solid foundation reduces the risk of subsequent delays in the procedure. The criteria on the basis of which it is decided whether there are sufficient grounds to carry out an in-depth investigation include, among others, the extent and likelihood of consumer harm, the strategic nature of the policy area or the sector concerned, the significance of the impact on the functioning of competition in the internal market, the extent or complexity of the investigation required, the possibility for bringing the case before a national court in a Member State, and whether the potential infringement investigated has terminated or is still ongoing.

2.6.2. Focus on investigative techniques

Given the increased focus on effects, investigations are becoming more fact-intensive and case files are growing bigger. This requires new approaches and skills in the handling of antitrust, merger, and state aid cases. DG Comp is constantly trying to improve its practices in collecting evidence and presenting facts in decisions.

Efficient investigative techniques (how best to gather reliable evidence) are essential for the success of any antitrust procedures. In order to better focus investigations and reduce case-handling time, we try to plan the details of the investigation at an early stage of the proceedings—(i) the quality and quantity of evidence needed to prove the case; (ii) the identification of possible sources where the evidence is located; and (iii) the resources to be assigned to this task.

Best practice in drafting (how best to present evidence to construct a sound decision) is another important tool. In order to discharge the burden of proof imposed on the Commission, case teams must thoroughly and accurately incorporate the results of the investigation into the final decision, demonstrating that the standards of proof are met. The final decision must address all the relevant issues the Commission investigated during the proceedings, incorporate all the relevant evidence gathered during the investigation, and lay down the reasoning of the Commission in a clear and consistent fashion.

2.6.3. Organizing peer-review panels

In order to ensure the quality of its interventions, DG Comp applies a particular form of scrutiny for major antitrust, merger, or state aid cases, from their factual basis through the legal reasoning to economic analysis. It consists of organizing a peer-review panel at key points during the investigation—for example, after the sending of the Statement of Objections and the hearing, where a peer review team looks at all aspects of a case with a 'fresh pair of eyes'.

The primary objective of this exercise is to provide assistance to the case team in particularly complex cases with a view to ensuring that the foundations of the case are robust. The peer review panel may identify areas where further work is necessary to sustain an objection and how this might be carried out.

2.6.4. Advocacy and competition screening of legislative proposals by other Commission departments

As a result of internal advocacy and communication efforts, competition policy and our objective of making markets work better for the benefits of consumers and businesses play an increasing role in the Commission's overall economic policy.

A competition test was included in the Commission's revised Impact Assessment Guidelines of 2005. All legislative and policy initiatives included in the Commission's annual work programme must pass this test. The basic 'competition test' applied in the context of competition-policy screening involves asking two fundamental questions at the outset. First, what restrictions of competition may directly or indirectly result from the proposal (does it place restrictions on market entry, does it affect business conduct, etc.)? Second, are less-restrictive means available to achieve the policy objective in question? This screening exercise may result in the choice of less-restrictive regulatory or market-based methods to achieve certain policy objectives, thereby helping avoid unnecessary or disproportionate restrictions of competition.

2.7. Current Management Challenges

2.7.1. *Measuring performance and impact*

It is impossible to know whether objectives are correctly set, whether the institutional structures and processes are well defined and ultimately whether the actions of a competition authority produce the desired outcome if the performance of the institution is not measured in one way or another.

Working back from the overall objective of making markets work better for the benefit of consumers and business, we intend to use the following three performance measurements: productivity, quality, and impact.

Productivity tries to measure the efficiency of the organization; it indicates whether we are successful in coping with the incoming workload, in minimizing inputs, and in maximizing output. For that purpose, we compare on a regular basis, on the one hand, workload (incoming cases) and inputs (resources, etc.) with, on the other hand, outputs (decisions, texts adopted, etc.).

For a competition enforcer such as DG Comp to achieve its public interest objectives, the quality of its output is arguably at least as important as productivity. There are different sub-dimensions to that. We look at (a) the legal and economic soundness of our enforcement; (b) the timeliness of our procedures; (c) compliance with due process; and (d) how well we communicate on our enforcement.

In order really to know whether we achieve our ultimate objective of making markets work better, we need to measure the impact of our decisions on those markets. For that purpose, we intend to distinguish between the measurement of the direct impact of our action on markets and on the different stakeholders (consumers, competitors, etc.) and of the indirect effects (precedent effect, deterrence, etc.). As a first step, a project team dedicated to the *ex post* evaluation of DG Comp's enforcement activity was set up in 2007 as a part of the Policy and Strategy Directorate of DG Comp.

2.7.2. *Demonstrating the added value to citizens*

Closely linked with measuring performance is the challenge of demonstrating the added value of competition policy to ordinary people. It is not sufficient to know what the impact of competition policy action is: the benefits need to be communicated effectively.

We have recognized that communication is core business. Communicating effectively about our work has a preventive effect. We can explain the law and highlight the penalties for not respecting the law. In addition, explaining what DG Comp, entrusted with public resources and powers, does, ensures its accountability. Communication is also about good policymaking. Through dialogue, DG Comp can learn to re-evaluate the things about which it is communicating. Finally, external communication on concrete actions of competition policy can demonstrate a Europe of results. These simple principles are the core of our proactive communication strategy for which we have also recently created a dedicated Communications Policy unit.

2.8. Resources

2.8.1. The 'Comp 2010' project

In 2006, Commissioner Kroes and I set up an internal working group to take stock of where the Commission's competition policy as well as DG Comp's organization and resources stood, and where they should go in the medium term (until 2010). The working group produced a report which (i) provided the Commissioner and the management of the Directorate-General with a detailed picture of current work and output; (ii) identified relevant trends for the next years; (iii) determined the likely impact of those trends on work and output; and (iv) discussed options as to how the challenges could be addressed.

The working group found that the enforcement architecture and internal organization stemming from the 2003 and 2007 reforms produced reasonably good results in terms of focusing resources where DG Comp can bring the greatest added value. However, based on the analysis of expected trends that influence competition policy and on comparisons with other competition agencies, it identified a resource gap between what DG Comp should, and will have to, do in the future and what it is able to do on the basis of its current resources.

One of the main findings was that DG Comp was understaffed when compared to other competition authorities, such as the United States Department of Justice and Fair Trade Commission or the Japan Fair Trade Commission (see Figures 2.1. and 2.2.). Understaffing was even more evident if account was taken of DG Comp's responsibility for state aid issues.

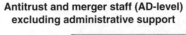

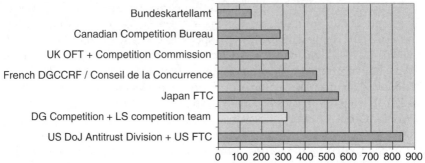

Figure 2.1. Antitrust and merger staff (AD-level) excluding administrative support (2006)

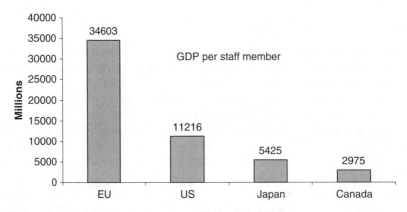

Figure 2.2. Gross domestic product per staff member (2006)

2.8.2. *Human resource strategy*

The issue of resources is not only about mechanically increasing staff numbers. It is increasingly challenging to attract, improve, and retain talent. DG Comp is focusing on very specific staff—lawyers specializing in competition law and economists specializing in industrial organization. For both of these categories, DG Comp is competing on the labour market with law firms and economic consultancies which are offering salary packages much higher than can the Commission. Organizing Commission competitions for higher-entry-level grades could somewhat reduce this salary gap, at least during the first years of a career. Organizing Commission competitions specifically addressed to candidates having the right profile (not lawyers or economists in general, but those having a specific competition background) could also improve recruitment. Accelerating recruitment procedures is a further challenge.

It is essential to ensure that staff recruited continue to have the skills and competences required to meet DG Comp's quality standards. This is guaranteed by a training programme adapted to real needs. Knowledge areas that are strategically relevant for DG Comp and so should be the focus of training programmes are law and procedures, economics and accountancy, sectoral knowledge, investigative techniques, drafting, communication, languages, and IT. The internal training offered by DG Comp and the use of external resources must continue to be improved.

Finally, keeping talent is only possible through a transparent and motivating career development system. Within the constraints of Commission-wide staff regulations, we recently introduced additional systems of recognition of expertise, through job titles for experienced case handlers and assistants. We also plan to activate a Career Guidance Function within DG Comp to give factual information to staff on career opportunities, and to facilitate the identification and building of career paths. It is particularly challenging to find a correct balance between promoting staff mobility to sustain motivation and the needs of DG Comp to guarantee the stability and continuity of its activities.

2.8.3. *Managing knowledge better*

One of the key assets of DG Comp is its accumulated knowledge of the markets as well as its expertise in applying the legal instruments at its disposal. Managing knowledge, so as to keep it up to date and accessible to all those who need it, is a major challenge for the Directorate-General. This will be of key importance if DG Comp is to better contribute its market knowledge to policies developed in other Directorates-General within the Commission. The organizational structure described above is instrumental in fostering the exchange of knowledge between colleagues. However, further action will be required to improve the management of in-house knowledge through updating the existing document management systems and case management applications.

2.9. Conclusion

The growing number of competition policy institutions in the world reflects the need for public institutions to safeguard and promote competition in an economy that is becoming increasingly globalized. In order to fulfil their role effectively these institutions must constantly assess and re-assess their mission, objectives, structures, processes, and performance. It is only through coming to terms with and adapting to changes in their environment and by carrying out the necessary improvements that their competences, powers, budgets, and ultimately existence can be justified before a wider public.

Note

[1] The author is Director General of the Directorate-General for Competition at the European Commission. The views expressed are personal to the author and do not necessarily reflect those of the European Commission. The author would like to thank Thomas Deisenhofer, András Inotai, and Kevin Coates for assisting him in preparing this chapter.

3

Article 81 EC Revisited: Deciphering European Commission Antitrust Goals and Rules

Matthew Bennett and A. Jorge Padilla[1]

3.1. Introduction

After many years making headlines on DG Comp's website and in its competition newsletters, interest in Article 81 appears to have subsided.[2] The consensus view seems to be that the reform of Article 81 was successfully culminated with the publication of the 'Guidelines on the Application of Article 81(3) of the Treaty' in April 2004.[3] The focus of recent antitrust debate is now on the reform of (or, perhaps, the lack of reform of) Article 82.[4] The Article 82 debate opposes, on one hand, those who defend the rule of law virtues of the per se illegality rules that have characterized the application of Article 82 since the 1950s and 60s and have been endorsed once and again by the Community courts and, on the other, those who consider that the unilateral practices of dominant firms should be assessed using a pure effects-based approach.[5] The Article 82 controversy has also reopened the discussion about the ultimate goal of competition policy—fairness, consumer welfare, the competitive process, single market integration, or all of the above.

The debate about Article 82 would benefit significantly from a detailed study of the reform of Article 81 and its application over the last few years. This is not simply because there is a greater wealth of case law built up within Article 81, but also because issues such as the objective of antitrust intervention and the practical application of the rule of reason in competition matters have played a central role in two recent Article 81 cases: *Glaxo*[6] and *02 (Germany)*.[7]

In *Glaxo*, the Court of First Instance (CFI) clarified that 'competition law...is concerned only with [the] impact [of certain business practices] on the welfare of the final consumer'.[8] This is a significant departure from previous case law, where Article 81 appeared to be a mere tool for the achievement of market integration.[9] In *02 (Germany)* the CFI adjudicated on the important question of how to determine whether an agreement is reducing competition. The CFI found that what matters is a comparison of the 'competitive situation' in the absence of the agreement versus competition under the agreement. The CFI stated:

Working on the assumption that O2 was present on the mobile communications market, the Commission did not therefore deem it necessary to consider in more detail whether, in the absence of the agreement, O2 would have been present on the 3G market. It must be held that that assumption is not supported in the Decision by any analysis or justification showing that it is correct, a finding that, moreover, the defendant could only confirm at the hearing. Given that there was no such objective examination of the competition situation in the absence of the agreement, the Commission could not have properly assessed the extent to which the agreement was necessary for O2 to penetrate the 3G mobile communications market. The Commission therefore failed to fulfil its obligation to carry out an objective analysis of the impact of the agreement on the competitive situation.[10]

Also in *Glaxo* the CFI clarified the Commission's 'legal burden of proof' in the context of an Article 81 case. Once the defendant has discharged its 'evidentiary burden of proof' in connection with the gains in efficiency produced by the agreement under consideration, it is incumbent upon the Commission to assess first the evidence in support of those efficiencies and then, if the gains in efficiency have been substantiated, to balance those efficiencies against the potentially anticompetitive effects of the agreement. More precisely, the court stated:

The Commission was required, first, to conduct an appropriate examination of [Glaxo-SmithKline's] factual arguments and evidence [regarding the pro-competitive implications of the allegedly restrictive clauses of its contracts], in order to be in a position to carry out, second, the complex assessment necessary in order to weigh up the disadvantage and the advantage associated with [those clauses].[11]

Thus, the CFI's ruling also clarified the structure of the competitive assessment of horizontal and vertical agreements under Article 81: an agreement will be considered legal unless it can be shown that it is likely to restrict competition; in which case the Commission (and not the defendant(s)) has to balance its anticompetitive and pro-competitive effects prior to concluding that the practice is anticompetitive overall. The CFI also noted the complexity of such a 'balancing exercise', which requires the Commission to take all relevant facts into account and not just the defendant's market share before concluding that the net effect of a contested agreement is anticompetitive.[12]

The remainder of the chapter is structured as follows. Section 2 provides an overview of Article 81 and how it has been implemented in the case law. Article 81 involves a series of screens designed to determine whether conduct is legal per se, illegal per se, or needs to be assessed according to its likely effects. Section 3 considers the objectives of Article 81 by looking at the recent ruling of the CFI in *Glaxo*. In Section 4, we review the recent CFI ruling in *02 (Germany)* to understand when an agreement should be regarded as anticompetitive. This case demonstrates the importance of selecting an appropriate competitive counterfactual when assessing the competitive nature of an agreement among competitors. Section 5 considers the structure of Article 81 from an error-cost perspective. While in principle Article 81 could be interpreted as either a structured rule of reason or a qualified per se illegality rule, depending on how the fourth limb of the Article 81(3) test was implemented, the recent CFI judgment in *Glaxo* suggests that it should be regarded as a structured rule of reason. Section 6 concludes with a discussion of the implications of the analysis developed in Sections 3 to 5 for the current debate on Article 82.

3.2. A Brief Overview of Article 81

Article 81 of the European Commission Treaty prohibits agreements and concerted practices which prevent, restrict, or distort competition unless the agreement is justified by improvements in efficiency. More precisely,

Article 81(1) prohibits all agreements between undertakings, decisions by associations of undertakings and concerted practices which may affect trade between Member States and which have as their object or effect the prevention, restriction or distortion of competition.

As an exception to this rule, Article 81(3) provides that the prohibition contained in Article 81(1) may be declared inapplicable in case of agreements which contribute to improving the production or distribution of goods or to promoting technical or economic progress, while allowing consumers a fair share of the resulting benefits, and which do not impose restrictions which are not indispensable to the attainment of these objectives, and do not afford such undertakings the possibility of eliminating competition in respect of a substantial part of the products concerned.[13]

3.2.1. *The structure of Article 81*

The implementation of Article 81 involves several stages: (1) hardcore practices, such as price-fixing or market-splitting agreements, are presumed to have the potential to restrict competition; (2) *de minimis* agreements are automatically exempted—that is, are regarded as per se legal;[14] (3) all other agreements which are capable of affecting trade between Member States are assessed under Article 81(1) to determine whether they have an anticompetitive object or actual or potential anticompetitive effects; (4) some agreements which are found to be capable of restricting competition benefit from a block exemption under Article 81(3) provided they meet certain category market share thresholds; and (5) for all other agreements which are found to be capable of restricting competition, the pro-competitive benefits produced by that agreement, if any, are evaluated to determine whether these pro-competitive effects outweigh the anticompetitive effects. Each of these stages is discussed in more detail below.

PRESUMED ANTICOMPETITIVE EFFECTS OF HARDCORE INFRINGEMENTS

Hardcore infringements are generally considered restrictions of competition by 'object' and are presumed to have the potential of restricting competition.[15] They are regarded as per se illegal. The Article 81(3) Guidelines state: 'Once it has been established that an agreement has as its object the restriction of competition, there is no need to take account of its concrete effects.'[16] This is because they 'have such a high potential of negative effects on competition that it is unnecessary for the purposes of applying Article 81(1) to demonstrate any actual effects on the market'.[17] The hardcore category includes three horizontal restrictions—price fixing, output restrictions, and the allocation of markets or customers—and five vertical restrictions—resale price maintenance, territorial and customer restrictions, selective distribution network sales restrictions, selective distribution network cross-supply restrictions, and spare parts restrictions.[18]

Price Fixing

The Commission has taken a strong stance on price fixing: it is almost generally regarded as per se illegal. In *Reims II*, however, the Commission granted an exemption to an agreement between most European public postal operators on the cost of onward delivery in each others' territories.[19] The Commission considered this to be price fixing of an unusual nature and identified the reduction of double marginalization as the main result of the agreement.[20] Economists have supported a per se illegality rule regarding price fixing, given the small probability that price fixing generates benefits to consumers.[21] However, (a) the economic literature has struggled so far to provide a clear-cut explanation of why companies operating in transparent oligopolistic industries engage in explicit coordination and why communication among competitors makes such a difference for market outcomes;[22] and (b) the empirical literature on the actual impact of a harsh cartel policy is mixed. Sproul 1993 looked at twenty-five cartel cases between 1973 and 1984 to examine pricing behaviour post indictment. He found that contrary to expectations prices actually rose after indictment. Block, Nold, and Sidak, in an earlier paper (1981), looked at prices for local bread markets. They found that whilst the presence of an enforcement action in the city did reduce mark-ups, the percentage change was relatively small (minus 4.6 per cent).[23]

Output Restrictions

The Commission also treats 'quantity fixing', under a per se illegality rule. However, there have been exemptions to the rule. The Commission has not prohibited agreements involving output restrictions when (a) the restriction was ancillary to a beneficial specialization or R&D agreement and met criteria laid out in the Article 81(3), or (b) the parties notified a 'crisis cartel' aimed at facilitating a coordinated reduction in overcapacity over a limited time period.[24]

Market Sharing

The Commission takes the view that market sharing not only restricts competition but also impedes the single market objective. As with other hardcore restrictions, the Commission will generally prohibit these agreements and only in exceptional circumstances will these agreements be found to fulfil the conditions set out in Article 81(3).

Resale Price Maintenance

This category includes agreements which have as their direct or indirect object the fixing of resale or retail prices.[25] For example, agreements seeking to fix prices indirectly, such as minimum distribution margins or requiring implementation of 'recommended' prices, are considered hardcore infringements, but that is not so for agreements involving discretionary recommended prices or maximum retail prices.[26] As with all hardcore restrictions, the Commission and the Community courts appear to believe that it is highly unlikely that conditions of Article 81(3) will be satisfied.[27] However, this is not the view held by many, if not most, economists. Nearly fifty years ago, economists such as Telser and Bork argued that resale price maintenance (RPM) was a competitive tool that dealers used to promote the efficient level of effort from downstream retailers.[28] Most recently, relying on that literature and also on evidence showing that upstream firms without market power commonly fixed the prices to be applied by retailers of their products, a group of leading IO economists urged the US Supreme Court to overrule its precedents on minimum RPM mandating a per se illegality rule and subject minimum RPM agreements to a rule of reason analysis.[29] The US Supreme Court in *Leegin* v *PSKS* (2007) did overturn the 1911 *Dr Miles* ruling, by finding that RPM is not per se unlawful but must be judged under a 'rule of reason'.[30]

Territorial and Customer Restrictions

These are agreements that have as their direct or indirect object the allocation of territories or customers among competitors. That is, their object is to restrict intra-brand competition. Whilst in general these agreements are banned, there are four types of territorial or customer restrictions which may be permitted under European Commission competition law: (i) upstream firms are allowed to restrict downstream firms from actively searching customers in different sales areas, but cannot restrict firms from selling to customers who actively seek them out (passive sales);[31] (ii) downstream wholesalers are allowed to restrict active and passive sales to end users; (iii) active and passive sales to unauthorized distributors by members of selective distribution systems can be restricted; (iv) it is possible to restrict the buyers of components from selling them to customers using them to manufacture goods that compete with those of the supplier. Once again, there is no support in economics for a per se illegality rule against agreements specifying territorial constrains. These agreements should be analysed under the rule of reason since they are likely to give rise to both pro-competitive and anticompetitive effects. Like RPM, the granting of exclusive territories can be an effective way to ensure the dealer has the correct incentives to maximize effort so that end-consumer demand is fully exploited.[32] However, as shown by Rey and Stiglitz, territorial exclusivity may also result in a reduction in inter-brand competition by facilitating tacit collusion among upstream manufacturers.[33] Given that a per se ban against territorial exclusivity cannot be defended on pure efficiency grounds, one might argue that the relatively tough stance of the Commission in connection with these agreements is a reflection of their potential impact on the Commission's objective to promote trade between Member States.

Selective Distribution Network Sales Restrictions

A producer with a selective distribution network cannot restrict active or passive selling by the authorized distributors to end users. However, the producer can restrict authorized distributors from selling to specific locations.[34]

Selective Distribution Network Cross-Supply Restrictions

A producer with a selective distribution network cannot restrict its distributors from buying/selling its goods from/to other authorized distributors within the network.

Spare Parts Restrictions

A buyer which buys parts from a component manufacturer and incorporates these parts into its own product cannot restrict the component manufacturer from selling the parts as spare parts to end-users, independent repairers, or service providers. It is far from clear why these restrictions should be considered to infringe Article 81(1), let alone a hardcore infringement. There is an extensive literature showing that firms seldom have an anticompetitive incentive to refuse to supply the repair market.[35]

In short, while the per se prohibition of price- or quantity-fixing agreements and market sharing under Article 81 is justified as a matter of economics, this is not the case for the other hardcore restrictions. RPM, exclusive territories, and selective distribution should be considered under the rule of reason. There is no doubt that these vertical agreements restrict intra-brand competition (competition among distributors of the same brand) but may not be able to affect inter-brand competition (competition between suppliers of competing brands), and oftentimes may give rise to substantial efficiencies.

EXEMPTIONS UNDER THE *DE MINIMIS* RULE

Article 81(1) prohibits agreements that have an 'appreciable' effect on competition.[36] The Commission has provided safe-harbour market thresholds for non-hardcore agreements to secure exemption from Article 81(1). The Commission's Notice on agreements of minor importance states that agreements between competitors will not fall under Article 81(1) if: (a) the aggregate market share held by the parties to the agreement does not exceed 10 per cent on any of the relevant markets affected by the agreement where the agreement is between actual or potential competitors; or (b) the market share held by each party does not exceed 15 per cent on any of the relevant markets where the undertakings are not actual or potential competitors. It should be noted, however, that in practice those thresholds have not always been observed.[37]

LIKELY ANTICOMPETITIVE EFFECTS

For agreements which do not have as their object the restriction of competition, the Commission must show that the agreement is likely to affect competition in the market so that there are negative market effects on prices, output, innovation, or the variety or quality of goods and services that can be expected.[38] Account must be taken of its actual or potential effects. The Commission must provide a relatively detailed analysis of those effects and such effects must be appreciable.[39] It must consider the likely impact of the agreement on both intra-brand competition and inter-brand competition.[40] The key question is: does the agreement restrict competition that would have existed in the absence of the agreement or of some of the contractual restraints that are part of the agreement?[41]

Fundamental in such an analysis is the degree of parties' market power. An agreement is considered likely to produce appreciable anticompetitive effects when it 'contributes to the creation, maintenance or strengthening of that market power or allows the parties to exploit such market power'.[42] However, the question of what degree of market power is required remains somewhat ambiguous. The Article 81(3) Guidelines state that the degree of market power required in Article 81 cases is less than the degree of market power required for a legal finding of dominance under Article 82.[43] Why this should be the case is unclear—indeed one would expect a higher standard of proof in the case of vertical agreements, which are often driven by efficiency considerations. Note in this regard that there is a vast empirical literature on vertical restraints showing that on balance most vertical restraints do not cause consumer harm.[44]

BLOCK EXEMPTIONS UNDER ARTICLE 81(3)

There are some types of restrictions that can benefit from an automatic exemption under Article 81(3) even if they are found to be potentially restrictive of competition under Article 81(1). This is because there are reasons to believe that their net effect be pro-competitive. For example, horizontal agreements involving R&D cooperation may be exempted under the following conditions: (1) they must provide all parties with access to the research and all parties must be free to exploit the results of that research; (2) any joint exploitation of the innovation can only relate to results which are protected by intellectual property rights; (3) any individual firm specializing in production must supply all the other firms in the agreement; and (4) the firms that are part of the agreement cannot exceed a combined market share of 25 per cent on the relevant market.[45]

Likewise, the Commission exempts three categories of horizontal specialization agreements provided that the parties to the agreement have a combined share of no more that 20 per cent on the relevant market:[46] (1) unilateral specialization agreements, where one participant gives up the manufacture or provision of certain products/services; (2) reciprocal specialization agreements, where each participant agrees to give up the manufacture or provision of certain products/services; and (3) joint production agreements, where the participants agree jointly to manufacture or provide certain products/services. The rationale behind these exemptions is that the concentration of manufacturing activities may allow firms to produce and distribute goods more efficiently and hence more cheaply. As long as the agreement does not create market power (hence the threshold), these efficiencies will be passed onto consumers through competition. Finally, vertical restraints benefit from a slightly larger safe-harbour than horizontal agreements: 30 per cent of the upstream market.[47] This is reflective of the fact that vertical agreements between non-competing entities are generally seen as typically motivated by efficiency considerations.

BALANCING UNDER ARTICLE 81(3)

The Commission acknowledges that many agreements that restrict competition may also have pro-competitive effects and that such effects may outweigh any adverse effect on competition. Those agreements may allow the parties to lower their costs, increase their quality, or expand their innovation activities. When the pro-competitive effects of an agreement outweigh its anticompetitive effects, the agreement will be 'on balance' regarded pro-competitive and, hence, compatible with competition.

Article 81(3) establishes four conditions to determine whether an agreement, which does not constitute a hardcore agreement and is not exempted for other reasons, may be exempt from Article 81(1) owing to its efficiency effects. Under these conditions an agreement must: (i) contribute to improving the production or distribution of products or to promoting technical or economic progress; (ii) allow consumers a fair share of the resulting benefit; (iii) not impose restrictions which are not indispensable to the attainment of the above objectives; and (iv) not afford the possibility of eliminating competition in respect of a substantial part of the products in question.[48]

These conditions are cumulative: all four conditions must be fulfilled before an agreement may be said to enhance competition; if any of the conditions is not fulfilled, then the agreement is not exempt.[49] We consider below each of these conditions in some detail. Note, finally, that Article 81(3) applies equally to agreements that restrict competition by object and agreements that restrict competition by effect.[50]

Efficiency Gains

The first condition of Article 81(3) provides that the restrictive agreement must 'contribute to improving the production or distribution of goods or to promoting technical or economic progress'.[51] The Commission provides some guidance about the criteria it will use in assessing efficiencies.

The Commission will only take account of efficiencies if they do not arise as a result of anticompetitive actions.[52] For example, the Commission will not take into account any reductions in costs that result from a price-fixing agreement.

There must be a clear link between the efficiencies claimed and the agreement under scrutiny. Efficiency claims which are based on uncertain and/or remote effects will not be considered. For example, a restrictive agreement will not be exempted because the increase in the parties' market power and the corresponding increase in their profits could arguably enable them to invest more in R&D and hence benefit consumers in the future.[53]

The magnitude and likelihood of the claimed efficiencies must be clearly specified and documented. It is the parties' responsibility to calculate or estimate the value of the efficiencies alleged and describe in detail how that amount has been computed. The parties must also explain how and when each claimed efficiency would be achieved.

The Commission will consider both 'cost efficiencies [*such as cost reductions* resulting from the *development of new production or distribution methods, synergies* resulting from the *integration of existing assets, economies of scale, economies of scope, or simply more efficient inventory processes*] and efficiencies of a qualitative nature whereby value is created in the form of new or improved products, greater product variety, etc.'.[54]

Fair Share to Consumers

Consumers must receive a fair share of the efficiencies generated by the restrictive agreement under Article 81(3). This condition raises two questions: who are the consumers and what is a 'fair share'?

The Commission guidelines define consumers as: 'all direct or indirect users of the products covered by the agreement, including producers that use the products as an input, wholesalers, retailers and final consumers.'[55] This definition calls into question whether European Commission competition law is concerned with the protection of final consumers only or if it also cares about the well-being of competitors. For example, if a wholesaler is harmed but yet competition at the wholesale level remains vigorous, does this constitute harm to consumers? Likewise, should one be concerned by a vertical constraint that simply reallocates rents from the wholesalers to the manufacturers?

The second question is what is a 'fair share'? The Article 81(3) Guidelines state that the 'pass-on of benefits must at least compensate consumers for any actual or likely negative impact caused to them by the restriction of competition found under Article 81(1)'.[56] Thus, the Guidelines appear explicitly to recognize that the relevant standard is one that requires that the agreement makes no consumer worse off rather than a standard that would require the agreement to maximize consumer welfare. The Commission notes that those consumer benefits may not arise instantly and may be uncertain.

This condition incorporates a sliding scale.[57] The greater the restriction of competition found, the greater must be the efficiencies and the pass-on to consumers. In cases where the potential anticompetitive effects of the merger are very small or unlikely, it is improbable that the Commission will feel it to be necessary to embark on a detailed examination of the degree of pass-through inherent in this condition. On the contrary, when the restriction of competition is likely and substantial while the efficiencies are unlikely, uncertain, or simply small, no amount of pass-through will be regarded as sufficient from the viewpoint of Article 81(3).

Quantifying the degree of pass-through of benefits may prove difficult and, in any event, requires substantial information. The degree of pass-through, and hence the outcome of the balancing test, will depend on the following factors: (i) the characteristics and structure of the market; (ii) the nature and magnitude of the efficiency gains; (iii) the elasticity of demand; and (iv) the magnitude of the restriction of competition. The degree of competition remaining on the market and the nature of that competition will influence the likelihood of pass-on.[58]

Indispensability

To be exempted under Article 81(3), the restrictive agreement must be 'reasonably necessary' in order to achieve the claimed efficiencies.[59] The standard of reasonableness appears to be quite high: 'efficiencies [must] be specific to the agreement in question in the sense that there are no other economically practical and less restrictive means of achieving the efficiencies.'[60] However, businesses are not required to consider hypothetical alternatives. The claimed efficiencies will only be disregarded when it is reasonably clear that there are 'realistic and attainable' alternatives.[61] At that point the parties need only explain and demonstrate why those seemingly realistic and significantly less-restrictive alternatives to the agreement would be 'significantly less efficient'.[62]

Once it is established that the agreement as a whole is indispensable, the Commission may then look at whether there are individual restraints that are indispensable to the agreement. This step is used to ensure that there are not any unnecessary restrictions of competition. A restriction within the agreement is only considered indispensable if its absence would eliminate or significantly reduce the efficiencies from the entire agreement.

No Elimination of Competition

The fourth and final limb of Article 81(3) states that the agreement must not result in the elimination of competition in respect of a substantial part of the products concerned. The Commission explains that in its assessment of this condition it will take into account the degree of competition before the agreement. Hence, agreements producing effects in markets where competition is particularly weak will be subject to a tighter scrutiny.[63] This is perhaps the most controversial limb of the four parts of Article 81(3). The Article 81(3) Guidelines provocatively state: 'Ultimately the protection of rivalry and the competitive process is given priority over potentially pro-competitive efficiency gains which could result from restrictive agreements.'[64] But why should we give greater weight to the protection of rivalry than to consumer welfare? Indeed, why should an agreement be blocked when there are benefits that flow to consumers that outweigh the potential anticompetitive effects of the deal? The Guidelines state that '[w]hen competition is eliminated the competitive process is brought to an end and short-term efficiency gains are outweighed by long-term losses'.[65] That is, the Commission presumes that the negative long-term impact on consumer welfare caused by the elimination of actual competition will always be larger than the positive short-term benefits for consumers originating from an efficiency-enhancing arrangement. That presumption is, however, unjustified as a matter of economics. Whether the long-term effects of the agreement offset its short-term effects is an empirical matter that can only be resolved case by case. Furthermore, such an inter-temporal balancing exercise requires, to be properly conducted, discounting the future and adjusting for uncertainty, because while the short-term benefits of the agreement may be measurable and relatively certain, its future effects are unlikely to be measurable or certain.

3.2.2. The treatment of specific non-hardcore horizontal and vertical agreements

As noted above, vertical and horizontal restrictions which are not restrictions by object and do not benefit from a block exemption are evaluated using an effects-based approach. However, not all of those agreements are treated equally: some have been considered more harmful and less likely to satisfy the conditions in Article 81(3) than others. This section provides a brief overview of several different horizontal and vertical agreements and discusses how Article 81 has been applied to them in the past.

HORIZONTAL AGREEMENTS

'Crisis cartels': whilst horizontal price agreements are considered per se anti-competitive, given that their unambiguous object is to restrict competition, the Commission has shown some leniency towards so-called 'crisis cartels', in which firms operating in industries with declining demand have agreed to reduce capacity in a coordinated way.[66] The Commission has also permitted some 'restructuring' cartels when it has been able to show that the agreement would not substantially eliminate competition.[67]

'Information exchange agreements': these agreements include the exchange of opinions or experiences, joint market research, preparation of statistics and models, and joint comparative studies of enterprises or industries. Information exchanges may facilitate collusion but may also have significant pro-competitive effects.[68] For example, the exchange of default information among competing banks may mitigate the adverse selection and moral hazard problems that typically limit the development of efficient credit markets.[69] In *UK Tractors*, the ECJ identified several conditions for an information exchange to be likely to produce anticompetitive effects: (a) the market where the exchange takes place is concentrated and characterized by high barriers to entry; (b) the information exchanged is only made available to some market participants; (c) the exchange of information concerns the commercial behaviour of individual firms; (d) the information exchanged are prices and/or quantities; and (e) trade associations act as a medium to introduce contractual agreements.[70]

'Joint-selling agreements': these cover a range of coordination forms including: market prospecting, reciprocal distribution assistance, and joint selling. In general, the Commission's position is that joint-selling arrangements tend to restrict competition more than it may be necessary. The parties must therefore be able to demonstrate very large efficiency gains to be exempted under Article

81(3). Joint-sales agreements between the largest undertakings in an oligopolistic market are unlikely to be exempted,[71] as are agreements aiming to set prices collectively through joint-sales organizations, and joint-sales agreements that tend to restrict output.[72] On the other hand, the Commission has considered that joint-selling agreements between SMEs may encourage competition.[73]

'Joint-buying agreements': the Commission's position towards joint-buying agreements is less negative than towards joint selling. The Commission acknowledges that joint-buying agreements can lead to reductions in transaction costs, which may then be passed through to consumers provided there is sufficient competition downstream.[74]

'Joint-production agreements': joint-production agreements are exempted provided that the parties have a combined market share of no more than 20 per cent and do not contain hardcore restrictions.[75] However, even when market shares have exceeded this threshold, the Commission has still taken a rather lenient stance to these agreements.

'Standardization agreements': not all standardization agreements fall within Article 81(1). Situations where participation in the standards is free, unrestricted, non-discriminatory, and transparent are unlikely to produce any restrictions on competition and hence will not have any appreciable effect on the market. On the other hand, standardization agreements that coerce third parties, foreclose the market, or have the objective of excluding actual or potential competitors fall under Article 81(1).

'Environmental agreements': these are agreements in which parties undertake pollution abatement or seek to achieve any other environmental objectives. Examples of these agreements include recycling agreements, arrangements to promote reductions of emissions, or other energy-efficiency practices. Environmental agreements that restrict competition or limit the parties' ability to decide what or how to produce are likely to fall within Article 81(1). This likelihood will increase when the parties hold a significant proportion of the market. However, the Commission has a positive stance on agreements that are innovative and achieve environmental targets without negatively impacting product diversity or purchasing decisions.[76]

'Research and Development joint ventures': R&D agreements that do not contain hardcore clauses receive block exemptions provided that the market share of the parties concerned does not exceed 25 per cent. The Commission has tended in the past to take a lenient stance towards R&D agreements, rarely finding them restrictive of competition even when market shares are relatively high.[77]

VERTICAL AGREEMENTS

In general, the Commission's treatment of vertical agreements has been substantially more lenient than that of horizontal agreements. This is because, with no direct overlaps, the agreements are less likely to have an anticompetitive impact.

'Agency agreements': these are vertical agreements in which a person (the agent) is vested with the power to purchase or sell goods and services on behalf of another person (the principal). Genuine agency agreements for the purchase of goods or services by the principal (where the principal bears all risk) do not fall under Article 81(1). Where the principal bears all the risk, the agent is merely an extension of the principal and, hence, the agency agreement will have no impact on the competitive structure of the downstream markets. However, agency agreements which also contain exclusivity provisions limiting intra-brand and/or inter-brand competition may fall under Article 81(1). Examples of these are: (i) provisions preventing the principal from appointing other agents for particular transactions/customers/territories (exclusive agency provisions); and (ii) provisions preventing the agent from acting as an agent for the undertaking which compete with the principal ('non-compete clauses').

'Exclusive-distribution agreements': as discussed previously, exclusive-distribution systems are only regarded as hardcore infringements if they are coupled with territorial restrictions on passive sales. More generally, it has been acknowledged that some degree of exclusivity may be an indispensable feature for efficient distribution systems.

'Selective distribution agreements': when selective distribution systems provide scope for enhanced inter-brand competition the Commission has taken a favourable stance towards them.[78] This is the case when the products or services covered by the agreement are complex or heavily branded.

'Franchise agreements': in franchise agreements, the franchisor provides the franchisee with know-how, trade marks, designs, and intellectual property in return for a franchise fee. It is this transfer of knowledge that distinguishes a franchise from a standard distribution agreement. The ECJ recognizes that in order for a franchise system to work efficiently, the franchisor sometimes needs to lay down uniform commercial standards and impose terms on the franchisee to enforce these standards. In *Pronuptia de Paris* v. *Schillgallis*, for example, the ECJ concluded that restrictions to maintain common standards and to protect intellectual property rights were not prohibited under Article 81(1).[79]

'Exclusive purchase/non-compete provisions in distribution agreements': these are agreements to limit buyers dealing in competing goods. In general, the Commission has taken a relatively relaxed stance and states that non-compete clauses and purchase obligations must be fewer than five years in duration unless the distributor sells products from premises owned/leased by the supplier.

Economists belonging to the so-called 'Chicago School' showed in the 1960s that exclusive dealing is unlikely to be anticompetitive when retail competition is fierce, because then the upstream manufacturer has no incentive to act anticompetitively by restricting downstream competition. This is the 'single monopoly profit theorem'. In a vertical chain of production there is a single monopoly profit to be had. A firm that has a monopoly at one level of the vertical chain can secure a monopoly profit if it charges a monopoly price for its product and everyone else charges a competitive price for theirs. It would then prefer to have as much competition as possible at every other level of the chain because that will reduce the price of the final product, increase sales, and thereby maximize the total profit that it receives. The upstream monopolist has no incentive to monopolize competitive levels of the chain because it can never get more profit than it currently obtains from having a monopoly at one level.[80]

The 'Chicago School' also showed that an upstream monopolist may not have the ability to appropriate the rents resulting from the exclusion of potential competitors by means of foreclosing distribution.[81] This is because a downstream retailer which anticipates that the implication of an exclusive dealing agreement with its incumbent supplier is to foreclose future entry will demand better terms and conditions from its supplier prior to agreeing to become exclusive. In fact, it will demand to be fully compensated from the increase in market power caused by the agreement. This result holds true when: (a) one or more retailers are pivotal to exclude the entrant;[82] (b) even if no single retailer is pivotal for exclusion, they are able to coordinate their purchasing behaviour;[83] and (c) even if no single retailer is pivotal for exclusion and they are unable to coordinate their purchasing behaviour, they compete fiercely with relatively homogeneous products.[84]

3.3. The Goal(s) of Article 81

Now that we have provided an overview of Article 81 from law and economics perspectives, we turn to consider the *objectives* of Article 81. According to the Article 81(3) Guidelines,

The objective of Article 81 is to protect competition on the market as a means of enhancing consumer welfare and of ensuring an efficient allocation of resources. Competition and market integration serve these ends since the creation and preservation of an open single market promotes an efficient allocation of resources throughout the Community for the benefit of consumers.[85]

The Guidelines identify two 'instrumental' goals of Article 81—single-market integration and the protection of competition—both serving the 'ultimate' goal of enhancing 'economic welfare within the single market'.[86] The Commission assumes that the process of competition is vital to market integration and that market integration is a prerequisite for the efficient allocation of resources, and hence for the goal of enhancing consumer welfare, within the single market.

The objective of single-market integration has been one of the central tasks of the Community since its creation. As Gerber puts it: 'This "unification imperative" has shaped institutional structures and competences within the system, supplied much of its legitimacy and generated the conceptual framework for the development and application of its substantive norms.'[87] However, as explained below, it is not clear that the goals of single-market integration and the protection of competition are compatible with the consumer welfare objective.

3.3.1. *Many goals, conflicting goals*

The concern for market integration in Article 81 has manifested itself most clearly in the degree of attention granted to vertical restraints affecting trade across borders in European Commission competition law.[88] In *Nintendo*, the Commission found that the company had taken actions to prevent exports of game consoles from the UK to the Netherlands and Germany.[89] The Commission concluded: '[the infringement] had the object of artificially partitioning the single market, thereby jeopardising a fundamental principle of the Treaty.'[90]

Competition policy in Europe, and in particular Article 81, must serve the goal of protecting competition. One of the central objectives of the European Commission Treaty is to ensure a system of free competition. Article 4 of the Treaty states that the activities of the Community and its Member States should be: 'conducted in accordance with the principle of an open market economy with free competition'. Also, Article 98 requires the Community and its Member States to 'act in accordance with the principle of an open economy with free competition, favouring an efficient allocation of resources'.

In practice, protecting competition is taken to mean protecting rivalry and the competitive process. This is because it is believed that there can be no effective competition in the absence of actual competitors. Decisions and judgments apparently geared to protect competitors are actually intended to protect the competitive process and, sometimes, to consolidate the liberalization efforts of the Commission and the Member States. For most economists the emphasis on the competitive process is odd. Protecting competition means ensuring that markets work efficiently. There would be no issue if protecting rivalry and achieving efficiency were always mutually compatible objectives, but that is not the case.[91]

Economists have long debated whether the goal of competition law should be the protection of consumer welfare or aggregate welfare (the sum of consumer welfare and industry profits).[92] They have disagreed on whether competition law should focus on short-term consumer welfare or, instead, it should also take into account the impact of certain commercial practices on future generations of consumers.[93] And they have also disputed whether competition policy should concentrate on allocative efficiency (prices, quality, and output) or, instead, dynamic efficiency (innovation) should be considered the main goal of economically sound antitrust law.[94] But, there is a generalized consensus amongst economists, at least those who regard themselves as orthodox or mainstream, that companies' actions should be regarded illegitimate only when their impact on welfare is adverse.

3.3.2. Glaxo *and the objectives of antitrust*

In September 2006, the CFI partially annulled the Commission's finding that the dual pricing policy adopted by the Spanish subsidiary of GlaxoSmithKline (GSK) infringed Article 81. GSK's 'General Sales Conditions' allowed it to charge a higher price to wholesalers for products exported from Spain to other Member States than for products marketed within Spain. The higher prices for non-domestic consumption were specifically designed to eliminate wholesalers' incentives to obtain medicines at low prices in Spain and then sell them in higher-price European countries.

The Commission had found that GSK's dual pricing policy had the effect of restricting competition due to the restriction of opportunities for parallel trade. The Commission concluded that GSK's policy would infringe the competition laws whether or not it directly harmed patients. Indeed, the Commission claimed that the notion of the consumer is not restricted to the final consumer, that is, the patient. Therefore, the interests of wholesalers, pharmacies, national health budgets, insurance schemes can also be taken into account.[95]

The CFI disagreed and stated:

In effect, the objective assigned to Article 81(1) EC, which constitutes a fundamental provision indispensable for the achievement of the missions entrusted to the Community, in particular for the functioning of the internal market, is to prevent undertakings, by restricting competition between themselves or with third parties, from reducing the welfare of the *final consumer* of the products in question.[96]

It is therefore not sufficient to show that an agreement limits the freedom of action of the parties to the agreement (that is, GSK and the wholesaler) to conclude that it restricts competition—'it is still necessary to demonstrate that the limitation in question restricts competition, to the detriment of the final consumer'.[97] Hence, parallel trade must be given protection only 'in so far as it gives final consumers the advantages of effective competition in terms of supply or price'.[98]

The CFI judgment also indicates that the right welfare measure from the viewpoint of applying Article 81 is long-term consumer welfare. First, the CFI rightly points out that competition in the pharmaceuticals industry is mainly driven by innovation.[99] Furthermore, when reviewing the Commission's arguments in relation to the fourth condition under Article 81(3), the CFI held that it was necessary for the Commission to assess what form of competition (short-term price competition or long-term competition through innovation) should be given priority.

the fact that [the GSK pricing scheme] prevents the limited pressure which might exist, owing to parallel trade from Spain, on the price and the cost of medicines...must be related to the facts...that competition by innovation is very fierce in the sector. In those circumstances, it was still necessary...to assess what form of competition must be given priority with a view to ensuring the maintenance of effective competition.[100]

This was further demonstrated by the Court's special attention to innovation and the importance it attached to companies' ability to finance it: 'The importance of the medicines sector is characterised by the importance of competition by innovation. R&D is costly and risky and it is most frequently financed from an undertaking's own funds rather than from borrowing. This situation requires an optimum flow of income.'[101]

Finally, contrary to the Commission's position in the Article 81(3) Guidelines that 'Negative effects on consumers in one geographic market cannot normally be balanced against and compensated by positive effects for consumers in other unrelated geographic or product markets',[102] the CFI held that 'the agreement in question must enable appreciable objective advantages to be obtained...it being understood that these advantages may arise *not only on the relevant market but also on other markets*'.[103]

The CFI refers to *Compagnie Generale Maritime* in support of its interpretation.[104] The Commission's Article 81(3) Guidelines attempt to reconcile the CFI's ruling in *Compagnie Générale Maritime* with the policy stated in paragraph 43 of the Guidelines by noting that, although the restriction caused by the agreement in question and its beneficial effects occurred in different markets, 'the affected group of consumers were the same'.[105]

3.4. The Concept of 'Restriction of Competition'

As stated above, Article 81(1) prohibits all agreements which have as their object or effect the restriction of competition. But, when can it be said that competition has been restricted? What is the appropriate competitive counterfactual? Does the examination required under Article 81(1) require an assessment of the anticompetitive and pro-competitive effects of the agreement—does it require a rule of reason analysis?

3.4.1. *Defining the counterfactual*

The question of the appropriate counterfactual is of particular relevance because, as the recent *O2 (Germany)* case demonstrates, small changes in the way the counterfactual is defined can have significant differences in how Article 81(1) is applied.[106]

In February 2002, O2 and T-Mobile notified the Commission of an agreement concerning the sharing of some elements of their 3G infrastructure (in particular mast-/site-sharing) and the national roaming on each others' networks within the German market. The Commission found the site-sharing provisions did not appreciably restrict competition under Article 81(1) because the agreement was restricted to sharing basic network infrastructure such as masts, power supply, racking, and cooling. However, the Commission considered that national roaming between network providers limited network-based competition with respect to coverage, retail prices, quality, and transmission speeds. It therefore concluded that these provisions restricted competition 'by definition'.[107] However, the agreement was exempted under Article 81(3). The parties appealed the decision because being subject to Article 81(1)—even if exempted under Article 81(3)—implied that the agreement between the parties negatively effected competition and hence carried obligations which a finding of exemption from Article 81(1) would not carry.

In May 2006, the CFI partially annulled the Commission's decision because the Commission had failed to take proper account of the competitive situation in the absence of the notified agreement—that is the counterfactual. Regarding this counterfactual, the judgment states that 'The competition in question must be understood within the actual context in which it would occur in the absence of the agreement in dispute; the interference with competition may in particular be doubted if the agreement seems really necessary for the penetration of a new area by an undertaking.'[108]

The Court judged that the Commission's assessment of the roaming provisions relied on the assumption that O2 would have in any event rolled out its 3G network. The Commission decision was based on the assumption that O2 would have been present on the German 3G market even without the agreement. However, the Commission had not examined the extent to which the agreement was necessary for O2 to penetrate the 3G market.[109] The Commission had no specific evidence in connection with the agreement in question.[110] Furthermore, some of the Commission's considerations in its Article 81(3) assessment pointed towards uncertainty regarding O2's situation in Germany absent the agreement.

It is therefore apparent . . . [that] . . . O2's competitive situation on the 3G market would probably not have been secure without the agreement, and it might even have been jeopardised. Those assessments confirm that the Commission's presuppositions in its examination under Article 81(1) EC and Article 53(1) of the EEA Agreement have not been established.[111]

This case is of importance as it clarifies that the examination of competition in the absence of an agreement may be

particularly necessary as regards *markets undergoing liberalisation* or *emerging markets*, as in the case of the 3G mobile communications market here at issue, where effective competition may be problematic owing, for example, to the presence of a dominant operator, the concentrated nature of the market structure or the existence of significant barriers to entry.[112]

3.4.2. *Article 81(1) and the rule of reason*

In *O2 (Germany)*, the CFI clarified that the Commission's assessment under Article 81(1) should limit itself to consider the impact of the agreement on actual and potential competition taking into account the competitive situation in the absence of the agreement. It also clarified that such an assessment did not amount to an assessment of the pro-competitive and anticompetitive effects of the agreement.[113] That is, the balancing of anticompetitive and pro-competitive effects must be conducted exclusively within the framework laid down by Article 81(3).[114]

The CFI thus repeated the case law in *Métropole*, in which the court ruled that no balancing of anti- and pro-competitive effects may be carried out under Article 81(1).[115] This was important given that soon after *Métropole* the ECJ had adopted in *Wouters*[116] what Professor Nazzini has denoted as a 'bi-dimensional' framework test for Article 81(1) under which the anticompetitive effects of the agreement are balanced against its pro-competitive effects and other public policy objectives.[117]

3.5. Article 81: Structured Rule of Reason or Quasi per se Rule?

At first sight, the competitive assessment of agreements under Article 81 appears to be conducted under a 'structured rule of reason approach'. Under this rule, an agreement would be considered legal unless it can be shown to survive one or more screens aimed at establishing first the likelihood of anticompetitive effects, in which case the antitrust authorities still have to balance its anticompetitive and pro-competitive effects in a final stage prior to concluding that the agreement's overall impact is anticompetitive. This approach is illustrated in Figure 3.1.

The first stage in this structured analysis would be to determine whether the object of the agreement is to restrict competition; if that is the case its anticompetitive effects are presumed, in which case the analysis moves directly to

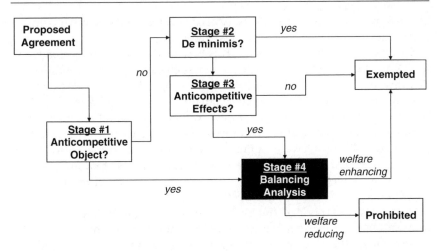

Figure 3.1. Article 81: a structured rule of reason approach

the fourth stage of the analysis. Agreements whose object is not to restrict competition may none the less produce appreciable anticompetitive effects. The second stage in the structured rule of reason analysis embodied in Article 81 would seek to identify and exempt those agreements that are unlikely to have an appreciable effect on competition and the market. The third stage of the analysis would require investigating the competitive impact of the agreement by considering the strength of competition in the absence of the agreement. If such analysis determined that the agreement has the potential to produce anticompetitive effects, then those welfare-reducing effects would need to be balanced against the potential pro-competitive effects of the agreement. Figure 3.1. clearly illustrates the importance of this balancing stage (Article 81(3)) in the context of the assessment of agreements under Article 81.

However, a closer look at the fourth condition in Article 81(3) raises serious doubts about the characterization of Article 81 as a structured rule of reason standard. As explained above, the fourth limb of Article 81(3) says that the protection of rivalry and the competitive process is given priority over the potentially pro-competitive efficiency gains which could result from restrictive agreements. That is, due to this condition, even if the parties to a potentially restrictive agreement could demonstrate that net effect on consumer welfare of such an agreement was positive, the agreement would none the less be prohibited if it was likely to cause a substantial reduction of competition. This implies that (a) agreements which have as their object the elimination of competition will be regarded per se illegal *de facto*; (b) agreements involving dominant firms or creating a dominant position will most likely be regarded per se illegal; and (c) agreements that involve some degree of price coordination but which generate significant network effects, two-sided externalities, or other demand efficiencies are also likely to be regarded per se illegal.

Once the fourth limb of Article 81(3) is properly taken into account, the legal standard embodied in Article 81 is best characterized as a 'quasi per se illegality rule'—that is, all agreements between undertakings, decisions by associations of undertakings, and concerted practices which may affect trade between Member States and which have as their object or effect the prevention, restriction, or distortion of competition will be regarded illegal unless: (i) they are unlikely to have an appreciable effect on competition; or (ii), if they have the potential to restrict competition (a) there is no significant lessening of effective competition and (b) the pro-competitive effects of the agreement are expected to exceed its anticompetitive effects.

The structure of this legal standard is depicted in Figure 3.2. As can be seen from this figure, the balancing test does no longer play a central role in the assessment of the agreement. Its prominent position is now occupied by the assessment of the impact of the agreement on the strength of market rivalry or, if you like, despite the ambiguity of the concept, the health of the competitive process.

What approach is preferable taking into account that the ultimate goal of Article 81 is meant to be the protection of economic welfare within the single market? The answer to this question is trivial unless we assess that: (i) competition authorities and courts will inevitably make mistakes when measuring and balancing the pro-competitive and anticompetitive effects of agreements among firms and (ii) 'administrability' and 'legal certainty' are key desirable characteristics in competition law. In the absence of (i) and (ii), the structured

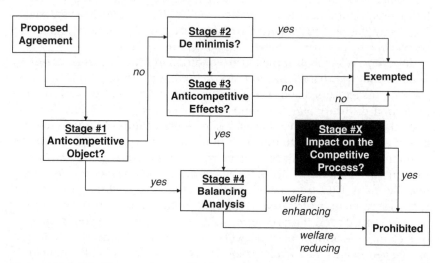

Figure 3.2. Article 81: a quasi per se illegal standard

Table 3.1. Possible errors in the assessment of horizontal and vertical agreements

	Illegal	Legal
Harmful to competition	Percent of cases correctly condemning anticompetitive agreements	Percent of cases falsely absolving legitimate agreements
Not harmful to competition	Percent of cases falsely condemning legitimate agreements	Percent of cases correctly absolving legitimate agreements

rule of reason is superior to the quasi per se illegality rule because the latter may prohibit agreements which are welfare enhancing. However, when the possibility of error is taken into account or when the simplicity and predictability of the rule are taken into consideration, the ranking of these two rules under the consumer welfare standard is no longer obvious.

One important factor in choosing between a rule of reason standard and a per se rule is the administrative and enforcement costs of implementing the legal standard. In principle, a qualified per se rule is arguably easier and cheaper to administer and enforce.[118] But this is not the case here given that the per se rule involves as many stages and analytical complications as the structured rule of reason approach. Thus, the key fact in comparing both standards should be the assessment of the likelihood and cost of error under each of the two approaches. Table 3.1 shows the standard error matrix with the shaded boxes reflecting the two possible errors that enforcement agencies and the judicial system can make: falsely condemning competitive agreements ('false convictions') and falsely absolving anticompetitive agreements ('false acquittals').[119]

Both rules may produce false acquittals and false convictions. And none of these two rules is a priori superior to the other in error terms because the expected cost of error of each of these two results will depend on their fine details. One might expect, however, that the qualified per se illegality rule would result in relatively more false convictions, while the structured rule of reason might cause relatively more false acquittals. In our opinion, given that the Commission can minimize the likelihood of false acquittals by rigorously applying the first three conditions of Article 81(3), the error costs of departing from the structured rule of reason approach are unjustified.

3.6. Conclusions

As mentioned in section 1, several aspects of the current debate on the reform of Article 82 would benefit significantly from a better understanding of the implications for Article 81 policy of the adoption of a more economic approach. Let us provide two examples of the potential benefits of such cross-fertilization. First, contrast the position of the CFI in *Glaxo* when it states 'competition law... is concerned only with [the] impact [of certain business practices] on the welfare of the final consumer'[120] with its position in *Microsoft*, where it says

it is settled case law that *Article 82 EC* covers not only practices which may prejudice consumers directly but also those which indirectly prejudice them by impairing an effective competitive structure... In this case, Microsoft impaired the effective competitive structure on the [relevant] market *by acquiring a significant market share in that market*.[121]

Second, while the current debate on Article 82 is characterized by the confrontation between those who defend an 'Ordoliberal' approach to antitrust enforcement (based on ambiguous concepts such as 'competition on the merits', 'normal competition', 'objective justification', or 'special responsibility') and those who defend an unstructured rule of reason, disregarding that 'administrability' and 'legal certainty' are key desirable characteristics in competition law,[122] the recent Article 81 case law provides an intermediate and more pragmatic approach to the competitive assessment of business practices—a structured approach that, while accepting the need to balance the pro-competitive and anticompetitive effects of those practices, recognizes the difficulty and the transaction and error costs associated with such complex balancing exercises.

We must confess that the disparities between Articles 81 and 82 are a mystery to us. In this chapter we have just taken note of them and have argued that they should be resolved in favour of the Article 81 approach. As to their origin and continued persistence, that is a question that exceeds the scope of this chapter but is one that we sincerely hope someone some day will be able to explain.

Notes

[1] This chapter was prepared for the IESE conference 'Fifty Years of the Treaty: Assessment and Perspectives of Competition Policy in Europe', held in Barcelona, 19–20 Nov. 2007. Matthew Bennett was working at LECG when this chapter was authored. Any opinions within this chapter are personal and are not a reflection of OPT Policy. We wish to thank Eduard Barniol, Katie Curry, and David Shaharudin for their invaluable help. We also wish to thank Xavier Vives for his comments and suggestions. The usual caveats apply.

[2] For an excellent review of Art. 81 and its reform, see Nikpay, Faull, and Kjølbye (2007).

[3] 'Guidelines on the Application of Article 81(3) of the Treaty', Official Journal C 101, 27.04.2004: 97–118.

[4] See Neelie Kroes, 'Preliminary Thoughts on Policy Review of Article 82', presented before the Fordham Corporate Law Institute, New York, 23 Sept. 2005; and European Commission, Directorate-General for Competition (2005).

[5] O'Donoghue and Padilla (2006).

[6] Case T–168/01, *GlaxoSmithKline Services Unlimited* v. *Commission*, 27 Sept. 2006.

[7] Case T–328/03, *O2 (Germany) GmbH & Co. OHG* v. *Commission*, 2 May 2006.

[8] *GlaxoSmithKline Services Unlimited* v. *Commission*, 27 Sept. 2006, para. 273.

[9] See, among many others, Cases 56 and 58/64, *Consten and Grundig-Verkaufs-GmbH* [1966] ECR 299, and Case 187/80, *Merck* v. *Stephar* [1981] ECR 2063.

[10] *O2 (Germany) GmbH & Co. OHG* v. *Commission*, 2 May 2006, para. 77.

[11] *GlaxoSmithKline Services Unlimited* v. *Commission*, 27 Sept. 2006, para. 307.

[12] Ibid. para. 313.

[13] 'Guidelines on the Application of Article 81(3) of the Treaty', paras 8 and 9 (nn. omitted).

[14] 'Notice on Agreements of Minor Importance which do not Appreciably Restrict Competition under Article 81(1) of the Treaty Establishing the European Community (de minimis)', Official Journal C 368, 22.12.2001: 13–15.

[15] 'Guidelines on the Application of Article 81(3) of the Treaty', para. 21.

[16] Ibid. para. 20.

[17] Ibid. para. 21.

[18] Ibid. para. 23.

[19] See *Reims II*, OJ [1999] L275/17.

[20] See also *Uniform Eurocheques*, OJ [1985] L35/43; *Visa International-Multilateral Interchange Fee*, OJ [2002] L318/17; and *IFPI 'Simulcasting'*, OJ [2003] L107/58. This argument also forms the basis for the US Department of Transportation's provision of antitrust immunity to the large airline alliances. See e.g. Brueckner (2001).

[21] See Hylton (2003: ch. 4).

[22] Whinston (2006: ch. 2).

[23] See Sproul (1993); Block, Nold, and Sidak (1981).

[24] This has been justified under the argument that it is better to permit a limited period of price fixing now than to have unfettered competition result in the loss of an otherwise viable competitor for ever onwards. See e.g. Craycraft, Craycraft, and Gallo (1999).

[25] See Case 43 and 63/82 *VBBB & VBVB* [1984] ECR 19.

[26] See *Guidelines on Vertical Restraints*, OJ [2000] C291, para. 225.

[27] See Case C-360/92P *Publishers Association* v. *Commission* [1995] ECR 1–23.

[28] See Telser (1960); Bork (1966).

[29] See Brief of Amici Curiae Economists in Support of Petitioner, *Leegin Creative Leather Products, Inc.* v. *PSKS, Inc.*, 22 Jan. 2007.

[30] See *Leegin Creative Leather Products, Inc.* v. *PSKS, Inc.*, Slip Op. No. 06–480, 28 June 2007.

[31] This distinction has become more complicated with the advent of the Internet. In general, the Commission views sales over the Internet as passive sales. However, sending out unsolicited emails would be seen as active marketing. See 'Commission Approves Selective Distribution System for Yves Saint Laurent Perfume', Commission Press Release IP/01/713, 17 May 2001 and 'Commission Clears B&W Loudspeakers Distribution System after Company Deletes Hard-core Violations', Commission Press Release, IP/02/916, 24 June 2002.

[32] See Mathewson and Winter (1984).

[33] See Rey and Stiglitz (1995).

[34] *Guidelines on Vertical Restraints*, OJ [2000] C291, para. 185.

[35] See, among others, Carlton and Waldman (2001); Ahlborn, Evans, and Padilla (2005).

[36] 'Guidelines on the Application of Article 81(3) of the Treaty', para. 16.

[37] See e.g. Case 30/78 *Distillers Co. Ltd* v. *Commission* [1980] ECR 229 [1980] 3 CMLR 121.

[38] 'Guidelines on the Application of Article 81(3) of the Treaty', para. 24.

[39] Ibid. para. 26.

[40] Ibid. para. 17.

[41] Ibid. para. 18.

[42] Ibid. para. 25.

[43] Ibid. para. 18.

[44] See Slade and Lafontaine (2008).

[45] 'Commission Regulation (EC) No 2659/2000 of 29 November 2000 on the Application of Article 81(3) of the Treaty to Categories of Research and Development Agreements', Official Journal L 304, 05.12.2000: 7.

[46] 'Commission Regulation (EC) No 2658/2000 of 29 November 2000 on the Application of Article 81(3) of the Treaty to Categories of Specialisation Agreements', Official Journal L 304, 05.12.2000: 3.

[47] 'Commission Regulation (EC) No 2790/1999 of 22 December 1999 on the Application of Article 81(3) of the Treaty to Categories of Vertical Agreements and Concerted Practices', Official Journal L 336, 29.12.1999: 21–5.

[48] 'Guidelines on the Application of Article 81(3) of the Treaty', para. 34.

[49] Ibid. para. 38.

[50] Ibid. para. 20.

[51] Ibid. para. 48.

[52] *Van den Bergh Foods*, OJ [1998] L 246/1.

[53] See, however, Chaps 3 and 5 below for a discussion of the CFI's ruling Case T–168/01, *GlaxoSmithKline Services Unlimited* v. *Commission*, contradicting this example.

[54] 'Guidelines on the Application of Article 81(3) of the Treaty', paras 59–72.

[55] Ibid. para. 84.

[56] Ibid. para. 85.

[57] Ibid. paras 90 and 91.

[58] Ibid. para. 96.

[59] Ibid. para. 73.

[60] Ibid. para. 75.

[61] Ibid.

[62] Ibid.

[63] Ibid. para. 107.

[64] Ibid. para. 105.

[65] Ibid.

[66] See e.g. *Synthetic Fibres*, OJ [1984] L 207/17.

[67] See *Stichting Baksteen*, OJ [1994] L 131/15. See also *Bayer/BP Chemicals*, OJ [1988] L 150/35.

[68] See Kühn and Vives (1995).

[69] See Padilla and Pagano (1997); also Padilla and Pagano (2000).

[70] Case C-7/95 P, *John Deere Ltd* v. *Commission*, 28 May 1998.

[71] See *Floral*, OJ [1980] L39/51.

[72] See *Ansac*, OJ [1991] L152/54.

[73] See *SAFCO*, OJ [1972] L13/44 and *Cekanan*, OJ [1990] L299/64.

[74] See *National Sulphuric Acid Association*, OJ [1980] L 260/24 and *National Sulphuric Acid Association*, OJ [1989] L 190/22.

[75] See *Fujitsu/AMD*, OJ [1994] L 341/66.

[76] See *CECED*, OJ [2000] L 187/47 and *DSD*, OJ L 319/1.

[77] See *Olivetti/Cannon*, OJ [1988] l52, 26.2.88.

[78] Case 26/76, *Metro* v. *Commission* [1977] ECR 1875.

[79] See Case 161/84, *Pronuptia de Paris GmbH* v. *Irmgard Schillgalis* [1986] ECR 353.

[80] In fact the monopolist has an incentive to destroy market power at other levels of the chain. A second monopoly, for example, would result in a higher price for the final product and reduce its sales. This result, known unhelpfully as 'double marginalization', dates back to Cournot 1838.

[81] Bork (1978); Posner (1979).

[82] Posner (1979).

[83] See Rasmusen, Ramseyer, and Wiley (1991); Segal and Whinston (2000).

[84] Fumagalli and Motta (2006).

[85] 'Guidelines on the Application of Article 81(3) of the Treaty', para. 13.

[86] See Nazzini (2006).

[87] See Gerber (1998: 347).

[88] See e.g. *Volkswagen*, OJ [1998] L 124/60.

[89] *Nintendo*, OJ [2002] L 255/33.

[90] Ibid. para. 374.

[91] See the discussion of the fourth limb of the Art. 81(3) test in 3.2.1.

[92] See Pitman (2007) and references therein. See also Padilla (2007).

[93] See Chang, Evans, and Schmalensee (2003).

[94] See Géradin, Ahlborn, Denicolò, and Padilla (2006), 'DG Comp's Discussion Paper on Article 82: Implications of the Proposed Framework and Antitrust Rules for Dynamically Competitive Industries' <http://ssrn.com/abstract=894466>.

[95] See *GlaxoSmithKline*, OJ [2001] L 302/1, para. 184.

[96] Case T–168/01, *GlaxoSmithKline Services Unlimited* v. *Commission*, 27 Sept. 2006, para. 118 (emphasis added).

[97] Ibid. para. 171.

[98] Ibid. para. 121.

[99] Ibid. para. 106.

[100] Ibid. para. 315.

[101] Ibid. para. 271.

[102] 'Guidelines on the Application of Article 81(3) of the Treaty', para. 43.

[103] Case T–168/01, *GlaxoSmithKline Services Unlimited* v. *Commission*, 27 Sept. 2006, para. 248 (emphasis added).

[104] Case T–86/95, *Compagnie générale maritime and Others* v. *Commission* [2002] ECR II–1011, para. 343.

[105] 'Guidelines on the Application of Article 81(3) of the Treaty', n. 57.

[106] Case T–328/03, *O2 (Germany) GmbH & Co. OHG* v. *Commission*, 2 May 2006.

[107] Ibid. para. 19.

[108] Ibid. para. 68.

[109] Ibid. para. 77.

[110] Ibid. para. 86.

[111] Ibid. para. 114.

[112] Ibid. para. 72.

[113] Ibid. para. 69.

[114] 'Guidelines on the Application of Article 81(3) of the Treaty', para. 11.

[115] Case T–112/99, *Métropole television (M6), Suez-Lyonnais des eaux, France Télécom and Télévision française 1 SA (TF1)* v. *Commission* [2001] ECR II–2459.

[116] Case C-309/99, *JCJ Wouters, JW Savelbergh and Price Waterhouse Belasting-adviseurs BV* v. *Algemene Raad van de Nederlandse Orde van Advocaten* [2002] ECR I–1577.

[117] Nazzini (2006: 521–5).

[118] Hylton (2003).

[119] We borrow the colourful acquittal/conviction terminology from the criminal context.

[120] Case T–168/01, *GlaxoSmithKline Services Unlimited* v. *Commission*, 27 Sept. 2006, para. 273.

[121] Case T–2001/2004, *Microsoft* v. *Commission*, 16 Sept. 2007 (emphasis added).

[122] Ahlborn and Padilla (2008).

4

Some Economics of Abuse of Dominance

John Vickers[1]

4.1. Introduction

European competition law and policy towards mergers and anticompetitive agreements have become much more soundly based in economic principles over the past decade. The law on abuse of dominance has not. The question now is whether, and if so how, the Commission will forge a more economics-based policy approach in this core area of competition law. The recent landmark *Microsoft* judgment certainly does not compel it to do so, but neither does it preclude it. Indeed, the judgment emphasizes that under EC law, the Court's 'review of complex economic appraisals made by the Commission is necessarily limited to checking whether the relevant rules on procedure and on stating reasons have been complied with, whether the facts have been accurately stated and whether there has been any manifest error of assessment or a misuse of powers'.[2] So there is much to play for.

   The aim of this chapter is to appraise from an economic perspective selected aspects of current law and policy on Article 82 concerning *exclusionary* abuse of dominance. The topic of exploitative abuse, important though it is, lies beyond its scope. Ideally, especially in a piece prepared for a conference celebrating fifty years of the Treaty, the chapter would trace the evolution of lines of case law on Article 82 (formerly 86), but here too I will be selective, and focus on three cases on which judgment has been given in 2007. Since, quite unlike the US, the evolution of EC law on abuse of dominance has been rather limited, history will not be lost from view.

Article 82 EC

Any abuse by one or more undertaking(s) of a dominant position within the common market or in a substantial part of it shall be prohibited as incompatible with the common market in so far as it may affect trade between Member

---

States. Such abuse may, in particular, consist in: (a) directly or indirectly imposing unfair purchase or selling prices or other unfair trading conditions; (b) limiting production, markets, or technical development to the prejudice of consumers; (c) applying dissimilar conditions to equivalent transactions with other trading parties, thereby placing them at a competitive disadvantage; (d) making the conclusion of contracts subject to acceptance by the other parties of supplementary obligations which, by their nature or according to commercial usage, have no connection with the subject of such contracts.

Two of the exclusionary abuses to be discussed involve pricing. Section 4.4 below looks at *predatory pricing* from the perspective of the *Wanadoo* case.[3] Section 4.5 concerns *discounts and rebates*, which were at issue in *British Airways*.[4] The *Microsoft* case concerned the 'non-price' abuses of *refusal to supply* and *tying and bundling*, which are considered in section 4.6. As will be seen, 'non-price' abuses often involve prices especially when it comes to remedies. The discussion of these abuses is preceded, in section 4.3, by a quick tour of the economics of anticompetitive exclusion. However, since there is no abuse without market dominance, a word on that is due first.

4.2. Dominance

Much could be said about dominance but I will limit myself to two points.[5] The first is the relationship between dominance and abuse, on which the Report by the EAGCP said: 'If an effects-based approach provides evidence of an abuse which is only possible if the firm has a position of dominance, then no further separate demonstration of dominance should be needed.'[6] On this view, separate verification of dominance needs less attention with an effects-based approach to abuse than if abuse is appraised formalistically.

However, serious prior dominance assessment is essential and natural in an approach to abuse oriented to economic effects. Abuse analysis is hard and error-prone on any approach, and dominance assessment has the great merit of efficiently screening out cases where it need not be undertaken (and correspondingly deterring the bringing of cases in which market power is less than strong). Likewise, dominance analysis is a healthy discipline. Unilateral conduct can easily look suspicious, especially to the economically untrained eye, but cannot reasonably be considered sinister without independent evidence of substantial market power. This is not to say that the conduct at issue should be excluded from the assessment of dominance. And the analysis of abuse, if the dominance threshold is crossed, should be carried out in a way that integrates the findings of the market power analysis.

Allegations of predatory pricing illustrate the point. Firms price below incremental cost for all sorts of reasons, mostly benign, especially for consumers. Without independent evidence of market power there is no good reason for competition policy scrutiny of such pricing. When the evidence shows such power amounting to dominance, however, further scrutiny makes sense. To make a finding of predatory pricing abuse, should it be necessary in Europe, as in the United States, to show not only below-cost pricing but also a dangerous probability of recoupment? Apparently not in EC law, and arguably not in terms of economics, provided dominance has been proven to a proper standard and the exclusion is from the dominated market. But, even then it would seem unwise for, say, an agency not to ask itself the recoupment question at least as a cross-check on its dominance finding. This issue will be taken further in section 4.4 below.

The second point concerns the standard of proof of dominance. In the period from 1990 to 2004, when the concept of 'dominance' did double duty because of its primary role in the Merger Regulation as well as in Article 82, there was some merit in the concept being treated with a degree of elasticity. Greater strictness is now called for, and will become all the more important if scope for private actions is to expand. The basic reason is that particular conduct by a firm with a mild degree of market power is far less likely to distort competition than the same conduct by one with great market power. So, on the whole, public authorities better spend their resources examining the latter than the former. Private actions are fine so long as their prospects of success are good when, and only when, the public interest tends to be promoted rather than retarded by them. So, a disciplined approach to dominance is important for the direction of private as well as public enforcement of Article 82.

Despite its many merits, the Staff Discussion Paper (DG Competition 2005) therefore caused some consternation when at paragraph 31, after commenting on high market shares as an indicator of dominance, it spoke of dominance being 'more likely to be found in the market share range of 40 per cent to 50 per cent than below 40 per cent, although also undertakings with market shares below 40 per cent could be considered to be in a dominant position'. The rider that firms 'with market shares of no more than 25 per cent are not likely to enjoy a (single) dominant position' hardly gave comfort.

Shares of properly defined markets are at most a way to screen out cases that deserve no more attention. High shares alone never imply dominance. Unless market definition has gone awry—in which case that is the problem to fix—there is no significant prospect of single-firm dominance with a share anywhere near 25 per cent, and dominance at 40 per cent would normally seem quite improbable. In my view, therefore, it would be preferable for the Commission to say that dominance is more likely to be found above 50 per cent than below, and not likely to be found below 40 per cent. Subject to the ever-present vagaries of market definition, this would indicate something of a safe harbour, as far as concerns unilateral conduct, for firms that might otherwise soften their competitive edge to the detriment of consumers for fear of competition law entanglement.

In sum, dominance analysis should precede abuse analysis and be undertaken in a disciplined way. In cases that proceed to abuse analysis, dominance assessment should, however, be integral to, not separate from, the analysis of harm to competition and consumers.

4.3. Some Economics of Anticompetitive Exclusion

We now turn from dominance to abuse, with a focus on exclusionary abuse. The fundamental question for law and policy to address in the area is how to draw the line between unilateral conduct that is 'competition on the merits' or 'normal competition', and, on the other hand, anticompetitive (competition-distorting) conduct. Only the latter should be condemned as unlawful. However, an immediate problem is that rivals to the dominant firm may be excluded from the market, or at least from serving portions of market demand, by competition on the merits (if the dominant firm is sufficiently superior at delivering what customers want) as well as by anticompetitive conduct. In a sense, then, the task is to distinguish between good and bad exclusion. This is surprisingly hard to do even in principle. It is harder still to craft administrable legal rules and precedents that are good at separating anticompetitive conduct from competition on the merits.

What does economics have to say about the fundamental question? Modern economic theory of anticompetitive behaviour is 'post-Chicago' in that it is underpinned by game theory and contract theory, not just price theory, and its conclusions are often at odds with the per se *legality* that some 'Chicago' scholars advocated for a range of unilateral (and vertical contractual) practices. But 'post-Chicago' does not mean 'anti-Chicago'; on the contrary, it has absorbed much of the 'Chicago' critique of 1950s and 60s interventionism in US antitrust law and policy. Indeed, much 'post-Chicago' economics starts by taking seriously, and answering, the challenge posed by 'Chicago' scholars of explaining why, since there is ultimately only one monopoly profit to be had in any market, a dominant firm would find it profitable to engage in efficiency-reducing behaviour such as the exclusion from related markets of rivals more efficient than itself.

The aim of this section is to give a brief guided tour of some economic theory relevant to the assessment of exclusionary abuse under five headings:[7]

- predatory pricing
- partial exclusion to exploit rivals
- divide-and-rule exclusion
- leverage of market power
- maintenance of market power.

Needless to say, the subject of anticompetitive exclusion receives much more thorough treatment in books such as Motta (2004) and Whinston (2006), and, in recent surveys, notably Kaplow and Shapiro (2007), and Rey and Tirole (2007).

4.3.1. *Predatory pricing*

Predatory pricing, in its simplest form, is below-cost pricing by a dominant firm to drive rivals from the market and thereby create monopoly power for the dominant firm to enjoy. In that stark form predatory pricing satisfies three principles, or tests, that have been advanced to distinguish anticompetitive conduct from competition on the merits—the sacrifice test, the as-efficient competitor test, and the consumer harm test.[8]

First, pricing below cost normally entails profit *sacrifice* by the dominant firm if by 'cost' is meant the avoidable cost of serving the demand at issue. Put differently, such pricing normally makes no business sense but for its anti-competitive effect. The caveat 'normally' is, however, important. There are settings where pricing below avoidable cost could be profitable for dynamic reasons other than causing competitors to withdraw from the market (or portions thereof). Examples include cost dynamics, such as learning-by-doing, and inter-temporal demand linkages, such as profitable after-market sales.

Second, pricing below avoidable cost tends to exclude *as-efficient competitors* from serving the demand in question. If the incumbent sets price below the cost of meeting that demand, then, even if the rival is slightly more efficient than the incumbent, it will not be able profitably to serve the demand (perhaps unless it has dynamic cost or demand reasons of the sort mentioned in the previous paragraph).

Third, although below-cost pricing benefits consumers in the short run, if the result is substantially greater monopoly power than would otherwise have existed, then the incumbent will recoup the losses from below-cost pricing by high prices to the overall detriment of consumers. Then there will be net *consumer harm*.

A tradition of economic thought often associated with the 'Chicago School' regards allegations of predatory pricing with doubt bordering on incredulity, and cautions against policy intervention to stop low pricing also because it risks promoting inefficient competitors and harming consumer interests. Why would a firm, especially one with market power, throw away money by below-cost pricing? If the threat to do so lacks credibility, as in the simplest of economic models, why would it deter a rival from entering or expanding in the market? The answer is that the simplest of economic models assumes away issues of asymmetric information and uncertainty. Once these are re-injected, realistically, into the analysis, there is ample scope for 'rational'—and hence 'credible' threats of—below-cost pricing.[9]

For example, aggressive pricing to build or sustain a *reputation* for toughness may be quite rational and hence credible. Short-term loss-making in one market might then be recouped by deterring entry in other markets in which the incumbent operates. Likewise, low pricing may be a credible *signal* of market conditions that deters entry. It could be used to play havoc with an entrant trying to test out market conditions, or with the principal/agent relationship between the entrant and its finance providers.[10] For all these reasons it seems right to approach allegations of predatory pricing with caution not incredulity. Exactly that approach was recommended by the US Court of Appeals in the 2003 *American Airlines* case (*US* v. *AMR Corp*), which observed that ' "post-Chicago" economists have theorized that price predation is not only plausible, but profitable, especially in a multi-market context where predation can occur in one market and recoupment can occur rapidly in other markets'. This point bears on the question, to be considered further in section 4.4, of whether proof of likely recoupment should be required before a finding of predatory abuse is made.

Predatory pricing can be defined more broadly than in relation to below-cost pricing. An alternative approach would be to say that low pricing *intended* to eliminate rivals is predatory. But, besides the practical difficulties of discerning intent, this faces the fundamental problem that all sorts of irreproachable business behaviour, including competition indisputably 'on the merits', may have eliminatory intent. Justice Breyer, when a Court of Appeals Judge, once drew the parallel with a boxer delivering a perfectly legal punch with eliminatory intent, who is not thereby guilty of attempted murder.[11]

Another view would say that low pricing could well entail profit sacrifice, or be conduct that makes no business sense but for anticompetitive effects, without price going below avoidable cost. The latter is sacrifice relative to zero profit, whereas a firm with market power can usually do a lot better than that. Moreover, pricing above avoidable cost, so long as not too much above, could cause the withdrawal of a rival that, though less efficient than the incumbent, would bring competition to the incumbent that would be beneficial for consumers.

True, but how to craft a legal rule on those lines? Even in principle, the issue is unclear since both the sacrifice test and the consumer harm test raise the question: relative to what? For example, it would seem absurd in principle, never mind practice, to require a dominant firm to maximize profit subject to rivals not altering the scale of their operations. And it would seem odd to ban a dominant firm from causing the exit (or shrinkage) of rivals whose presence (or non-shrinkage) would benefit consumers. On that basis, why not go the whole hog and require the firm to maximize consumer surplus?

Therefore, having below-cost pricing a necessary condition for a finding of unlawful predatory pricing, though unlikely to be the 'optimal' rule in every situation, has a good deal of common sense. Following the very influential

1975 paper by Areeda and Turner, below-cost pricing became a necessary—but far from sufficient—condition for a predatory-pricing violation in US law, and cost benchmarks feature prominently in EC law. As will be illustrated below, there remains plenty of scope for argument over (a) the relevant cost concept (Areeda and Turner favoured average variable cost, as a proxy for marginal cost); (b) how to measure cost; (c) the role, if any, for evidence on intent; (d) whether or not separate proof of recoupment should be required; and (e) what scope should be allowed for justifications of below-cost pricing.

4.3.2. Partial exclusion to exploit rivals[12]

Let us turn now to exclusive contracts—contracts under which customers (which themselves might be downstream firms selling to final consumers) agree not to deal with rivals to the dominant incumbent. At first blush these might seem 'obviously' anticompetitive since they restrict the buyers' freedom of choice. But, if a buyer freely and rationally entered into the exclusive contract, it would have been compensated for restricting its choice.[13] How then could it be in the interest of the incumbent to offer terms to the buyer attractive enough to persuade the buyer to restrict its freedom to buy instead from the rival, even though the rival might turn out to be more efficient than the incumbent?

Aghion and Bolton (1987) first gave the answer that by appropriately structuring the exclusive contract the incumbent–buyer pair might in effect sometimes be able to extract some of any efficiency advantage that the rival may have. In particular, by setting an appropriately calibrated *penalty* for breach of contract, payable by the buyer to the incumbent in the event that the buyer purchases from the rival, the rival, if it enters, will have to offer a sufficiently good deal for the buyer to pay the penalty for breach. If that happens, some of the rival's efficiency advantage will be received by the incumbent–buyer pair. It is as if they set and collected an entry fee from the rival. When the rival is not sufficiently more efficient to pay the fee, the consequence will be the exclusion of a more-efficient firm than the incumbent. But the aim here is not so much exclusionary as exploitative of the rival when it is sufficiently more efficient to pay the fee—indeed, that is when the incumbent does best. However, this argument does not work if, as in many legal systems, penalties for breach of contract are unenforceable or if the exclusive contract is easily renegotiable in the event of entry. Then the rival is never excluded if it is more efficient than the incumbent.

4.3.3. Divide-and-rule exclusion[14]

A second, and perhaps more important, reason why buyers might sign exclusive contracts even though that may foreclose a more efficient rival has to do with a possible coordination problem among buyers—hence 'divide-and-rule'. If the entrant has scale economies or there are network effects in demand, then by pre-empting enough buyers with exclusive contracts, the incumbent might be able to deny the rival so much potential demand that the rival cannot operate efficiently (even though, at any given output level, the rival may be more efficient than the incumbent). As Aghion and Bolton put it: 'What is crucial . . . is how the size of the entrant's potential market affects the probability of entry.'[15] If shrinkage of that potential demand substantially reduces the probability of entry, then each buyer offered exclusivity by the incumbent might accept it for fear that otherwise it will be left in a rump of 'free' buyers that is too small for entry to be viable.

Divide-and-rule exclusion is explored theoretically by Rasmusen, Ramseyer, and Wiley (1991) and reinforced by Segal and Whinston (2000), who show how the scope for exclusion may be greater if the dominant firm can discriminate among buyers, including sequentially. Of course, theories of divide-and-rule exclusion are plausible in fact only if there are scale economies and, as a result of the dominant firm's conduct, too few free buyers for rivals to achieve them.[16]

Sequential interactions with buyers are also a feature of Bernheim and Whinston's (1998) analysis of exclusive dealing, in which exclusive dealing with the first set of buyers may lessen competition to supply subsequent buyers.[17] Then, even if exclusive dealing is inefficient, it may come about because the first set of buyers can be compensated with part of the profit gain at the expense of the subsequent buyers. Again the theme is buyer disunity. Arguably, buyer disunity is at the heart of predatory pricing theory (discussed above). If consumers *en masse* spurned the incumbent's predatory price and paid a premium to sustain the rival, they might well pay lower prices in the long run. But, if each consumer has a negligible effect on the rival's survival prospects, none will want to pass up the good short-term offer from the incumbent.

4.3.4. *Leverage of market power*[18]

If a firm has a dominant position in the market for product A and bundles product B with product A, or ties them so that A can be bought only with B, it might seem superficially 'obvious' that the firm is leveraging or extending its market power from A to B. (For example, in section 4.6 below, the firm is Microsoft: A is its Windows operating system and B is its Media Player.) But the 'Chicago' counter is again to ask why a profit-seeking firm with market power would engage in such behaviour unless it was efficient. Unless consumers wanted the products bundled or tied, their willingness to pay, and hence monopoly profit, would seem to be reduced by it.

The point was crisply put by Judge Easterbrook, formerly a leading exponent of the 'Chicago School', writing for the US Court of Appeals for the Seventh Circuit in the recent case of *Schor* v. *Abbott Laboratories*, where the defendant was the supplier of a combination-drug therapy for HIV.[19] The central question in the case was whether there was a 'free-standing' (for example, independent from predatory) theory of monopoly leveraging that US antitrust law should recognize. It is worth quoting at length why Judge Easterbrook said not:

The problem with 'monopoly leveraging' as an antitrust theory is that the practice cannot increase a monopolist's profits.... The basic point is that a firm that monopolizes some essential component of a treatment (or product or service) can extract the whole monopoly profit by charging a suitable price for the component alone. If the monopolist gets control of another component as well and tries to jack up the price of that item, the effect is the same as setting an excessive price for the monopolized component. The monopolist can take its profit just once; an effort to do more makes it worse off and is self-deterring.... We appreciate the potential reply that it is impossible to say that a given practice 'never' could injure consumers. A creative economist could imagine unusual combinations of costs, elasticities, and barriers to entry that would cause injury in the rare situation.... But just as rules of per se illegality condemn practices that almost always injure consumers, so antitrust law applies rules of per se legality to practices that almost never injure consumers.[20]

This last point about rules being appropriate for conduct that meets an 'almost-always' test illustrates how considerations of administrability (often associated with Harvard Law School, notably Areeda, Turner, and Breyer) can go hand in hand with 'Chicago-School' precepts—the 'double helix' of Kovacic (2007).

How has 'post-Chicago' economics shown the coherence (albeit in Easterbrook's view insufficient plausibility for policy purposes) of pure leveraging theory? Whinston (1990) showed how tying B with A might be able to deter entry into the B-market by making the A-monopolist a more aggressive competitor in the B-market. This theory requires A and B not to be closely complementary products—there must be credible commitment to tying (perhaps through technological integration) and the tying must be such as to leave too little independent B-demand in relation to the rival's fixed costs for it to be viable. How common is the joint occurrence of these conditions is a matter for debate.

4.3.5. *Maintenance of market power*[21]

A distinct theory of exclusionary tying and bundling concerns not the leverage of market power from A to B, but rather the *maintenance* of market power in A—in other words, the extension of market power in time, not from product to product. This theory of exclusion is entirely consistent with the

'Chicago' point that there is only one monopoly profit—the issue is about its prolongation.

To see how the argument works, suppose that products A and B are demanded only in combination, that the incumbent has an A-monopoly for the time being, but that a potential A-rival is contemplating entry in due course. The incumbent also supplies Bs, and there are independent B-suppliers around, but suppose that they will go out of business if the A-monopolist ties or bundles its As and Bs together, denying them B-demand. Why would the incumbent do that unless it was efficient and in the interest of consumers to do so? Perhaps because the probability of the rival A-supplier entering is substantially lower if the independent B-suppliers have been eliminated.

Choi and Stefanadis (2001) analyse this point in a model of probabilistic entry after investment. Bundling by the A-incumbent diminishes the investment incentives of potential entrants into each market. Carlton and Waldman (2002) explore a related model in which the potential A-rival is also a B-supplier, and where economies of scope between As and Bs are such that the rival will in due course enter the A-market only if it has first competed on the merits in the B-market, which the incumbent's bundling thwarts.

It should be observed that this exclusionary logic is quite separate from the reasons, which are not developed further in this chapter, that a firm may have to engage in such practices as exclusive contracts in order not to lose power to *exploit* its dominance.[22] For example, an upstream firm might have an exclusive contract (or integrate) with a downstream firm as a way of committing not to go on to give better deals to other downstream firms, in which case its market power could unravel.[23] The incumbent's aim here is to prevent its 'one monopoly profit' from evaporating because of weak commitment power. In effect, the dominant firm contrives to stop competing with itself. Note that this point, unlike the theme of this section, is not about the exclusion of rivals to the incumbent, though it can entail exclusionary effects in vertically related markets.

4.3.6. *Economics of exclusion: concluding comment*

Notions that certain unilateral practices by firms with market power are 'obviously' exclusionary—in a sense that implies economic inefficiency—do not withstand the 'Chicago' critique. However, as has been illustrated above, the *coherence* of theories of inefficient exclusion, consistent with profit-maximizing firms, has been demonstrated by more recent economics. If factual circumstances consistent with those theories were thought almost never to arise, then *laissez-faire* would still have practical policy merit.[24] Otherwise, cases must depend on facts. In particular, a necessary condition for a finding of abuse should be a fact-consistent theory of harm to competition.

4.4. Predatory Pricing

On 30 January 2007, the Court of First Instance (CFI) in Luxemburg dismissed the appeal by France Télécom against the Commission's decision in 2003 in what is known as the *Wanadoo* case.[25] The Commission had found that Wanadoo Interactive, part of France Télécom, had abused a dominant position in the French market for high-speed internet access for residential customers by predatory pricing. The case provides a setting in which to consider the economics and EC law of predatory pricing.

Wanadoo contested various aspects of the Commission's decision, including the finding of dominance in this fast-growing market, which was very new in 2001 when the questioned pricing conduct began. The following discussion will, however, focus on the assessment of *abuse* (paragraphs 122–230 of the judgment). Paragraph 130 states the law:

It is clear from the case-law on predatory pricing that, first, prices below average variable costs give grounds for assuming that a pricing practice is eliminatory and that, if the prices are below average total costs but above average variable costs, those prices must be regarded as abusive if they are determined as part of a plan for eliminating a competitor.[26]

In carrying out its cost analysis, the Commission spread the 'non-recurrent variable costs' of acquiring customers over four years, somewhat less than the average duration of subscriptions in the event. On that basis the Commission found that Wanadoo priced below its variable costs until August 2001, and below full costs until October 2002. Wanadoo argued that comparison of costs and revenues over a longer period was required to test below-cost pricing, especially given the new and dynamic nature of the market, but the Court at paragraph 152 ruled that costs and revenues after the relevant conduct (that is, after October 2002) cannot be included in the calculations. On that approach much investment would appear to be at risk of being found 'predatory'. Assessment of abuse must concern the position of the firm at the time of the alleged abuse, but where investment-related activity is concerned that position includes reasonable expectations as to future revenues and costs; and how events turned out may be informative, though not decisively so, about the reasonableness of such expectations.

Wanadoo next argued that it had a right to align its prices on its competitors' prices. The Court at paragraph 187 denied such an absolute right and held that beyond some point price alignment might become abusive. That conclusion does make economic sense. For example, a more efficient rival could be inefficiently deprived of custom if an unqualified matching right existed.

Finally, on abuse, Wanadoo made related arguments that its pricing showed no predatory intent, that consumers benefited from low prices and were not harmed, and that the Commission failed to show (and in the circumstances of the market could not show) recoupment—the ability to recoup short-term losses by reducing competition in the longer term. The judgment at paragraph 197 said:

It is clear therefore that, in the case of predatory pricing, the first element of the abuse applied by the dominant undertaking comprises non-recovery of costs. In the case of non-recovery of variable costs, the second element, that is, predatory intent, is presumed, whereas, in relation to prices below average full costs, the existence of a plan to eliminate competition must be proved.

From an economic perspective, this passage is doubly perplexing. First, it suggests that eliminatory intent, independent of anticompetitive effect, is a basis for a finding of abuse (despite the Courts saying that abuse is an objective concept). Second, as indicated in section 4.3.1 above, besides the difficulty of discerning intent, all sorts of manifestly pro-competitive behaviour may be motivated by eliminatory intent, so that concept is not altogether helpful in drawing the line between pro- and anticompetitive conduct.

Is there, nevertheless, an economically defensible case for doing without a requirement to show probable recoupment before finding predatory-pricing abuse? Arguably there is if: (i) dominance was established to a stringent standard; and (ii) pricing is below variable (or avoidable) cost without objective justification; and (iii) the below-cost pricing is in the dominated market. Ability to recoup would seem to be more or less implied by the joint occurrence of (i) to (iii). For example, recoupment requires barriers to (re-)entry, but those must exist if dominance has been established to a stringent standard. Even so, there may still be merit in examining recoupment as a cross-check on the initial finding of dominance. Of course, if dominance is found only to a lax standard, then recoupment should be required to prove predatory abuse. Far better, though, to raise dominance standards generally.

What if (ii) does not hold, say, because the pricing is between avoidable and average total cost (presumably with some allocation of overheads in the multi-product case)? Then it would seem important to show recoupment in order to help distinguish between plans to eliminate competitors that are merely competition on the merits,[27] and plans to eliminate competition with a view to subsequent price increases to the detriment of consumers—the kind of elimination that competition law should, at least on an effects-oriented view, be concerned about. On this view, then, it would be necessary (but not sufficient) to demonstrate probable recoupment as an element of proving the existence of a plan to eliminate competition.

The relevance of (iii) is that conduct can sometimes be found to constitute abuse even if it does not occur in the relevant product market in which dominance has been found. Thus, the Court of Justice in *Tetra Pak II*, saying that it would be inappropriate in the circumstances of that case to require in addition proof of a realistic chance of recouping losses from below-cost pricing, held that:

Application of Article [82] presupposes a link between the dominant position and the alleged abusive conduct, which is normally not present where conduct on a market distinct from the dominated market produces effects on that distinct market. In the case of distinct, but associated, markets, application of Article [82] to conduct found on the associated, non-dominated, market and having effects on that associated market can only be justified by special circumstances. An undertaking which enjoys a quasi-monopoly on certain markets and a leading position on distinct, though closely associated, markets is placed in a situation comparable to that of holding a dominant position on those markets as a whole. Conduct by such an under-taking on those distinct markets which is alleged to be abusive may therefore be covered by Article [82] of the Treaty without any need to show that it is dominant on them.[28]

It is hard to know what to make of this. It would have been more straightfor-ward to show that the firm actually was dominant—not just infer that it was comparable to being so—on the markets as a whole. Then the issue of abuse on non-dominated markets need not have been opened up. Now that it has been, a very cautious approach towards predatory pricing abuse on non-dominated markets would seem appropriate, requiring a demonstration of recoupment among other things. Otherwise dominant firms in some markets would be unduly and unreasonably deterred from offering good deals to customers in others.

None of this is to say that the calculus of recoupment should be confined to the market in which the below-cost pricing occurred. As was highlighted by the judgment of the US Court of Appeals quoted in section 4.3.1, predatory pricing in one market can be rapidly recouped in others—for example, through reputation effects.

Wanadoo sought to justify its low pricing in terms of economies of scale and learning effects, but the Court ruled that these considerations did not call into question the finding of abuse because a firm that engages in predatory pricing 'may enjoy economies of scale and learning effects on account of increased production precisely because of such pricing'.[29] Though appeal to such econ-omies obviously cannot exempt a dominant firm from the requirements of Article 82, their dismissal in these terms is troubling. When learning effects matter, there is nothing intrinsically sinister about pricing low to sell more to get costs down. Indeed, on the face of it that is both pro-consumer in the short term and pro-efficiency in the longer run. In principle, the benefit of future cost reduction should be added to price, or subtracted from short-term cost, in formulating the below-cost pricing test in the first place. In any case, if such gains flow from the low pricing, that is a benefit of it, which should not be ignored.

France Télécom has appealed to the European Court of Justice against the *Wanadoo* judgment of the CFI. The grounds of appeal include the calculation of cost recovery, the time horizon for cost and revenue assessment, and the recoupment question. The Court of Justice therefore has an opportunity to develop and clarify EC law on predatory pricing.

4.5. Discounts and Rebates

In March 2007, the Court of Justice dismissed the appeal by British Airways (BA) against the 2003 judgment of the CFI upholding the Commission's 1999 decision, following complaints by Virgin that BA had abused a dominant position as a purchaser in the UK market for travel agency services. The abuse was bonus schemes that: (i) rewarded loyalty from travel agents and (ii) discriminated between them, with the object and effect of excluding competitors from UK markets for air travel services. The Commission fined BA €6.8 million. BA had appealed to the CFI on a number of grounds, including dominance—its share of air ticket sales through UK travel agents had declined to below 40 per cent, and other means of ticket sales were growing considerably. But BA's appeal to the Court of Justice focused on the question of abuse.

BA had, until 1998, operated marketing arrangements with UK travel agents with annual BA ticket sales above £500k that involved payments on top of basic commissions based on sales' increases from one year to the next. Three very large travel agents had a global agreement based on the growth of BA's share in their worldwide sales. In 1998, BA introduced a new performance reward scheme for travel agents with additional commissions on a sliding scale on sales between 95 per cent and 125 per cent of prior-year benchmarks. None of the bonuses was conditional on exclusivity.

Before the Court of Justice BA argued, first, that the CFI had wrongly analysed exclusion, having failed to distinguish between customer 'fidelity' based on good deals—a species of normal price competition—and fidelity that excludes by creating artificial barriers for rivals. The Court of Justice said that the case law does give indications as to when discount or bonus schemes, though not conditional on exclusivity, give rise to an exclusionary effect. These include payments linked to the attainment of sales objectives defined individually, the 'very noticeable effect at the margin' for a travel agent near a threshold (since discounts applied to all, not just incremental sales), and BA's size relative to others. BA then contended that its discounts were economically justified and efficient because they increased sales and so helped cover the fixed costs of airline operation. The Court of Justice dismissed the fixed-cost point because that was an issue of fact, so not for it to consider.

BA's second plea was that the CFI had failed to consider the probable effects of the discount schemes, and evidence of absence of significant effect on competing airlines. The Court of Justice held that a finding of fidelity-building effect could be made on the basis of the mechanism of the schemes, in particular those arising from the very noticeable effect at the margin and the resulting possibility of disproportionate reductions in commission at threshold points. BA's third plea that prejudice to consumers had not been considered was also dismissed briefly on the grounds that Article 82 is aimed not just at direct consumer harm but also detriment through the impact of practices on an effective competitive structure. BA was equally unsuccessful in its other pleas, including its claim that it was wrong to find discriminatory distortion of competition among travel agents just because two with the same BA ticket sales might get different commission levels (arising from different prior years).

The US courts, by contrast, took an entirely different view of related allegations that BA's incentive arrangements with travel agents and also corporate clients were predatory foreclosure. In *Virgin* v. *British Airways*, the Court of Appeals for the Second Circuit upheld summary judgment against Virgin for lack of factual evidence and failure to show consumer harm. The Court adopted an emphatically pro-consumer view of competition. It applied the *Brooke Group* test of predatory pricing, mentioned above, and held that Virgin had shown neither below-cost pricing nor recoupment. Virgin's monopoly-leveraging claim was likewise dismissed for lack of proof. Note that the trans-Atlantic contrast between these cases is not just that BA lost in the European Commission but won in the United States—it got summary judgment in the United States, so the case did not even reach a trial of factual issues.

It is no criticism of the European Court of Justice that it did not engage in factual questions, because that is not its role. Its defence of the CFI's non-engagement with facts is none the less striking. Inspection of the mechanism of the discount schemes, particularly 'the very noticeable effect at the margin', seems largely to have sufficed for the EC Courts to infer anticompetitive effect and indirect consumer harm. This approach is to avoid testing the theory of harm against the facts of the marketplace. It is to shun those facts and to stake all on inferences drawn from the inherent features of the discount scheme. It is also to shun a serious assessment of justifications of the schemes in terms of efficiency and the consumer interest. Discount schemes are natural and can well be desirable when there are substantial fixed costs. Of course, it is a matter of (sometimes self-evident) fact whether fixed costs are significant in a given industry, but that is no reason for even an appellate court to dismiss considerations arising from such costs. Moreover, one looks in vain in the judgments for the principles by which competition on the merits is to be distinguished from abuse. Customer loyalty by itself is as consistent with the former as the latter.

Perhaps a key to understanding the readiness of the EC Courts to uphold the finding of abuse is the oft-repeated very noticeable effect at the margin. It is true that at threshold points there can be well-below-cost, indeed negative, implied prices on small increments of sales. But that is not enough for a coherent theory of anticompetitive harm. One would also need to show that a large proportion of travel agents were very close to such threshold points. It might be said that the thresholds might have some effect even on agents not very close, and that larger increments of sales need to be assessed. But, then the 'very noticeable effect' softens. In sum, the very noticeable effect may apply to too few travel agents itself to be of competitive significance in the market as a whole. No short-cut answer is available from there being a sharp effect at some margins. A fuller analysis is needed.

None of this is to say that the European BA case necessarily reached the wrong outcome. The point is rather that the analysis used to reach conclusions that BA's discount scheme was abusive was seriously incomplete if economic effects to the detriment of consumers and/or as-efficient rivals are important in distinguishing between abuse and competition on the merits. It might be said that more factual analysis is too demanding. But if fact-light assessment is wanted, it is far from obvious that *laissez-faire* is worse than formalistic intervention to condemn discount schemes not conditional on exclusivity.

4.6. Refusal to Supply, Tying, and Bundling

The *Microsoft* judgment delivered by the CFI on 17 September 2007 upheld the Commission's decision in March 2004 that Microsoft had abused a dominant position in the worldwide market for client PC operating systems by: (a) refusing to supply and authorize the use of 'interoperability information' for rivals to develop competing products on the market for workgroup server operating systems; and (b) tying Windows Media Player with the Windows client PC operating system. The Commission imposed a fine of €497.2 million, with more to follow when Microsoft did not fully comply with the remedies imposed. Those required Microsoft: (i) to supply interface information to allow non-Microsoft workgroup servers to be fully interoperable with Windows PCs and servers; and (ii) to offer to OEMs a version of the client PC operating system without Media Player (on terms not less attractive than the bundled version, which Microsoft remained free to provide). On 22 October, Microsoft said that it would not appeal against the CFI judgment and announced a package of measures to comply with the Commission decision.

Before reviewing the economics[30] and EC law of the kinds of 'non-price' abuse at issue in this case, two prior cases deserve particular mention. First, there are striking parallels to note between the Microsoft case and the EC IBM case of the early 1980s, which also concerned issues of refusal to supply interface information and bundling by a major US corporation with market power by virtue of a prevailing *de facto* computer standard (relating to IBM's System/370 network architecture).[31] The IBM case was settled by an Undertaking in 1984, without the Commission issuing a decision. IBM undertook to release interface information in a timely manner and to offer System/ 370 CPUs without main memory (while retaining design freedom and the right also to offer CPUs with main memory). Second, there is of course the US Microsoft case.

4.6.1. *The US case*

It is particularly instructive to consider the Court of Appeals' judgment in June 2001 in the US Microsoft case.[32] The Court first upheld the finding that Microsoft had monopoly power in the market for Intel-compatible PC operating systems worldwide on the basis of its share of that market coupled with the 'applications barrier to entry'—the network externalities that ensure that applications software will tend to be written for the dominant Windows standard, thereby reinforcing its dominance.

As to abuse (to use the EC term), the Court said that '[t]he challenge for an antitrust court lies in stating a general rule for distinguishing between exclusionary acts, which reduce social welfare, and competitive acts, which increase it'. Five principles from US jurisprudence were then stated to help address that question: (i) to be condemned as exclusionary a monopolist's acts must harm the competitive process and thereby consumers; harm to competitors will not suffice; (ii) the plaintiff must demonstrate such anticompetitive effect; (iii) then the monopolist may proffer a pro-competitive justification; (iv) if that stands unrebutted, the plaintiff must then show that anticompetitive harm outweighs pro-competitive benefit; (v) the focus is on effects not intent; evidence on intent is relevant only insofar as it helps predict effect.

Central to the US case was whether Microsoft had unlawfully thwarted Netscape's Internet Navigator browser (and Sun's Java technology) in order: (a) to protect its Windows operating system's monopoly ('monopolization'), and/or (b) to extend its Windows operating system's monopoly to browsers ('attempted monopolization'). A further question was whether Microsoft had unlawfully tied its Internet Explorer browser to its Windows operating system.[33]

As to (a), the Court upheld many of the findings of the lower court (in a manner rather consistent with the maintenance of market power theory of section 4.3.5 above):

Microsoft's efforts to gain market share in one market (browsers) served to meet the threat to Microsoft's monopoly in another market (operating systems) by keeping rival browsers from gaining the critical mass of users necessary to attract developer attention away from Windows as the platform for software development.[34]

These efforts of Microsoft, which lacked pro-competitive justification, included aspects of the following: restrictive licensing conditions with OEMs (that is, PC makers, so a key route to market); the integration of Internet Explorer with Windows; agreements with internet access providers; dealings with internet content providers, independent software vendors, and Apple; and actions to thwart Java. The Court, however, dismissed the claim that Microsoft had unlawfully attempted to monopolize the browser market on the grounds that the plaintiff had not proven a dangerous probability of achieving monopoly power in that (putative) market. (This is like a recoupment point.) In short, the Court did not find leverage theories (of the sort sketched in section 4.3.4 above) demonstrated by the facts.

As to the tying claim, the question before the Court was whether per se or rule-of-reason analysis was appropriate for platform software products. They said the latter. The separate-products principle laid down by the Supreme Court in *Jefferson Parish*[35] is that there is no tying subject to per se liability unless there is sufficient demand for the tied product separate from the tying product to identify a distinct product market in which it is efficient to supply the tied product separately. This test, applied to integration of platform software products, did not suggest that they were not separate, but the Court concluded that as a general matter their bundling could not be said to have so little 'redeeming virtue' as to warrant per se condemnation. The Court accordingly remanded the tying question back for (structured) rule-of-reason, rather than per se, assessment.

Following the Court of Appeals' judgment, the US Justice Department (and some but not all States) agreed a settlement with Microsoft in November 2001, which received court approval in a Final Judgment a year later. Microsoft agreed, among other things: (a) to specify and license to third parties some communications protocols needed to interoperate with Windows client PC operating systems; and (b) to allow OEMs and end-users to substitute competing alternatives to Microsoft's 'middleware'—software that bridges between the operating system and applications. Many have doubted the effectiveness of the US settlement, but the Court of Appeals in 2004 upheld the District Court's approval of the remedies[36] and the view of the Justice Department is that they have succeeded in promoting competition and consumer choice.[37]

4.6.2. The European Commission case: refusal to supply interoperability information

Microsoft denied that its refusal to supply interoperability information was abusive on the grounds that the information was protected by intellectual property (IP) rights, and that the narrow criteria in the case law for holding the refusal to license IP to be abusive were not satisfied by the facts of the case. In any event, it argued, the refusal was objectively justified by consideration of innovation incentives. The Commission, while not conceding that the information was protected by IP rights, adopted its decision on the assumption favourable to Microsoft that it was.

A line of cases has established that although firms are generally free to choose with whom they deal, there are certain circumstances in which a refusal to supply can be an abuse. Only exceptionally, however, has refusal to supply IP been found to be abusive—rightly so since the essence of IP is the right to exclusive use.[38] In *Magill*, television companies were held to have abused dominance by refusing to supply (copyrighted) weekly programme listings so that third parties could supply multi-channel weekly TV guides, and *IMS Health*, where the Court of Justice gave a preliminary ruling on points of law, concerned IP rights over the geographical format or 'brick structure' by which German pharmaceutical sales data were presented.[39]

The Microsoft judgment, summarizing this and related of jurisprudence, says at paragraph 332 that circumstances are exceptional if three tests are met—indispensability, exclusion of effective competition, and prevention of the appearance of a new product for which there is potential demand. The last of these conditions is found only in the case law on refusal to supply IP rights: in other contexts abuse can be found without it holding.

The Commission in its decision, while contending that the three *IMS* tests were met, had warned that their automatic application would be problematic, saying that the entirety of the circumstances must be subject to comprehensive examination.[40] For the Commission, these included the disruption of previous supply of interoperability information, the great importance of interoperability in software markets, Microsoft's extraordinary power arising from its client PC operating system standard leading to the rapid attainment also of dominance in workgroup server operating system. In that regard, the Commission decision (at paragraphs 764 ff.) explicitly addressed the 'one monopoly profit' argument. As to the leverage of monopoly (see section 4.3.4 above), the Commission said that the 'one monopoly profit' argument relies on strong assumptions that do not hold in the case at hand. But, then the Commission stressed incentives to maintain monopoly (see section 4.3.5):

[A] future competitor in the client PC operating system market will need to provide products interoperable with Microsoft's dominant workgroup server operating system. As such, by strengthening its dominant position in the workgroup server operating system market, Microsoft effectively reinforces the barriers to entry in the client PC operating system market.[41]

In economic terms, this point is very much in line with the monopoly maintenance theory of harm to competition upheld by the US Court of Appeals.

Despite the Commission's emphasis on the desirability of appraising the entirety of the circumstances, the CFI proceeded straight to consider Microsoft's refusal to supply against the three *IMS* tests, deferring the wider exceptional circumstances invoked by the Commission for consideration only if one or more of the *IMS* tests was not satisfied (para. 336). The Court found that the Commission had not erred in concluding that each test was satisfied. First, interoperability on an equal footing is indispensable for rivals to compete viably. Second, otherwise there is a risk that competition will be eliminated. Third, the Commission was not manifestly incorrect to find that the refusal to supply would limit technical development—hence new products—to the prejudice of consumers. As to objective justification, the Court considered that Microsoft had failed to show that requiring disclosure of interoperability information would have a negative effect on its incentives to innovate.

In sum, the Court judged that 'the exceptional circumstances identified by the Court of Justice in *Magill* and *IMS Health*... were also present in this case' (para. 712). Thus, the automatic application of the *IMS* tests, which the Commission had warned would be problematic, sufficed to dismiss Microsoft's plea, and there was no need to consider the wider exceptional circumstances invoked by the Commission.

Indeed, the Court commented (at para. 559) that even if the Commission had been wrong to find that Microsoft had a dominant position in the market for workgroup server operating systems, that would not have undermined a conclusion of abuse because the abuse stemmed from, and concerned 'leveraging' of dominance in the market for client PC operating system software. The Court saw the *IMS* test relating to the prevention of a new product rather broadly in terms of Article 82(b), which prohibits limiting production, markets or technical development to the prejudice of consumers. As to prejudice to consumers, the Court (at para. 664) noted that indirect prejudice via market structure is possible and then made the extraordinary statement that 'Microsoft impaired the effective competitive structure on the workgroup server operating systems market by acquiring a significant share on that market.'

The earlier cases of *Magill* and *IMS Health* had concerned information in the public domain—TV listings and a map grid—that appear to have been largely by-products of other activities requiring little if any creative effort. The context of Microsoft's interoperability information is very different. Yet, the Court found with relative ease that the 'exceptional circumstances' of those cases, and the *IMS* test in particular, were satisfied by the facts in *Microsoft* (without even needing to attend to some truly exceptional features of Microsoft's position). This suggests that such circumstances are not nearly as exceptional as previously thought.

All this leaves two major questions for the future. What now is the principle that limits dominant firm duties to supply their rivals with access to important inputs? When such a duty applies, at what price must the input be supplied?

4.6.3. *The European Commission case: bundling of Media Player*

The Court upheld the Commission's four-part test to determine the question of bundling/tying abuse. First, Microsoft had a dominant position in the tying product (client PC operating system software). Second, the tied product (Windows Media Player) was separate by reference to consumer demand. Third, consumers could not buy the tying product without the tied product. Fourth, competition was foreclosed because Microsoft offering original equipment manufacturers (OEMs) Windows with Media Player bundled gave it an unparalleled distribution advantage, with the result that third-party media players could not compete on their merits through OEMs. (This conclusion was reached notwithstanding the fact that OEMs and end-users are free to instal third-party media players, which have had considerable success in the marketplace, including through the OEM channel.) The Court held that Microsoft had bundled without objective justification, noting that it remained free to offer a bundled version so long as an unbundled version was offered too.

Following the Commission's decision, Microsoft has indeed offered an unbundled version—albeit it at the same price as the bundled version—for which there has been (unsurprisingly) little demand. A remedy requiring an unbundled version, while allowing continued bundling, is of questionable effectiveness without a required price difference between the two versions. Some would go further and say that the ineffectiveness of the remedy itself calls into question the finding of abuse. What could the required price difference have been? One candidate is avoidable cost, but the avoidable cost of adding Media Player to Windows is likely to be very small indeed. It is arguable that a required price difference larger than avoidable cost would have been an appropriate remedy, especially bearing in mind that remedial measures may well go further than requiring cessation of abuse. But the Commission did not enter the business of price-difference regulation.

All this suggests that the bundling abuse finding in the EC Microsoft case is of less significance than that relating to interoperability, being relatively easy but largely ineffective to remedy, at least without the apparatus of (price-difference) regulation. Matters would have been quite different if it had been found abusive for Microsoft to supply a bundled version at all, and so had been required to supply unbundled software only. But, then Microsoft would have had a powerful objective justification in terms of efficiency and consumer welfare.

It will be apparent from the above that the 'non-price' abuses of refusal to supply and tying/bundling are necessarily to do with price. If it is held to be abusive to refuse to supply in some context, the remedy is presumably an obligation to supply. But, that obligation is without practical meaning unless the price of supply is capped. Then it would seem that the abuse is refusal-to-supply-on-reasonable-terms—a price abuse, in other words. Likewise, the bundling abuse is a form of refusal to supply—namely refusal to supply an unbundled version. But, if a bundled version can be supplied in parallel, the issue again comes down to price, in particular the price difference between the bundled and unbundled versions. The fact that pricing obligations are difficult to specify and enforce is a further reason to be cautious about imposing obligations to supply.

4.7. Article 82: The Future

The EC Courts were a helpful spur to the reforms of European policy and practice towards mergers, especially between 2002 and 2004. There is no indication from the *Microsoft* judgment, nor from *Wanadoo* nor *British Airways*, that they will play a similar role in relation to Article 82. So, after fifty years of the Treaty are we stuck? That now depends primarily upon the Commission. That the *Microsoft* Court has not taken a lead in reforming the policy and practice of Article 82 makes it all the more important that the Commission does so.

With the *Microsoft* case in train, the Commission has been understandably reticent about Article 82 policy for the past two years. But, on 28 November 2007, the Commission adopted guidelines on non-horizontal mergers (European Commission 2007). Guidelines on the application of Article 82, at least as regards exclusionary abuse, would do well to mirror some broad features of the non-horizontal merger guidelines.[42] The first is that they are explicitly consumer-oriented throughout, with competitor protection explicitly rejected: 'the fact that a merger affects competitors is not in itself a problem' (para. 16). Accordingly, the focus of concern is anticompetitive foreclosure—that is, where as a result firms can profitably increase price. Second, the guidelines are clear that non-horizontal mergers provide substantial scope for efficiencies. The same is also true of a range of unilateral practices by firms with market power. Third, they spell out the principal mechanisms of harm to competition (as to which see section 4.3, above) and identify some of the crucial questions of fact that theories of harm to competition must face.

The importance and impact of Article 82 over the next fifty years will of course turn on technological and market developments as well as on what happens in competition authorities and courts. The Commission, nevertheless, has an unusual opportunity now to shape the contours of future public policy towards firms with market power, and to complete the economics-based reform of EC competition law enforcement.

Notes

[1] This chapter was prepared for the IESE conference 'Fifty Years of the Treaty: Assessment and Perspectives of Competition Policy in Europe', held in Barcelona, 19–20 Nov. 2007, more than a year before the Commission published its guidance on enforcement priorities in applying Article 82 to exclusionary abuse. For comments on an earlier version I thank, without implicating them in any way: Steve Anderman, Daniel Beard, David Evans, Ian Forrester, Ben Gauntlett, Philip Marsden, Massimo Motta, Joe Perkins, Patrick Rey, Xavier Vives, and Anthony Whelan.

[2] *Microsoft* v. *Commission*, T–201/04 [2007], para. 87, with the point repeated, paras 379 and 482.

[3] *France Télécom SA* v. *Commission*, T–340/03 [2007].

[4] *British Airways* v. *Commission*, C-95/04 P [2007].

[5] Fuller discussion is in Vickers (2006).

[6] Economic Advisory Group on Competition Policy 2005: 13.

[7] These headings (and one on foreclosure via vertical integration) formed the structure of the Cleary Gottlieb lecture I gave in London in Sept. 2006 and the Telecom Italia lecture in Milan in Nov. 2006.

[8] Vickers (2005) discusses these principles in more detail. They are by no means the only ones that have been suggested.

[9] For a full analysis and critique of the stance of US antitrust law towards allegations of predatory pricing since 1993, see Bolton, Brodley, and Riordan (2000).

[10] A point explored by Bolton and Scharfstein (1990).

[11] Quoted at Kovacic (2007: 49).

[12] See further Rey and Tirole (2007: sect. 4.1).

[13] As this point indicates, the freedom argument cuts both ways. Policy intervention to ensure freedom *ex post* denies an element of freedom *ex ante*—namely, freedom to agree not to exercise some options *ex post*. It therefore seems unlikely that freedom per se can be much help in distinguishing between pro- and anticompetitive behaviour.

[14] See further Rey and Tirole (2007: sect. 4.2).

[15] Aghion and Bolton (1987: sect. III).

[16] Fumagalli and Motta (2006) and Simpson and Wickelgren (2007) are two recent articles that extend the analysis, with mixed results, to the case where the multiple buyers are firms competing to sell to final consumers.

[17] Bernheim and Whinston (1998: sect. IV).

[18] See further Rey and Tirole (2007: sects 3.1 and 5.2) and Tirole (2005).

[19] More specifically, plaintiff Schor contended that Abbot's price for its Norvir component was too high in relation to the price for its Kaletra combination containing Norvir, and that Abbott was thereby unlawfully leveraging its Norvir monopoly to other components. There was no contention of predatory pricing: the imputed price for the non-Norvir components of Kaletra was above average variable cost.

[20] Schor v. Abbott Laboratories, No. 05–3344 (7th Cir. 2006).

[21] See further Rey and Tirole (2007: sect. 3.2) and Tirole (2005).

[22] See further Rey and Tirole (2007: sect. 2.1).

[23] Policy intervention to ban discrimination could in this setting counterproductively help the dominant firm to *bolster* its market power.

[24] Recall Judge Easterbrook's position on whether US antitrust law should recognize a pure theory of leverage.

[25] *France Télécom SA* v. *Commission*, T–340/03 [2007].

[26] Citing *AKZO* v. *Commission*, C-62/86 [1991], and the *Tetra Pak* cases, above all *Tetra Pak* v. *Commission*, C-333/94 P [1996].

[27] Prices below avoidable cost by a dominant firm are presumptively not competition on the merits in the absence of objective justification, whereas prices above avoidable cost, even if below total cost, might be competition on the merits without further justification.

[28] *Tetra Pak* v. *Commission*, C-333/94 P [1996].

[29] *France Télécom SA* v. *Commission*, case T–340/03: para. 217.

[30] One of a number of economic analyses of the EC Microsoft case is Kühn and van Reenen (2007).

[31] Vickers (2008) compares the European IBM and Microsoft cases.

[32] *United States* v. *Microsoft*, 253 F.3d 34 (DC Cir. 2001). Economic analyses of the case include Whinston 2001 and Rubinfeld 2004.

[33] The tying allegation came under sect. 1 of the Sherman Act, which concerns anti-competitive agreements, rather than sect. 2, which concerns monopolization.

[34] *United States* v. *Microsoft*, 253 F.3d 60 (DC Cir. 2001).

[35] *Jefferson Parish Hospital Dist. No. 2* v. *Hyde*, 466 US 2 (1984).

[36] *Massachusetts* v. *Microsoft*, 373 F.3d 1199, 1243 (DC Cir. 2004).

[37] Press release of 30 Aug. 2007 in connection with the Department of Justice's review of the Final Judgments. The remedies were due to expire in Nov. 2007 but some (e.g. relating to protocol licensing) have been extended. In an amicus brief filed on 9 Nov. the Department of Justice urged the District Court to deny motions from certain States, including California and New York, calling for general five-year extensions of the Final Judgments.

[38] The Courts have distinguished between the exclusive right and its exercise. It is the latter which may be abusive in exceptional circumstances.

[39] *RTE and ITP* v. *Commission*, C-241&242/91 P [1995] ('*Magill*'), and *IMS Health*, C-418/01 [2004].

[40] See e.g. para. 316 of the CFI judgment. The immediately preceding paragraph records Microsoft's reliance on the *Magill/IMS Health* tests. Ironically, the Court adopted precisely the tests urged by Microsoft, but of course reached the opposite conclusions on them.

[41] *United States* v. *Microsoft*, 253 F.3d 34 (DC Cir. 2001): para. 769.

[42] The Commission finally issued guidance on its enforcement priorities in applying Article 82 to exclusionary abuse on 8 December 2008. Official publication in all Union languages followed in February 2009.

5

Cartels in the European Union: Economics, Law, Practice[1]

Massimo Motta

5.1. Introduction

Collusive practices allow firms to exert market power they would not other-wise have: they artificially restrict competition and increase prices, thereby reducing welfare. Accordingly, they are prohibited by any antitrust law, and a large part of the antitrust authorities' (AA) efforts are devoted to fighting such practices. However, there might be divergences across jurisdictions (and within the same jurisdiction there may be changes over time) as to the stand-ard of proof required to prove the infringement of the law. Indeed, while any AA would agree that a written agreement or the creation of a central office to fix prices, allocate quotas of production, or share markets would be illegal, differences often exist as to how to treat situations in which firms manage to keep industry prices high without overtly colluding.

The main purpose of this chapter is to identify the chief mechanisms behind collusion, to study the factors which facilitate them, and to explain which behaviours should be treated as an infringement of the law and which ones should not. I shall also analyse what actions antitrust authorities should take in order to deter and break collusion, and more particularly I shall analyse EC cartel law and experience in this respect.

This chapter is structured as follows. Section 5.2 sketches the main features of collusion from an economic point of view, and briefly reviews factors that make collusion more likely to occur. Section 5.3 deals with the 'practice' of collusion in the European Union. First, I describe the EU institutional and legal frameworks, then I discuss the legal standards for finding firms guilty of collusion and argue that to a large extent EU practice coincides with what economic thinking recommends. Finally, I review some empirical evidence in the EU fight against cartels, and discuss what could be done to increase deterrence. Section 5.4 concludes the chapter with some summarizing notes and a brief discussion of the policy initiatives that the European Commission should undertake in the domain of cartel law.

5.2. Economic Analysis of Collusion

In this section I briefly characterize the economic concept of collusion. In economics, collusion is a situation where firms' prices are higher than some competitive benchmark.[2] In other words, for economists, collusion coincides with an outcome (high-enough price), and not with the specific form through which that outcome is attained. Indeed, as I explain below, collusion can occur both when firms act through an organized cartel (explicit collusion) and when they act in a purely non-cooperative way (tacit collusion).

To avoid misunderstandings, let me emphasize that in this section I will not use the term 'collusion' as a synonym for a collusive agreement that should be outlawed, but in the economic theory sense, that is, high prices. Later, in section 5.3, I will argue that although in economic theory collusion is defined as a market outcome, antitrust authorities and judges should consider illegal only those practices where firms *explicitly* coordinate their actions to achieve a collusive outcome.

5.2.1. What are the main ingredients of collusion?

Firms may be unable to achieve a collusive outcome, even if they could freely agree on the prices they should set. This is because each firm would have the temptation unilaterally to deviate from a collusive action, as by doing so it would increase its profit.

Consider an industry consisting of two fruit sellers in a street market. Imagine they both sell pears of identical quality, and that they each pay €1 per kilo to their suppliers. Imagine also that each seller thinks that €2 per kilo is the monopoly price, and believes the other thinks in the same way. When a seller arrives at his stall, he has to decide the selling price. Suppose that he thinks the rival is setting a price of €2. If he charges €2 for his pears, he will get roughly half of the buyers, as people who want to buy pears are indifferent between buying from him or from the other vendor. But he will have a strong temptation to *deviate*, that is to charge a lower price than his rival: if he sets a price of, say, €1.90, consumers will all buy from him (why pay more for an identical product?). As a result, he will still enjoy a high unit margin but he will sell more units: in short, he will make more profits than if he sold at the collusive price of €2.[3]

The acknowledgment that any collusive situation naturally brings with it the temptation to *deviate* from it and therefore to break collusion, leads us to the identification of the two elements which must exist for collusion to arise. First, its participants must be able to *detect* in a timely way that a deviation (a firm setting a lower price or producing a higher output than the collusive levels agreed upon) has occurred.[4] Second, identifying the deviation is not enough: there must also be a *punishment*, which might take the form of rivals producing much higher quantities (or selling at much lower prices) in the periods after the deviation, thus depressing the profit of the deviator.[5]

Only if a firm knows both that a deviation will be identified quickly and that it will be punished (i.e., it will have to forgo enough profits because of the market reaction of the cartel members), might it refrain from deviating, so that the collusive outcome will arise.[6]

To continue our example, after having seen why a fruit seller has a temptation to cut prices below the collusive level of €2, let us see under which conditions he will deviate. If the street market is small enough, and if the sellers post the prices of the fruit they sell, detection of the price cut will be immediate. After the price cut has been identified, one can bet that a seller who has so far sold at the price of €2 will immediately retaliate, and probably will start to sell at a price lower than €1.90 per kilo. The result will be a price war which will reduce the profit of both. A seller contemplating a deviation will certainly expect that the rival will retaliate. As a result, the prospect of selling for some time at very low prices will deter him from deviating in the first place. In other words, the awareness that a deviation will be easily detected and that a market punishment will ensue, will make each seller refrain from deviating and convince him to stick to the collusive price instead.

To summarize, for collusion to occur, first, there must be the possibility to *detect* deviations from a collusive action in a timely way. Secondly, there must be a credible *punishment* which follows a deviation.

It is important to stress that in the example the two fruit vendors do not talk to each other, neither directly nor through intermediaries: collusive prices will arise through purely non-cooperative behaviour of the sellers. In other words, if detection of deviations is rapid, and if (market) punishments of deviations are likely and credible, then *tacit collusion* can arise: firms do not necessarily have to talk to each other, let alone agree on complicated schemes, for a collusive outcome to be sustainable. All that is needed is the awareness that a deviation will be identified, and that a 'punishment' will follow.

5.2.2. Coordination: the difference between tacit and overt collusion

A difficulty with the example above is that it is not clear how the collusive price is chosen. Imagine that, for some reason, each seller thinks that the other would set a price of €1.50, rather than a price of €2. Then, a collusive situation might again occur in equilibrium, but this time with sellers setting a price lower than the monopoly price. In other words, the collusive mechanism I have described works for many different prices and results in firms getting quite different levels of profits.[7]

This result raises the important issue of *coordination*. Firms that are tacitly colluding might arrive at the fully collusive price, but this is just one of the many possible equilibrium outcomes (one of these also being the competitive outcome, i.e., the one-shot game equilibrium price). So, is there an outcome that is more likely than the other? And, since firms have an interest in coordinating on an outcome with the highest possible profits, how can they achieve that outcome? Under *tacit collusion*, it is difficult for the firms to solve the coordination problem. If firms cannot communicate with each other, they can make mistakes, and select a price (or a quantity) which is not jointly optimal for the firms, and which might be difficult to change. Using the market to signal intentions to coordinate on a different price might be very costly. If a firm believes the right price for the industry is higher and increases its own price to signal it, it will lose market share in the adjustment period. If a firm decreases its own price to try and coordinate on a lower equilibrium price, this move might be understood as a deviation and trigger a costly price war. Therefore, experimenting with price changes to coordinate on another collusive equilibrium might be too costly.

Under *explicit collusion*, instead, firms can talk to each other and coordinate on their jointly preferred equilibrium without having to experiment with the market, which is costly. Furthermore, if there are some shocks which modify market conditions, communication will allow the firms to change to a new collusive price without the risk of triggering a period of punishment.

Suppose, for instance, that, in the example above, one seller knows that demand for pears has decreased, so that he thinks the optimal price is now lower, say €1.80. Absent communication with the other vendor, our seller faces a problem: if he reduces the price to €1.80, as new market conditions suggest, collusion might break. Indeed, the rival vendor might have a different perception of market demand, and/or misinterpret the new low price as a 'deviation', and start a price war as a punishment. However, if he sticks instead to the usual price of €2, he will make lower profits, because demand is lower.

Explicit collusion avoids this problem: our vendor could simply tell his rival that he thinks it would be better to decrease the price, and communication will allow them to decide on a new price that suits them both, without risking any price war or a lengthy adjustment period.

Market allocation (or market-sharing) schemes—according to which a firm sells in a certain region (or serves customers of a certain type), whereas the rivals sell in other regions (or serve customers of a different type)—whether achieved by explicit collusion or historical accidents, have the advantage of allowing for prices to adjust to new demand or cost conditions without triggering possible price wars. A market allocation scheme avoids the possibility that, if a shock reduces production costs or market demand, a price reduction might trigger a price war. As long as each firm does not serve segments of demand (explicitly or tacitly) allocated to rivals, prices can change without the collusive outcome being disrupted. This probably explains why such collusive schemes are often used.[8]

I shall come back to the issues of communication and coordination among firms, and on why competition policy should focus on explicit collusive practices (that is, when some communication and coordination exists) in section 5.3. Before doing that, however, I would like to conclude this part on the economics of collusion by briefly discussing the practices which facilitate collusion.

5.2.3. *Factors that facilitate collusion*

The analysis of collusion in modern industrial economics is based on the so-called *incentive constraint* for collusion: each firm compares the immediate gain it makes from a deviation with the profit it gives up in the future, when rivals react. Only if the former is lower than the latter will the firm choose the collusive strategy. In general, collusion is more likely to arise the lower the profit that a firm would obtain from deviating, the lower the expected profits it would make once the punishment starts, and the more weight firms attach to the future (when the loss from deviation occurs).

A large part of the literature on collusion studies the factors which foster collusive outcomes, by relying on the framework just delineated (that is, the condition that says that a firm is better off colluding than deviating): if a given factor relaxes the incentive constraint of the firms, then it facilitates collusion; if it makes it more binding, it hinders it; if the effect is ambiguous, then the factor does not have a clear impact on collusion.

The study of facilitating factors is important for two reasons. First, it allows one to identify the practices that facilitate collusion so that antitrust authorities can intervene so as to eliminate them whenever possible. Second, in merger analysis, it allows one to evaluate whether a particular industry is prone to a collusive outcome or not, and therefore it gives indications as to whether a given merger should be prohibited or not. For the purpose of this chapter, however, since we are interested in how to act against cartels, we can restrict attention only to those facilitating factors that can be controlled by the firms themselves, and we do not need to dwell upon *structural* facilitating factors that are exogenous to the firms, and which therefore are less relevant for detection and deterrence of cartels.[9]

In what follows, I first emphasize the role played by agreements to exchange information about past and current individual data; such agreements allow firms to improve observability of prices and quantities, and therefore to *enforce* collusion. Next I discuss the role of communication among firms, stressing that announcements on future actions help firms *coordinate* on a particular collusive outcome. Finally, I will make some brief considerations on pricing clauses that may also facilitate collusion.

OBSERVABILITY OF FIRMS' ACTIONS

Detection of deviations is a crucial ingredient for collusion, and Stigler (1964) argued that collusive agreements would break down because of *secret* price cuts. In fact, Green and Porter (1984) show that if actual prices (or price discounts) are not observable collusion would be more difficult to sustain, but it could still arise at equilibrium. Their important contribution can be summarized in the following way. Imagine an industry where sellers cannot observe the prices charged by rivals and where market demand levels are also unobservable. Then, a seller would not know if a lower than expected number of customers served is due to a negative shock in demand or to a price cut by a rival which has stolen some (or all) of his business. Green and Porter show that if the discount factor is high enough, there exists a set of collusive strategies that represent an equilibrium. The strategies are such that each firm sets a collusive price (which might be the price that maximizes joint profits) as long as every firm faces a high level of demand. When a firm faces a low (or zero) demand, then the punishment is triggered and each firm sets the one shot equilibrium price for a finite number of periods. After this finite punishment phase, all firms revert to the collusive price.

Therefore, the model implies that collusion can be sustained at equilibrium, but unlike the standard model with perfect observability, collusive prices and profits will never be observed forever, even if no firm deviates. Indeed, the punishment is triggered whenever a low level of demand is observed, and will last for a certain number of periods, after which firms revert to the collusive prices.[10] The model has therefore an important implication. The observation of some periods with low prices is not sufficient to exclude that the industry is at a collusive equilibrium. Rather, price wars simply are the indispensable element of a collusive strategy when rivals' prices and market demand realizations are unobservable.[11]

Since observability of prices and quantities helps firms reach the most collusive outcomes (under perfect observability, price wars that are costly for the firms would not occur), competition policy should pay special attention to practices that help firms monitor each other's behaviour. One example of such a practice is given by information exchange agreements, which I discuss next. I shall also address other pricing practices that increase observability of firms' actions, such as resale price maintenance and best price clauses.

INFORMATION EXCHANGE I: DATA ON PAST OR CURRENT PRICES AND QUANTITIES

It is often the case that via trade associations or in other ways, firms in a given industry exchange data on prices, quantities, or other variables such as capacities, customer demand, costs, and so on. In the light of the discussion above, it becomes important to identify the collusive potential of such communication among firms.[12]

First, we have seen above that exchange of information on past prices and quantities (or of verifiable information on prices and quantities set in the current period) of each individual firm facilitates collusion, as it allows one to identify deviators and better target market punishments, that become then more effective and less costly for the punishing firms.

In the absence of disaggregate information on past prices and quantities, availability of more precise estimates of aggregate (market) demand would also help, as it allows firms to see whether a decrease in individual demand is due to cheating of rivals or to a negative shock in market demand. In turn, this implies that there would be no need for punishment phases which are triggered not by deviations but by a general decrease of market demand.[13]

Exchange of information about past (and current) prices and quantities helps firms sustain collusion, but it is possible that there might also be efficiency effects behind exchange of such data. For instance, better information about demand might allow firms to increase production in markets, times, and areas where demand is higher. The literature on information exchange has ambiguous findings.[14] Theoretically, it is possible in certain circumstances that exchanging information improves welfare. However, it is unlikely that firms need to exchange individual and disaggregate data in order to achieve whatever efficiency there might be. Kühn (2001) also argues that information about the industry might help firms devise incentive schemes for their personnel, based on relative productivity, but, again, for such schemes to work firms do not need detailed data at a disaggregate level.[15]

Kühn (2001) convincingly concludes that while both types of information exchange help firms to collude, the observation of past and present quantities and prices of firms is a more effective collusive device than the exchange of private information about market demand. Further, if efficiency gains of information exchange exist, they would be reaped already with the exchange of aggregate data. This should lead competition policy to a more severe treatment of agreements concerning exchange of information about individual prices and quantities (especially the more disaggregate and the more recent). Indeed, his conclusion that communication between firms about such individual firm data should be forbidden is compelling.

COORDINATION ISSUES: THE ROLE OF COMMUNICATION

When firms repeatedly meet in the marketplace, if the discount factor is large enough, any price between marginal cost and fully collusive price might be sustained. This raises the issue of which price is likely to arise as the market outcome. Habit, history, or particular events might provide firms with a *focal point* on which to coordinate.

Consider, for instance, a situation where two firms are told by a regulator that their prices cannot be higher than a certain level, say 100. In this case, this price will provide a clear benchmark (the focal point) for the firms, and one can bet that 100 will be the price that they will set.[16]

History might also provide hints. Many European markets have been protected from foreign competition for a long time, resulting in several national monopolies in many industries. Once tariff and non-tariff barriers started to fall, this created a potentially pan-European market. However, a situation where each firm stays in its own market without entering foreign ones would provide a good collusive equilibrium, which is just the continuation of something which has happened for a long time. Instead, starting to export might be considered a deviation and might trigger a retaliation in the home market, with rivals exporting in turn. Therefore, the status quo might be a focal point, and only when demand and technology conditions substantially change might firms be tempted to break the current situation.[17]

Whatever the reason, if firms have coordinated in the past on a certain collusive price or divided markets in a certain way, it might be too risky for them to experiment so as to change it. Firms might simply update such a price more or less mechanically with inflation or when raw materials commonly used in the industry become more expensive.

If firms were colluding explicitly they would simply communicate with each other and they could achieve higher collusive prices (provided that firms are symmetric enough, they would have similar preferences over prices) and/or more efficient market sharing rules. But, even if they did not overtly collude, they could still try to overcome coordination problems by transmitting information to each other, as I discuss in what follows.

INFORMATION EXCHANGE II: ANNOUNCEMENTS OF FUTURE PRICES

Announcement of future prices (or production plans) might help collusion in that it might allow firms better to coordinate on a particular equilibrium among all the possible ones.[18] Farrell (1987) was the first to show the role of non-binding and non-verifiable communication (known as 'cheap talk') in achieving coordination among players in games with multiple equilibria.[19] Since then, both theory and experimental evidence seem to indicate that announcements about price intentions might help firms to coordinate, although not under all circumstances.[20]

However, not all announcements about future actions should be treated in the same way. One should distinguish between two different situations, according to whom the announcements are directed: (1) *'private' announcements* directed to competitors only (these include communication in auctions); (2) *'public' announcements* with commitment value to consumers.

'Private' announcements: in the first case, announcements are directed to competitors only. To help fix ideas, think of a firm sending a fax to rivals where it is stated that from next month it intends to set a certain price. As Kühn 2001 remarks, it is hard to imagine any efficiency reason behind such announcements. Most probably, they just help rivals coordinate on a particular collusive price, and therefore help them collude by avoiding costly periods of price wars and price instability.

Advance notice of price changes: as long as it does not fully commit the firm to the price announced, it might also be a tool to avoid costly experimentation with the market.[21] A firm might announce a price increase effective, say, in sixty days, but then revert to the current price if the other firms did not follow suit with similar announcements of price changes.[22] In this way, firms might arrive at a commonly agreed price without incurring the risk of losing market shares or triggering price wars during the period of adjustment to the new prices.[23]

'Public' announcements: in the second case, price announcements are public, and therefore seen by rival firms as well as consumers. Think, for instance, of a firm advertising the prices of its products in newspapers. On the one hand, it might be argued that transparency of prices still helps collusion, for the reasons indicated above. On the other hand, though, market transparency is good for consumers, as it allows them to shop around for the best offer. The latter positive effect is generally considered stronger than the collusive effects of the announcements. Both theoretical arguments and empirical evidence suggest that price advertising in this sense is generally beneficial and brings prices down.[24] Therefore, when prices are transparent for both consumers and firms, this should not be considered as an anticompetitive practice.

To conclude, whereas announcements directed to rivals only should be forbidden, announcements about current and future prices which carry commitment value vis-à-vis consumers should be regarded as welfare-enhancing.

PRICING RULES AND CONTRACTS

Firms might be able to write contracts and adopt pricing rules that help them sustain collusion. In what follows, I will briefly discuss some examples of such practices.

Meeting-competition clauses state that if the buyer receives a better price offer from *another* seller, the current seller will match that price.[25] In this case, the potential for collusion is high, and twofold. First, the clause works as a device to exchange information: whenever a buyer is offered a better price, it will have an incentive to report that information to the current seller. This will make firms immediately aware of a deviation from a collusive outcome in the industry, and we know that timely detection of deviations is a crucial element for collusion. Second, the clause reduces the incentives to deviate in the first place: if rivals can retain their current customers due to a meeting-competition clause, the price decrease can only attract new buyers, but cannot steal existing buyers from other firms.

Meeting-competition clauses might have efficiency explanations,[26] but the pro-collusive impact of meeting-competition clauses seems so strong that antitrust agencies should probably adopt a rebuttable presumption that they are anticompetitive. In other words, the burden of proving that such clauses are not harmful should be on the firms using them.

Resale price maintenance (RPM) is a vertical agreement whereby a manufacturer imposes upon its retailer(s) the price at which the good should be sold in the final market. There are a number of reasons why RPM can be pro-competitive,[27] but RPM might also facilitate collusion among manufacturers. The intuition is clearly conveyed in the following quote:

> With a competitive retail market and stable retail cost conditions, manufacturers could assume agreed-upon retail prices by fixing their wholesale prices appropriately. In reality, however, variation over time in the costs of retailing would lead to fluctuating retail prices. If wholesale prices are not easily observed by each cartel member, cartel stability would suffer because members would have difficulty distinguishing changes in retail prices that were caused by cost changes from cheating on the cartel. RPM can enhance cartel stability by eliminating the retail price variation.[28]

Jullien and Rey (2007) have recently formalized this argument, and showed that indeed RPM allows manufacturers better to identify deviations from a collusive action, as the quote above suggested, and therefore better to sustain collusion.

Uniform delivered prices might also facilitate price observability among rivals. Consider a situation where producers are located in different geographic areas, and serve consumers that are also spread out over the territory. In these circumstances, it might be difficult for firms to compare prices and to detect price changes, since prices vary with transportation costs. Under uniform delivered pricing, a firm would set the same price inclusive of transportation cost throughout its territory, and independent of the customers' locations. Somebody located next to a firm's plant would pay exactly the same as somebody located hundreds of kilometres away. The practice, however, would make it much easier for competitors to check the prices charged to the clients, thereby fostering collusion.[29]

5.3. Cartels in the European Union: Law and Practice

In this section, I first briefly describe cartel law in the European Union, and then discuss the way it has been enforced by the European Commission, which is an administrative authority whose decisions can be appealed to the European Community Courts, that is, the Court of First Instance (CFI) and the European Court of Justice (ECJ).[30]

First, I describe the legal framework and the general enforcement of the law (section 5.3.1). Then, I turn to some crucial substantial issues, such as how EU case law has dealt with the standards of proving collusive infringement (section 5.3.2). Finally, I provide some empirical evidence on the way cartel law has been enforced in the European Union, and in particular discuss the issue of deterrence (section 5.3.3).

5.3.1. *Legal framework*

The main EU law provision on cartels is represented by Article 81 of the European Community Treaty,[31] which recites:

(1) The following shall be prohibited as incompatible with the common market: all agreements between undertakings, decisions by associations of undertakings and concerted practices which may affect trade between Member States and which have as their object or effect the prevention, restriction or distortion of competition within the common market, and in particular those which: (a) directly or indirectly fix purchase or selling prices or any other trading conditions; (b) limit or control production, markets, technical development, or investment; (c) share markets or sources of supply; (d) apply dissimilar conditions to equivalent transactions with other trading parties, thereby placing them at a competitive disadvantage; (e) make the conclusion of contracts subject to acceptance by the other parties of supplementary obligations which, by their nature or according to commercial usage, have no connection with the subject of such contracts.

(2) Any agreements or decisions prohibited pursuant to this Article shall be automatically void.

(3) The provisions of paragraph 1 may, however, be declared inapplicable in the case of: any agreement or category of agreements between undertakings; any decision or category of decisions by associations of undertakings; any concerted practice or category of concerted practices, which contributes to improving the production or distribution of goods or to promoting technical or economic progress, while allowing consumers a fair share of the resulting benefit, and which does not: (a) impose on the undertakings concerned restrictions which are not indispensable to the attainment of these objectives; (b) afford such undertakings the possibility of eliminating competition in respect of a substantial part of the products in question.

A full discussion of Article 81 is not within the scope of this chapter, but a few remarks are in order.

First, one should note that the European legislator does not restrict attention to *agreements*: indeed, the reference to *concerted practices* allows the European Commission possibly to deal with collusive situations where firms have not explicitly agreed with each other. This term is deliberately vague enough so as to capture very different situations and institutional arrangements, including cases where firms have not explicitly agreed on, or even discussed, prices, quotas, or market sharing: most of the discussion on the standard of proof (see below) could be rephrased as a discussion of what elements define a concerted practice.

Secondly, Article 81 refers to agreements and practices that either have the effect or the *object* of distorting competition. This implies that once a cartel or a concerted practice has been identified, it is not necessary to investigate whether it has had any anticompetitive effect. If, for instance, firms have set up a collusive scheme to fix prices, it is completely irrelevant to European Union law whether firms have been successful in their design or not: even if it was proved that firms did not manage to affect prices at all, this would not spare them a finding of infringement, nor would this conceivably have much effect on the fine they should pay (as we shall see below, fines are not calculated in proportion to actual damages to clients and consumers).

Thirdly, Article 81(3) admits the possibility that some agreements among competitors may be allowed under EU competition law. However, both the Commission and the Courts have been clear that agreements to fix prices, outputs, or markets will very rarely benefit from that provision: they are considered restrictive of competition by their object, and therefore it would be very hard for firms to escape a finding of infringement. In other words, cartels are (almost) per se prohibited. However, very restrictive agreements that contain some perceived beneficial elements may exceptionally be authorized by the European Commission.

For instance, the Commission has granted exemptions from competition rules for so-called *crisis cartels*—namely, agreements where firms engage in reciprocal reductions in capacity and output—provided such reductions in overcapacity are permanent, favour specialization, and are implemented in such a way that they minimize the social costs of the unemployment which results from the cutback of production.[32] Here, the European Commission has considered that competition can be sacrificed to avoid the social costs that industry restructuring left to the market would cause.[33]

Another example where a restrictive agreement has been allowed because of perceived environmental gains is provided by the CECED decision concerning an agreement among producers and importers of washing machines which together account for more than 95 per cent of European sales. The agreement aims among other things at discontinuing production and imports of the least energy-efficient washing machines, which represent some 10–11 per cent of current EU sales. The agreement removes one of the dimensions along which sellers compete, and as such it might negatively affect competition and increase prices (as a general rule, the most polluting machines are also the least expensive ones). However, the Commission considered that the agreement will benefit society in environmental terms, reducing energy consumption, and that such an objective would not have been attained without the agreement. This is because consumers do not properly take into account all the externalities involved in their purchase and consumption decisions, and firms would not give up a tool of market competition unless bound by an agreement.

A final example of the same nature is given by agreements of *shipping conferences*, which have benefited for a long time from a block exemption. By virtue of this exemption, ship-owners have been able to operate as a cartel along some specific routes. According to the European Commission, the counterpart of allowing the shipping companies to operate as a cartel should have been the establishment of stable and certain shipping services: the provision of regular scheduled maritime services on routes to and from the European Union would otherwise have been at risk owing to the possibility of having to operate well below capacity.[34] This unusually lenient treatment of maritime transportation services was, however, put to an end last year (the abolition of shipping conferences entered into effect only in October 2008).[35]

Apart from the aforementioned cases, which are to some extent exceptional and which arguably are only partly collusive, the European Commission (and the European Courts) have consistently found them illegal since the early cases (such as the *Quinine* cartel and the *Dyestuffs* cartel, both decisions dating from 1969).

ENFORCEMENT OF CARTEL LAW

As indicated above, the European Commission is the main enforcer of the law against cartels in the European Union. The European Commission's powers are established by Council Regulation 1/2003 (which replaces Council Regulation 17, dating from 1962). The European Commission has extensive investigatory powers, which include the possibility to conduct inspections not only on the firms' premises but also on the homes (and private vehicles) of the firms' managers and employees, the latter possibility not being allowed under the old Regulation 17, and introduced because experience showed the European Commission that often compromising cartel documents have not been kept in offices but in private homes.

FINING POLICY

Under EU competition law, fines can be imposed only on firms (although national laws in some European countries do allow for criminal penalties, and/or administrative sanctions to be imposed on firms' managers), and Regulation 1/2003 establishes that fines may not exceed 10 per cent of the firm's turnover (although actual fines rarely go anywhere close to such a ceiling), and that they should be fixed with regard to the gravity and the duration of the infringement of the law.

The Commission has still considerable discretion in the determination of the fines, but it has progressively been more transparent about the way it imposes fines. In January 1998, it released a Notice which established some of the criteria that it uses to set the fines. In September 2006, it published new Guidelines on its fining policy.[36] According to the new Guidelines, the Commission will use a two-step procedure to set fines. As a first step, the basic amount of the fine will be set. To do so, the Commission will: (1) determine an initial variable amount of the fine as a percentage (maximum 30 per cent) of the firm's relevant market turnover; (2) multiply it by the number of years the infringement has taken place for; (3) add a fixed component of the fine which equals 15–25 per cent of the annual turnover. As a second step, the basic amount of fine thus obtained might be modified taking into account aggravating or mitigating circumstances. Among the first category, there is recidivism (a firm might receive a 100 per cent increase in the fine for each instance of earlier infringement of the same type, whether at the EU level or in national Member States), obstruction of investigation (for instance, denying facts which turn out to be supported by objective evidence, or refusing inspections by Commission officials[37]), and for having played the leading role in instigating or policing the cartel. Among the second category, there may be evidence that the firm had terminated the infringement as soon as the Commission intervened, that it had a substantially limited role in the cartel, and that the anticompetitive conduct had been authorized or encouraged by national public authorities or legislation.[38] In any case, the resulting fine cannot exceed 10 per cent of the previous business year's total turnover. Note that for large multi-product and multinational firms the risk that the fine may be higher than the 10 per cent threshold will be much lower than in the case of smaller and more 'specialized' firms. In exceptional cases, which presumably could take place only for the latter type of firms, the Commission might also reduce the fine if the firm can prove inability to pay, that is if it could offer 'objective evidence that imposition of the fine as provided for in these Guidelines would irretrievably jeopardize the economic viability of the undertaking concerned and cause its assets to lose all their value'.[39]

As an example of how the European Commission will calculate the fine, consider a firm which has been found involved in a cartel which lasted for six years. Suppose the Decision is taken in August 2007 and that in the relevant product and geographic market within the European Economic Area it had a value of sales of €100 million in 2006. The basic amount of the fine might be calculated as (30 per cent) (of 100) $\times$ (6) + (25 per cent) (of 100) = €180 + €25 = €205 million. If any of the aggravating or attenuating circumstances listed above are present the fine would be modified upwards or downwards. For instance, if the same firm has been involved in a cartel in the past, the fine might be doubled and become €410 million.

However, if the total fine thus obtained is above 10 per cent of the worldwide turnover of the company, then the fine would be capped at that level. Suppose, for instance, that the relevant product market is at the EU level and that the worldwide turnover of the company in the previous year was €1,000 million, then the firm could not receive a fine higher than €100 million.

In practice, and as we shall see below, the available evidence supports this claim; it is widely believed that the Commission has toughened its stance against cartels over time (whether fines have reached a level at which they are a real deterrent for cartels is subject to debate, however, as we shall also discuss below). Increased fines have not been the only sign that—from the second half of the 1990s—fighting cartels has become the priority for the Commission. Indeed, two other important changes which are worth stressing have occurred in the EU competition law. First, the Commission has started a process of 'modernization' which has led to some of its powers being given to national competition authorities and national courts, with the aim of better employing its resources and devoting them to important cases (such as cartels) rather than on minor agreements. Second, it has introduced a leniency policy which has arguably been the main novelty in the fight against cartels.

LENIENCY POLICY

Leniency programmes grant total or partial immunity from fines to firms that collaborate with the authorities. They work on the principle that people who break the law might report their crimes or illegal activities if given proper incentives.[40] In competition law, the Antitrust Division of the Department of Justice (DoJ) in the United States have been the first to introduce such a law, in 1978, granting immunity from criminal sanctions if certain conditions occurred. (In August 1993, this scheme was thoroughly redesigned by the DoJ, giving rise to a stream of firms applying for leniency and giving evidence which led to the uncovering of a number of cartels.)

The European Union introduced a leniency policy in 1996. It established that a fine might have been very substantially (75–100 per cent) reduced if a company informed the European Commission before an investigation started; and substantially (50–75 per cent) reduced if cooperation took place after an investigation had started but before the European Commission had obtained sufficient grounds for initiating the procedure; in both cases, the company had to be the first to report, terminate all cartel activities, and must not have been the instigator of the cartel. The fine might have been significantly (10–50 per cent) reduced if the company cooperated with the European Commission in the investigations (for instance, by not challenging the European Commission findings and allegations) without the previous conditions for more generous reduction of fines being met.

Although successful, this policy did not give the results one could have hoped for, mainly for two reasons. First, leniency was given in a discretionary way by the European Commission (rather than being automatic like in the United States), and firms did not know what fines they would get until the final Decision was adopted by the Commission. This clearly reduced the benefit from disclosing evidence. Second, firms did not receive immunity if an investigation had already begun.

In February 2002, the European Commission adopted a new leniency policy. It improves on the first point since it introduces transparency and certainty: complete immunity from fines is given to the firm first reporting a cartel and, upon providing evidence, the firm will receive (conditional) immunity in writing from the Commission.[41] Further, the new rules specify that any firm can apply for immunity as long as it had not coerced other firms to participate in the cartel (the previous condition, requiring a firm not to be an instigator of the cartel, left room for interpretation).

It also improves on the second point, since immunity is given to a firm that provides evidence that enables the European Commission to establish an infringement even when the European Commission is already in possession of enough information to launch an inspection (but not to establish an infringement).[42] The Leniency Notice was further revised in December 2006, but without substantial changes relative to the 2002 Notice.

The use of leniency programmes in antitrust has been studied first by Motta and Polo (1999; 2003).[43] They show that such programmes might have an important role in the prosecution of cartels provided that firms can apply for leniency *after* an investigation has started. This is because as soon as an investigation starts a firm's expected probability of being found guilty suddenly increases, thus modifying the balance between cost and benefit from a cartel. If given the possibility to apply for leniency, the firm might then decide to give up its participation in the cartel in exchange for a total or partial reduction of the fine.

Leniency also helps in that it saves resources of the authority: building up a convincing enough case to be defendable in courts is very costly, but the cost of this prosecution stage can be avoided or greatly reduced by leniency, since the firms would bring themselves enough evidence to the authority.

In practice, there is no doubt that the 2002 Leniency Programme has been an extremely effective device in uncovering cartels and in facilitating the Commission's task to prosecute the companies involved in such cartels. In the period from its entering into force in February 2002 to end-December 2006, the Commission received 104 applications for immunity (that is, for a zero fine) and granted (final or conditional) immunity in 56 cases, rejected 34 applications, while the remaining were still pending in early 2007.[44] However, not all conditional immunity granted by the Commission will necessarily translate into a Final Commission Decision. In many cases, the Commission might decide not to pursue the cartel because the infringement is very minor or long past, because it believes that it would not have enough elements for successful prosecution, or because it prefers to let a National Competition Authority prosecute the case, focusing instead only on major international cartels. Even so, it is remarkable that a number of cartel cases in the last years have been initiated by cartel participants which at a certain point decided to apply for leniency.

5.3.2. Standards of proof: which practices violate European Union law?

In section 5.2 above I have already stressed that a collusive outcome might arise without firms agreeing or communicating to coordinate their behaviour. This raises the crucial issue of whether 'tacit' collusion, and not only explicit collusion, represents a violation of competition law.[45] In what follows, I discuss how the European Commission and the Courts have dealt with this important issue.

PARALLEL BEHAVIOUR IS NOT PER SE UNLAWFUL

Perhaps the prototypical case of 'tacit' collusion is given by a situation where firms behave in a parallel way over time, that is tend to imitate each other in their price decisions. Suppose, for instance, that—even without common shocks on demand or input prices—one day a seller increases prices by 10 per cent, and that the next day a rival follows suit. Absent any other documentary evidence (such as proof that the firms have agreed on prices), does this price parallelism represent evidence that firms have infringed Article 81? Or, in the terms of EU law, is this evidence that the firms have engaged in a concerted practice?[46]

The answer is that the Commission has been tempted to answer positively this question, but the European Court of Justice, especially in its *Wood Pulp* judgment, which is the most recent on this issue, seems to exclude this possibility.

THE *WOOD PULP* JUDGMENT

In 1984, the European Commission adopted a decision (*Wood Pulp*) that found that forty wood pulp producers and three of their trade associations had infringed Article 81 (previously Article 85) of the Treaty by concerting on prices. In 1993, the European Court of Justice issued a judgment (*Ahlström and others v. Commission*) that annulled most of the Commission decision, partly on procedural grounds and partly on substantive issues.

The Commission found an infringement of Article 81 due (among other factors) to parallel behaviour, which consisted of: (i) a system of quarterly price announcements; (ii) the simultaneity or quasi-simultaneity of the announcements; (iii) the fact that announced prices were identical. As the ECJ rightly argues, absent documents which *directly* establish the existence of collusion between the producers concerned, the problem was to understand whether the three elements (i), (ii), and (iii) are proof of collusion (constitute a firm, precise, and consistent body of evidence of prior concertation) or can instead be explained by normal competitive behaviour:

In determining the probative value of those different factors, it must be noted that *parallel conduct cannot be regarded as furnishing proof of concertation unless concertation constitutes the only plausible explanation for such conduct.* It is necessary to bear in mind that, although article 85 (now article 81) of the Treaty prohibits any form of collusion which distorts competition, *it does not deprive economic operators of the right to adapt themselves intelligently to the existing and anticipated conduct of their competitors.*[47]

To establish whether parallel conduct was in this case proof of collusion, the ECJ commissioned two experts' reports, whose conclusions were devastating for the European Commission, in that they indicated that parallelism could well have been the result of the normal oligopolistic interdependence among competitors.

(i) The European Commission believed that the system of quarterly price announcements and the fact that all firms quoted prices in the same currency were practices expressly adopted by the wood pulp producers so as to increase the transparency of the market, thus rendering collusion easier. The experts found that it was the purchasers who, after the Second World War, demanded the introduction of that system of announcements in order better to estimate their costs. Further, they found that the US dollar price was first introduced by the North American producers during the 1960s (before the period of the alleged concerted practices), and subsequently adopted by other producers; they also found that this development was welcomed by the buyers.

(ii) According to the European Commission, the close succession of price announcements could only be explained by a concerted practice. However, it had another, innocent, plausible explanation according to the experts' reports. Several market features, including the existence of common agents that work for several producers, implied that information on announced prices would spread very quickly.

(iii) The third element in the European Commission's construction was that the prices announced by the wood pulp producers involved were the same (or very similar) although they had different production costs, different rates of capacity utilization, different costs of transportation to a given market; and they were at an artificially high level in some years, whereas the low prices in two particular years corresponded to a punishment phase. However, the experts and the ECJ noted that the same pattern of prices could also be consistent with an alternative explanation—that is competitive behaviour in an oligopolistic industry. First, the fact that (average) prices were high in some years and low in others might be explained by specific demand and supply shocks (such as the introduction first—and discontinuation later—of storage subsidy schemes by the Swedish government, the evolution of the Canadian and US market, and relative exports to European markets). Second, the experts argued that the fact that prices over the economic cycle were the same (or similar) across producers was compatible with the firms behaving independently: a competitor decides to set the same price as its rivals simply because it fears the reactions that would take place if it did not do so.[48]

In the light of the experts' reports, the ECJ arrived at the conclusion that *concertation is not the only plausible explanation for the parallel conduct.*[49] At this point, one can ask the broader question of whether one can ever find an infringement of antitrust laws by simply looking at parallel conduct. The answer is that this is possible, but the standard of proof is (rightly) high, as one should prove that communication and/or coordination of some kind among the firms must be the *only plausible explanation* for parallelism. In another important case, *Dyestuffs*, price rises were so simultaneous that it is impossible that they had not been previously agreed upon:

In Italy, apart from Ciba who had already ordered its Italian subsidiary to increase prices, all other producers, with the exception of ACNA, sent by telex or fax—from their headquarters, seated in places very distant from each other—instructions to their respective agents in the afternoon of 9 January: Sandoz at 17.05, Hoechst at 17.09, Bayer at 17.38, Francolor at 17.57, BASF at 18.55, Geigy at 19.45, and ICI at an undetermined time, since instructions were given by phone.[50]

Therefore, in that case, even absent documentary evidence, the Court agreed with the Commission's finding of a concerted practice.

TACIT MARKET-SHARING SCHEMES?

Another example of possibly tacit collusion is given by situations where each firm limits itself to selling in one particular market. Indeed, a market outcome where two (or more) firms sell in, say, their domestic markets only may be the result of an explicit market-sharing agreement but could also be due to 'tacit collusion': each firm is happy to limit its sales to the domestic territory because it anticipates that if it started to sell also abroad a retaliation would follow, resulting in overall competition and the loss of the domestic monopoly.

An important case in this respect is *Soda-Ash*, which deals with an alleged concerted practice of market allocation. (Note that the Commission decision was taken after the *Wood Pulp* Commission decision, but before the *Wood Pulp* judgment.) Soda ash is a commodity used as a raw material in the production of glass. ICI, a British company, and Solvay, a Belgian company, are the main producers in the industry. The two firms had a long history of *explicit* market-sharing agreements (at times when cartels were not illegal), started in the 1870s and renewed immediately after the Second World War with a so-called 'Page 1000' agreement, which divided Europe (and some overseas markets) into spheres of influence—for instance, ICI was to sell in the United Kingdom and Solvay in Continental Europe.

The agreement (that the defendants indicated as being out of date since 1962) was terminated as of 31 December 1972 when the UK entered the European Community (so as to comply with the antitrust rules of the Treaty). But, as the European Commission said in its decision:

The alleged desuetude of the 'Page 1000' arrangement did not however manifest itself in any significant change in the commercial policy of Solvay or ICI in the soda-ash sector, either in 1962 or at any later stage. Neither ever competed with the other in their respective home markets in the Community. Similarly in overseas export markets each continued to respect the other's sphere of influence.[51]

What is noticeable is that each firm admitted that it had no intention of invading the other's home market, but simply because it feared retaliation if it had done so.[52] They therefore justified a collusive outcome as the result of independent decisions that made sense from a business viewpoint. In this case, continuing to share markets was an easy way to reach tacit collusion.

The other interesting point here is whether tacit collusion is an infringement of Article 81 (previously Article 85). In this case, the Commission decided that it was, and that the term 'concerted practice' mentioned in Article 81 among the prohibited practices covered also tacit collusion: 'The Commission fully accepts that there is no direct evidence of an express agreement between Solvay and ICI to continue to respect the "Page 1000" cartel in practice. However, there is no need for an express agreement in order for article 85 to apply. A tacit agreement would also fall under Community competition law.'[53]

The CFI annulled the Commission Decision, but on procedural grounds, while being silent on the merits of the question.[54] Interestingly, the European Commission later readopted the decision, and the case is still pending at the Court. In the light of the *Wood Pulp* judgment, absent documentary evidence, it would be difficult for the Commission to persuade the Court, since—in the words of the Court—Article 81 'does not deprive economic operators of the right to adapt themselves intelligently to the existing and anticipated conduct of their competitors'.

To sum up, the EU jurisprudence requires documentary evidence for the finding of a cartel law infringement. Absent documentary evidence, proof of a concerted practice can be found from market outcomes (such as parallel behaviour) only to the extent that the coordination of competitors' decisions is the only plausible explanation for those outcomes.

This approach, based on observable elements which are verifiable in a court of law, seems very sensible to me, in that it privileges legal certainty and avoids the uncertainty that would inevitably follow if firms had constantly to second-guess what would happen if they behaved independently but in a similar way to their competitors. Clearly, though, not everybody might be happy with this approach, which minimizes Type I errors (the possibility to find 'guilty' firms which are not), but permits Type II errors (as firms which are colluding but do not leave traces behind would not be found in violation of the law).

One may argue that such an approach is too lenient with the firms—since they know that they could reach a collusive outcome even without an explicit agreement and that such tacit collusion is not unlawful, how could one ever believe that collusive outcomes could be successfully avoided? There are at least two answers to this concern.

First, it is true that tacit collusion *might* be sustained by firms. However, we have also seen that there are very good reasons why firms would like to communicate and/or to coordinate their actions. They might want to avoid unnecessary and costly experiments with the market and choose instead the best (for the firms) prices, or they might want to create facilitating practices and more generally an environment which improves observability of firms' actions so as to favour collusion. This will lead firms to try and communicate among themselves so as to coordinate their actions, thereby leaving traces of hard evidence behind them. Firms have known for a long time that they will be found guilty if there is any written proof of their coordination, and yet antitrust authorities keep on uncovering such hard evidence in cartel cases.[55]

Second, in order to make sure that cartel violations do not persist, antitrust authorities (and more generally governmental institutions) have also another instrument, which is to intervene so as to render the market environment less prone to collusive outcomes. A tough stance on practices that allow firms to exchange information so as to monitor each other's behaviour is an example of this approach.[56]

AGREEMENTS TO EXCHANGE INFORMATION AS A CONCERTED PRACTICE

According to a very authoritative commentator, '[a]n important element in establishing the existence of concerted practices is contact between the parties, which must involve intentional communication of information between them, either directly or through an intermediary'.[57] It is important to note that such exchanges of information which would give rise to a concerted practice do not necessarily take the form of communications on the prices that firms intend to charge, nor do they need to be part of a precise agreed-upon scheme. In the *Peroxygen* judgment (1985), for instance, the ECJ found that the firms had engaged in a concerted practice:

Full exchange was made of information about production, so that each knew the others' general commercial policy. It was held that these arrangements constituted a concerted practice: although the parties had not necessarily agreed a precise or detailed plan in advance, it was sufficient that by their mutual involvement they had departed from the basic requirement that each must determine independently the policy which it intended to adopt on the market.[58]

As emphasized in section 5.2 above, the ability to observe the market decisions of competitors is a crucial ingredient to sustain collusion, and this calls for a prohibition of the exchange of sensitive commercial information among rivals. The European Union jurisprudence seems entirely consistent with this approach, since the presence of exchange of information of a detailed and disaggregate nature is sufficient to a finding of concerted practice. In *Fatty Acids*, three producers of oleine and stearine were fined for having set up a system to exchange information on market shares, prices, and orders.[59] In *VNP/Cobelpa*, Belgian and Dutch paper manufacturers exchanged—through their national trade associations—detailed data at the individual firms' level on prices, discounts, terms of supply, sales, and payments.[60] In *UK Tractors*, the Commission fined seven UK producers or importers of agricultural tractors for a sophisticated agreement to exchange information on sales at a very disaggregate level, both in geographic terms (sales were broken down at such a fine level that one could even in some cases identify the buyers) and in product terms (information was provided on which type of tractor was sold). Both the CFI and ECJ upheld the Commission's decision, clearly establishing the principle that setting up a scheme to monitor each other's sales data amounts to a concerted practice.[61]

These judgments are important because they indicate that it is possible to prove infringement of the law even absent documentary evidence of meetings and agreements, provided that there is enough evidence that firms have intentionally created an environment where collusion can be more easily sustained.[62]

Interestingly, there also seems to exist some awareness that transparency is bad when it takes place on the supply side only, whereas transparency which involves also the demand side should be positively looked at—as argued above. In *Covisint*, a decision which concerned the creation of an automotive Internet marketplace (set up by agreement of six car manufacturers), the Commission dismissed objections that the agreement could have made collusion easier by making prices more transparent, and found instead that B2B marketplaces would have pro-competitive effects.

5.3.3. *Evidence in the fight against cartels*

In this section, I briefly review some empirical evidence on the fight against cartels in the European Union, and discuss enforcement issues.

Table 5.1—obtained from information collected from European Commission and Community Courts' documents and websites—details for each year since 1969 (when the first cartel cases were decided by the Commission) the number of cases decided by the Commission, the total number of firms involved, and the average fine. For the same cases, it then tracks the outcome of the Community Courts' Judgment. Obviously, the Judgment for a given case will be given by the Courts in a later year, but it is the original year of the Commission Decision which is included in the statistics. After the introduction of the CFI, there may be two appeals for the same case: whenever both Judgments have been given, it is the final one which is included in the Table. In cases where the ECJ Judgment is still pending, it is the fine given by the CFI which is included in the statistics. The last-but-one column of Table 5.1 also provides the names of the cartel cases for each year and indicates with an asterisk (*) those cases where leniency applications were granted. One can therefore notice at first sight that from the year 2000 onwards the Leniency programme has played a crucial role in the fight against cartels.

The data in Table 5.1 are also used to draw some figures which should illustrate at first sight some relevant information. Figure 5.1 indicates the number of firms which have been found to have infringed cartel law in the EU. This shows that the frequency of cartel cases tends to increase in the last years, although a large number of firms have been involved in cartel cases also from the mid-80s.

Figure 5.2, however, clearly indicates that from the mid-90s onwards there has been a dramatic increase in the total fines given by the European Commission. Figure 5.3 confirms this data by looking at the average fines imposed by the Commission on cartel participants, but it also reveals that the turning-points seem to be 1998 (the year in which the first Guidelines on fines was published) and, above all, 2007 (the revised Guidelines on fines were published on 1 September 2006, so there was no case in 2006 in which the new method of setting fines was used).[63] Figure 5.3 also offers additional information—namely, the fines imposed in appeals by the Community Courts. (Note that for cases since 2002 the data on Court Judgments are incomplete or missing altogether because cases referring to recent Commission Decisions are still pending at the CFI. Accordingly, the Court fines from 2002 onwards are obviously underestimated.) However incomplete, the Figure tells us that the Community Courts tend to reduce the fines, although not dramatically so. A reading of the Court Judgments, however, shows that the Court in general approves the Commission's attitude towards cartels and its fining policy. In general, when the Court fines diverge from the Commission fines it is because the Court has decided to annul a Commission Decision on procedural grounds, or because it thinks that the Commission has not given proper consideration to all the factors which should affect the calculation of the fines.[64] On issues of substance, however, there does not seem to be

Table 5.1. Cartel decisions and court judgments: numbers of firms and fines (€m)

year	number of cases	total number of firms involved	total fines given	average fine given by the EC	total fines as confirmed by Community courts***	average fine given by the Community courts***	name of cases (parties involved)	notes
1969	2	16	0.99	0.06	0.95	0.06	Quinine (6), Dyestuffs (10)	
1970	0	0	0.00	0.00	0.00	0.00		
1971	0	0	0.00	0.00	0.00	0.00		
1972	0	0	0.00	0.00	0.00	0.00		
1973	1	23	9.00	0.39	1.59	0.07	European Sugar (23)	two firms also fined under art 82 (cannot distinguish)
1974	1	4	0.36	0.09	0.00		Belgian Wallpaper (4)	collective boycott (collective refusal to supply) referenced by 'Jones and van der Woude' as cartel
1975	1	6	0.10	0.02		0.00	Tinned Mushrooms (6)	no appeal
1976	0	0	0.00	0.00		0.00		
1977	1	9	0.12	0.01		0.00	Vegetable Parchement (9)	no appeal
1978	0	0	0.00	0.00	0.00	0.00		
1979	0	0	0.00	0.00	0.00	0.00		
1980	0	0	0.00	0.00	0.00	0.00		
1981	0	0	0.00	0.00	0.00	0.00		
1982	2	8	2.38	0.30	1.43	0.18	SSI -Dutch Tobacco (6); Zinc (2)	

Year							
1983	1	26	1.25	1.25	0.05	0.05	Cast Iron Steel Rolls (26)	no appeal
1984	4	62	20.43	17.68	0.33	0.29	Flat Glass -Benelux (8); Zinc Producer Group (6); Peroxide Products (5); Wood Pulp (43)	Flat Glass -Benelux, Zinc Producer Group, Peroxide Products no appeal
1985	0	0	0.00	0.00	0.00	0.00		
1986	4	31	65.57	62.28	2.12	2.01	Polypropane (15); Roofing felt (8); Meldoc (5); Fatty Acids (3)	Polypropane two appeals; Meldoc and Fatty Acids no appeal
1987	0	0	0.00	0.00	0.00	0.00		
1988	3	34	74.00	6.02	2.18	0.18	Flat glass (3); PVC (14); LdPE (17)	Flat glass three firms infringed art 82 (but fines are for infringement of art 81); PVC two appeals (second initiated by the Commission);
1989	1	14	9.50	7.47	0.68	0.53	Welded Steel Mesh (14)	Welded Steel Mesh two appeals
1990	2	4	18.00	4.00	4.50	1.00	Solvey/ICI (2); Solvay/CFK (2)	Solvay/CFK two appeals; readopted in 2000 no appeal since
1991	0	0	0.00	0.00	0.00	0.00		

(Continued)

Table 5.1. (Continued)

year	number of cases	total number of firms involved	total fines given	average fine given by the EC	total fines as confirmed by Community courts***	average fine given by the Community courts***	name of cases (parties involved)	notes
1992	4	48	44.76	0.93	39.76	0.83	Dutch Building cartel (28); Eurocheques-Helsinki (2); French African Shipping (17); Railway Tickets Lloyd's (1)	Dutch Building cartel two appeals; French African Shipping no appeal; Railway Tickets Lloyd's two appeals (second initiated by the Commission)
1993	0	0	0.00	0.00	0.00	0.00		
1994	5	86	399.106	4.64	236.81	2.75	Carton board (19); PVC II (12); Cement (41); Far Eastern Freight (13); Ford Agricultural UK tractor (1)	Carton board, PVC II two appeals; Ford Agricultural no fine imposed, no appeal
1995	1	2	11.80	5.90	11.60	5.80	Dutch cranes (2); Ferry services (5)	no appeal
1996	1	5	0.65	0.13	0.65	0.13		
1997	0	0	0.00	0.00	0.00	0.00		
1998	5	41	451.89	11.02	162.09	3.95	Alloy surcharge (6)*; British Sugar II (4)*; Pre-Insulated Pipe (10)*; Trans Atlantic Conference Agreement (15); Greek ferries (7)*	Alloy surcharge, British Sugar II, Pre-Insulated Pipe cartel, Greek ferries two appeals; Alloy surcharge readoption for one party in 2006 pending

Year							Cases	
1999	1	8	99.00	12.38	86.22	10.78	Steamless steel B (8)*	first appeal (3.8m); Alloy surcharge under art 65 of ECSC; two appeals
2000**	1	5	112.90	22.58	102.58	20.52	Aminoacids(5)*	Aminoacids two appeals; pending
2001	9	59	1780.29	30.17	1483.69	25.15	SAS/Maersk (2)*; Graphite Electrodes (8)*; Vitamins (13)*; Citric Acid (5)*; Luxembourg Brewers (4)*; Bank Charges(5); Interbrew and Alken Maes (5)*; Zinc Phosphate (6)*; Carbonless Paper (11)*	second appeal: Citric Acid; Graphite Electrodes, Interbrew and Alken Maes, Zinc Phosphate, Carbonless Paper two appeals pending
2002	9	47	944.87	20.10	212.60	4.52	Industrial Glass (7)*; Austrian Banks (8)*; Methione (4)*; Fine art auction houses(2)*; Methyglycamine (2); Food Flavour Enhancers (4)*; Specialty Graphite (8)*; Plasterboard (8)*; Concrete Reinforcing Bars (8)*	second appeal: Austrian Banks (37m); Methione (118m); pending first decision: Plasterboard (478m); Concrete Reinforcing Bars (85m); Fine art auction houses, Methygly-camine, Food Flavour Enhancers no appeal

(Continued)

Table 5.1. (Continued)

year	number of cases	total number of firms involved	total fines given	average fine given by the EC	total fines as confirmed by Community courts***	average fine given by the Community courts***	name of cases (parties involved)	notes
2003	5	28	404.78	14.46	153.34	5.48	Industrial Tubes (5)*; Organic Peroxides (6)*; Sorbates (5)*; French Beef (6); Electrical and Mechanical Carbon and Graphite Products (6)*	pending first appeal: Industrial Tubes (39m); Organic Peroxides (0.001m); Sorbates (99m); Electrical and Mechanical Carbon and Graphite Products (96m); pending second appeal French Beef (16m)
2004	5	33	354.20	10.73			Copper Plumber Tubes (13)*; Choline Chloride (6)*; Spanish Raw Tobacco (9)*; French Brewers (2); Needles (3)*	pending first appeal: Copper Plumber Tubes, Choline Chloride, Spanish Raw Tobacco, Needles; French Brewers no appeal

2005	5	682.32	16.64	Monochloroacetic Acid (5)*; Thread (10)*; Italian Raw Tobacco (6)*; Industrial bags (16); Rubber chemicals (4)*	pending first appeal: all cases
2006**	5	1833.11	32.73	Synthetic Rubber (11)*; Copper Fittings (12)*; Butimen Netherland (14)*; Methacrylates (5)*; Hydrogen Peroxide (14)*	pending first appeal: all cases
2007	3	2014.81	106.04	Gas Insulated Switchgear (11)*; Elevators (5)*; Dutch Beer (4)*	

* denotes cases where leniency has been granted and therefore fines after leniency are reported
** denotes a year where there are readoption decisions; readoption decisions are not included in the count
*** For the Commission Decisions taken since 2003 Court data are incomplete because most cases are still pending

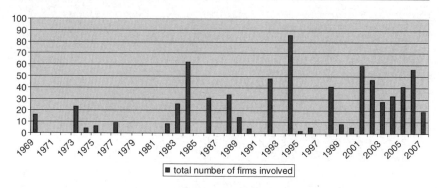

Figure 5.1. Cartel infringements in the EU: total number of firms involved

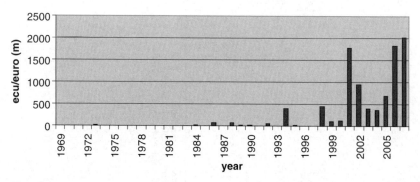

Figure 5.2. Cartels in the EU: total fines given

divergence between the Commission and the Court on the way to treat cartels. The *Wood Pulp* case discussed above is to my knowledge the last one where the Court's Judgment diverges from the Commission Decision on substantive grounds.

Finally, Figure 5.4. shows that in most of the recent cartel decisions the leniency programme exercised a crucial role: the figure shows the cases where an applicant was given full immunity, i.e. had either initiated the investigation or given a fundamental contribution to the Commission at a stage in which it had not enough evidence for an infringement decision.

Some additional evidence on the fight against cartels comes also from an empirical paper (Langus and Motta 2007) which estimates the effect of European Union antitrust fines and investigations on the share prices of the firms which have violated antitrust laws. By using event study methodology, this paper shows that on average the stock market reacts to a surprise inspection by lowering the valuation of the firm by about 2 per cent, to a Commission infringement decision by lowering it by about 3 per cent, and to a Court

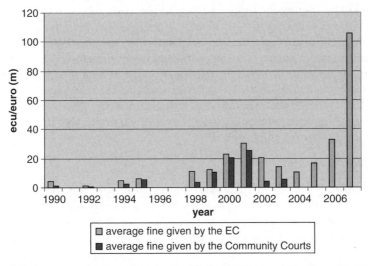

Figure 5.3. Average cartel fines given by the EC (1990–2007) and (for the same cases) by the community courts

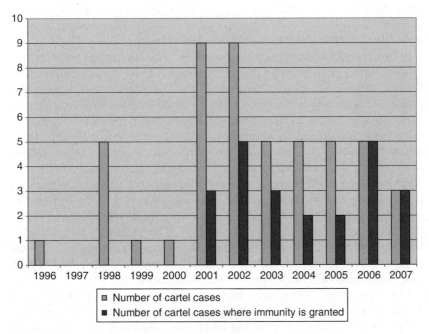

Figure 5.4. Leniency programme

Judgment upholding the Commission's Decision by lowering it by about 1 per cent. What is perhaps more noticeable, though, is that the fine—averaging 1 per cent of the firm's capitalization—accounts only for a small part of this 6 per cent loss in the valuation of the firm. It seems likely, therefore, that most of the loss in market value is due to the market anticipating that the firm will not be able—after the European Union investigation—to earn the same profits as it would make when the cartel was operating. Indirectly, therefore, this is evidence that after a cartel investigation the firms will not be able to sustain such high prices as during the cartel.

DETERRENCE

Clearly, the EU Leniency Programme is one of the reasons why the Commission was able to uncover several large international cartels in the recent years. Unfortunately, however, it does not seem that the Programme has been able to cut significantly the time the Commission needs successfully to prosecute the case: still too long a time elapses between the moment a leniency applicant first reveals the existence of a cartel to the Commission and the moment the Commission adopts an infringement decision, occupying too many of the scarce resources of the Commission. Currently, however, the Commission is studying the adoption of settlement procedures (similar to the plea-bargaining adopted in the United States) which might allow the Commission to use its resources more efficiently to the discovery of new cartels.

If leniency programmes might be (as indeed they appear to) crucial to break existing cartels, their effect on the prevention of cartels is more ambiguous. On the one hand, to the extent that they simplify the collection of the evidence necessary for the successful prosecution of cartels (but we have seen that this effect does not seem to have been extremely important so far), a leniency programme could help an antitrust authority devote more resources to the discovery and investigation of new cartels, therefore increasing the probability of discovery and prosecution, and hence (*ceteris paribus*) deterrence. On the other hand, however, the very nature of leniency implies that one or more firms will receive a reduction in fines in exchange for cooperation with the authority (in most cartel cases, several firms end up receiving significant reductions in the fines, although no more than one can receive full immunity). *Ex ante*, therefore, a firm might expect that when leniency programmes are in place the average expected fine will decrease, making the trade-off between expected benefits and expected costs of cartel participation tilt towards the former.

Motta and Polo (2003) argue that when antitrust authorities have tight budget constraints the effect of freeing resources from prosecution onto investigation and discovery is the dominant effect, thus suggesting that—in the real world where authorities are severely constrained—leniency programmes will also help deter formation of cartels. However, if, due to procedural issues, it is difficult to free an authority's resources, leniency programmes might help disrupt existing cartels while increasing the chances that new ones will be formed. A tightening on the fining policy (an increase in the fines) might therefore be a useful complementary measure to be taken after the introduction of leniency programmes. In this sense, the recent increase in fines imposed by the Commission helps avoid that leniency might come at the cost of lower deterrence.

Whether fines are now large enough to deter cartels is, however, an open question. On the one hand, until the recent revision of the Guidelines, the Commission's fines were probably much lower than they should be, as argued by several commentators,[65] and as revealed also by the number of repeat offenders that one finds when looking at the EU cartel cases. On the other hand, the 2006 Guidelines impose sizeable fines, especially to firms which have already been involved in cartel cases in the past (both under EU law or in national jurisdictions of the European Union's Member States): under the new rules, a firm which has been caught violating cartel law four times in the past, and which has been now involved in a cartel for five years, may receive an annual fine equal to 140 per cent of the affected commerce,[66] to be multiplied by the five years of the duration of the infringement. Even considering the most pessimistic hypotheses on the price overcharges that a cartel is able to sustain (see, for example, Connor 2005, which estimates them to be not less than 25 per cent), and the fact that a cartel will not be uncovered with a probability close to 1, such a large fine is likely to provide a good deterrent.

Certainly, it would be difficult to argue that fines should be increased further, for at least two reasons. The first one is that setting fines arbitrarily high may run against the legal principle of proportionality (it would be unfair to impose an extremely large penalty for a minor infringement, for instance); the second is that imposing very large fines might also entail social costs—for instance, if the firm had to give up profitable projects because after paying the fines it would not have enough financial assets to secure financial funds from outside investors.[67]

Therefore, it would be advisable to use other mechanisms, rather than further increasing the fines, in order to increase deterrence. In the United States, unlike the European Union, deterrence is substantially increased by prison sentences and by treble damages in private actions.

Making collusion a criminal offence would provide a stronger deterrent of collusion as managers would find it very risky to collude. However, it is unlikely that there will be sufficient support by EU Member States for a reform of competition law which introduces criminal penalties. Perhaps something could still be done, though, to give managers incentives to respect antitrust laws. For instance, they could be given administrative fines (and firms should be forbidden to reimburse them) and be disqualified from top managerial positions for some years. Otherwise, those who are taking the decisions to participate in a cartel would not pay any consequences for their violations of the antitrust laws.

A well-designed system of private actions for the recovery of antitrust damages may also represent a complementary instrument to increase deterrence. If buyers and final consumers have the right to obtain compensation for the loss they have incurred, and appropriate steps are taken to make it easy for them to sue for damages, this will add to the costs that a firm faces when it is involved in a cartel, and should help increase deterrence. Note, however, that the excess of the US system, which leads to excessive litigation, should be avoided. For instance, awarding of treble damages is likely to invite unmeritorious claims, and should accordingly be avoided.

Finally, it would be recommendable for antitrust authorities to improve deterrence by fostering competition culture. Among other things, firms should adopt antitrust compliance programmes and codes of conduct. Firms often write 'codes of conduct', where they commit to follow environmental, social, and labour laws, and such codes form a sort of 'contract' with consumers and investors that they would find it costly to violate. Making sure that compliance with antitrust laws is also included in such codes could help increase deterrence.

5.4. A Brief Summary

In this chapter, I have briefly analysed the economics of collusion, explaining what collusion is, what the main ingredients necessary for the firms to sustain it are, and which factors facilitate it. I have then reviewed the EU experience in fighting cartels, by focusing in particular on the standards of proving infringement of EU competition law, and on its enforcement policy. In this part, I have argued that to a large extent EU cartel policy is in line with economic thinking, and that the requirement to rely on documentary evidence to prove infringement of Article 81 is well motivated.

I have also reviewed the recent experience of the European Commission with a particular view to understanding what can be done to break existing cartels and deter the formation of new ones. I have argued that the EU leniency programme has been very successful in uncovering cartels, but it has unfortunately not allowed the Commission to make the prosecution of cartels quicker. Accordingly, whether in the form of a settlement procedure, or a different design of leniency programmes, the Commission should try to speed up the dealing of cartel cases, so as to free precious resources and energy that it could use to investigate new cartels (for instance, by identifying sectors where cartels are more likely to exist).

Finally, I have argued that after the introduction of the 2006 Guidelines fines have probably reached a high enough level to have some deterrence effect on the formation of cartels. However, deterrence could still be dramatically improved not only by trying to raise the probability that they will be investigated (see above), but also by increasing the costs that firms incur when a cartel is uncovered. From this perspective, the recent initiatives taken by the European Commission to promote private actions for the recovery of damages look particularly promising (although care should be taken not to induce excessive litigation, which would be inefficient).

Notes

[1] This chapter was prepared for the IESE conference 'Fifty Years of the Treaty: Assessment and Perspectives of Competition Policy in Europe' held at IESE Business School, Barcelona, 19–20 Nov. 2007. Comments from Barbara Gabor, Vivek Ghosal, Mario Mariniello, and Wouter Wils are gratefully acknowledged. I am also very grateful to Dimitrios Magos for his superb work as research assistant. Sect. 2 of this chapter is partly based on Motta (2004: ch. 4) (with the permission of Cambridge University Press). For a formal analysis, please refer to that chapter.

[2] In technical terms, the benchmark is usually the equilibrium price of a game where firms meet only once in the marketplace (a situation where collusion would not arise). For instance, in a homogenous goods game—where firms choose prices—a collusive outcome would exist whenever prices are higher than the one-shot Bertrand equilibrium price—where firms choose quantities—whenever they are lower than the one-shot Cournot equilibrium quantities.

[3] A necessary assumption for this simple example to hold is that at the collusive price of €2 the seller does not manage to sell all the pears he comes to the market with. Otherwise, he would not have an incentive to cut his price in order to increase sales.

[4] As noted by Stigler (1964), detection of a deviation is not always easy: in many markets, firms' prices and outputs are not directly observable.

[5] Note that a punishment should be thought of as a more aggressive market behaviour, and not as a direct monetary (or physical!) punishment. A punishment also hits the punishing firms, and not just the deviating firm, precisely because it has to rely on market mechanisms (a low price affects all the firms' profits). It is therefore crucial that firms are willing to take part in the punishment.

[6] In turn, this implies that collusion can be sustained only if firms meet repeatedly in the marketplace. Otherwise, a punishment cannot take place. In technical terms, collusion will never arise in a one-shot game. This is why collusion should be modelled through dynamic (repeated) games.

[7] The 'folk theorem' (Friedman 1971) says that in games with an infinite horizon if the discount factor is large enough firms can have any profit between zero and the fully collusive profit at the collusive equilibrium.

[8] Market allocation schemes are particularly frequent in the European Union, as we shall see below: in many cartel cases, firms have simply divided the European markets along the national borders.

[9] Among such structural factors which facilitate collusion, there are industry concentration, difficulty of entry, regularity and frequency of the orders, lack of buyer power,

symmetry, and multi-market contacts. See Motta (2004: sect. 4.2) for a discussion of such factors.

[10] Charging a price equal to marginal cost forever—that is an infinite punishment—would clearly be suboptimal here; since the punishment is triggered even if nobody has actually deviated, it would not make sense to condemn the industry to zero profit forever whenever a low level of demand is observed.

[11] On the other hand, as I discuss below, the alternatives of high and low price levels are no proof either of a collusive outcome, since an industry at a non-collusive equilibrium might have lower prices under negative demand (or common input) shocks or increased capacities.

[12] On collusion and exchange of information between competitors, see Kühn (2001).

[13] Porter (1983) shows that exchange of private information about market demand reduces demand uncertainty and allows more collusive outcomes to be sustained. In a similar vein, Kandori (1992) shows that as demand uncertainty decreases firms can attain higher collusive outcomes (and punishment phases become more severe), and Kandori and Matsushima (1998) also find that communicating information about past realizations helps collusion. Technically, the last article differs from Green and Porter (1984), Porter (1983), and Kandori (1992) in that it assumes that firms receive private rather than public signals, so that each firm might have a different belief of what has happened in the industry (has there been a demand shock, or has somebody deviated?). Other articles that deal with collusion under imperfect monitoring and private signals are Compte (1998) and Athey and Bagwell (2001).

[14] The incentives for firms to exchange private information and more importantly the welfare effects of such exchanges are not robust, as they crucially depend on whether the firms compete on prices or quantities, or whether the uncertainty concerns costs or demand. See Kühn (2001) or Raith (1996).

[15] Some exceptions about detailed data might occur in particular sectors. In banking and insurance, for instance, markets are characterized by asymmetric information. If firms had information about clients' solvency history, this would be efficiency-enhancing as it would lessen adverse selection problems and foster competition by helping customers to switch firms. See Padilla and Pagano (1997). Note, however, that although disaggregate, this is not information about prices set or quantities produced by firms.

[16] Schelling (1960) was the first to introduce the notion of focal points (or conventions) and to show how they can help people to coordinate.

[17] See below for a discussion of the *Soda-Ash* case, which can be interpreted as a tacit collusive outcome with history providing an easy focal point for firms.

[18] Unilateral announcements help players to select a jointly optimal price, on which it would otherwise be difficult to coordinate if a focal price (that is, an obvious price to be chosen) does not exist.

[19] Farrell (1987) analysed a game with different features from 'supergames'. He looked at a 'battle of the sexes' situation, where there are two asymmetric equilibria, as in an industry where at equilibrium only one of two firms could profitably enter, whereas if both entered they would make losses.

[20] See Farrell and Rabin (1996) for a non-technical discussion of the possible role of cheap talk in different games, and of the conditions one should expect it to affect equilibrium outcomes or equilibrium selection. A number of experiments have been

performed on this issue; see, for instance, Cooper, et al. (1992). See Kühn (2001) for other references on experiments on the collusive effects of information.

[21] However, advance notice of *effective* price changes could be in the interest of consumers who might want to know in advance the prices they will have to pay, and so reduce uncertainty.

[22] See Hay (1999) for the Ethyl case, where this was one of the allegedly anticompetitive prices used by the firms.

[23] See Borenstein (1999) for an account of the Airline Tariff Publishers (ATP) case in the United States, an example of how firms can manage to coordinate on prices through a succession of announcements which do not have commitment value with respect to consumers. See also Klemperer (2002) and Cramton and Schwartz (2001) for a discussion of how firms manage to 'communicate' in auctions, managing to achieve collusive bidding.

[24] For a survey of both the theoretical and the empirical literature on price advertising, see Fumagalli and Motta (2001).

[25] A 'meet-or-release' clause gives the seller the possibility to match the price or free the customer from the contract.

[26] If gathering information about prices is a costly process, these clauses might speed up purchase since they ensure the early buyer is not missing better deals. They may also introduce some price flexibility in long-term contracts by ensuring that shocks that affect outside options are internalized in the contracts. See Salop (1986: 283–4) and Crocker and Lyon (1994).

[27] See Motta (2004: ch. 6) for a discussion.

[28] Mathewson and Winter (1998: 65).

[29] A similar effect is achieved by 'basing point pricing', a system whereby each producer sets the final price as the mill price at the common basing point (which might be the seat of plants of one or more firms or it might be completely arbitrary) plus transport cost from that point to the final destination. Again, this allows increased transparency on the producers' side, in that it allows prices to be better compared.

[30] Discussion of how the National Competition Authorities and National Courts of the twenty-seven Member States of the European Union deal with cartels is beyond the scope of this chapter. To a large extent, however, national laws and policies follow EU law and case law.

[31] Note, however, that Article 81 covers both horizontal and vertical agreements; furthermore, not all horizontal agreements are cartels and indeed Article 81(3) gives conditions for agreements among competitors to be accepted.

[32] Goyder (1993: 162–5).

[33] Although crisis cartels allowed by the Commission are far from being a frequent phenomenon, Goyder (2003: 153) argues that in bad periods they may have a comeback and mentions the *Stichting Baksteen* as a recent decision (1995) where the Commission has authorized an agreement in the Dutch brick industry to cut down excess capacity.

[34] This does not appear as a particularly compelling economic argument: after all, there are many industries which have not been granted any exception and in which firms might have to operate below capacity in some periods. More probably, the explanation is historical: shipping conferences have existed for a very long time and in many

jurisdictions, and the European Union might have found it politically difficult to break with past rules.

[35] See Benini and Bermig (2007).

[36] 'Guidelines on the Method of Setting Fines Imposed Pursuant to Article 23(2)(a) of Regulation No. 1/2003' [2006], OJ C210/2. For a discussion, see also de Broca (2006).

[37] For instance, in *Bitumen Netherlands*, the Commission increased the fine imposed on KWS by 10 per cent for having twice denied Commission inspectors access to its premises. In *Copper Fittings*, Advanced Fluid Connections (and other cartel participants) received a 60 per cent increase in the fine for having continued the infringement even after the Commission's inspection. The same firm received a further 50 per cent increase because of giving misleading information to the Commission.

[38] For instance, in *French Beef*, the Commission reduced the fines by 30 per cent because of the role played by the French Minister of Agriculture in promoting the agreement.

[39] 'Guidelines on the Method of Setting Fines Imposed Pursuant to Article 23(2)(a) of Regulation No. 1/2003' [2006], OJ C210/2, at para. 35. According to the case law, the inability to pay is relevant only in a 'specific social context'—for instance, if the payment of fines may lead to higher unemployment. See Wils (2007: 229).

[40] Similar schemes are routinely used in several fields other than antitrust, such as fiscal law and environmental law. In Italy, the so-called turncoat laws (*leggi sui pentiti*) have been successfully used to fight organized crime such as the Mafia and 'terrorist' organizations such as the 'Red Brigades'. Of course, there are ethical issues involved because punishment is abandoned in exchange for deterrence of further crimes: criminals might be set free (and sometimes even rewarded) in exchange for information that results in imprisoning other criminals.

[41] Immunity in the final decision will be confirmed if the firm has fully cooperated throughout the process. For instance, in the *Raw Tobacco Italy* case, the firm Deltafina saw its conditional immunity (granted at the beginning of the procedure) withheld because in breach of cooperation it had informed its competitors of its leniency application and that an investigation was open before the surprise inspection. Eventually the firm was still given a 50 per cent reduction in fines.

[42] A reduction of fines is granted to firms that do not fulfil the previous conditions but provide evidence that has *significant value added* for the investigation. For an assessment of the EC leniency policy, see also Géradin and Henry (2005). See also van Barlingen and Barennes (2005) and Suurnäkki and Tierno Centella (2007) for a discussion on how leniency works in practice.

[43] See also Spagnolo (2000), Rey (2003), and Harrington (2008).

[44] See European Commission (2007e: 12–13). When more firms involved in the same cartel apply for immunity, only the first one is entitled to receive it, and the other firms will be classified by the European Commission as applying for reduction of fines. The statistics reported are therefore not inflated by the fact that several cartel participants might report more or less simultaneously to the Commission.

[45] In Motta (2004: sect. 4.4) I discuss the issue in more detail. I argue that there should be infringement of the law only when firms explicitly coordinate their behaviour. In other words, tacit collusion does not run against article 81, and evidence on market data (for instance, that prices are 'too high', that there is parallel behaviour, and so on) can

represent only complementary evidence: only hard evidence (such as minutes of agreement, faxes, recording of phone calls and meetings and so on) should constitute a proof of violation of competition law. The suggested approach is consistent with the EU practice as indicated by the discussion in the text below.

[46] The ECJ defined the term 'concerted practice' in the *Sugar Cartel* judgment as follows: 'The concept . . . refers to a form of coordination between undertakings which, without having been taken to the stage where an agreement properly so-called has been concluded, knowingly substitutes for the risks of competition practical co-operation between them' ([1975] ECR 1916).

[47] *Ahlström and others* v. *Commission*, para. 71 (emphasis added).

[48] The experts referred to the 'kinked demand curve' hypothesis, according to which there is price rigidity in the markets because a firm expects that if it increases prices the rivals will not follow and therefore will lose market shares, and that if it decreases prices the rivals will immediately follow and therefore will not benefit from the price cut. Therefore, the same price would continue to hold unless major shocks have intervened. Nowadays, we would rephrase the arguments by appealing to the tacit collusion model described in sect. 5.2. No firm would lightheartedly want to change prices relative to its competitors, fearing that this would trigger a reaction which would be detrimental to its profits.

[49] *Ahlström and others* v. *Commission*, para. 126 (emphasis added). This is not the only case in which the Court disagreed with the Commission about evidence of concerted practice. In *Compagnie Royale Asturienne des Mines and Rheinzinc* v. *Commission* (Cases 29–30/83 [1984] ECR 1679), the Court found that the reason why two suppliers refused to sell to a buyer (Schlitz) was the poor credit record of the buyer, not a concerted behaviour.

[50] Motta (2004: 188) (my translation).

[51] C–277/87 *Sandoz* v. *Commission* [1990] ECR 27.

[52] Ibid. 43–4.

[53] Ibid. 55.

[54] Judgment of 29 June 1995, Case T–30/91 [1995] ECR II–01775.

[55] Noteworthy is a stream of high-profile international cartels prosecuted by both United States and European Union authorities in the late 1990s, including *Citric Acid*, *Lysine*, *Vitamins*, and *Graphite Electrodes*.

[56] Merger control may also play an important role in that it could prevent the formation of industrial structures where collusion would probably be sustained. Further, in Motta (2004: sect. 4.4) I argue that there are a number of initiatives that authorities could take in order to prevent collusion—from the careful design of public procurement auctions to the outlawing of certain business practices which foster collusion.

[57] Goyder (2004: 75).

[58] Ibid. 76–7.

[59] [1989] 4 CMLR 445.

[60] [1977] 2 CMLR D28.

[61] Of course, this does not mean that firms cannot exchange any statistical information. What the Commission and the Courts object to is, rightly, the exchange of very detailed and individual (pricing or sales) data.

[62] In the Court's language, the exchange of information allowed the firms to 'replace practical co-operation for the normal risks of competition'.

[63] The 2007 data refer to the period up to 1 Aug. 2007.

[64] In those cases, however, the Commission can readopt the Decision after having redressed the procedural wrongs. To avoid double-counting, though, readopted Decisions are not included in either the Table or the Figures. This explains possible divergences between official Commission statistics and the ones offered here. For instance, European Commission 2007e reports that in the year 2006 the Commission took 7 cartel Decisions. Two of them, however, were cases of readoption after the Court had annulled the Decision on procedural grounds.

[65] See Buccirossi and Spagnolo (2006) for a discussion.

[66] The basic fine may be up to 30 per cent of the relevant market turnover, plus a fixed component, which could be up to 25 per cent of the relevant market turnover or a yearly pro rata of 5 per cent. This yearly 35 per cent may then be increased by 400 per cent, as each previous infringement may raise the fine by 100 per cent.

[67] The literature on imperfect financial markets stresses that the ability of a firm to borrow funds from outside investors crucially depends on the assets it owns. Therefore, if the payment of a large fine considerably reduces its assets, its borrowing ability will be reduced accordingly, and some profitable projects may not be financed. In principle, it is also possible that the payment of a large fine may lead the firm to bankruptcy. However, recall that under EU law no fine can be above 10 per cent of the firm's worldwide turnover (which for large multinational and multiproduct firms can be much higher than the turnover of the relevant market) and that a firm may be granted a fine reduction if it can prove inability to pay.

6

An Economic Assessment of European Commission Merger Control: 1958–2007[1]

Bruce Lyons

6.1. Introduction

Mergers are a major means of restructuring—potentially allowing a more efficient allocation of resources as market conditions and firm-specific capabilities change over time. They provide a swift way to experiment with new ideas when the transaction costs of coordination, incentives, and exchanging ideas are expected to be lower within an organization than when using market transactions. This can enhance the efficiency of the merging firms, leading to increased competition, a spur to rivals, and improved competitiveness on the world stage. Potentially, both consumers and producers can gain from mergers.

However, mergers may also dampen the competitive process, by reducing the number of effective competitors, by softening competition, by impeding entry, and by reducing the incentives to innovate. This can harm both domestic consumers and international competitiveness. Effective merger regulation is the essential *ex ante* means of filtering merger proposals so that efficient ones are allowed while anticompetitive ones are not.

The Commission's jurisdiction for merger control includes only firms with a fairly large turnover and which have at least one-third of European sales outside a single Member State. Ninety per cent of such merger proposals falling within the Commission's scrutiny are allowed without any conditions. Headlines are made when a merger is prohibited, but this has happened only twenty times in seventeen years, during which time over 3,500 mergers have been appraised. Clearances subject to conditions (that is, remedies) happen over ten times as frequently as prohibitions, so the overall intervention rate since 1990 has been 7.5 per cent.[2]

This is only the tip of the iceberg. Merger control is a powerful signal to firms contemplating mergers and they modify their proposals in anticipation of the merger regime. This is why the underlying logic for each intervention is so important. It is also why there are so few 'slam dunk' prohibitions. Merger control is so difficult because, in the presence of an effective regime and given compliance costs to the firms, only the beneficial or marginal mergers would be proposed. This means that, in an effective regime, all cases other than obvious clearances are likely to be difficult.

Seven-eighths of an iceberg is unseen below water. How many inappropriate mergers does European merger regulation deter? I am unaware of any EU-level evidence but a recent UK estimate (Deloitte 2007) surveyed over 200 senior competition lawyers and over 200 firms. Following external legal advice, five mergers were abandoned or modified for every merger that was blocked or modified by the UK competition authorities.[3] However, external legal advice was taken in only 25 per cent of cases where firms modified or abandoned mergers on anticipated competition grounds, so the five-to-one ratio is an underestimate.[4] It is likely, then, that there is at least as much 'below-the-water' or 'deterrence' effect for the ECMR as there is for an iceberg. This deterrence may be either positive or negative. Positive deterrence is where anticompetitive mergers are modified or abandoned, or alternative merger partners are found. Negative deterrence is where efficient mergers are abandoned or made less effective by modification or choice of a less suitable partner. More positive and less negative deterrence can simultaneously be achieved only by applying a clear 'economic effects' approach to merger appraisal.[5] And, to spread the message, it is necessary to signal this approach in clearly argued decisions as well as in broad messages contained in guidelines and speeches.

One of my themes in this chapter is that over the last fifty years competition economics has been evolving as a discipline and, more recently, there has been a constructive interaction with the law. Law and economics are beginning to learn from each other. In section 6.2 I sketch the development of competition economics as a background to legal developments in European merger control. One of the lessons I draw is that the economics has been continuously developing over the last fifty years and it is sensible to bear this in mind when evaluating policy.[6] A further subsection ('Trends in merger activity') provides some additional background from the perspective of shareholder returns and merger waves during the period. Section 6.3 picks up on the three key economic areas of merger appraisal: non-coordinated effects in horizontal mergers; coordinated effects in horizontal mergers; and non-horizontal mergers. These are ranked in decreasing order of the difficulty of economic analysis. A further subsection ('Merger interventions and remedies') considers the crucial and, until recently, under-researched area of the appropriateness of the remedies applied to mergers that have been found to be anticompetitive.

Commission practice is evaluated in each of these areas throughout section 6.3. In section 6.4 I turn to a broader statistical evaluation of the efficiency of DG Comp's merger regulation, in particular drawing on some simple ideas from bargaining theory, before concluding briefly in section 6.5.

6.2. Historical Context

6.2.1. *A brief history of competition economics*

It is relatively easy for an economist to criticize particular merger decisions. We can dip into our magnificent theoretical and econometric toolboxes to pull out the latest research technology and it is not hard to find a lack of sophistication of the practitioner's old-fashioned hammer. That is sometimes fair criticism but it can also be unfair because many of our new tools are very new and some are relatively untested for policy applications. The purpose of this section is to place the evaluation of European Union merger policy in the context of the development of economic ideas. The intention is to provide a more even-handed critique of policy and practice by acknowledging some gaps in the academic literature.

The branch of economics that provides the foundations for competition policy is known as 'industrial economics' or 'industrial organization'. In the formative years before the 1957 Treaty, there were many different national traditions in the field, not all of which were founded in the microeconomics of individual markets. For example, the German approach was heavily influenced by 'Ordoliberalism'. Founded in the disasters of the first half of the last century which culminated in an unholy alliance between Nazism and cartels, Ordoliberalism saw competition policy as essential to protecting individual freedom, with clear and strong legal rules necessary to provide a bulwark against political and corporate repression.[7] In contrast, Anglo-Saxon economics focused on microeconomic efficiency. There were many anecdotal case studies of how competition operated. A classic example from the time was a major US work providing the first systematic treatment of barriers to entry (Bain 1956). There was no internationally dominant advanced textbook on the subject.[8]

During the 1960s and 70s, US economists developed a theoretical framework known as Structure–Conduct–Performance (SCP) which drew a link between market structure (for example, concentration, entry barriers), the way firms behaved (for example, collusion versus more competitive pricing), and performance (for example, efficiency of production, consumer welfare). Case studies were supplemented by econometrics as computers became available to academics, with the emphasis of looking for broad trends across industries to support the SCP approach. This approach was brilliantly brought together in Scherer 1970, an advanced textbook that also had some influence on this side of the Atlantic. However, it was based essentially on US research and evidence. Also, some of the theoretical foundations of SCP were a little *ad hoc* by modern standards of rigour. The approach was also challenged by a strongly non-interventionist 'Chicago School' of thought which became highly influential, not least because it worked so closely at the interface between law and economics (for example, Posner 1976 and Bork 1978—the writers both became influential judges). Entering the 1980s, however, industrial economics was about to change and leave its fragmented schools of thought substantially behind.

In the period up to the introduction of the European Community merger regulation (ECMR) in 1989, but too novel to influence it, there were two revolutions emerging in industrial economics. First, 'game theory' was finally providing a unifying framework for investigating strategic interaction between firms. Since the deepest idea comes straight from Cournot (1838), it is not clear why it took so long for game theory to come centre stage, but that is not a question to dwell on here. Game theory proved a fantastically flexible tool for testing whether some of the claims from SCP were consistent with rational behaviour and for investigating new ideas. Many of the SCP insights were confirmed, but the sensitivity of some results to apparently minor assumptions made industrial economists think very hard about the foundations of how firms compete. An interesting feature of this development was that European economists (often working in US universities) were at least as important to developing these ideas as were Americans. Game theory was a unifying idea in more ways than one. The early fruits of this approach were brought together in a remarkable text by Tirole (1988), which has since served generations of graduate students on both sides of the Atlantic. From now on, the intellectual story is largely one of transatlantic consensus.[9]

These terse academic ideas were not yet ready to be influential for merger policy. There was much too much of an 'anything can happen' about them, and not enough attention to real policy issues. Furthermore, there was little in the way of empirical foundation. This was just around the corner and developed through the 1990s. New datasets on specific markets combined with rigorous theoretical models and powerful computers to provide new ways to understand competition in actual markets. In the context of merger appraisal, this ability to model how a market currently competes appeared to be just one step away from the holy grail of predicting how the market could be expected to operate post merger.

Moving into the current century, there is an increasing interaction between policy cases and academic industrial economics. Economists realize the value of real cases not least as a way of gaining understanding of the business practices that matter. It is no longer good enough to develop a toolkit and tell practitioners to use it. The process is more interactive. Real policy issues,

138

including merger cases, are stimulating theoretical developments within a common and fairly stable framework of analysis. A new sub-discipline of competition economics, much more nuanced to legal ideas and practical policy, has emerged.

In the context of this history of fast-changing ideas, the fact that practical merger control in Europe seriously engages with new research is something to be applauded. However, this comes with a health warning. The new toolkit is powerful and convincing because it is sensitive and subtle. This means that a strong training is necessary to use it properly. This is not to say that it is beyond the comprehension of a good competition lawyer or the firms themselves. Good economic analysis is sensible and intuitive once properly explained. But, it is to say that a strong training is necessary to understand when a superficially sensible theory may be profoundly misleading. Consequently, there is a danger that ideas are applied inappropriately.[10] Some of the fault lies with economists (not economics)—for example, too many economists are too ready to identify an 'equilibrium' outcome without spelling out the essential elements underpinning that equilibrium (for example, empirically verifiable assumptions), let alone the dynamics of getting there. This is an issue on which economics can learn from the law. The legal approach of making an argument in bite-sized steps is important for confirming whether each step applies to the case in hand. This has been recognized by the CFI (for example, *Airtours/First Choice*). Where this decomposition of steps is not possible, as is the case for some highly sophisticated simulation models, economists need to be very careful to explain whatever steps they can, to be honest about the limitations of their tools and to be particularly cautious in interpreting their conclusions. It is unwise to rely on analysis that is not explained intuitively step by step.

Next, I turn to what was happening to merger regulation in Europe during the same fifty years that competition economics was evolving as a discipline.

6.2.2. Evolution of EC merger control

1957–89: PRE-ECMR

The Treaty of Rome made no explicit provision for merger control. Nevertheless, both Articles 81 and 82 (originally 85 and 86 respectively) were applied to mergers in a limited way. The legal basis under Article 82 was established by the Court in *Continental Can* (1973) and this seems to have allowed some degree of influence by the Commission over potentially very unattractive mergers. However, it could only be used against a firm that was already considered dominant, and could not prevent the creation of a dominant position (Whish 2003). The Commission also tried to apply Article 81 to mergers, and in *BAT* (1987) the Court found that the acquisition of a minority shareholding might be an infringement if it brought anticompetitive influence. It was only in December

1989 that ECMR brought explicit merger control at the European level, and the focus of this chapter is on what has happened since.

Nevertheless, it is worth recalling the combination of economic and political factors that created the climate to introduce explicit merger control at that time. Insiders in the Commission (DG IV) had wanted the power to control mergers for some time, but faced resistance from firms arguing that size was necessary to compete against America and Japan. National competition authorities were also anxious to preserve their competences. This stalemate was part of a much wider languishing of European common policy over the previous decade. However, things were about to change. DG IV under the leadership of Irish commissioner Peter Sutherland was able to capitalize on the opportunity created by a number of factors in the mid-1980s. A remarkable and unlikely combination of Commission leadership (Delors and Cockfield) with the confluence of domestic agendas of the most powerful heads of state at the time[11] resulted in the Single European Act of 1985.

This aimed to create a single European market by the end of 1992. It did not introduce merger regulation, but it reinvigorated the idea of common policy and it put the benefits of competition centre stage. The economics of market structure suggests that the number of firms that can survive in a market depends on the size of that market and the toughness of competition. In particular, a larger market supports a less than proportionately greater number of firms because prices are driven closer to marginal costs. The process of integration must consequently be expected to see a period of exit or consolidation between firms. In markets where the geographic market at which competition was anticipated to take place rose from the national to the European level, concentration would rise. This is exactly what we observed (Lyons 2001). Associated with this, the late 1980s saw a significant merger wave (though nowhere near as big as the 1990s wave) and the expectation was that this would grow as firms prepared for the single market.[12] It was important to control this process to ensure it did not go too far.

Finally, firms themselves were beginning to see the benefits of European-level merger control. They were increasingly worried by the prospect of double jeopardy in multiple filings if they wanted to complete a cross-border merger. Their advisers were also aware of the recent ECJ decision over BAT, which opened up the horrifying possibility that a merger might at some future date be declared void because it breached Article 81.

1989–2002: ESTABLISHING THE NEW ECMR

Organizational Issues

The new ECMR was operated by a specialist unit within the then DG IV—the Merger Task Force (MTF). It had to work to a very precise and tight timetable with time limits both for its initial Phase I scrutiny (basically one month) and for its more extended Phase II investigations (a further four months). There were only around fifty-five cases per annum until 1993, after which there was an unprecedented merger boom reaching around 330 cases annually at the turn of the century. The relatively quiet early years gave the opportunity to develop processes and an *esprit de corps*. Nevertheless, by necessity, cases had to be dealt with rapidly. It is perhaps not surprising that there were some significant inconsistencies and elements of poor economic analysis in the early years (Neven, Nuttall, and Seabright 1993). However, a combination of case overload and possible complacency was to mean that bad practice was not weeded out (see Kühn 2005 for examples), resulting in the reversals of 2002. It also became apparent that the tight timetable left too little time to consider sensible, effective remedies short of prohibition.

There are four distinct stages in the application of merger policy: decision to clear (possibly subject to agreed remedies) or to investigate in depth (Phase I); in-depth investigation (Phase II); decision to clear, prohibit, or require remedies (formally taken by the full college of the European Commissioners); and possible appeal (CFI and ECJ). Since the full set of Commissioners is entirely non-specialist and all but one has their eyes fixed on their own portfolios, this leaves the Competition Commissioner in a potentially very powerful position. It is very hard for an outsider to judge how this power is wielded, but it must be difficult to push too far from the 'house' (that is, 'staff') opinion except in exceptional cases. Nevertheless, the Competition Commissioner has weekly meetings with DG Comp staff, at which his or her views on particular cases can be made clear, and other Directorates with sectoral expertise are widely consulted throughout the investigation, and can probably be influential.[13]

Leaving aside this limited amount of political influence, the process is such that the first three of the four stages identified above are all conducted by DG Comp (formerly known as DG IV), which is investigator, prosecutor, and jury. The dangers are compounded by the practice of the same teams taking cases from Phase I to Phase II, so any preconceptions or prejudices carry through. It almost invites an investigation team to get locked into a provisional judgment it had to make during the early weeks of Phase I. Human nature is that we prefer to prove ourselves right rather than wrong, so the temptation must be to spend Phase II trying to justify the Phase I decision to refer. Thus, it is crucial to have an effective appeal system if good economic analysis is to be sustained.

Unfortunately, the distance of the appeal provided only a limited constraint, at least before 2002. The parties to a merger can appeal to the CFI. A further appeal, limited to legal questions, may also be possible to the ECJ. Both are traditionally lengthy processes, and business realities mean that it is extremely difficult to resurrect a merger prohibition that has been overthrown on appeal. An important 2001 reform introduced the expedited procedure, particularly for merger appeals, in the CFI (with the intention of deciding on appeals within twelve months). However, accelerated appeals are not universally allowed and there can still be substantial delays.[14] European merger control is very much more distant from the courts than is the US procedure, where the courts cast a continual shadow on the FTC or DoJ, even though the parties typically settle out of court.[15] Both sides in the US system must continuously ask themselves: 'how would the courts interpret the evidence we are providing to support our arguments?' In contrast to the USA, the court in Europe does not attempt fact finding. The question it asks is one of judicial review, so DG Comp must only ask itself: 'would the court find that we have failed to adopt the correct procedure in collecting evidence, and have we been sufficiently diligent in trying to interpret it?'[16] Despite a shot across the Commission's bow in *Kali & Salz* (1998), where the Court called for closer examination of the merger, this does not seem to have had a major impact on reforming internal procedures.

One final element of procedure deserves honourable mention. A major advantage of the EU system is that reasoned (and relatively readable) decisions are published. In the US, because it is adversarial, far too much remains unpublished and there is no clearly argued case to review. As any academic knows, written publication is a major discipline for clear thinking, as well as for the dissemination of appropriate analysis. While this does not completely compensate for the lack of internal checks and balances, its value should not be underestimated.

Substantive Issues

A unique feature of the ECMR, by international comparisons, is that because of the 1957 Treaty, the Commission must be concerned with market integration. Even now, post introduction of the euro, economic integration is still very much less advanced in Europe than in the United States. Integration issues impinge on mergers in two principal ways. First, some national corporate governance rules impede the market for corporate control. Second, and most relevant to competition policy, the national application of merger control can potentially distort the market in much the same way as nationalistic state aids. The scope of the ECMR was intended to pick up any merger with a 'Community dimension', but there have been gaps. The commendable idea was to apply the principle of subsidiarity to mergers with operations predominantly in a single country. However, the combination of an absolute size threshold and a proportionate sales distribution across member states (The Commission does not have jurisdiction if less than one-third of turnover is outside the home market) was to cause significant problems in a very limited number of important cases. In particular, it leaves some very significant European mergers in the hands of national authorities who have revealed themselves to have more interest in 'national champions' than in preserving competition. Despite attempts at reform, this problem has endured and continues to undermine good merger regulation in a few important cases.[17]

Another area of concern was the substantive test in the original ECMR (which has since been revised and improved). The original test by which mergers were to be appraised is provided by Article 2(3) of the ECMR (1989): 'A concentration [i.e. merger or acquisition] which creates or strengthens a dominant position as a result of which effective competition would be significantly impeded in the common market or in a substantial part of it shall be declared incompatible with the common market.' This is commonly referred to as the dominance test (DT). The primary importance of establishing 'dominance' is that it encouraged a formalistic approach based on market share. The DT contrasts with the United States' 'substantial lessening of competition' (SLC) test, which is currently interpreted as 'whether the merger is likely to create or enhance market power or to facilitate its exercise' (US Merger Guidelines 1997).[18] The semantic difference between the DT and the US SLC test may seem minor but in practice it did make a difference in giving too much weight to market shares, and so market structure, over economic effects.[19]

On its own, the DT was not a bar to good economic analysis. As I have argued in section 6.2.1, economic ideas were moving along at a rapid pace. How were economic ideas able to penetrate into the Commission? Economists were embedded in the case teams, but few had the PhD-level training in industrial organization that is necessary to check the quality of sophisticated economic analysis. There was little formal training in competition economics, and only a very informal academic advisory group (from around 1997). Meanwhile, both the Commission and merging parties were being offered a new weapon. External economic consultancies had first appeared in London during the mid-1980s and these were available to advise on merger control. The Commission began to use them for commissioned reports into various issues such as market definition and quantitative techniques. Merging parties began using them to hone their defence on particular mergers. By 1995, Neven (2006) estimates that the total amount of fees for the three largest competition consultancies was c.£2.5 million, including both EU and national advice. The Commission's market definition notice of 1997 was important in its explicit use of economic concepts and this appears to have been a trigger for the consultancies to grow. By 2004, turnover had grown nearly tenfold, with around 150 professional economists working in European consultancies—which is very many more than were working in the Commission.[20] There was a clear imbalance of economic expertise and the Commission was struggling with the economic analysis.

The 2002 Appeals

The Commission suffered a series of high-profile reverses in the European CFI in the following judgments:[21]

- *Airtours/First Choice*: DG Comp did not conduct a sufficiently rigorous economic analysis of the incentives for and ability to coordinate behaviour as a consequence of the proposed merger.[22]
- *Schneider/Legrand*: DG Comp failed to take account of the different degree of competition in each of the national markets it identified, and did not provide Schneider with enough information to offer an appropriate remedy.
- *Tetra Laval/Sidel*: DG Comp should have: (a) taken account of the fact that its concern over leveraging market power between two otherwise separate markets would have required tactics that are illegal under Article 82; (b) provided a proper appraisal of behavioural commitments before resorting to its favourite structural remedy (divestiture); and (c) adopted a higher standard of proof.[23]

As can be seen, these appeals raised a range of concerns, including both inadequate economic analysis and procedural weaknesses. Such concerns have since been reinforced by a 2005 CFI judgment relating to a controversial 2001 decision:

- *GE/Honeywell*: although the prohibition decision was upheld due to a relatively minor horizontal part to DG Comp's case, the Court strongly condemned their analysis of conglomerate effects (i.e. the theory that the merger would result in exclusionary effects due to opportunities to bundle products).[24]

Table 6.1. provides some context for the way in which these Court landmark decisions related to the timing of Commission-led initiatives in merger policy.[25]

2003–7: REFORM

It would be wrong to attribute all the reforms to the CFI reverses of 2002. Indeed, the Green Paper on reform had been published in 2001. The truth is that the CFI hastened and sharpened the reforms, but change was already on the way. Ten new Member States were due to join the European Union in May 2004 bringing a potentially large increase in caseload at the same time as a merger boom. Much of this caseload might relate to state aid and other areas, but there would also be merger concerns because of the multiplicity of national geographic markets until the new members on the perimeter of the European Union become more economically integrated. DG Comp needed more-efficient procedures to deal with this. It was also a fairly natural time to reflect on the ECMR, with an active Commissioner Monti and a significant amount of experience following the reviews of the first decade. It would have been surprising if change was not necessary. Possibly most important in the long run, however, was the economic analysis being used increasingly to inform competition decisions across the globe. It presented a serious challenge to integrate top class economic analysis centrally into merger appraisal.

Table 6.1. Soft law and precedent in EC merger control since 1989

Date	Commissioner*	Commission led	Court landmarks†
1989	Sutherland	ECMR	
1990	Brittan		
1991			
1992			
1993			
1994	Van Miert	Joint ventures	
1995			
1996			
1997		Revisions to ECMR on full function joint ventures, Phase I remedies and procedure. Relevant market notice; access to file	
1998			Kali & Salz (ECJ)
1999			
2000	Monti	Simplified procedure for small, low market share mergers	
2001		Green Paper on ECMR reform; Remedies notice; role of hearing officer	*CFI expedited procedure (<1 yr)*
2002		EU–US cooperation agreement	Airtours/First Choice; Schneider /Legrand; Tetra Lavel/Sidel
2003			
2004		Major revisions to ECMR (inc. substantive test and efficiencies). Horizontal guidelines; procedural best practice guidelines	
2005	Kroes	Ancillary restraints notice; referral to/from national authorities; access to file	GE/Honeywell
2006		Revisions to access to file	Impala appeal over Sony/BMG
2007		Non-Horizontal guidelines; [consultation on revised remedies notice]	

Notes: *at beginning of year; † involving significant criticism of the Commission.

Some of the reforms were organizational or procedural. The MTF was dismembered and folded into other mainly sectoral units. Devil's advocate panels (known as 'a fresh pair of eyes') were introduced to provide an internal critique of the arguments provided by case teams. This does not eliminate the problem of a single case team taking the case from start to finish, but along with the chief economist's team, it was a step in the right direction. The merger appraisal timetable was extended to allow more time to develop remedies appropriate to the expected competitive harm.

Other reforms were targeted directly at developing better and more consistent economic analysis. First, the important new post of Chief Competition Economist (CCE) was created and filled by an independent-minded academic economist, Professor Lars-Hendrik Röller. He was provided with a small team of ten well-trained economists to help case teams with more technical economic analysis. It appears that the Chief Economist's Team (CET) has been broadly welcomed by case teams (not least for easing their workload) and has provided helpful advice, but it remains small and has duties wider than casework.[26] In addition, the CCE acts as an independent adviser to the Commissioner with the power to offer 'final advice' also to the College of Commissioners immediately prior to a final decision. This is a potentially very powerful procedure in the event that the CCE disagrees with the case team and relevant senior officials in DG Comp. Second, horizontal merger guidelines were published, explaining the circumstances in which a merger might be expected to result in competitive harm. These provide an important discipline within the 'house', as well as providing external guidance and principles for positive deterrence. Last, but not least, there was a subtle change to the substantive test.

THE NEW SIEC TEST

The European Commission Green Paper (2001) reviewing the merger regulation spent only four pages of a fifty-eight-page document on substantive issues (the dominance test, merger-specific efficiencies, and simplified procedure), with the rest going into great detail on jurisdictional and procedural issues. But it turned out that the substantive issues were the most important for reform. In particular, the dominance test was replaced by a standard apparently much closer to the US SLC. The 'new' standard was that a merger should not be a 'significant impediment to effective competition'.[27]

Was it necessary to change the substantive test? The US experience possibly suggests not. The 1968 US guidelines state that 'the primary role of Section 7 enforcement is to preserve and promote market structures conducive to competition'. This sounds like a very structural interpretation of an SLC. But the major revision to the guidelines in 1982 is far more specifically economic effects based: 'mergers should not be permitted to create or enhance market power or to facilitate its exercise'. This wording has essentially survived in subsequent revisions. Now is not the place to try to explain the role of economic ideas in the evolution of US merger control, but the timescale of ideas between the 1914 Clayton Act and the 1982 revision is on a completely different scale to the time span between 1989 and 2002. The ECMR needed a more substantial kick than a set of guidelines.[28]

One interpretation of the DT is that it could be seen formally as establishing whether the competition authority was considering either an independent effect or a coordinated effect of the merger. The former would be traditional dominance by a single firm, and the latter would be a case of collective dominance. However, this fails to appreciate that a merger to create the second or third biggest firm may have unilateral as well as coordinated effects. In essence, there were two problems.[29]

First, the DT could be 'too harsh' on merging firms that would create an efficient new enterprise with an incentive to cut price or improve quality to such an extent that this might make an existing rival unprofitable (or at least reduce its market share). This would 'create dominance' only by *increasing* competition, but it still might fall foul of a crude interpretation of the DT because of the reduced number of competitors. This led to accusations that DG Comp was protecting competitors more than consumers in some cases (Neven, Nuttall, and Seabright 1993: ch. 3.5). While it is possible to imagine situations where the preservation of a less-efficient firm in the market might be desirable for long-term competition considerations, such situations are very exceptional and a competition authority should be made to justify such a judgment on competition grounds, and not on easy appeal to crude dominance.

Second, the DT could be 'too generous' to merging firms because of the double hurdle for the competition authorities. In particular, the DT could allow an undesirable merger that significantly impedes competition, but which does not meet the dominance criterion. The doctrine of collective dominance was sometimes tortured into filling the gap—for example, *Airtours/First Choice* (see sect. 6.3.2 below).[30]

The SIEC test was exactly the right change to make. It built on the existing test, and changes only what was necessary for a more efficient and effective system of merger control. It allowed the maximum use of good case law and signalled continuity, thus minimizing uncertainties during transition. It had the additional benefit that it is semantically almost indistinguishable from the SLC test and so contributed to an emerging world standard (see also Vickers 2004). Any transatlantic disputes over merger appraisal should no longer hide behind legal wording. I have already argued that the academic literature on competition economics has converged. Consequently, transatlantic disputes must be due to either a difference of issues that the merger raises in European as distinct from American markets or from mistakes by one side of the Atlantic in their economic analysis (or from national protectionism encroaching on the discretionary range of interpretation of a lessening of competition).

6.2.3. *Trends in merger activity*

There is no reliable data on trends in European mergers prior to the mid-1980s, but there appears to be no evidence of substantial activity on continental Europe from 1957 until this time. UK data do reveal a substantial peak in activity in the early 1970s.[31] This happens to be the time that the UK joined the European Union, but this merger wave was probably more tied to the concurrent merger wave in the USA and, to an extent, a delayed effect of the 1956 Restrictive Trade Practices Act which outlawed cartel agreements.[32]

Two and a half genuinely European merger waves are discernible since the mid-1980s, and these also broadly coincide with peaks of M&A activity in the USA. Mergers can be measured in different ways, but one set of figures suggests the 1980s European peak by value of deals was in 1989, having risen steadily from the mid-1980s. Measured by number of deals, the first peak was in 1991. This peak was exceeded by 1995 and increased rapidly until the turn of the century before falling away (see Martynova and Renneboog 2006a: Figs. 2.1 and 2.2).[33] Our period ends with the beginning of a third wave in the mid-2000s, starting around 2004.

In Figure 6.2 (see section 6.3.4) we measure activity relevant to merger control by the number of Phase I decisions. This measure combines a value effect (because of the notification threshold) with a numbers effect (since it is a simple count), along with a requirement for the mergers to have an effect on trade between Member States. The pattern broadly reflects other measures of M&A activity, though it demonstrates a much stronger upward trend overlaying the waves of activity. For example, the number of deals in Martynova and Renneboog (2008a) roughly doubles between the 1991 and 2000 peaks, while the number of Commission decisions rises sixfold.

Martynova and Renneboog (2008b) characterize this period of European mergers as increasingly involving cross-border activity and mainly between firms in the same broad industry. There were some huge equity-funded deals in the turn of the century peak compared with more buyouts in the earlier period and private equity in the most recent period. Each merger wave has ended with a stock market crash.

Even if not of direct relevance to merger control, it is interesting to consider the average private pay-off to mergers. There have been numerous event studies of stock market reactions to merger announcements. These are founded on the assumption of efficient markets. Event studies look at the few days around a merger announcement and usually separate the impact on the bidder from that of the target. Measured against market trends, they estimate cumulative abnormal returns, CARs, which can be attributed to the news of the merger. The CARs therefore reflect the capitalized market expectation of enhanced profitability due to the merger. This may be due either to enhanced efficiency or enhanced market power. Recent examples based mainly on the European turn of the century merger boom include Campa and Hernando (2004), Goergen and Renneboog (2004), and Martynova and Renneboog (2006a; 2008b). On average, these find an increase in CARs for the target in the order of 10–20 per cent, more or less zero for the acquirer, and around 1 per cent combined. However, studies looking at how stock market returns evolve over the following years are much more pessimistic. There has been less European research of this nature, and such studies inherently cannot look at the most recent period, but more studies find a negative impact than find a positive effect. A similarly pessimistic picture emerges from studies of post-merger operating performance (for example, profitability, growth).[34]

Overall, the financial markets continue to support merger activity which consequently continues with trend growth overlaying distinct merger waves. Event studies suggest most of any capitalized expected benefits are captured by

the acquired firm's shareholders, but long-term studies suggests that anticipated benefits are not always achieved.[35] From the perspective of merger
control, however, none of this is particularly relevant. A competition authority is not a management consultancy. Its role is to ensure that mergers do not
harm competition and consumers. Inasmuch as many mergers destroy value,
shareholders and policy makers must develop appropriate corporate governance to look after the interests of the firms' owners and employees.

6.3. Merger Appraisal and Interventions

This part reviews EU merger appraisal according the relevant theory of harm.[36]
There are three broad categories. We have a very settled theory of non-coordinated effects with canonical models and clear predictions. This has allowed
the development of quantitative techniques leading up to full simulation
models. The unambiguous price-raising tendencies of horizontal mergers
also focus attention on merger-specific efficiencies. The theory of coordinated
effects is much newer and though it has rapidly achieved a consensus canonical model, there are still major gaps, not least its silence on how a particular
equilibrium is achieved. The theory of non-horizontal effects is very delicate
and often insecure, especially as applied to mergers. It should be treated with
great caution, not least because rival firms have perverse incentives in lobbying the Commission. A fourth section appraises some aspects of the
Commission's practice in merger remedies.

6.3.1. Non-coordinated (unilateral) effects

SIMULATION MODELLING

Quantitative techniques are fundamental to unilateral effects horizontal merger appraisal. The crudest is simple market share analysis. At various times, the
Commission has been accused of using a simple 40 per cent or 50 per cent rule
on joint market share to find dominance.[37] Although it has never been that
simplistic, it can look that way especially when remedies are hastily agreed in
Phase I in mergers with multiple market overlaps.

The Commission typically supplements joint market share with consideration of the market shares of leading rivals. The argument is that a large rival
suggests a greater ability to compete against a newly merged firm with a large
market share. This may be because it has low costs or a particularly attractive
product offer.[38] Beyond this, the Commission's analysis is far less systematic.

A big gap in Commission practice is that there is no systematic analysis of
demand elasticities and cross-elasticities.[39] In even the most basic economic
models, the industry elasticity of demand is important in converting market

share into market power. With differentiated products, the cross-elasticities of demand are also important. Economic theory provides a framework for linking all these concepts, and econometrics provides a way of estimating the elasticities. Merger simulation blends these together in order to ask the central 'what if?' question: what would happen to prices if the merger was allowed unremedied? Notice the several significant steps as one moves from market share analysis to simulation. The process of constructing a simulation model provides a disciplined framework for the case team to implement an effects-based policy. It forces them to think deeply about the theory of harm and so identifies the relevant questions and data requirements. Much can be learned by taking these steps individually—in fact, much more than can be learned from each step than from a simple summary prediction, which is the standard bottom line of a merger simulation. The predictions from such models should be far less important than the process of getting there. In fact, the headline predictions can be an unfortunate distraction.[40]

Alongside this lack of a systematic approach to calibrating demand elasticities and cross-elasticities in general, full simulation models have begun to be used in the quantification of unilateral effects by both the merging parties and the Commission (for example, *Volvo/Scania*: see Ivaldi and Verboven 2005a and 2005b and Hausman and Leonard 2005; also *GE/Instrumentarium*, for a simplified quantification). Such simulations were first used explicitly in a merger decision in *Lagardere/Natexis/VUP*, though the simulations appear to have been parachuted in. The simulation was of only a small part of the concerns of the merger and does not appear to have been decisive.

Nevertheless, this is a mighty bound in economic analysis. Full-blown simulation can be a dangerous black box. As such, it is either believed uncritically or dismissed/ignored as black magic. This should not blind us to the virtues of going through the steps underlying a basic simulation, because this gives exactly the right information on which to base a good decision. If each of these steps can be verified as making sense in relation to the pattern of substitutability and pricing in a market, then it is natural to complete the simulation but still interpret the results with caution, particularly if, as is typical, the predictions are extrapolations into unobserved market structures and not interpolations within past experience.[41] Nevertheless, it is important for an in-house expertise to develop in order to understand what can and what cannot be learned from simulations, and to have the ability to challenge external experts.

A quite separate criticism of full-blown merger simulations is that they are expensive and time-intensive.[42] An alternative way to achieve a simple feel for the harm a merger may cause is to calibrate elasticities using expert opinions or surveys. This makes the methodology practicable and not excessively demanding in its data requirements. It is explicitly approximate and so makes it easier for non-experts to place in context. Davies and Lyons (2007) apply such 'basic simulation' techniques to a number of actual decisions for which the Commission required remedies. We show that for a series of paper and pharmaceuticals mergers, combined market shares range from around 20 per cent to 90 per cent, yet the predicted price rises are only loosely correlated with market share. In fact, we predict a price rise for the merger with the smallest market share and a possible decline for the merger with the largest market share. Clearly, the different elasticity estimates make a very significant difference, as do expected efficiencies. It must be admitted that some of these substitutability effects are implicit in the text of a decision, but the beauty of a basic simulation is that it allows the analyst to combine issues of substitutability and market share in an appropriate (though still approximate) way.

EFFICIENCY DEFENCE

Firms merge for many different reasons, including efficiencies, experimenting with product combinations and connections, family reasons, inappropriate managerial incentives, and hubris. Market power is another motive. Whether it is a deliberate motive or an incidental effect does not matter for merger control, but it is clear that it is not the only motive for merger. And, of all the other motives for merger, efficiency enhancement is economically the best (that is, for social welfare). In fact, in the absence of positive efficiency effects, it is hard to justify the much-less-hostile competition policy towards horizontal mergers in contrast to cartels.

In the early days of the ECMR, there were severe concerns by merging firms that the Commission was hostile to efficiency-enhancing mergers. The logic could be found in the idea of a dominance test—a merger that not only combines market shares but also forms an efficiency base for extending shares might appear to be doubly dominating. This view was given support by some early decisions (starting with *AT&T/NCR*; Neven, Nuttall, and Seabright 1993). This fear of claiming efficiencies has become known as the efficiency *offence*.

The efficiency offence was meant to have been eliminated by the revised ECMR and Horizontal Merger Guidelines which came into force in May 2004. The new position, quite sensibly, is supposed to be that merger-specific efficiencies are a good thing, at least inasmuch as they reduce marginal costs because this tends to reduce price (or at least moderate any tendency for price to rise post-merger), which is beneficial to consumers. To this extent, there is now an official efficiency *defence*.[43]

Another perspective on the evolving change in emphasis is provided by looking at the annual reports of DG Comp. These suggest a slower change. Through the 1990s, the emphasis in the mission statement was on integration: Single European Market then European Economic and Monetary Union (EMU). Only very recently has efficiency become an explicit part of the mission statement:

The mission of the Directorate General for Competition is to enforce the competition rules of the Community Treaties, in order to ensure that competition in the EU market is not distorted *and that markets operate as efficiently as possible*, thereby contributing to the welfare of consumers and to the competitiveness of the European economy.[44]

Is there any evidence that the efficiency offence has been left behind and replaced by an efficiency defence? The words 'efficiency' or 'efficiencies' are not mentioned in DG Comp's Annual Report reflecting on 2004 (that is, the first following the revised ECMR and guidelines); there were plenty of mentions in 2005, but none in the section on mergers; and in 2006 there was a significant section reflecting on the efficiency defence in three mergers.[45] In *Korsnäs/AD Cartonboard*, the Commission accepted there would be efficiencies and that these would be significantly passed through, but only because of a term sheet agreement with a very strong buyer, Tetra-Pak. In *Inco/Falconbridge*, the Commission thought that the efficiencies could have been achieved without the merger and in any case were unlikely to be passed through to customers. In *Metso/Aker Kvaerner*, the Commission did not accept that the efficiencies would outweigh the anticompetitive effects. Overall, while these cases suggest there remains a high hurdle for firms to achieve an efficiency defence, it does seem that the efficiency offence may have been eliminated for horizontal mergers.[46]

There are several reasons why we may not observe firms offering an efficiency defence more often. First, it may be that mergers rarely achieve efficiencies that could not be attained by some other means. There is a paucity of academic evidence on merger-specific efficiencies, not least because it is difficult to measure the efficiency of mergers directly. The nearest proxies that can generally be measured are profitability and shareholder returns. Of course, these could include elements to reflect enhanced market power as well as reduced costs, but since only a very small fraction of all mergers are found to impede competition, we can at least draw some cautious implications about efficiency by studying a large enough sample of mergers. This evidence, summarized below in section 6.4.2, suggests that European mergers raise joint market value by around 1 per cent, which is consistent with rather modest efficiency gains. A further issue is that cost efficiencies only benefit consumers if they are passed through in lower prices. Again, there is remarkably little evidence on firm-specific cost pass-through (as distinct from industry-wide cost pass-through). The US case of *Staples/Office Depot* showed just 15 per cent firm-specific pass-through, thus requiring six or seven times the cost reductions compared with any enhanced-market-power price-raising effect (Ashenfelter, et al. 2006).[47]

Overall, while progress has been made in relation to the treatment of efficiencies in merger control, practice is still evolving and it appears that firms and their advisers remain cautious in deploying an efficiency defence.

6.3.2. *Coordinated effects (collective dominance)*

THE COMMISSION AND THE ECONOMICS

There is a modern consensus on the economics of coordinated effects (see Ivaldi, et al. 2003b, or Motta 2000). This consensus is based on a canonical repeated game model of the sustainability of collusion. This has the following essential elements: (a) sufficient price transparency to identify deviations from coordinated behaviour; (b) lags in detecting and responding to such deviations; (c) the ability to impose a rational 'punishment strategy' on deviants; (d) discounting of future profit streams. The essential model is simple and powerful. It can be adapted to bring out numerous insights relating to, for example, market shares, number of firms, demand growth, product differentiation, cost asymmetries, and multi-market contact. It is a neat model that adds credible punishment to more traditional transparency concerns. In thirty years, it rose from an abstract idea in game theory to the conventional wisdom implicitly accepted by the CFI in *Airtours/First Choice* in 2002.[48] This is quite remarkable for a new idea in economics.[49]

Perhaps inevitably, there have been, and remain, a number of problems with the use of the repeated game model. First, the model needs very careful adaptation to the individual circumstances of a merger, particularly in the presence of capacity constraints. This was not done in *Nestlé/Perrier*, where the importance of the distribution of capacities across firms was not properly appreciated at the remedies' stage (see Compte, Jenny, and Rey 2002). Another example is *UPM/Kymmene/Haindl* where the Commission published fairly implausible concerns over coordination in capacity expansion. However, to its credit, it did eventually listen to well-reasoned economic advice and accepted a carefully articulated theoretical and empirical argument that coordination would not be enhanced by this particular merger (see Kühn and van Reenen in Lyons 2009).

When carefully applied, the repeated game model is an excellent way of summarizing our current understanding of the sustainability of tacit coordination. However, there remains a serious gap in our understanding of how tacit coordination is initially achieved. In particular, the economists' canonical model is the same for explicit as for tacit collusion, yet the Commission regularly discovers that cartels with a dozen firms can be stable while, with the single exception of the overturned Airtours decision, it has never expected tacit coordination between more than two firms. This is quite consistent with the model which admits multiple equilibria (that is, even when coordination is sustainable, it will not necessarily be achieved because more competitive outcomes are always also sustainable). However, it does highlight that the model is silent on the process by which a coordinated price is achieved. The concern is not that the canonical repeated game model is wrong or misleading, but that it tells only half of the story of tacit collusion. It may be that this is an area where sociology or organizational psychology can help.[50] The point is that, following the Airtours decision, the Commission should neither ignore nor over-rely on the 'Airtours conditions'. They are necessary for the stability of coordin-ated effects but not sufficient for coordinated effects to actually emerge.

THE COURT AND THE COMMISSION

In this section, I investigate the influence of the Court on the Commission's attitude to coordinated effects, or collective dominance as this form of behav-iour was known until 2004. In Table 6.2, I identify some landmark Commission and Court decisions. One very imperfect but simple way to 'measure' the importance attributed to coordinated effects by the Commission is to identify the number of merger decisions which non-trivially mention either collective dominance or coordinated effects.[51] This information was collected by some of my colleagues for another purpose (Davies, Olczak, and Coles 2007). In Figure 6.1 I summarize these 'significant mentions' as a percentage of all de-cisions, grouped in relation to those Table 6.2 landmark decisions that indicate significant changes in the direction of confidence of the Commission.[52]

The number of CD/CE 'significant mentions' in each period is not particu-larly large and there were events other than decisions by the Commission and

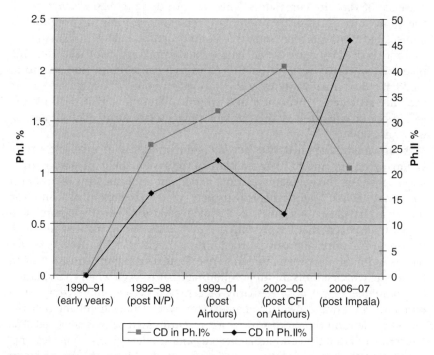

Figure 6.1. Trend incidence of collective dominance analysis

CFI that will have been an influence. Also, the proportion of mergers genuinely causing coordinated effects may differ from year to year and will be endogenously determined by the deterrence effect of Commission decisions. Nevertheless, a rather interesting story of law and economics emerges.

- *Early years of ECMR*: the Commission did not consider collective dominance, but began to develop the idea of a strong second firm as a counterbalance to a merger creating or enhancing a leading market share.
- *Nestlé/Perrier (1992)*: the possibility of collective dominance in merger cases becomes established, and this heralded a period of serious consideration of collective dominance. *Gencor/Lonrho* further raised the profile and even though *Kali & Salz* was reversed in the Court, the principle of collective dominance in mergers was importantly confirmed.
- *Airtours/First Choice (1999)*: emboldened by the earlier decisions and further success with *Gencor/Lonrho*, confidence grew, including that '4 to 3' mergers might create collective dominance. During this period, there were seven cases where both single and collective dominance were found and remedies were required.[53]
- *CFI strikes down A/F decision (2002)*: the shock of the Court reversals, particularly *Airtours*, brought about a period of retrenchment. While it seems that first phase decisions still considered collective dominance, there was much greater caution in Phase II.
- *Impala appeal against Sony/BMG clearance (2005)*: the CFI shocks the Commission in the opposite direction, opening up the possibility of coordinated effects in a '5 to 4' case. Commission responded with enormous caution in Phase II cases to ensure serious consideration of coordinated effects in nearly half of all Phase II cases.

This analysis requires a particularly cautionary note for recent cases.[54] The new substantive test was introduced in May 2004,[55] and this is likely to have changed how the Commission looks at non-leading mergers in the last period. For example, two 2006 decisions were prosecuted as non-coordinated effects while it is likely that the Commission would have felt it had to tackle these as collective dominance cases under the DT. *T-Mobile/tele.ring* (Phase II) would have created the second firm in the market with 30–40 per cent, behind Mobilkom with 35–45 per cent and with ONE as the third player with 15–25 per cent. There was also *Linde/BOC* (Phase I), in which three firms (including BOC) each had market shares of 25–40 per cent and Linde was an aggressive entrant. It is not clear whether it prosecuted them under non-coordinated effects because this is easier to prove (or at least less likely to fall foul of appeal) or whether the reform allowed the Commission to act on the theory of harm it genuinely believed.

Finally, I should be clear that a statistical analysis like that in Figure 6.1. says little about how good individual decisions were. Its purpose is to highlight trends that are missed by delving into individual case detail.

Table 6.2. Some landmark decisions in collective dominance/coordinated effects

Case	Date of decision	Table 2 code	Decision	Essential case notes
Nestlé/Perrier	1992	N/P	By Comm.: allow s.t divestment	'3 to 2' merger in bottled water, with 'remedy' creating more equal market shares
Gencor/Lonrho	1996	G/L	By Comm.: prohibition	Would have been a '3 to 2' merger in two rare minerals; first prohibition on CD grounds
Kali & Salz	1998		By ECJ: quashed on merits	ECJ confirms principle of collective dominance, but not '3 to 2' when merger would create 23% share and the '2' would have a combined share of 60%
Gencor/Lonrho	1999		By CFI: upholds prohibition	Upholds principle of CD due to oligopolistic interdependence —structural links unnecessary
Airtours/First Choice	1999	A/F	By Comm.: prohibition	Would have been a '4 to 3' merger in package holidays
A/F appeal in CFI	2002	A/F CFI	By CFI: referred back to Commission for proper analysis	CFI severely criticises Commission analysis
Impala appeal in CFI over Sony/BMG clearance	2006	Impala CFI	By CFI: referred *clearance* back to Commission for proper analysis	Proposal was a '5 to 4' merger in recorded music. Court criticises Commission's analysis of transparency and retaliation. Commission confirmed (in 2007) its 2004 clearance decision

6.3.3. *Non-horizontal mergers*

The EAGCP (2006)[56] subgroup set out five key principles as to why non-horizontal mergers (NHMs) are different from horizontal mergers (HMs).

1) The competitive impact of NHMs is fundamentally different. HMs directly remove a competitor producing a substitute product. NHMs bring together complementary products and so may reduce competitive distortions (for example, double marginalization). The competitive effects are therefore entirely different.

2) The sources of competitive harm in NHMs often require a change in strategy and the impact on competition is indirect. While price rises can be expected for HMs in the absence of efficiencies or continuing competitive constraints, any adverse effects of NHMs require the introduction of a new strategy (for example, bundling). In order to find such a new strategy anticompetitive, it needs to be profitable and to harm competitors to the extent that their consumers are also hurt.

3) There are many forms of NHM so there is a large variety of ways in which different (competitive and anticompetitive) effects may occur. In fact, the canonical model of NHMs is the 'Chicago' view that there should be a presumption of benefits unless a carefully specified and specific harm can be proved.

4) Market power in an existing market is an essential prerequisite for competitive harm from foreclosure. In its absence, efficiency arguments should be presumed to prevail.

5) There are stronger efficiency arguments for non-horizontal mergers than for horizontal mergers. NHMs are often motivated by the minimization of transaction costs in order to facilitate efficient coordination and specific investment, neither of which is a likely benefit in HMs.

One aspect of the *Tetra Laval/Sidel* appeal was that the CFI required a high standard of proof in cases of conglomerate and vertical effects. There is good economic justification for this in the following sense. Suppose that the standard of proof requires at least a 51 per cent chance/expectation of an impediment to competition in order to intervene (that is, prohibit or require remedy). In a horizontal case, there is essentially a single issue to prove—that rivals would provide a lesser competitive constraint than they do pre-merger. Non-horizontal arguments are more complex and may require two or three essential steps in order to establish an expectation. If each step is essential, it is necessary to be more sure of each in order to reach the 51 per cent overall expectation of harm. For example, with two essential steps, each step would require an average of 72 per cent expectation on average ($0.72 \times 0.72 = 0.51$) and, if three steps are essential, each would need 80 per cent expectation ($0.8 \times 0.8 \times 0.8 = 0.51$).

Although non-horizontal mergers are far less frequently at issue than are horizontal mergers, there have been too many examples where these principles have been ignored. Controversy particularly surrounds so-called 'portfolio effects' which have been claimed to be anticompetitive due to the opportunity a conglomerate merger provides to bundle products purchased by the same consumers to the relative disadvantage of competitors. This is also the area which has caused most transatlantic disputes. The CFI has recently severely criticized two important Commission decisions invoking such effects (*Tetra Laval/Sidel* in 2002 and *GE/Honeywell* in 2005) but there was evidence of problems much earlier (for example, some of the analysis in *Guinness/Grand Met*, 1997).[57]

Worryingly, some of the problems with the analysis of conglomerate mergers seem to be stubbornly ingrained. For example, post the 2002 CFI decisions, merger reforms, and even CET, there is some poor reasoning in *Lagardere/Natexis/VUP* (Jan. 2004). This merger was allowed subject to remedies and there were probably sufficient horizontal issues to justify this. However, my concern is that efficiencies related to vertical and conglomerate aspects of the merger were discussed as highly problematic because they would harm competitors. These efficiencies include: efficient marketing and distribution; ease of moving from hardback to 'pocket book' format; higher advances to authors; and financial resources to allow long-term policies. Merger policy should not act against a publishing merger because the merged firm might be able to pay its authors more! The efficiency offence is as important to eliminate for non-horizontal as for horizontal mergers.

More careful analysis is essential, and the best way to enhance the accuracy and predictability of decisions is to provide clear guidelines. These cannot be as precise as for horizontal mergers because of the subtlety with which anticompetitive effects might manifest themselves. Nevertheless, case handlers, firms, and their advisers all need to know the parameters within which they operate. In view of the misconceptions, good guidelines are more important here than anywhere else. Guidelines for vertical and conglomerate mergers were promised 'during the course of 2004' (33rd Annual Report on Competition Policy 2003, #223) but were held up first by the awaited appeal over *GE/Honeywell* (2005) and then by the abuse of dominance appeal by *Microsoft* (2007). They were finally agreed in late 2007.

There is no space for specific comment on the guidelines, but the EAGCP principles seem to have been appreciated and some appropriate procedures are set out. For example, in relation to foreclosure issues created by a merger, the Commission will establish: first, the enhanced ability to foreclose (that is, to reduce a rival's profits); second, the incentive to do so (that is, consequently to enhance the merged firm's profits); and third, whether a foreclosure strategy would have an anticompetitive effect downstream 'in ways that cause harm to consumers' (#15) (that is, to raise price or otherwise harm consumers).[58] This provides a strong structure for the analysis of non-horizontal mergers.

6.3.4. *Merger interventions and remedies*

INTERVENTION TRENDS

The top line in Figure 6.2 shows the trend in mergers decided by the Commission (right-hand scale). In order to avoid double counting, this trend is based on Phase I decisions. It shows the great merger boom at the turn of the century, with the number of mergers qualifying for scrutiny doubling between 1997 and 2000, followed by a dip then record numbers of qualifying mergers in 2006 and again in 2007. All other trends are measured on the left-hand scale. Four levels of intervention are identified: prohibitions are the most extreme but also least frequent; withdrawals during Phase II are often due to the parties deciding that their merger proposal was likely to be prohibited; more frequently, undertakings may be agreed short of prohibition (for example, divestitures) in order to eliminate the competitive harm in a proposed merger; and these undertakings, which are known as merger remedies, may be agreed early (that is, in Phase I) or late (that is, in Phase II).

In order to clarify the trends, Figure 6.3 expresses interventions relative to merger decisions and groups them into three periods. The first, 1990–7, can be thought of as a period of settling into the new regulation during a period with a steadily growing number of qualifying mergers, and finished with the first revision of the ECMR in 1997, which included a significant procedural change

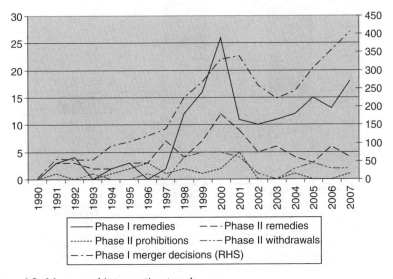

Figure 6.2. Merger and intervention trends

affecting Phase I remedies. The next four years, 1998–2001, was a period of acceleration in mergers combined with growing confidence of the MTF. Thirdly, the most recent six-year period began with the Court reverses and Monti reforms.

Figure 6.3 includes two extra dimensions of intervention in addition to the four in the previous figure. First, a clearance in Phase II can be thought of as an intervention in that it imposes costs on a merger that might potentially have been cleared in Phase I. Second, some Phase I withdrawals may be due to the parties anticipating that their merger proposal would be referred to Phase II.[59] These 'softer' categories of intervention are separated by a solid line in the figure. In general, Figure 6.3 arranges interventions with the strongest (that is, prohibitions) at the bottom and the weakest at the top of each column.

Prohibitions are on trend decline. They peaked with five prohibitions in 2001 (that is, one-quarter of all prohibitions in just one year), three of which were subject to major appeals in the Court,[60] since when there has been just two prohibitions.[61] However, adding withdrawals in Phase II and remedy decisions changes the picture. The intervention rate rose from 7.5 per cent in the first period, to 10.8 per cent during the confident turn-of-the-century period, before falling to 6.4 per cent. Adopting the broader concept of intervention (that is, including Phase II clearances and Phase I withdrawals) presents a similar trend with the exception that Phase I withdrawals have been

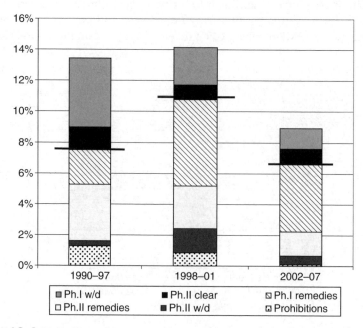

Figure 6.3. Intervention rate

declining steadily over the years. The high rate of Phase I withdrawals in the first period may have been a learning effect on the part of firms who did not properly appreciate the implications of the ECMR in its early years. Finally, two other trends are not so readily discerned from the figure: the Phase II referral rate has halved from 7 per cent to 6 per cent to 3.5 per cent over the three periods; and the ratio of remedies to prohibitions has grown very rapidly from 5 to 10 to 53.[62]

Overall, there appear to be three overlaying trends, the first two being monotonic over time and the third not so. First, more is being agreed in Phase I and less referred to Phase II. Second, more mergers are being remedied as opposed to prohibited. Third, the peak of intervention in 1998–2001 has seen a very substantial reversal in recent years.

EFFICACY OF REMEDIES

It is clearly important that agreed remedies should be effective in restoring competition that would otherwise be impeded by a merger. In 2005, DG Comp completed its own in-house study of past merger remedies. The study analysed forty decisions containing ninety-six different remedies, adopted by the Commission between 1996 and 2000. These cases were sampled to pick up on a range of alternative remedies and different industrial sectors, as well as Phase I and Phase II agreements. The study used interviews with the parties selling and purchasing divested assets and with trustees. They carried out a total of 145 full interviews.

In terms of the design and implementation of divestitures, the most frequent problem was insufficient scope of assets transferred such that the business could not stand alone from its previous parents. This afflicted 80 per cent of the divestitures and one-third of the problems remained unresolved after three to five years. Carve-out of assets from a previously integrated business was mentioned as a problem about half as much. Transfer issues and inadequate interim preservation of assets pending transfer were the next most frequent problems, together afflicting up to two-thirds of divestitures though most such problems were resolved in three to five years. The unavailability of a suitable purchaser was problematic in around one in five cases. Moving away from divestitures, there was limited evidence on access and other non-divestment remedies. The sample was small, but three out of four infrastructure remedies failed due to the market developing very differently from what had been anticipated. Technology access agreements were often flawed due to the licensor being able to limit transfer of essential support technology. Overall, the fundamental difficulty of setting suitable access terms was the single most important element impeding access as an effective remedy.

Combining the above findings with a limited number of market indicators such as market share, the study was able to provide a basic assessment of the effectiveness of remedies. On the simple criterion of whether divested assets were still in business three to five years later, the DG Comp study found that 6 per cent were not (7 per cent of which had been transferred to new ownership).[63] Only 18 per cent of divested businesses increased market share, with one-third remaining the same. Compared with the market share performance of assets retained by the merging parties, only 23 per cent of divestitures did better, with 57 per cent doing worse. The Commission's own assessment was that, 57 per cent of divestitures were considered effective, 24 per cent partially effective, 7 per cent ineffective, and 12 per cent unclear. Access remedies were least effective.

In Davies and Lyons (2007), we were able to analyse the competitive consequences of remedies applied to some mergers in more depth. Our research drew on both detailed interviews from the DG Comp study and our own modelling of the remedied markets. Most of the mergers we looked at were between firms with multiple market overlaps, and nearly all of the remedies involved what we call 'prohibition within the market'. In other words, once a trigger threshold of impediment to competition is assessed to have been reached, one or other of the merging parties' businesses was required to be divested in its entirety. One of our key findings was that the restoration of market structure does not necessarily mean the restoration of competition. While the Commission took care to ensure that buyers were suitably established firms, it did not necessarily take other important issues into account— for example, the incentives to market and develop products when brand ownership is split across geographic markets due to selective divestiture.

At the time of writing, the Commission was consulting on draft revised remedy guidelines. These generally improve remedy practice. However, there are four issues on which the Notice could be improved. The first two relate to remedy selection and the second two to implementation.

First, licensing agreements in remedies have used terms like 'adequate compensation' and 'normal and non-discriminatory commercial conditions'. These terms are open to abuse leading to ineffective remedies. Much clearer guidance is necessary to determine commercial terms and licence duration such that competition will be fully restored.

Secondly, our research revealed a significant minority of cases where there is a national geographic market and where the anticompetitive overlap is very small. In such cases, some form of price and production commitment would almost certainly have been the better option to divestiture. This seems to be particularly the case where the merger has numerous product and geographic markets and the parties may be so keen to get the main part of the merger approved that they propose a divestiture when that is not in their customers' best interests (for example, there is no buyer with a serious interest in a small product, even though they can be tempted by an appropriately low purchase price). We suggest the Commission should be much more willing to accept behavioural guarantees when: the market is very small; there is a significant risk that potential purchasers of a divestiture will not invest in the product; and where the identity of customers makes it sufficiently easy for them to monitor undertakings.

Thirdly, at the time of negotiations between the merging parties and a potential purchaser of divested assets, the seller and buyer will agree a deal that maximizes their joint profits. The distribution of such profits will be reflected in the purchase price. Joint profits will normally be maximized by a purchaser who does not intend to use the assets to compete directly with the merging parties. There is, therefore, a serious danger that a seller and purchaser collude to avoid the restoration of competition to the pre-merger level (Farrell 2003). In this context, we welcome the proposal that the Commission proposes to discuss business plans with potential purchasers. However, the Commission should take steps to ensure that these plans are credible and that they do restore competition.

Fourthly, two weaknesses in relation to trustees are not sufficiently addressed in the new draft. First, the merging firms both propose the trustee and determine the mandate, albeit with the approval of the Commission. My concern is not one of explicit bias, but of the failure of the Commission to be the first to instruct the trustee on the reason for the divestiture. In the past, many have not been aware of the competition concerns, let alone the requirements necessary to restore competition. Indeed, this is typically not their expertise. Second, trustees are paid by the merging parties. Combined with being appointed and instructed by them, this sets in stream a natural loyalty to the merging firms and to their shareholders. This holds even when the trustee is an experienced auditor. Therefore, in addition to being the first to instruct a new trustee, it would be better if the Commission or some third party could pay them and claim back costs from the firms.

6.4. Merger Policy Evaluation

How efficient is the Commission in reaching merger decisions? Recent 'peer review' type league tables place it close to the best in the world.[64] Although little reliance can be put on such beauty shows, it does establish that the Commission is doing a reasonably good job by international standards. This is all the more impressive in that it is not particularly generously resourced. Nevertheless, as I have already argued, it could do significantly better.

In the following section, I propose a very simple summary measure of the efficiency of EC merger control based on elementary bargaining theory. In a second section, I review some recent statistical evaluations based on shareholder value and changes in response to Commission decisions.

6.4.1. *A bargaining failure approach to inefficient merger control*

The first principle of bargaining theory is that, in the absence of asymmetric information, if there is a mutually beneficial deal to be done, it will be agreed.[65] The details of who gets what depends on bargaining power, particularly relative costs of delay and outside options. In the presence of asymmetric information, mistakes will be made in that negotiations break down but this should be infrequent if there is an effective information-gathering process. The second principle is that the deal should be reached very quickly. Delay imposes a deadweight loss during which the beneficial agreement is not implemented, in addition to which there are direct compliance and investigation costs of Phase II.[66]

In the context of merger appraisal, bargaining theory suggests that an efficient system should be able to

- reach a deal between the agency and the merging parties; and
- reach it reasonably quickly (that is, more often in Phase I than in Phase II).

Breakdown in negotiations can be manifested in either a prohibition or the parties walking away. A prohibition arises either if the Commission is unduly harsh, or if the merging parties made a mistake in proposing an irredeemably uncompetitive merger or in offering an insufficient remedy for a potentially beneficial merger. Either way, all prohibitions are mistakes by one side or the other, even though it is not possible to attribute blame for such mistakes. Unilateral withdrawals by the merger parties are a little more complex. In particular, withdrawal may be due to outside reasons like a change in market conditions. Nevertheless, some will be due to the expectation, developed during the investigation, that the agency will not agree with what the merger parties believe would be an acceptable deal.

Figure 6.4 shows the trend in merger decisions against failures to agree, along with remedy agreements for context. To avoid double counting of Phase II, the baseline trend is again represented by the number of Phase I decisions. First look at the total number of failures to agree defined as prohibitions plus withdrawals in either phase (that is, the columns below the bar). This shows a trend improvement in reaching agreement, suggesting an increasing efficiency of communications between merging firms and the Commission. Reasons for this include experience, more written guidance, a more economic approach, and the impact of the Courts. In relation to the last of these it certainly seems significant that there was a zero failure to agree in 2003 (that is, in the year that followed the three great reverses to the Commission in 2002!). Looking at the components of the failures to agree, Phase I withdrawals are always the largest contributor, but they are also probably the most influenced by external factors. More interesting is that prohibitions generally outweighed Phase II withdrawals until 1997, since when the reverse has been true.[67]

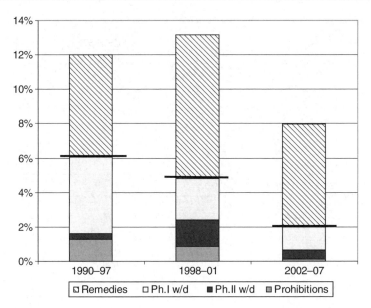

Figure 6.4. Failure to agree

The main measurable dimension of speedy agreement is remedies agreed in Phase I as compared with Phase II. This trend is shown in Figure 6.5. There is a significant legal reason for the distinct change in the pattern from 1998 because the 1997 amendment to the ECMR clarified the legal position of remedies agreed in Phase I.[68] In the former period, more remedy agreements were achieved in Phase II than in Phase I, and only 38 per cent were not subject to these costly delays. In contrast, the last decade has seen an improved efficiency such that 69 per cent are agreed in Phase I (1998–2006). Needless to say, the efficiency interpretation of this crude analysis must be taken with a very large health warning.[69] Apart from the revision to the ECMR, it is quite possible that more mistakes are made in Phase I remedies than in Phase II. Nevertheless, it does seem that negotiating efficiency has improved. It takes both sides to reach agreement, so the credit for this must be shared between the merging firms (or their advisers) and the Commission.

Putting together the reducing failure-to-agree rate and the early-agreement rate, we can reconsider the positive deterrence effect of the ECMR—the hidden benefits of merger regulation in deterring harmful mergers from being proposed in the first place. If firms completely ignored the ECMR when making merger proposals, we would expect a large number of anticompetitive mergers to be proposed, with a consequently large number of prohibitions. We do not observe this, so the true benefits of the ECMR are grossly underestimated by

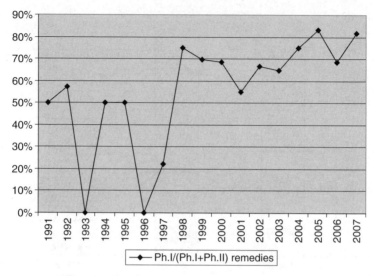

Figure 6.5. Speed of agreement

looking only at actual mergers. Firms act with foresight and take account of the prospect of the merger control when making proposals.

Overall, this very simple bargaining approach is consistent with a more positive deterrence effect in the last decade, but little continuing improvement. This may be because some sort of optimum has been reached, or it may be that the Monti reforms will take a little longer to be absorbed into rational expectations.

6.4.2. Other statistical evaluation approaches

The event study framework, discussed in section 6.2.3 above, can be developed to estimate the effectiveness of competition policy. Duso, Neven, and Röller 2007 and Neven and Röller 2002 use the Eckbo 1983 methodology which focuses on the share price response of competitor firms. The argument is that if they can expect to benefit from a reduction of competition in the market, then their valuation will rise; but if the merger is expected to create a fierce or efficient new competitor, then their valuation will fall. For horizontal mergers, the effect on rivals is, in theory, a sharp indicator of whether a competition agency should intervene in a merger or not.[70] In practice, stock-market valuations are likely to be very imprecise as an indicator of competitive effects. Even professional investors may need time to identify the extent of overlap markets and evaluate complex competitive impacts. Effects will also be reduced to the extent that they build the anticipated regulatory response into their valuations.[71] The authors look at all Phase II mergers up to 2001 and a randomly matched sample of Phase I cases. Competitors were identified from the decisions. Weighted average CAR gains for the merging parties are again around 1 per cent and they find just over half of mergers are pro-competitive judged by competitor impact. They found that four out of fourteen prohibitions in their sample were wrong (type 1 error) judged by competitor impact (these include the appealed *Airtours/First Choice*, *Tetra Laval/Sidel*, and *GE/ Honeywell*). The Commission also made type 2 errors by clearing one-quarter of anticompetitive mergers without remedy. Thus, there was a roughly equal balance of type 1 and type 2 errors. They also found no United States effect but weak evidence for more excessive intervention on firms from small countries and insufficient intervention for national and EU markets (compared with a global relevant market). However, their strongest result was that many more errors are made in Phase I decisions. They conclude: 'The probability of waving an anticompetitive merger through [in phase I] is some 75 per cent higher, which is a high price to pay. This suggests that allocating more time and resources to phase I, as well as opening phase II more frequently, may reduce type II errors considerably.'[72] A similar caution against Phase I agreements in complex mergers can also be found in the pharmaceuticals case studies in Davies and Lyons (2007).

Aktas, de Bodt, and Roll (2007) estimate a 'probability of intervention' equation to supplement their stockmarket impact analysis. Based on a sample of EU mergers 1990–2000 they find that foreign acquirers are subject to more frequent 'regulatory intervention' than domestic acquirers, but only when local EU competitors are 'being harmed'. They define regulatory intervention as either Phase I remedies or referral to Phase II, so clearance in Phase II is included as an intervention. 'Being harmed' means a decline in CARs around the merger event window. They conclude that the Commission has been operating a protectionist policy, intervening disproportionately when EU firms expect to lose out to a more efficient competitor. There are some substantial problems with this study, not least in the very broad interpretation of the competitor set (not taken from decisions) and in the absence of variables to reflect the degree of overlap in competition-relevant markets or market shares. Nevertheless, it provides food for thought.[73] Note that both the Duso, Neven, and Röller (2007) and Aktas, de Bodt, and Roll (2007) studies were based on pre-2002 mergers and so exclude mergers since the Monti reforms.

Other econometric studies have used information from within published decisions to investigate the market structural determinants of an intervention. Without the supplement of stockmarket valuations, such studies can only investigate the consistency of decisions—they have no independent estimate of whether decisions are right. Lindsay, Lecchi, and Williams (2003) examine 245 mergers decided 2000–2 and find, not surprisingly, that high market shares and barriers to entry are the main determinants of an adverse decision.[74] They also look for nationality effects, but find neither US nor Nordic ownership mattered. Bergman, Jakobsson, and Razo (2005) separate the decision to go to Phase II from the conditional decision to prohibit, given Phase II. Market share is important for both, particularly for the Phase II decision. The only other significant variable for prohibition is if the firm was a world leader. Entry barriers and fears of coordination are significant for Phase II referral. No effect was found to do with individual commissioners or firms from large EU Member States, but US firms were less likely to be referred to Phase II.

Davies, Olczak, and Coles (2007) focus on collective dominance cases prior to 2004. They develop an econometric model of Commission decisions to find that, although the combined market share of the largest two firms has a similar quantitative effect on an adverse finding, size symmetry (measured by the ratio of the share of the second firm to that of the largest) has a negative effect on a finding of single dominance but a positive effect on a finding of collective dominance. These effects are statistically highly significant which suggests that the Commission is at least selecting between unilateral or coordinated effects in more or less appropriate configurations of market shares.

6.5. Conclusions

Actual decisions are only the tip of the iceberg in terms of the impact of merger control, because these decisions along with guidelines and policy pronouncements influence the type of mergers that firms propose. Given the costs of delay and compliance, firms have a considerable incentive to propose mergers that will be acceptable. This makes it crucial to publish the right argument behind a decision. If this guidance is sufficiently clear and if firms rationally anticipate merger control, they will only propose acceptable or marginally harmful mergers—this is why Phase II merger control is, or should be, very difficult to call. In this sense, the analysis is more important than the decision itself.

The right analysis is based on the expected economic effects of a proposed merger. Competition economics is an evolving discipline and has made major progress in the second half of the fifty years under review. Although many ideas are now well established, this does mean that some of the economics is relatively new and it is not surprising that some earlier decisions were not as good as they might have been.

When the ECMR was introduced in 1989, the Commission (DG IV) had a reputation for slow decision-making. The new MTF was legally required to act speedily and it achieved this. The evidence suggests it grew a little careless during the turn-of-the century merger boom and this reinforced the Monti reform package. Institutional reforms within the Commission (for example, 'fresh pair of eyes', chief economist's team) have improved merger control and the Court has, on the whole, been a positive influence. Reform of the ECMR and the provision of guidelines have also been important and certainly positive.

Turning to the substantive analysis used by the Commission, the analysis of non-coordinated effects is becoming more receptive to efficiencies, but there is still work to be done in implementing the publicly stated policy. Also, the Commission has yet to clarify its attitude to highly sophisticated economic analysis, in particular to merger simulation. Simulation has both benefits and limitations and it should proceed cautiously. It needs to avoid relying on a 'black box' grinding out price predictions, but it should utilize the steps underlying simulation (for example, estimation of cross-elasticities) to gain a more accurate understanding of the market.

The Commission has had an interesting relationship with the Court in relation to coordinated effects, and there is evidence that it may have swung too far in response to each new decision. Nevertheless, the revised substantive test and recent Airtours decision should encourage it to analyse mergers in the way it genuinely believes they may cause harm. Bearing in mind the 'iceberg effect' of decisions on merger proposals, it is more important to make the right argument than to live in fear of being overturned on appeal.

Commission practice on non-horizontal merger appraisal has been the weakest part of its analysis. This has been recognized by the Court, but there continue to be worrying signs in some recent decisions. The new guidelines are long overdue and urgently needed.

The efficacy of merger remedies has received considerable attention recently, and this research will no doubt improve future practice. Divestitures have too often been insufficient to establish a competitive, as distinct from simply viable, business, and licensing remedies are often rendered ineffective because insufficient attention is paid to specifying the terms of a licence. Furthermore, the Commission should not be shy of simple behavioural remedies in cases where small, typically national, markets are involved. These could save transaction and incentive costs associated with small divestments while ensuring a better outcome for consumers. More generally, the Commission should become more proactive with divestiture trustees and buyers to ensure there is no collusion or neglect in running down the assets.

Finally, we considered some wider evaluations of EC merger policy. Clear anticipation of merger control should lead to fewer anticompetitive mergers being proposed (so fewer prohibitions) and quicker agreement of remedies. The early years of the ECMR are consistent with a period of learning which mergers are, and which are not, acceptable. This process almost certainly applied to both the Commission and merging firms. Separate event study evidence is consistent with both type 1 and type 2 decision errors being made by the Commission. Such studies and other case study evidence also caution against the presumption that Phase I remedies are necessarily more efficient than agreements in Phase II as they suggest that more mistakes are made in the former.

Overall, the Commission's merger regime is maturing fairly well. It has shown itself to be capable of self-criticism and able to reform. It has established a good reputation, recovered from a difficult time with the Court in 2002, and is well positioned to improve further—but there is still work to be done and no room for complacency.

Notes

[1] An earlier version of this chapter was prepared for the IESE conference 'Fifty Years of the Treaty: Assessment and Perspectives of Competition Policy in Europe', held in Barcelona, 19–20 Nov. 2007. The support of the Economic and Social Research Council is gratefully acknowledged. Many thanks also for helpful comments from Michael Harker, Kai-Uwe Kuhn, Carles Esteva-Mosso, and Xavier Vives, none of whom is responsible for the views expressed in this chapter.

[2] If we include Phase II withdrawals, the intervention rate is 8.8 per cent. See sect. 6.4.1 for further discussion of withdrawals.

[3] Note that the UK system does not require notification and it is possible that this may affect the comparability of these figures.

[4] The report also suggests a number of other reasons why there will be a greater 'below the water' effect than these figures suggest. It also provides evidence that the negative deterrence (or 'business chilling') effect is limited to small beneficial mergers withdrawing rather than facing the costs of a Phase II investigation by the Competition Commission.

[5] Although the economic approach is sometimes thought to reduce the legal certainty obtained by applying rigid rules, the latter certainty would come at the expense of sensible decisions. Nevertheless, there is a role for 'safe harbours' as a way of limiting the fear of intervention when market shares are sufficiently small.

[6] Explicit merger control in the competence of the European Commission was only introduced in 1989 so the main focus of the chapter is on the period since then. The starting date in the title is, therefore, a little misleading because most of the chapter is about only the last third of the period.

[7] See Gerber (1998).

[8] It is worth noting that Luce and Raiffa's classic early textbook on game theory was published in 1957, but this approach was still far removed from practical competition policy. It is only with hindsight that we can note its importance.

[9] Of course, this is a somewhat heroic generalization. Other lines of thought, including transaction cost economics and the emerging field of behavioural IO, are important influences, and there are a few national differences, but these do not detract from the general conclusion that recent generations of industrial economists draw on essentially the same toolkit for their understanding of competition issues.

[10] The same is probably true of the law and legal precedent.

[11] Kohl was the new boy keen to build a reputation by acting on the European stage, Mitterrand was looking for something to distract attention from a doomed domestic macroeconomic policy that had been humiliated by international financial markets, and Thatcher had finally found something European she could support after years of obstructionism.

[12] Of course, there were many other influences behind this merger wave, which was also happening in the USA. See sect. 6.2.3 below.

[13] Political influence is thus more subtle than in the US Department of Justice and FTC which have political appointees.

[14] Even under the expedited procedure, the CFI judgments have taken twelve months beyond the initial Commission Decisions, which themselves were five to six months after original notification of the merger proposals. Few merger proposals are resurrectable after such a period. In the absence of the expedited procedure, the appeal takes much longer. For example, *Airtours/First Choice* took just under three years from Commission decision to CFI judgment; and from notification of merger to CFI judgment took nearly five years in *GE/Honeywell*.

[15] In the United States, the Department of Justice and Federal Trade Commission (whichever is given responsibility for a particular merger) combine stages 1 and 2 (i.e. second request), before presenting their case to the court for a preliminary injunction (i.e. decision). In practice, most cases are settled before going to court, but the immediacy of the courts has a major impact and discipline.

[16] Notwithstanding this focus on judicial review, the CFI has shown itself willing to engage in some serious economics, as in *Airtours/First Choice*.

[17] For example, the Commission's protracted dispute with Spain since 2005 over *Gas Natural/Endesa* and *EON/Endesa*.

[18] The Clayton Act prohibits any acquisition, the effect of which 'may be substantially to lessen competition, or to tend to create a monopoly' (Clayton Act #7, 1914).

[19] Some examples of apparently rigid market share rules used by the Commission in relation to pharmaceuticals mergers are given in Davies and Lyons (2007), for example, in ch. 8.

[20] Economic advice accounted for some 15 per cent of merger-control-related fees—similar to the split in the USA, but still leaving lawyers with the lion's share!

[21] *Schneider/Legrand* and *Tetra Laval/Sidel* both came through the new expedited procedure.

[22] See Garces, Neven, and Seabright (2009) for a discussion of this case.

[23] DG Comp immediately appealed to the European Court of Justice fearing some of these issues could undermine merger control. The appeal was rejected in Feb. 2005.

[24] See Vives and Staffiero (2009) for a discussion of this case.

[25] For completeness, and to anticipate that not everything has been solved by the reforms about to be discussed, in 2006 a third-party appeal over a 2004 clearance was upheld (i.e. referred back to DG Comp, who did more analysis and cleared it again in 2007). This was *Impala over Sony/BMG*: inadequate assessment of potential coordinated effects.

[26] It began in 2003 with ten PhD-level economists and in 2007 planned to grow towards twenty members. See Röller and Buigues (2005) for more detail on the CCE and CET.

[27] I put 'new' in inverted commas because the essential change was to reverse the ordering of a sentence. The 2004 revision of Article 2.3 of the ECMR reads in full:

'A concentration which would significantly impede effective competition, in the common market or in a substantial part of it, in particular as a result of the creation or strengthening of a dominant position, shall be declared incompatible with the common market.' This compares with the 1989 original: 'A concentration which creates or strengthens a dominant position as a result of which effective competition would be significantly impeded in the common market or in a substantial part of it shall be declared incompatible with the common market.' Nevertheless, this remains an important signal of priorities, not least in the common shorthand of SIEC compared with DT.

[28] Kuhn (2002) disagrees that a revised substantive test for the ECMR was necessary.

[29] The following paragraphs are based on a submission I made in response to the public consultation on the 2001 Green Paper and in which I argued that a SIEC test should be adopted.

[30] Recital 25 of the revised ECMR clarifies that filling this gap is an aim of the new test.

[31] An official data series on 'Acquisitions and Mergers of Industrial and Commercial Companies' started in 1967. Unlike the later merger waves, many of the UK mergers at this time were driven by diversification.

[32] As Symeonidis (2000) shows, the consequent increase in competition was slowly eroded by an increase in concentration over the next twenty years. Other studies (e.g. Prais 1981 and Hannah and Kay 1981) attribute a disputed proportion of the increase in concentration at that time to mergers.

[33] See also Ilzkovitz and Meiklejohn (2006: ch. 1) and Martynova and Renneboog (2008a; 2008b).

[34] Another feature of international mergers is that they can bring new ideas in corporate governance. See, for example, Bris, Brisley, and Cabolis (2008), Martynova and Renneboog (2008b), and Burkhart and Berglof (2003).

[35] In Lyons (2001) I argue that this pattern of findings is consistent with mergers being a response to anticipated adverse market conditions and does not necessarily mean that they are 'unsuccessful'.

[36] Lyons (2009) includes six excellent case studies of mergers and merger appraisal in Europe.

[37] The Commission does not adjust market shares for an expected contraction of output post merger, which is a necessary condition for harm to consumers (Farrell and Shapiro 1990). The 50 per cent figure is consistent with the ECJ in an Article 82 case, *Akzo 1993*, where it is taken to establish dominance in the absence of exceptional circumstances. Other Article 82 appeal cases accept a share closer to 40 per cent and occasionally lower. Merger findings of dominance have tended to use similar thresholds (see Whish 2003: chs. 5 and 21).

[38] However, in the early years of the ECMR, the Commission made the mistake of forgetting that the same benefits of a strong rival are not relevant if coordinated effects are at issue—in fact, quite the opposite (e.g. Nestlé/Perrier).

[39] Some implicit discussion of these concepts is often found under 'market definition'. A closely related concept to elasticity and cross-elasticity is the diversion ratio, which is often a more intuitive way of getting at the same thing.

[40] See the case studies of merger simulations by Slade and by Gollier and Ivaldi in Lyons (2009).

[41] Slade (in Lyons 2009) provides an incisive critique of the sensitivity of simulations to often arbitrary technical assumptions.

[42] Though sophisticated simulations can sometimes be achieved within the constraints of a merger inquiry (e.g. Ivaldi in Lyons 2009).

[43] I have no space to go into the important issue of whether this defence should be on the basis of a consumer welfare standard, as implied here, or a total welfare standard, such that even if consumers lose out a little this can be more than compensated for by enhanced profits (i.e. the famous 'Williamson trade-off'). I favour the consumer welfare standard for mergers because this is more likely to encourage positive deterrence and the self-selection of beneficial mergers by firms (see Lyons 2002; Farrell and Katz 2007). Fixed-cost savings would become important under a total welfare standard.

[44] DG Comp 2007 Annual Management Plan: 4 (emphasis added). The italicized text on efficiency was first added only in 2006.

[45] The 2007 report was not available at the time of writing.

[46] Sadly, the same may not yet be true of non-horizontal mergers. See below.

[47] Stennek and Verboven provide another example in Ilzkovitz and Meiklejohn (2006), but they rather implausibly estimate greater than 100 per cent pass-through of costs, which is hardly likely for cost reductions. Another possibility is that firms are still scared to claim efficiencies. Unpublished research currently under way at the CCP by Peter Ormosi looks at what merging firms report to their shareholders as compared with what is said about merger-specific efficiencies in a merger decision. He finds that firms report much more positive cost savings in annual reports than is reported in decisions. While there may be some reporting bias if evidence is presented by firms but not reported in a Commission decision, he argues that firms still prefer to offer remedies in Phase I rather than risk a costly Phase II investigation in the hope of a successful efficiency defence.

[48] The germ of the idea can be traced back to Luce and Raiffa (1957) but was applied seriously to the abstract theory of tacit collusion only in the 1970s (starting with Friedman 1971, and culminating in Abreu's work in the mid-1980s). The model is not mentioned in sixty-five pages devoted to coordination in Scherer (1970). Important applied theoretical and econometric work during the 1980s (Rotemberg and Saloner; Green and Porter; Porter; Slade) soon established its value, and it is central to Tirole's (1988) treatment of tacit collusion, and remains so in Motta (2005).

[49] New ideas need academic testing both for theoretical robustness and on real world data. Once properly understood, the knowledge must be transferred to practitioners (through recruitment of recent graduates who have learnt the new ideas, commissioning of review papers, and conferences) who must feel confident enough to apply the knowledge. Finally, the judges must find the ideas sufficiently intuitive and compelling to be accepted by the court.

[50] See Scott Morton (1997) for an example of sociological influence on cartels.

[51] Or joint dominance or oligopolistic dominance or tacit collusion.

[52] Apart from the first period (1990–1), there were between 762 and 1,031 Phase I and between 24 and 58 Phase II decisions in each period in Fig. 6.1.

[53] Garces, Neven, and Seabright (2009) provide a good discussion of the importance of this case for the analysis of collective dominance/coordinated effects.

[54] In fact, most of the jump was in 2006, where two-thirds of Phase II cases seriously considered CE. This had dropped back to one quarter in 2007. However, there were only

a small number of decisions in each of these years (twelve each). There is apparently a surprising drop in Phase I analysis, but this may be due to a change in the method used for Phase I cases (data since 2004 is subject to revision).

[55] Hence, the change of terminology from CD to CE.

[56] The Economic Advisory Group on Competition Policy provides independent academic advice to the European Commission. The author was one of the subgroup members drafting this advice.

[57] See the chapters by Stenbacka and Vives and Staffiero in Lyons (2009) for critiques of cases involving vertical and conglomerate effects.

[58] It is positive to observe that the Commission's success in the Microsoft appeal in relation to exclusionary effects has not diluted the draft guidelines.

[59] And so incur compliance costs and the risk of prohibition or deal-breaking remedy requirements. Other reasons for withdrawal include changes in stock market conditions and adverse responses by shareholders.

[60] *Tetra Laval/Sidel*, *Schneider/Legrand*, and *GE/Honeywell*.

[61] ENI/EDP/GDP, which would have brought together the very dominant gas and electricity suppliers in Portugal. There is also the 2007 prohibition of Ryanair/Aer Lingus.

[62] There is no obvious change in the nature of proposed mergers that would explain these trends.

[63] On this minimal criterion, European merger remedies appear to have been more successful than in the USA, where an earlier FTC study suggested a much smaller survival rate. However, the comparison is unfair because Europe was able to learn from the US experience. It is also the case that exit generally is slower in Europe than in the USA.

[64] Every three or four years, the UK government conducts an independent peer review of national and international authorities, mainly by lawyers but also consulting competition economists and firms. For the merger regime in 2007, the EC ranked fourth behind the USA, UK, and Germany. Relative to the USA, it scored 94 per cent in 2001, falling to 86 per cent in 2003/4, before recovering to 91 per cent in 2007. *Global Competition Review* conducts an annual survey of competition lawyers and in their mergers survey DG Comp has risen to joint first place alongside the FTC and UK Competition Commission.

[65] With symmetric ignorance, both parties may wish to gather information so that they can be more sure that a mutually beneficial deal exists.

[66] A study of fifty companies involved in over 500 mergers worldwide, conducted by PricewaterhouseCoopers (PwC) and jointly commissioned by the International Bar Association and American Bar Association, found a typical cost for the firms of €3.3 million for a cross-border merger even when scrutinized by a single authority.

[67] The one exception in the last decade was in 2001 when an exceptional five mergers were prohibited (three of which were significantly reversed in the CFI).

[68] See revision to Art. 6(1) in Council Regulation (EC) No 1310/97 of 30 June 1997 amending Regulation (EEC) No 4064/89 on the control of concentrations between undertakings (OJ L 180, 9.7.1997: 1–6). A change in the 2004 revisions to the ECMR may also have had some effect because it no longer requires firms to notify one week after the conclusion of the deal. However, the earlier rule was not often respected and the suspension provides sufficient incentives to ensure that firms normally notify without excessive delays. I am grateful for Carles Esteva-Mosso's opinion that this change has not had a significant impact in remedy negotiation. First, it is uncommon that companies

are ready to start negotiating remedies in pre-notification. Second, even before the 2004 modification, the Commission was happy to discuss remedies in pre-notification (e.g. *Unilever/Bestfoods*). As ever, they engage in discussions without prejudice of the results of Phase I investigation. If new concerns arise during the investigation or during 'market testing', parties could be required to improve the remedies.

[69] In current work with Luke Garrod, we provide more sophisticated econometric investigation of the speed of agreement and link this with the type of error to be expected (i.e. whether agreements are too tough or too soft).

[70] Only where the merger is expected to lead to exclusionary effects (in non-horizontal mergers) would a decline in rival value be associated with anticompetitive effects.

[71] Some UK and US studies have looked at the stock market response at each stage of merger investigation in order to trace the impact of new information, but the results tend to be rather noisy. See Beverley (2008) and references therein.

[72] See also Duso, Neven, and Röller (2007) and Duso, Gugler, and Yurtoglu (2006b) for a similar analysis of merger remedies.

[73] See also Aktas, de Bodt, and R. Roll (2004).

[74] However, the mention of entry barriers in a decision may not be an independent measure as it could be mentioned or not in order to bolster a decision based on other factors.

7

State Aids: Economic Analysis and Practice in the European Union

David Spector

7.1. Introduction

Compared with the other branches of competition policy, state aid control has been the focus of little economic research until recently.[1] Part of the explanation probably lies with the lack of interest for this question in the United States, where state aid control does not exist. But a more fundamental reason is probably at play: an economic assessment of state aid control does not involve a small number of well-defined questions (like unilateral and coordinated effects in the case of merger analysis, or exclusionary strategies in the case of most abuses of a dominant position), but rather a broad array of fields of economic theory.

First, there are many different mechanisms by which aid can be beneficial or harmful: the possible benefits are related to the need to correct some form of market failure, which may result from informational asymmetries, positive externalities, or market power; as to the possible harm, it may be related to the risk of creating static inefficiencies in production (by encouraging production by inefficient firms), dynamic inefficiencies (by changing firms' expectations and thus their behaviour), or to the risk of making market structures less competitive. The overall weighing of all these effects also depends on the cost of public funds, itself a complex issue and the focus of a vast literature in the field of public finance.

Second, the assessment is made more complex by the fact that the economic analysis of state aid control is not the same thing as the analysis of state aid. State aid control is after all a control over the decisions of national governments, and an economic analysis must therefore address the determinants of national aid policies. Justifying state aid control by the possibly inefficient character of state aid is indeed not convincing. National governments can and sometimes do make inefficient choices in all branches of policy, but this obvious fact is not usually viewed as sufficient to warrant control at the Community level. In general, one may consider that the mere fact that a given policy is inefficient should deter a national government from following it; and even when this is not the case, there is no reason to assume that the European Commission would necessarily be better inspired than national governments. An economic analysis of European state aid control must therefore not only provide guidance as to the identification of the beneficial and harmful effects of state aid. It must also identify in which circumstances national governments are likely to grant state aid which should in fact not be granted. In other words, while the analysis of state aid tends to emphasize market failures, the analysis of state aid control must also account for the possibility of government failure.

7.2. Why Should State Aid be Prohibited?

7.2.1. State aid control cannot be justified only by the inefficiency of state aid

Even though the subsidiarity principle is not legally applicable to state aid control, the very existence of a Community control is sometimes justified on the grounds that the granting of aid entails significant negative cross-country externalities, which can be internalized only at a supranational level.[2] It can thus be helpful to distinguish, among the factors likely to induce governments to make inefficient decisions about the granting of state aid, between those resulting from cross-country externalities and those induced by purely internal effects. This distinction matters because the necessity of state aid control at the Community level is more obvious when the inefficiencies result from cross-country externalities than when they do not—although, even in the latter case, some convincing justifications for Community control exist (see below).

7.2.2. Paternalistic justifications for state aid control

Irrespective of any cross-country effects, governments can decide to grant inefficient state aid for a variety of reasons. The most obvious one is incompetence. But the possible (and, in some cases, no doubt very real!) incompetence of national governments falls short of justifying state aid control at the Community level, for two reasons. First, with all due respect, there is no reason to assume a priori that officials are systematically more competent at the European Commission than in national governments. Second, even if they were, this superior competence could in theory be applied to many fields of policy. It does not imply that state aid should be subjected to the control of the European Commission, while other branches of economic policy would remain entirely in the hands of possibly incompetent national governments. Two other sources of inefficiencies make for a more convincing justification for state aid control.

STATE AID CONTROL AS A TOOL TO HELP GOVERNMENTS RESIST INTEREST GROUPS

The ability of private interest groups to distort economic policy in their favour has been amply documented.[3] For example, empirical studies in the United States have shown the degree of tariff protection enjoyed by various industries to be directly correlated to the level of donations to political parties.[4] As for aid to private firms (which is not prohibited in the United States), their costs appear to be disproportionately large when assessed against their alleged benefits, especially if the latter are measured according to the number of jobs created. For instance, the aid granted in the 1990s by the State of Michigan to various firms on job-creation grounds cost more than 2 million dollars per job; the aid granted by the State of Alabama to Daimler-Benz amounted to 168,000 dollars per job.[5] In particular, sector- or firm-specific public policy seems to be often tilted in favour of declining industries, in the United States at least.[6]

There is little doubt that similar inefficiencies can be found in European countries—for example, regarding trade policy. In the case of state aid, recent research has shown that the allocation of aid is largely determined by political rather than economic factors.[7] Whether such inefficiencies, which reflect the imperfections of national political institutions, are enough to justify a control at the Community level is a moot point. One could argue that the Commission's role is not to prevent a government from engaging into wasteful public spending: the citizens of a democratic country should be left free to have their government spend public funds inefficiently if this pleases them, as long as there is no harm to other countries. Beyond this cynical view, one could also claim that countries willing to limit the power of interest groups can do so by using, for example, constitutional clauses constraining the ability of their governments or parliamentary majorities to favour arbitrarily selected private firms. Such clauses could be seen as an extension of the general anti-discrimination and equality clauses present in many constitutions.

If all state aid were inefficient, a constitutional prohibition in each country would be sufficient and there would be no need for supranational control. But this solution would be unsatisfactory because, in the real world, some state aid is desirable. The best solution may thus be an institutional set-up combining flexibility—that is, the possibility to grant state aid in some circumstances—with sufficient insulation from the pressures of domestic politics.

European state aid control bears a striking similarity to this theoretical solution.[8]

A recent event, outside of the realm of state aid, casts light on the merits and limits of this justification. It regards the discussions between European countries about whether each country should be free to set VAT rates in the restaurant sector at the level of its choosing. In the name of the subsidiarity principle, France asked to have the right to lower its rate, claiming that, since restaurant meals are an immobile good, their taxation involves no cross-country externalities and should be left in the hands of national governments. The European Commission broadly agreed with this view. It claimed that, though the lowering of VAT rates on restaurants is not a good policy in its view, it had no problem in leaving the decision to national governments, and that European coordination should focus on mobile goods, for which cross-country tax externalities may be present. But several European countries successfully opposed this. In particular, the German minister of finances stressed that, if he were left free to set the rate of VAT, he would not be able to resist the lobbying of restaurant owners and would be forced to lower VAT, even though he viewed such a lowering as economically inefficient. In other words, he asked the European Commission to tie his hands in order to insulate a purely German economic policy decision from the pressures of German interest-group politics. The logic of this position is very similar to that justifying a European state aid control policy by the necessity to protect national governments from themselves, or at least from powerful domestic interest groups. Interestingly, as is revealed by its stance on the VAT front, the Commission seems to be reluctant to play such a role, presumably because it does not enjoy being scapegoated by national governments which happily shift the blame to 'Europe' in order to justify unpopular decisions. This understandable reluctance means that state aid control cannot be primarily justified by the need to overcome the imperfections of national politics.

STATE AID CONTROL AS A COMMITMENT DEVICE FOR NATIONAL GOVERNMENTS

Another possible justification for state aid control, unrelated to any cross-country externalities, is the existence of a commitment problem facing national governments. The problem is that if governments were free to grant aid as they pleased, the expectation of this possibility would affect firm behaviour even before any aid being effectively granted. For example, if it is expected that failing firms will be rescued by governments with some probability, companies may be encouraged to undertake overly risky investments, or to adopt lax management practices. More generally, a firm's incentives to become more efficient so as to cut costs, raise quality, or innovate are likely to be dampened if it expects that the resulting competitive advantage will be offset by the granting of aid to its lazier rivals. This idea has been formulated by the economist Janos Kornai when analysing attempts by the Hungarian government to partly liberalize the economy:

Although state-owned enterprises were vested with a moral and financial interest in maximizing their profits, the chronic loss-makers among them were not allowed to fail. They were always bailed out with financial subsidies or other instruments. Firms could count on surviving even after chronic losses, and this expectation left its mark on their behaviour.[9]

State aid thus has a diffuse and indirect cost, beyond the sector to which aid recipients belong. Every time an aid is granted, this confirms agents' belief that they live in an economy in which aid may be granted in the future. Irrespective of the criteria for receiving aid, this is likely to distort firm behaviour. If aid is granted in priority to failing firms, this is likely to decrease incentives to innovate; if it is channelled mostly to support R&D, this may lower incentives to undertake R&D out of private funds; more generally, the possibility of state aid encourages firms to divert resources away from productive uses into lobbying.

Since national governments typically have short horizons (that is, until the next election), they may be tempted to forego the benefits of not granting aid (that is, contributing slowly to changing firms' expectations and behaviour) in order to enjoy the short-term benefits of aid.

This type of problem is by no means limited to state aid. In the same spirit, governments approaching an election are often tempted to follow lax budget policies towards the end of their terms, because the benefits from a budgetary expansion are immediate, while the costs fall on future generations which will have to repay government debts—or, at the very least, to next year's taxpayers.[10]

In some American states, the constitution imposes a balanced-budget clause, precisely in order to prevent governments from succumbing to the temptation just before elections. Could the same be done about state aid, through a simple prohibition at the national level? The problem with this solution is, again, that some flexibility may be desirable if state aid is considered an efficient instrument in some circumstances. In this case, Community control may constitute a good compromise between insulation from domestic political cycles and the need for flexibility.

THE COST OF RENT-SEEKING

Firms' expectations that they could possibly benefit from state aid induces them to divert resources away from productive activities to unproductive rent-seeking ones.[11] According to various estimates, the cost of these rent-seeking activities is very high. In the United States, total expenditures on transfer activity have been estimated at 25 per cent of GDP.[12] Other estimates, based on regressions of gross national output on the relative number of lawyers (supposed to be a proxy for the magnitude of rent-seeking activities) and physicians or engineers (supposed to be a proxy for the magnitude of productive activity) point to similar or even higher costs of rent-seeking.[13] Of course, lobbying to be granted state aid is but one of many forms of rent-seeking activities, and the above figures do not refer specifically to state aid. But they are sufficiently impressive to make one consider the costs of the induced rent-seeking activities as an important adverse effect of state aid.

Does this warrant supranational state aid control? The answer is quite similar to that in the previous section. On the one hand, the mechanism at play is purely national, in that if a country develops a reputation for granting state aid while its neighbours do not, the rent-seeking activities will take place in that country, and the corresponding costs will not be incurred abroad. This precise mechanism does not generate any cross-country externality. On the other hand, since it relies on a reputation effect unfolding over the long run, short-sighted national governments may lack the proper incentives, and supranational control may represent a substitute for a constitutional ban—maybe a slightly better one, given the flexibility it affords.

7.2.3. Non-paternalistic justifications: internalizing cross-country externalities

While purely domestic problems could, in theory at least, be dealt with at the national level, a pan-European policy is the only possible way of internalizing externalities. Accordingly, several economists have claimed that state aid control should focus on aid-inducing negative cross-country externalities—that is, on aid which has negative effects on the countries other than the one granting it.[14] This view is also sometimes held by Commission officials.[15] It is thus particularly important to identify in detail the mechanisms giving rise to negative cross-country externalities. Two of them can be singled out: wasteful subsidy races, and cross-country rent-shifting in oligopolistic markets. Interestingly, the notion of 'distortion of competition', which is so prominent in the law of state aid control and appears to be staging a comeback after years of oblivion, pertains only to the latter (see below).

STATE AID, LOCAL EXTERNALITIES, AND INEFFICIENT SUBSIDY RACES

The Nature of the Externality

A firm's decision to set up, expand, or maintain a plant in a country often generates sizable benefits for the host country: tax revenues (levied directly, on the firm, or indirectly, on employees' salaries), possibly a decrease in unemployment and in the associated costs, increased demand for the output of local suppliers, etc. It may also result into a transfer of skills to the local workforce, which can then benefit the economy more broadly as workers change firms. Each national government thus may have an interest in granting aid in order to lure firms into its territory. Absent state aid control, competition across governments wanting to attract the same firms might result into large volumes of aid, shifting the location of firms' activities rather than creating new ones.

If public funds had no 'deadweight cost', that is, if a transfer of €100 to a firm cost only €100 to the country granting the aid, state aid would raise distributional issues, but it would be neutral from an efficiency viewpoint. However, in reality, raising tax revenues is costly because taxes distort economic agents' incentives and decrease total wealth. According to some empirical estimates, raising €100 for the government entails a deadweight cost between €18 and €24: when the government raises €100, other economic agents lose not €100, but between €118 and €124.[16]

The existence of a sizable deadweight cost of government funds implies that competition across governments wanting to attract firms by means of financial incentives is likely to result into excessive aid, that is, into amounts of aid that reduce overall social welfare (including the recipient's welfare in the calculation). The following simple example illustrates this point. Assume that a firm hesitates between locating in countries A and B, and that the benefit derived from its presence is €1,200 for the country it chooses. Assume also that, for each government, raising €1,000 in taxes involves a deadweight cost of €200. Clearly, no government will want to offer more than €1,000 to the firm, because offering €1,000 involves a real cost of €1,200 (€1,000 transferred to the recipient of aid, plus a deadweight cost of €200): €1,000 is the absolute maximum that a rational government will want to offer. If the firm manages to exploit the rivalry between the two governments, it may succeed in obtaining this maximum amount. The outcome can thus be that one of the governments pays €1,000 to the firm. This aid reduces welfare because the loss to the country granting the aid (€1,200) is greater than the benefit to the recipient (€1,000). Notice that the benefit derived by the country from having the firm locate on its territory (€1,200) should not be taken into account when evaluating the impact of the aid because we assumed that the firm would have located in one of the two countries anyway, even without aid.

This reasoning is an illustration of the famous game-theoretic notion of the 'prisoner's dilemma'. It is by no means limited to state aid. It is in fact a simple instance of the far more general phenomenon of tax competition, which causes governments to cut taxes on mobile factors (such as corporate income) and to make up for these cuts by raising taxes on immobile factors (such as labour). In fact, the granting of aid can be interpreted as a selective cut in corporate taxes.

TWO CAVEATS

This analysis of state aid in terms of inefficient subsidy races lends itself to two criticisms—one economic, the other political. From an economic viewpoint, the criticism is based on the claim that, in some circumstances, competition between governments to attract firms may raise, rather than decrease welfare. This may be the case if two conditions are met: the deadweight cost of taxation is low and the benefit derived from a firm's presence varies greatly across locations. In such a case, the countries or regions in which the presence of a firm would yield the largest benefits are willing to 'bid' greater amounts than regions in which these benefits would be smaller. Just like price competition, cross-country competition thus reveals where the external benefits are greatest, and it causes firms to locate where their presence is most valuable, which is desirable. In addition, this comes at little cost if the deadweight cost of taxation is low.[17]

Which model is more relevant is an empirical question. The available literature about the United States, where aid is not prohibited, lends support to a rather negative view of competition across states to attract firms. States tend to engage into costly competition simply in order to shift activities from neighbouring states to themselves, without much creation of new activities.[18] This destructive cross-state competition also seems to have intensified lately,[19] and this has prompted some American authors to recommend a federal control over state aid.[20]

The other caveat is that justifying European state aid control by the need to prevent inefficient competition between Member States for the attraction of firms is a bit paradoxical, given the absence of any coordination of corporate taxation. Governments can indeed compete in two ways in order to attract firms. One is to offer firm-specific aid, and the other is to cut corporate taxes across the board. If the inefficiencies generated by such competition are considered a serious problem, then the solution is to have some supranational control over both state aid and corporate tax rates. But this is not the case: there is no coordination over corporate taxation in Europe (if one excepts very recent progress towards harmonizing the definition of the tax base), and vigorous tax competition has led some EU countries to adopt zero corporate tax rates. This remark does not imply that the need to limit tax competition is not a convincing justification for state aid control, but rather that, if this is the case, there is some inconsistency between this justification and the lack of European-wide fiscal coordination. Of course, the symmetric paradox exists in the United States: while competition between States unleashes large volumes of often inefficient aid to firms, the existence of a federal tax on corporate profits, at a rate of 35 per cent, effectively solves the tax competition problem.

STATE AID, DISTORTION OF COMPETITION, AND STRATEGIC TRADE POLICY

In oligopolistic markets, state aid may also generate cross-country externalities by having an impact on the investment decisions of the rivals of the aid recipient. The underlying mechanism has been studied in the economic models of strategic trade policy,[21] and can be summarized as follows. In an oligopoly, in which firms earn rents derived from their market power, a firm's profit increases if its rivals decrease their investment (to be understood in a broad sense, including R&D, advertising, set-up costs in order to operate in a new country, etc.) Therefore, a national government may have an interest in inducing the foreign rivals of one of its national champions to scale down their investments. State aid may achieve this result in some circumstances. For example, if country A grants investment aid to a firm, competitors in country B may expect a capacity expansion by the recipient of the aid, and thus a reduction in the residual demand facing them. This expectation may in turn induce them to scale down their investment. The overall result is a shift of part of the oligopoly rents towards the recipient of the aid, at the expense of its rivals.[22]

The granting of aid may thus allow the recipient to pre-empt a part of the demand which, absent any aid, would have been served by foreign rivals. This mechanism involves a cross-country negative externality because when a government grants aid, it fails to take into account the harm to foreign competitors.

However, the analysis should not stop there, because the granting of aid may also generate a positive cross-country externality: if the recipient of aid expands production or investment, consumers may benefit, not only in the country whose government granted the aid, but also abroad. A government caring only about the welfare of domestic economic agents would fail to take this effect into account. If this positive externality is more important than the abovementioned negative one, it could be the case that, even absent state aid control, governments grant too little, rather than too much aid!

Recent papers by David Collie[23] indeed show that if the deadweight cost of taxation is low, then the prohibition of state aid reduces social welfare. The reason is that the various governments' attempts to distort competition end up cancelling out, but welfare is increased in the process because subsidies cause firms to act on the basis of perceived costs that are lower than real costs, which induces them to expand output and cut prices. This partly counteracts the fact that under imperfect (that is, oligopolistic) competition, firms tend to choose inefficiently low output levels and/or set inefficiently high prices. However, if the deadweight cost of taxation is high, then governments are induced to grant too much state aid from a supranational viewpoint and a ban on state aid increases welfare.

These analyses rely on a highly stylized model, and in particular they consider only some specific forms of aid. They are nevertheless important for several theoretical and empirical reasons.

First, they show that the very notion of distortion of competition, which lies at the core of state aid control policy, is quite ambiguous in economic terms. When state aid is motivated only by each national government's desire to induce foreign firms to produce less and shift production to domestic firms, it may in the end cause welfare to increase as long as the deadweight cost of taxation is small enough. In this sense, the very idea that distortion of competition is bad, and that state aid should be allowed only when this 'bad' is outweighed by some 'good', is not always justified.

Second, the resulting rationale for state aid (in cases where the deadweight cost of taxation is low) could be framed in terms of market failures, in accordance with the current wording of state aid control policy.[24] The market failure simply results from the presence of oligopolistic, rather than perfect, competition, which causes firms to base their decisions on marginal revenue rather than marginal cost calculations.

Finally, Collie's analyses show that the more differentiated a market is, the less likely it is that state aid might cause harm, at least if one assumes that national governments are rational and one does not take into account the various commitment problems mentioned above. The reason is that in a highly differentiated product market, aid to a firm does not cause much harm to foreign competitors, but it benefits foreign consumers, so that the overall net effect on foreign agents is likely to be positive. Since the overall net effect on domestic agents (including the government, taking the deadweight cost of taxation into account) is necessarily positive (otherwise the government would not grant the aid in the first place), this implies that the effect of aid on total welfare (that is, domestic and foreign combined) is positive as well. This points towards some practical guidance: the more differentiated a market is, the more lenient the assessment of aid should be.

STATE AID MAY DECREASE COMPETITION

Aid may be harmful because it risks making market structure less competitive in the long run. For example, an aid may allow a firm to engage into a predatory strategy which will cause rivals to exit or to be forced to merge with the recipient of the aid. Or, if the sector under consideration is subject to significant credit constraints, it may allow the recipient of the aid to gain access to a large volume of essential inputs, thereby raising rivals' costs and making them compete less aggressively. A variant of this effect is a situation in which the recipient of the aid ends up being the only one able to purchase smaller rivals and gain access to their assets, which may prevent a more balanced distribution of assets. This mechanism may in some cases entail a cross-border externality since the decrease in competition may generate a large transfer of surplus away from foreign consumers and competitors towards the recipient of the aid. Notice, however, that state aid may also change market structure in the opposite direction, making it more competitive (see below).

7.3. When Can State Aid be Beneficial?

7.3.1. *State aid may correct different types of market failure*

Just like other public policies, state aid may in some circumstances alleviate market failures, which may be caused by the presence of externalities (for example, in the case of public goods), by informational asymmetries, or by lack of competition. The various types of externalities justifying, in some circumstances, corrective aid measures are discussed in many excellent articles, and will thus be listed very briefly.

EXTERNALITIES AND PUBLIC GOODS

Externalities arise when a transaction has an impact on other agents than the parties to the transaction. Externalities can be negative—for example, in the case of pollution. Positive externalities may arise for a variety of reasons. One of them, in the case of R&D, is the presence of knowledge spillovers: a company's R&D efforts may benefit other companies because new knowledge diffuses outside the company undertaking R&D, through social and business interactions, or as a consequence of employees moving across companies. Several empirical studies have found the magnitude of such knowledge spillovers to be significant. They may explain, in particular, the success of clusters such as the Silicon Valley or its many imitations.[25] Another possible externality may result from the location of a firm in a region undergoing an economic crisis, through its impact on the regional unemployment rate as well as through possible 'Keynesian' effects. Public goods can be seen as a particular type of externality, since any potential consumer can enjoy the consumption of the good without being a party to any transaction, due to the non-exclusionary nature of the good.

Markets fail in the presence of externalities because the external effects (be they positive or negative) are not taken into account by economic agents, in the absence of a transaction by which the external gainers would pay or the external losers would be compensated. This may warrant a corrective public policy, which can take the form of a tax (in the case of pollution), or, symmetrically, a subsidy. In some cases, the most efficient subsidy may have to be explicitly or implicitly selective, when the activity generating a positive externality is due to one specific firm.

INFORMATIONAL ASYMMETRIES

Informational asymmetries may cause markets to unravel, in particular as regards the provision of insurance or credit to firms. For example, if firms or potential innovators are better informed than investors about the true prospects of their projects, firms may lack access to capital. Jumping to the conclusion that governments should then replace failing markets may seem naive at first glance, because the replacement of private investors and banks with a government would not cause the informational asymmetry to disappear: the government would not be better than private investors at distinguishing good projects from bad ones. However, this objection is only partly valid. Economic theory has shown that in the presence of asymmetric information, public intervention may raise overall welfare, even if the government is not better informed than private agents. In a nutshell, the reason is that private investors in general cannot appropriate the full value generated by the projects they fund—if they did, entrepreneurs would be left without any incentives to succeed, since they would not reap the benefits of success. As a result, subsidizing entrepreneurs may raise overall welfare even when it is not privately profitable. This type of consideration may justify subsidies to firms in nascent high-technology sectors, in which informational asymmetries are likely to be large.

STATE AID AS A MEANS TO CREATE COMPETITION

Finally, state aid may help a new company to get off the ground and create or increase competition, to the benefit of consumers. In some circumstances, it is conceivable that the creation of a second firm, in the case of a monopoly, is not privately profitable, because set-up costs are too high relative to the flow of future profits. But, when market structure shifts from monopoly to duopoly, consumers gain, and this gain is not taken into account when deciding whether to create a new company. This may in some cases justify the granting of state aid. A famous example is Airbus: it has been estimated that because of the increased competition in the aircraft sector fostered by the creation of Airbus, the corresponding subsidies significantly raised European welfare.[26]

However, this argument lacks generality. Economic theory does not come to the conclusion that there is in general too little entry because of potential entrants' failure to internalize consumer welfare. The reason is that this positive externality of entry is compensated by a negative externality, called the 'business-stealing' effect: an entrant fails to take into account the decrease in incumbent profits induced by its potential entry.

STATE AID AS A MEANS TO ACHIEVE 'PERSONALIZED CORPORATE TAX RATES'

An additional possible justification for state aid is barely ever mentioned. Like all kinds of taxation, corporate taxation distorts firms' behaviour. For instance, corporate taxation affects the cost of capital (through quite complex channels[27]), which has a strong impact on investment, with an elasticity estimated between -0.5 and -1.[28] Corporate tax rates also appear to have a significant impact on firms' choices of organizational form.[29] The same could be said about other taxes paid by companies, such as taxes levied on firms' wage bills, which are known to have highly distortive effects.

But the impact of taxation on firms' investment, employment, or organization decisions varies a lot across sectors, and probably across firms in each sector—just like the impact of personal income taxation on labour supply varies a lot across individuals. This may justify in theory 'personalized' taxation. Rather than lower taxes on all firms, including those whose behaviour is little affected by them, it could be more efficient to target those most sensitive to taxation and offer tax breaks to these firms only. If they are granted with enough selectivity, such tax breaks would be considered as state aid.

Again, this rationale for state aid could be expressed in terms of the remedying of a market failure (albeit a government-created one) in that tax breaks targeted towards firms with the greatest sensitivity to taxation is justified by the divergence between socially and privately optimal decisions, which results from the existence of a tax wedge.

This justification for aid relying on the occasional superiority of 'personalized' tax rates over uniform ones implies that selectivity need not be bad by itself, even in the absence of any market failure beyond those induced by corporate taxation.

7.3.2. Caveats

The likely presence of market failures in the real world should not be construed as a blanket justification for state aid. To start with, almost no real-world market fits the textbook paradigm of perfect markets, and in that sense, market failures are ubiquitous. Some discipline is thus needed in order to assess whether the nature and the magnitude of a particular market failure, as well as the imperfections (for example, due to informational asymmetries) of policies, make state aid a suitable corrective measure. In particular, other tools are often more appropriate than state aid. For example, many externalities can be dealt with using general, non-selective instruments such as taxes or subsidies, and, similarly, public services may often be provided through transparent tender processes.

Second, asymmetric information may render public policy very inefficient. For example, aid to R&D may miss its goal and crowd out private R&D rather than stimulate new investment.[30] More generally, firms may misrepresent the extent to which the decisions supposedly generating positive externalities (that is, R&D, but also the choice to locate in a region undergoing economic hardship) are sensitive to the granting of aid, which may cause governments to grant inefficient aid.

Finally, as regards aid to R&D, much has been said about the inefficiencies of policies aimed at 'picking winners', and about the intrinsically unpredictable nature of innovation. This can be illustrated, *inter alia*, by a comparison of the identity of the largest private companies in Europe and in the United States. While the top companies in Europe today are, with a few exceptions, the same as twenty-five years ago, this is not true in the United States, where large companies (such as IBM) have been dethroned, while new companies in the high-technology sector were rising to prominence, such as Microsoft, Sun, or Google. This casual observation invites a lot a caution over the idea that governments can identify companies and technological endeavours worthy of state aid: if the largest and most sophisticated corporations failed to identify and produce the most path-breaking innovations in the last two decades, which came instead from unexpected quarters, why should we expect governments to be more enlightened?

7.3.3. *Correcting geographic disparities*

The goal of redressing economic disparities across regions figures prominently in Article 87(3) of the Treaty. 'Aid to promote the economic development of areas where the standard of living is abnormally low or where there is serious unemployment' (point (a)) and 'aid to facilitate the development of certain economic activities or of certain economic areas' (point (c)) may indeed be considered to be compatible with the common market.

Economic analysis cannot make a normative statement about the weight that public policy should put on the reduction in regional disparities, relative to other policy goals such as overall economic efficiency. It can, however, attempt to assess whether, and to what extent, state aid to companies is a proper tool to meet this goal.

Some empirical evidence shows that the knowledge spillovers flowing from efficient firms are very localized.[31] In Europe, they seem to be much stronger within than across regions.[32] This may provide a rationale for state aid as an instrument to reduce geographic inequalities.

However, according to a recent study, while regional policies aiming to attract firms to poor or peripheral locations apparently succeeded, they were very costly because the distortion of firms' location choices resulted into inefficiencies.[33] The case for state aid as a tool for the alleviation of regional inequalities might thus not be very strong, and alternative policies, such as direct income transfers could be more efficient in many cases.[34]

7.4. The Limits of Economic Analysis

7.4.1. *Theoretical analyses offer few clear-cut prescriptions*

THE ROLE OF MARKET POWER

Reflecting the variety of possible theories of harm and of the possible benefits of state aid, the various theoretical contributions described above cannot easily translate into a 'check-list', that is, into the identification of conditions making state aid more likely to be harmful, or, on the contrary, beneficial. Consider, for example, the issue of whether state aid should be considered more harmful when affecting markets in which firms have market power. Among the various theories of harm, the 'inefficient subsidy race' theory does not require the aid recipient to enjoy any market power. If a firm, even without any market power, is offered aid by a country willing to attract it in order to increase employment or tax revenues (even though the choice of location is neutral in terms of overall welfare and the firm would have located somewhere in the European Union even with no aid), then the granting of an aid entails an inefficiency from a European-wide viewpoint (if taxation has a deadweight cost, which is the case in practice). It would nevertheless be rational from the viewpoint of a benevolent national government. A rule authorizing aid as soon as the recipient enjoys little market power would fail to solve this inefficiency, even though it results from the lack of internalization of cross-border externalities by national governments and thus seems to be a prime candidate for supranational control.[35] Some other theories of harm, however, apply only if the recipient enjoys a lot of market power. This is the case, for instance, when the concern is that the recipient of aid might use its financial strength to engage into predatory strategies. This is also the case if aid is motivated by a national government's desire to shift rents from foreign to domestic firms. As seen above, such aid is not necessarily harmful from the overall European viewpoint. A necessary condition for it to be harmful is that the deadweight cost of taxation be high enough. Another one is the presence of some market power (for there would be no rents to start with otherwise). But the abovementioned theories offer complex guidance regarding the impact of market power, because they also stress that when product differentiation is maximal (a situation usually associated with a lot of market power), state aid is unlikely to be harmful. To sum up, according to the existing theories of state-aid-as-rent-shifting (one of many theories of harm, and one of several theories of harm-cum-cross-border-externalities), a ban is most likely to be justified (under a total welfare criterion) when the degree of competition is intermediate, that is, when the recipient enjoys market power (so that there are rents) but there is a significant amount of competition between it and its rivals (so that rents can be shifted).

Also, since large firms (often—but not always—enjoying significant market power) are more likely than small ones to have political clout, the 'interest group theory of harm' would lead one to be wary of aid granted to large, politically powerful firms.[36] Finally, empirical studies of the link between market power and innovation do not provide firm guidance, since firms' R&D efforts appear first to rise and then to fall with market power,[37] making it difficult to know for which level of market concentration there is the greatest lack of innovation, and thus the greatest need for public support.

SHOULD STATE AID CONTROL BE BIASED IN FAVOUR OF AID TO R&D?

All the praise lavished on aid to R&D notwithstanding, there is no compelling case for a particularly lenient control of aid to R&D, in the light of economic analysis, both theoretical and empirical. True, R&D combines externalities (due to knowledge spillovers) and informational asymmetries (which may result in underfunding). But these asymmetries, as noted above, also imply that aid to R&D may be inefficient for two reasons—namely, because of the crowding-out effect (governments may find it difficult to ascertain whether the subsidized R&D would have been undertaken without aid) and because of the possible inability of governments to pick winners effectively. This is not to say that aid to R&D is never desirable. The point is simply that economics offer no definitive argument to the effect that aid to R&D should be treated more favourably than, say, aid to a non-technological firm which could easily locate outside of Europe and conditions its presence (and the associated positive externalities, like, for example, tax revenues) on the granting of aid. To make matters even more confused, a recent theoretical model suggests, against much conventional wisdom, that the risk that unconstrained governments might grant too much aid is greater when the aid is targeted towards R&D than when it takes the form of a simple production subsidy.[38]

7.4.2. Some of the effects of state aid do not lend themselves to measurement

The assessment of the impact of an aid bears some similarities to the assessment of mergers. In both cases, the goal is to assess how the market will be affected by a given change. However, in the case of state aid, this exercise is far more complex than in the case of mergers.

The assessment of unilateral effects, which lies at the heart of horizontal merger control, provides for a helpful comparison. Its ambition, compared with the scope of the questions raised by the analysis of state aid control, is relatively narrow: it is limited to short-run effects, and takes market structure as given (except for the merging parties, of course). It lends itself to the econometric technique of merger simulation, which yields quantitative predictions based on parsimonious data requests. Yet, even within this well-delineated framework, merger control is often seen as unpredictable, especially as regards the assessment of efficiencies.[39]

But the questions which need to be addressed in order to assess a state aid measure are both more numerous, and often less liable to quantification than unilateral effects. Consider, for example, aid to R&D. One of the main justifications for the granting of aid to R&D is the existence of a positive externality due to knowledge spillovers. But how can the likelihood of such spillovers be proved in an individual case? The empirical research on this topic almost never proceeded by identifying the presence of spillovers in individual cases; but rather by studying large datasets and identifying the existence of knowledge spillovers on average, using sophisticated statistical techniques. Besides, even this approach fails to end up on firm ground, since the findings of the various studies are significantly divergent. In the case of mergers, the study of past mergers in the same market can often be considered to have some predictive value. But in the case of R&D, such an approach is less promising, because of the difficulty of finding relevant precedents, especially when the goal is to assess an innovation which has not yet occurred and the nature of which is uncertain by definition. This difficulty is reminiscent of the one faced by firms making efficiency claims when defending a merger. Such claims are often rejected for want of verifiability up to competition authorities' high standards. But the problem should be even more acute for state aid control, since the innovations purportedly encouraged are more radical, and thus more uncertain and less verifiable, than the incremental improvements representing the majority of efficiency claims in merger control. And even if spillovers could be shown to be likely, one should also ascertain whether the amount of R&D is sensitive to the volume of aid. Answering this question requires one to know not only the cost of funds available to the firm and the possible credit constraints facing it, but also the list of alternative possible investments for the recipient of the aid, the impact of the R&D effort on the firm's future production costs, as well as an estimate of market demand and rivals' marginal costs, so as to calculate how a given cost reduction, if achieved thanks to R&D, will affect profits. In many cases, the question is even more complex because R&D often aims to create new products rather than to decrease the cost of producing existing ones. Therefore, in order to calculate whether the firm's behaviour is likely to be impacted by the aid, one needs to make assumptions about the demand function in the hypothetical post-R&D world—that is, for example, about the elasticity of substitution between rivals' goods and the hypothetical, not-yet-existing new good which the subsidized R&D might—or might not— bring into existence.

This difficulty is by no means limited to R&D, as can be seen by moving to the question of dynamic inefficiencies—which is often, and probably rightly, mentioned as a justification for state aid control. There is simply no way of quantifying to what extent the granting of an aid will change economic agents' expectations in the long run, and thus their investment and innovation behaviour. Answering this question would require one to assess the impact of any given aid on other firms' expectations as to the likelihood of being granted state aid in the future under different types of circumstances, and to measure the impact on this change in expectations on firms' future behaviour (excessive risk-taking or 'X-inefficiency', diversion of resources from productive to rent-seeking activity, etc.)

Finally, any quantitative assessment of the welfare impact of a state aid must start by making an assumption about the cost of public funds, because, when calculating the overall impact of an aid on welfare, the loss to taxpayers is usually a major element. In fact, in all simple models of distortionary state aid, as well as in simple models of subsidy races, there is no harm at all unless this deadweight cost of taxation is large enough.

7.4.3. The relationship between welfare standards and assessment rules

The issue of the desirable welfare standard for state aid control has been discussed in several recent contributions.[40] For example, H. Friederiszick, L.-H. Röller, and V. Verouden recommend to focus on the combined surplus of consumers and taxpayers, on the grounds that these two categories of agents are politically less powerful than firms, so that omitting firms in the welfare criterion could offset this unbalance. In some cases, when all the relevant effects of the aid under scrutiny can be quantified, the welfare standard may offer precise guidance as to how to balance positive effects against distortionary ones. For example, in the case of a restructuring aid aimed at preventing a firm in an oligopolistic market from going bankrupt and exiting (legally falling under Article 87(3) point c), the abovementioned criterion would mandate a comparison between, on the one hand, the gain to consumers from a continuation of the recipient's activity (implying both an assessment of entry barriers, and an estimate of the remaining firms' behaviour after the recipient's exit, given the magnitude of entry barriers, cost structure, and demand characteristics) and the loss to taxpayers (measured with reference to a predetermined value for the deadweight cost of taxation). In principle, this comparison could be undertaken using the same market-estimation techniques as those routinely used for merger simulation.

However, in other, probably more frequent cases, the definition of a welfare standard cannot translate directly into predictable enforcement, because several important effects of state aid, both positive and negative, are difficult to measure. This problem can only be handled by complementing an abstract welfare standard with much more detailed policy rules defining filters, safe harbours, and 'shortcuts', and allowing the Commission to reach a decision without having to undertake a full-fledged balancing exercise in each case. In other words, the theoretical and practical limits of the economic analysis of any given state aid call for a 'structured rule of reason', which could be far easier to administer than a pure rule of reason.[41]

The proponents of the aforementioned welfare standard themselves acknowledge that it is more about general principles than about providing detailed guidance for enforcement, and they advocate a practical rule largely departing from a pure rule of reason guided only by the compass of the consumer-plus-taxpayer welfare criterion. First, they recommend a combination of block exemptions for low-intensity aid and *per se* prohibition for high-intensity aid, leaving economic analysis to play a role only in intermediate situations. Second, they stress that 'state aid control should concentrate on a small set of well-defined market failures and specify those clearly in its guidelines'. This is exactly the agenda of the ongoing overhaul of state aid control, as exemplified, for instance, in the recent Community Framework for State Aid for Research and Development and Innovation (the 'R&D&I Framework'),[42] which lists specific types of market failures for the assessment of the positive effects of an aid and specific types of distortions for the assessment of the negative effects, leaving aside many, possibly important but hard-to-measure effects, such as, on the positive side, the increase in production due to a decrease in perceived costs, and, on the negative side, the cost to taxpayers or the impact on all firms' expectations and future behaviour. Whichever welfare standard is chosen, if any, state aid control outcomes will continue to be determined primarily by detailed procedural rules, reflecting presumptions about the magnitude and likelihood of these unmeasurable effects.

7.5. Past Enforcement and the Current Overhaul

7.5.1. *The uncertain meaning of competition distortion and trade affectation in the case law*

In practice, up to the issuance of the state aid action plan (the SAAP), the Commission only rarely engaged into an economic, case-by-case, effects-based analysis of the justifications for specific aids. Whether a given measure met the definition of state aid, with reference to the two conditions of selectivity and transfer of state resources, was often the main issue. Presumptions about the likelihood of positive effects in different situations led to the definition of various thresholds. For example, industrial research, presumably generating greater spillovers (and thus prone to market failures) and fewer distortions, could be publicly funded according to the R&D Framework of 1996 up to 50 per cent, against 25 per cent for pre-competitive research.

In contrast, the question which generated the most inconsistency in Commission enforcement and Court rulings has been, for decades, the exact meaning and importance of the 'competition distortion' and 'trade affect-ation' conditions.

THE EVOLUTION OF THE STANDARD OF PROOF
ACCORDING TO THE CASE LAW

The Commission's handling of the competition distortion and trade affect-ation criteria has notoriously been inconsistent. First, until the CFI's *Philip Morris* ruling,[43] the Commission tended to consider that these conditions were necessarily met as soon as aid was granted and thus did not warrant a specific investigation—which is obviously false, since a pure lump-sum transfer to a firm facing no credit constraints is unlikely to have any impact on any market.

At first glance, the *Philip Morris* ruling brought some clarification, since it stressed that the Commission needed to address the criteria of competition distortion and affectation of trade between Member States. Moreover, the Court discussed the economics of the affected sector and the possible effect of the aid, in the following terms:

It is common ground that when the applicant has completed its planned investment it will account for nearly 50 per cent of cigarette production in the Netherlands and that it expects to export over 80 per cent of its production to other Member States. The 'additional premium for major schemes' which the Netherlands government proposed to grant the applicant amounted to HFL 6.2 million (2.3 million EUA) which is 3.8 per cent of the capital invested. When state financial aid strengthens the position of an undertaking compared with other undertakings competing in intra-community trade the latter must be regarded as affected by that aid. In this case the aid which the Netherlands government proposed to grant was for an undertaking organized for inter-national trade and this is proved by the high percentage of its production which it intends to export to other Member State. The aid in question was to help to enlarge its production capacity and consequently to increase its capacity to maintain the flow of trade including that between Member States. On the other hand the aid is said to have reduced the cost of converting the production facilities and has thereby given the applicant a competitive advantage over manufacturers who have completed or intend to complete at their own expense a similar increase in the production capacity of their plant.[44]

The above quotation gives the impression that a detailed assessment is in order. The Court indeed presented a detailed reasoning focusing on the likely impact of the aid. It mentioned that (i) the amount of the aid represented a significant percentage (3.8 per cent) of the planned investment; (ii) the aid was meant to have an impact on production capacities, and therefore on the market, as opposed to a pure lump-sum transfer that could in theory end up in the shareholders' pockets without affecting the firm's behaviour; and that (iii) this market impact was likely to affect trade between Member States, not only because of the cross-border flows of trade prior to the granting of the aid, but also because most of the additional production resulting from the investment benefiting from the aid was going to be exported.

It may seem a bit paradoxical, therefore, that the *Philip Morris* ruling has been interpreted as laying out an almost *per se* criterion according to which a selective measure benefiting a company is most of the time automatically presumed to distort competition and affect trade between member states. This interpretation relies on the focus on the single sentence claiming that 'when state financial aid strengthens the position of an undertaking compared with other undertakings competing in intra-community trade the latter must be regarded as affected by that aid'. However, this restrictive interpretation is confirmed by most subsequent rulings.

In contrast to *Philip Morris*, the Court held in *Tubemeuse*[45] that neither the importance of intra-European trade in the affected market, nor the magnitude of the aid, mattered for the finding of a risk of trade distortion or affectation of trade between Member States. In that ruling, the Court confirmed a Commission's decision prohibiting an aid granted by the Belgian government even though the recipient was selling mostly outside of the European Community. It also claimed that 'the relatively small amount of aid...does not as such exclude the possibility that intra-Community trade might be affected'. The Court did not go as far as claiming that there was no need to pay attention to the economic mechanism by which competition distortion and trade affectation could occur. For instance, in *Maribel*, the Court explained that

when state aid strengthens the position of an undertaking compared with other undertakings competing in intra-Community trade, the latter must be regarded as affected by the aid, even if the beneficiary undertaking is itself not involved in exporting.... Domestic production may...be maintained or increased, with the result that undertakings established in other Member States have less chance of exporting their products to the market in that Member State.[46]

The same point has been made in several subsequent decisions such as *Altmark*,[47] *Heiser*,[48] and *Xunta de Galicia*.[49]

In a nutshell, the Court's view, at least until very recent rulings discussed below, seems to have been that while the Commission needed formally to address the competition distortion and affectation of trade conditions, it was subject to a very low standard of proof, in that it was enough for the Commission to show that distortion of competition or affectation of trade could not be ruled out a priori. For instance, it stated in *Altmark* that 'it is *not impossible* that a public subsidy granted to an undertaking which provides only local or regional transport services and does not provide any transport services outside its State of origin may none the less have an effect on trade between Member States.'[50] Similarly, it claimed in Heiser that it was '*not inconceivable*... that [dentists] may be in competition with their colleagues established in other Member States'.[51] In *Ramondin*,[52] the Court also concurred with the Commission's view that the distortion of competition and affectation of trade conditions did not have to be assessed under a demanding standard of proof.

It must be noted, however, that in several recent decisions such as *Dorsten*[53] and *Brighton Pier*,[54] the Commission considered that it could not prohibit an aid because the obviously local nature of the affected market implied that there was no affectation of trade between Member States. Based on the same type of reasoning, in a largely local market (in a French overseas territory), the Court's *Le Levant*[55] ruling annulled a Commission prohibition decision.

The recent *Wam*[56] ruling may represent a turning point. While it is not the first ruling annulling a prohibition decision by the Commission, it did so by setting a standard of proof that appears to be more demanding than in most of the abovementioned case law. The Court stated indeed that the fact that the aid recipient was engaged into intra-European trade was not by itself sufficient for the Commission to conclude that the aid was going to affect trade between Member States: 'The mere observation that Wam participates to intra-community trade is insufficient to conclude on trade affectation or distortion of competition, and an in-depth analysis of the effect of aids is necessary.'[57]

THE FLUCTUATING ASSESSMENT CRITERIA
ACCORDING TO THE CASE LAW

In addition to the uncertainty regarding the standard of proof, the Commission and the CFI have been using inconsistent criteria. First, the very definition of a distortion has been unstable. In *Philip Morris*, the CFI held that competition distortion relates to a change in the position of an undertaking compared with other undertakings in intra-Community trade. But in the R&D&I Framework, the Commission also mentions (in passing) changes in the location of economic activity as a possible distortion,[58] even though such changes may occur independently of any impact on competitors (for instance in the case of the granting of aid to a monopoly not threatened by potential entry). Similarly, the CFI broadened the definition of trade affectation in the *Tubemeuse* ruling[59] (relative to *Philip Morris*), as it held that Article 87(1) may be violated even though the recipient sells mostly outside of the European Community.

To make things even more complicated, even the 'narrow' definition in terms of an impact on rival undertakings can be interpreted in several ways, either in terms of the impact on profits, or in terms of the impact on sales. This makes a big difference in highly competitive markets, in which a large shift in sales need not be synonymous with a big shift in profits, since per-unit profits may be low.

Beyond the definition of competition distortion and trade affectation, the Commission's views as to which market structures make competition distortion more likely have been contradictory. In many cases (e.g. *Imepiel*[60] and *Ramondin*[61]), distortion was considered more likely if the affected market was highly competitive. This was even stated as a point with general relevance in the motor vehicle guidelines, as the Commission recalled in the *DAF Trucks* Decision:

Under aid for modernization and innovation, the guidelines stipulate that 'in the context of a genuine internal market for motor vehicles, competition between producers will become even more intense and the distortive impact of aid will be greater. Therefore, the Commission will take a strict attitude towards aid for modernization and innovation'.[62]

However, in its recent R&D&I Guidelines, the Commission takes a very different view, claiming that the distortion of dynamic incentives or State-aid-driven market power creation are less likely in highly competitive markets.[63]

7.5.2. Interpreting the competition distortion and trade affectation conditions in the light of economic analysis

These inconsistencies probably reflect some underlying uncertainty as to the main economic mechanism by which state aid is likely to cause harm.

According to a commonly held view, the competition distortion and trade affectation conditions, if properly interpreted, should prevent the Commission from engaging into paternalistic policies by forcing the Commission to focus on aid having cross-country effects, and the Commission's recurrent temptation to forget these two conditions is nothing but the expression of its impulse to infringe on national governments' sovereignty. This is true, but depending on the precise 'theory of harm', the corresponding definition of competition distortion and trade affectation should be modified.

If one believes that harm is most likely to result from governments' attempt to shift rents across countries—a motive making aid socially harmful only if the deadweight cost of taxation is high enough—then it makes sense to define competition distortion with reference to the impact on rivals' profits. In that case, since rent-shifting presupposes significant market power, distortions can occur only in markets which are not too competitive. The traditional Commission position was thus contradictory, in that, on the one hand, it framed state aid control almost entirely in terms of harm to Foreign firms, and, on the other hand, it treated intense competition as an aggravating factor.[64] This confusion may be explained by the fact that in highly competitive markets aid is likely to have a big impact on rivals' *sales* (but not their profits).

But, if one believes that the harm caused by state aid often results from inefficient subsidy races driven by each government's desire to shift the location of economic activity towards its territory because of local or nationwide externalities (including employment or tax revenues), then cross-country shifts in output volumes are relevant—for instance, because they may be associated to shifts in jobs, even in the absence of any rent-shifting. This may thus justify some concern in highly competitive markets.

But, in addition, under the subsidy-race theory of harm, neither rent-shifting nor output-shifting across firms is a necessary condition. If the subsidy race is about attracting a monopolist's plant, there may be harm absent any impact on rival undertakings. It could thus make sense to consider distortions in location decisions across Member States as a distortion under Article 87(1), as is the case in the R&D&I Framework (as well as in Friederiszick, Röller, and Verouden 2006[65]).

7.5.3. The 'refined economic approach': the 'Trojan horse' of paternalism?

One could have expected that the refined economic approach touted in the SAAP and the R&D&I Framework would spell the end of the quasi-automatic presumption that almost any aid distorts competition and affects trade. Indeed, the R&D&I Framework contains a detailed description of the economic mechanisms by which state aid might decrease economic efficiency, and it calls for these mechanisms to be assessed on a case-by-case basis, without presumptions of any sort.

However, the road taken seems to be the opposite one. In the SAAP, it is stated that 'state aid should only be used when it is an appropriate instrument for meeting a well defined objective, when it creates the right incentives, is proportionate and when it distorts competition to the least possible extent.'[66] This claim appears to be at odds with Article 87(1) of the Treaty, which provides for the prohibition of any aid 'which distorts or threatens to distort competition . . . in so far as it affects trade between Member States', unless some justifications for the aid can be provided, as per Articles 87(2) and 87(3). In other words, whatever the definition of competition distortion and trade affectation, the Treaty states that aid neither distorting competition nor affecting trade is not prohibited, even if it is very inefficient economic policy from the viewpoint of the country granting the aid. In contrast, according to the SAAP 'aid should [not] be used' if it is not 'an appropriate instrument for meeting a well-defined objective', even if it does not distort competition. The assessment method proposed in the R&D&I Framework is in line with this view. Except for some specific categories of aid (aid below certain thresholds, aid for young innovative enterprises, etc.), aid measures will ... be declared compatible ... only if (i) they fulfil all the conditions and parameters mentioned in Chapter 5 [dealing with the appropriateness of the aid as a tool to solve a market failure] and (ii) the balancing test pursuant to Chapter 7 [dealing with a detailed assessment of the distortion of competition and trade] results in an overall positive evaluation.[67]

The cumulative nature of these conditions implies that aid not solving a well-identified market failure should be banned, even in the absence of any distortion.

One may wonder to what extent this approach is compatible with recent CFI rulings, such as *Le Levant*, which emphasized that competition and trade distortions are necessary conditions for aid to be illegal. Leaving legal niceties aside, there are convincing economic justifications for the Commission's openly paternalistic approach because it is difficult for national governments to tie their hands, not only for bad reasons (political cowardice, corruption, special interests) but also because, owing to the short time horizon of national governments, nothing short of a constitutional ban could work, and a constitutional ban devoid of any flexibility could be less efficient than supranational control (see above 'Paternalistic justifications for state aid control').

Ironically, while the Framework paves the way for a paternalistic policy meant to encourage national governments to spend their money wisely, which should be fine for economists, but maybe not for legal experts caring about compliance with the Treaty, recent proposals by economists appear to be more respectful of the letter of the Treaty. For instance, T. Besley and P. Seabright propose a seven-step rule by which aid to firms lacking market power, or aid unlikely to generate net cross-border negative externalities would be authorized, without the need to investigate the existence of a market failure in need of correction or whether the aid makes any economic sense at all.[68] Similarly, the three-leg test advocated by H. Friederiszick, L.-H. Röller, and V. Verouden appears to imply that aid not generating any distortion would be legal.[69]

In the end, this contradiction between economists defending the Treaty and official Commission documents departing from it (possibly on good economic policy grounds) will probably be arbitrated by Courts in the coming years.

Notes

[1] This has changed lately. Major recent contributions on the theoretical side include Collie (1998; 2002; 2005); Dewatripont and Seabright (2006). For an empirical assessment, see Neven (2000). For broad surveys, discussing theory, empirics, and policy, see e.g. Besley and Seabright (1999); and Röller, Friederiszick, and Verouden (2007).

[2] Besley and Seabright (1999); Fingleton, Ruane, and Ryan (1999).

[3] Cf. Persson and Tabellini (2000).

[4] Goldberg and Maggi (1999: 1135).

[5] See Tannenwald (2002: 467).

[6] Hufbauer and Rosen (1986); Hufbauer, Berliner, and Elliot (1986).

[7] Neven (2000).

[8] For a related argument, see Dewatripont and Seabright (2006).

[9] Kornai, Maskin, and Roland (2003: 1095). See also Kornai (1986).

[10] See Persson and Tabellini (2000) for an analysis of the impact of electoral cycles on economic policy.

[11] For an introduction to the concept of rent-seeking, see Tullock (1987).

[12] Laband and Sophocleus (1992).

[13] Magee, Brock, and Young (1989); Murphy, Shleifer, and Vishny (1991).

[14] Besley and Seabright (1999); Fingleton, Ruane, and Ryan (1999).

[15] Kleiner and Alexis (2005: 45).

[16] Ballard, Shoven, and Whalley (1985); Jorgenson and Yun (1990; 1991).

[17] Tiebout (1956); Besley and Seabright (1999).

[18] Tannenwald (2002).

[19] Chi and Leatherby (1997).

[20] Enrich (1996).

[21] Brander and Spencer (1985).

[22] In some circumstances, the causality may be reversed. For example, a firm facing a decrease in its residual demand may have greater incentives to engage in R&D so as to re-establish a better market position.

[23] See n. 1, above; also Garcia and Neven (2005).

[24] See e.g. the State Aid Action Plan, pt 23: 'One key element [in assessing compatibility] is the analysis of market failures.'

[25] Caballero and Jaffe (1993); Agrawal, Cockburn, and McHale (2006); Moretti (2004).

[26] Besley and Seabright (1999).

[27] See Auerbach (2005).

[28] Caballero and Haltiwanger (1995).

[29] Goolsbee (2004).

[30] For a survey of empirical research on this topic, see David (2000). Their conclusion is mixed, meaning that a strong crowding-out effect cannot be ruled out.

[31] Audretsch and Feldman (1996).

[32] Bottazzi and Peri (2004).

[33] Midelfart-Knarvik and Overman (2002).

[34] Ulltveit-Moe (2007).

[35] We thus beg to differ with Besley and Seabright 1999 who recommend that market power be considered 'a necessary condition of the identification of cross-border externalities' (p. 40).

[36] This point is made in Röller, Friederiszick, and Verouden (2007).

[37] Aghion, et al. (2005: 701–28).

[38] Collie (2005: 231).

[39] Gifford and Kudrle (2005).

[40] Röller, Friederiszick, and Verouden (2007); Martin and Strasse (2005); Kleiner and Alexis (2005: 45–9).

[41] On the notion of structured rules of reason, see e.g. Easterbrook (1984).

[42] 'Community Framework for State Aid for Research and Development and Innovation', 2006/C 323/01, 30 Dec. 2006.

[43] Case 730/79 [1980] ECR 2671.

[44] Ibid.

[45] Case 142/87 *Commission* v. *Belgium* [1990] ECR I–959.

[46] Case C-75/97 *Belgium* v. *Commission* [1999] ECR I–3671.

[47] Case C-280/00 *Altmark Trans GmbH, Regierungspräsidium Magdeburg* v. *Nahverkehrsgesellschaft Altmark GmbH* [2003].

[48] Case C-172/03 *Wolfgang Heiser* v. *Finanzamt Innsbruck* [2005] ECR 1627.

[49] Case C-71/04 *Administración del Estado* v. *Xunta de Galicia* [2005] ECR I–7419.

[50] Emphasis added.

[51] Emphasis added.

[52] Joined cases T–92/00 and T–103/00 ECR II–1385.

[53] OJ C-172/2001.

[54] N 56/01.

[55] CFI, 22 Feb. 2006, *Eurl Le Levant* v. *Commission*, case T–34/02.

[56] CFI, 6 Sept. 2006, *Italy and Wam SpA* v. *Commission*, case T–304/04.

[57] Author's translation of 'le seul constat de la participation de Wam aux échanges intracommunautaires est insuffisant pour étayer une affectation desdits échanges ou une distorsion de concurrence et, dès lors, nécessite une analyse approfondie des effets des aides' (pnt 74).

[58] R&D&I Framework, pt 7.4.

[59] Case 102/87 [1988] ECR 4067.

[60] OJ L 172/76, 27/06/1992.

[61] OJ L 318/36, 16/12/2000.

[62] OJ L 015, 20/01/1996 P. 0037–0045.

[63] Sects 7.4.1. and 7.4.2.

[64] This point has been made in Besley and Seabright (1999).

[65] Ibid.

[66] SAAP, pt 11.

[67] R&D&I Guidelines, sect. 1.4: 8.

[68] Besley and Seabright (1999).

[69] Röller, Friederiszick, and Verouden (2007). The author of the present chapter, however, is not entirely sure that the balancing test described by these authors would have this consequence. Under their test, an economically absurd aid generating no cross-country externalities would score zero on both the 'benefits' part of their test (legs (a) and (b)) and on the 'harm' part (leg (c)). Which decision would ensue is not clear.

8

Competition Policy and Sector-specific Regulation for Network Industries[1]

Martin Hellwig

8.1. Introduction

This chapter discusses the respective roles of sector-specific regulation and competition policy in network industries. The term 'network industries' refers to industries like telecommunications, electricity, gas, and rail transportation that involve important elements of a natural monopoly because the provision of services to customers presupposes the use of a fixed network infrastructure the costs of which are largely sunk.[2] If one wanted to be more precise, one would have to go into details of the scale economies and sunk costs in these infrastructure technologies. For instance, one might ask whether the postal sector is a network industry: Whereas there are significant scale effects in mail distribution, the main input here is labour; the costs of this input are not sunk, but involve significant learning-by-doing effects, which can foreclose competition in ways that are very similar to the foreclosure effects of sunk costs. In the analysis here, however, such details will be neglected. While acknowledging that the different network industries differ from each other in important and relevant ways, I will focus on questions that are common to all of them.

Over the past three decades, the organization of network industries in Europe and the United States has undergone significant changes.[3] In the past, these industries had mostly been organized as vertically integrated monopolies. Management of the network and provision of services through the network were usually handled by the same institution. Natural monopolies in networks supported monopolies in services, in some instances by statutory regulation, in others by market foreclosure based on vertical integration. In Europe, most of the vertically integrated monopolies were held in state ownership, in the United States, most of them were in private ownership subject to sector-specific regulation. Prices charged to final customers were usually computed on some kind of cost-plus basis.[4]

By now, these industries have been thoroughly reorganized. The vertically integrated monopolies have come under strong pressure; in some cases, they have completely disappeared. The changes differ from industry to industry and from country to country, but a few common elements can be named. Developments have involved the *privatization* of companies that used to be in state ownership, the *liberalization* of entry into the provision of services on the basis of the networks, finally, also some *vertical disintegration* between the operation of the network and the provision of services.

The liberalization of entry into the provision of services has been accompanied by the introduction of statutory rules requiring network operators to open their networks at regulated prices to competing service providers. It would therefore be misleading to merely refer to the change as 'deregulation', as is sometimes done in invocations of the holy triad of 'privatization, liberalization, and deregulation'. Whereas some regulations have been lifted, others have been newly imposed—the overall system of governance for network industries is simply different.

8.1.1. *Paradigm changes for network industries*

These developments have partly been driven by a change of paradigm for the governance of these industries. The vision of network industries run by vertically integrated monopolies has been replaced by a more complicated vision that involves monopolies upstream, in the organization and management of networks, and competition downstream, in the provision of services through the networks. The new vision is based on the recognition that natural-monopoly elements of the industry extend less far than had previously been thought. Whereas the networks themselves are natural monopolies in the technical sense of the word, the same cannot be said of the downstream activities that are based on the networks.

Characteristic examples are found in the telecommunications and electricity industries. In telecommunications, the local loop of the fixed-line network involves significant fixed costs. Because of these costs, a reduplication of the local loop would be highly wasteful; because these costs are sunk before any sales occur, they warrant the classification of the 'last mile' as a natural monopoly. In contrast, the provision of telecommunications services through the network does not warrant this classification. The technology here exhibits hardly any scale economies and hardly any sunk costs. If access to the network can be guaranteed, there is nothing to prevent the functioning of competitive markets. Even for fixed lines, at a high level of the network hierarchy—that is, for long-distance lines—one observes that, although costs are sunk, at relevant levels of use, duplication of long-distance lines is economical, and competition can be viable. Thus, in Germany, there are by now more than a dozen companies that have their own long-distance networks as a basis for competing in long-distance service provision. Investment in these networks has been very active, extending remarkably far down the overall network hierarchy.[5]

In the electricity industry, transmission and distribution grids are natural monopolies. For a transmission grid, there can be only one system operator in charge of maintaining a constant level of tension. For distribution grids, the inefficiency involved in duplicating the last mile would be even greater than in telecommunications. In contrast, the production of electricity, its transportation through the transmission and distribution grids, and its sale to final users exhibit no technical features that would warrant their classification as natural monopolies.

Another paradigm change concerns the role of the networks themselves. In the telecommunications industry, the natural-monopoly features of the traditional fixed-line networks seem to be losing in importance as technical progress facilitates the development of alternative networks as a basis for service provision. Network monopolies are being replaced by systems of networks that are in competition with each other. The paradigmatic example is provided by mobile telecommunications where, in any given country, we see a handful of operators building up networks and acquiring customers in competition with each other. We also see competition between fixed-line and mobile telecommunications, or between fixed-line and cable networks. Telecommunications services through different kinds of networks may not be perfect substitutes, but, even so, the imperfect substitutes that are available can impose effective constraints on the behaviours of the presumed network monopolists.[6] If so, we should be thinking about the industry as being in oligopolistic competition between network providers, rather than network monopolists holding sway over facilities that are essential to the provision of services downstream.

8.1.2. Changes of public policy towards network industries

The change in paradigm concerning the nature and implications of natural monopolies in network industries has also led to a change of public policy towards these industries. The change has been marked by: (i) a tendency to privatize previously state-owned companies in network industries; (ii) the opening of network industries to competition; and (iii) a reorientation of regulatory oversight, away from the direct control of final output prices and towards the promotion of competition in the industry.

These changes in public policy were to some extent motivated by the observation that the vertically integrated state-owned monopolists of the past had been slow in making use of new technological opportunities and that this was endangering the competitiveness of firms relying on services from these infrastructure industries.[7] To some extent, they were also promoted by finance ministers hoping to benefit from privatization proceeds or simply the cost reductions of downsizing under the threat of competition.[8] Given that competition tends to erode profits, there is an inherent conflict between these two aims, but, as long as it was just a matter of reform rhetoric, the conflict was played down. In political practice though, this conflict has been and continues to be quite important.

Within the European Union, the European Commission has been a major promoter of change. Under the auspices of the Internal Market Programme, it has initiated a series of directives designed to eliminate statutory monopolies in the different network industries and to create EU-wide internal markets, at least at the level of downstream activities, which are not natural monopolies in themselves and merely use the network infrastructures as essential inputs.[9] These directives have been instrumental in imposing change on national legislation in the different member states.[10]

Whereas, in the past, the main objective of government oversight over network industries had been to restrain the use of market power to charge high prices for their outputs, under the new paradigm, regulatory control of final-output prices has moved into the background. The main task of regulatory institutions for network industries today is to promote the development of competition in these industries—namely, competition in downstream markets and competition between networks where this is possible.

Competition in downstream markets is promoted by *access regulation* requiring the owner of the network to provide downstream service providers with the opportunity to use the network at whatever conditions are deemed to be reasonable. Thus, the owner of the local loop in fixed-line telecommunications is mandated to provide interconnection to competing providers of long-distance services or even local services. He may even be mandated to provide a competitor with access to the copper wire leading into a customer's house so that the latter, rather than the incumbent himself, can provide the customer with basic service.

For the promotion of network competition, the role of access regulation is somewhat ambiguous: on the one hand, access regulation reduces barriers to entry by allowing competitors to enter the fray with some investment without having to duplicate the entire network of the incumbent monopolist. On the other hand, access regulation reduces incentives to build competing infrastructures. There is thus a tension between the promotion of competition in downstream activities through access regulation upstream and the promotion of competition in upstream activities themselves. To be sure, the promotion of competition upstream will also serve the promotion of competition downstream, if only because the competing infrastructures upstream provide a basis for downstream competition. However, the effects are likely to take longer than the effects of access regulation permitting downstream entry without upstream investments.

With all this enthusiasm about the promotion of competition, we should note that, in the absence of competition among networks, there still is a problem of monopoly power to worry about. If the owner of an electricity distribution grid ceases all electricity generation on his own account and merely sells the transmission through his grid to outside generators, final customers have a choice between electricity generators, but this competition between generators does not reduce the grid owner's monopoly power. Thus, the traditional task of sector-specific regulation—namely, to restrain the use of power of network monopolists without endangering the viability of the networks, has *not* become obsolete.

8.1.3. *Sector-specific regulation versus competition policy: the issues*

The changes that have occurred raise questions about the appropriate statutory and institutional framework for regulatory oversight of the network industries. Under the *ancien régime*, regulatory oversight involved direct interventions designed to protect customers in final-output markets. This was the maintained purpose of statutory oversight over output prices under sector-specific regulation in the United States, as well as the various forms of government involvement in Europe. Under the new paradigm, competition itself is deemed to be the major force for customer protection. The notion that competition is the major force for customer protection is of course at the heart of traditional competition policy. One may therefore ask what is, or what should be, the relation between statutory oversight over the network industries and traditional competition policy.

At a very basic level, the question is whether anything more than traditional competition policy is needed. If we believe that customers end up being protected by competition itself, is it not enough to foster competition and, for this purpose, rely on the well-known tools of competition policy, antitrust policy and merger control? Couldn't we simply use the prohibition of exclusionary abuses under antitrust law in order to make sure that competitors in downstream markets are given access to upstream infrastructures? Or, to put the question differently, what are the comparative advantages and disadvantages of traditional competition policy as opposed to sector-specific regulation in dealing with the problem of natural monopoly in network infrastructures?

Further questions arise when a given industry is subject to sector-specific regulation and competition policy at the same time. There are two reasons why this can happen. First, different activities and different markets may be subject to different forms of statutory oversight. If we believe that the network infrastructure is a monopoly whose power needs to be effectively constrained and the downstream market is intensely competitive, we may want to subject the former to sector-specific regulation while leaving the latter to competition policy. In this case, the question is how one can ensure that public policy towards the industry as a whole is consistent. This is partly a legal question, concerning the consistency of norm interpretation across regimes, and partly an institutional question, concerning relations between the different institutions that are charged with the different forms of oversight.

Second, in the European Union, the *same* activities are sometimes subject to antitrust law *and* sector-specific regulation at the same time. This is due to the peculiar interaction of European Law and national law in the European Union. Sector-specific regulation, though narrowly circumscribed by European directives, is a matter of national law. At the level of national law, the existence of sector-specific regulation under a sector-specific law tends to preclude the application of general antitrust law. However, national laws cannot override the Treaty. Therefore, national laws concerning sector-specific regulation cannot preclude the application of Articles 81 and 82 of the EC Treaty to the very activities that are the subject of sector-specific regulation.[11]

An example is provided by the Commission's assessing a fine of some €12 million against Deutsche Telekom on the grounds that the price which final consumers were charged for basic service on analogue lines was predatory, being hardly above—for some time even below—the (regulated) price that Deutsche Telekom was charging for access to the bare wire that a competitor would need to provide such service himself.[12] The very same price that the Commission treated as an exclusionary abuse under Article 82 EC had previously been approved by the German Regulatory Authority.

In such cases, where regulation and antitrust policy concern the same activities, the problem of consistency of public policy comes up with a vengeance. There also is an issue of competition between European and national, antitrust, and regulatory authorities.[13] In the *Deutsche Telekom* case, the European Commission argued that it was not actually contesting the Regulatory Authority's decision. If it had done so, it would have had to initiate Treaty infringement proceedings against Germany. To avoid this roundabout and lengthy way of dealing with the matter, the Commission observed that one of the prices that were considered to be abusive belonged to a basket of prices under a price-cap regime and argued that it was not contesting the price cap that the Regulatory Authority had imposed, but only the use that Deutsche Telekom had made of the leeway it had in setting individual prices under this price-cap.[14] In fact, however, the Commission was overriding the Regulatory Authority's decision not to apply the prohibition of predatory pricing which existed under the German telecommunications law as under Article 82 EC.[15]

One might think that such instances of one institution overriding another are natural occurrences in a system involving a legal appeals process. However, this is not what we are seeing. Whereas a legal appeals' process would have a single hierarchy of legal institutions consider the proper application of a single law to a given case, the coexistence of national sector-specific regulation and

European antitrust law gives rise to *two* hierarchies of legal institutions apply-ing two different laws to the same aspects of a given case. This is where the consistency problem comes in with a vengeance.

These issues have a dynamic, as well as a static, dimension. Whereas the static dimension concerns the regulation and the functioning of the industry at any one point in time, the dynamic dimension concerns the development of the industry and its regulation over time. There are good reasons for seeing network industries as being in a state of transition. Whereas, at the time of market opening, these industries have highly concentrated market structures in all activities, one should expect that, as time goes on, the industry becomes more competitive, at least in downstream markets. In some industries, one may even expect to see competition between different networks. Such devel-opments may call for a reassignment of the tasks of sector-specific regulation and of competition policy, taking some activities and some markets out of the domain of sector-specific regulation and putting them under the auspices of competition policy. The European Union's framework for regulating the tele-communications industry under the Telecommunications Directives of 2002 is actually based on this notion and calls for regular reviews of whether markets are sufficiently competitive for sector-specific regulation to be re-placed by competition policy.

The notion of replacing sector-specific regulation by competition policy raises, first of all, the same questions as before—namely, what are the com-parative advantages of the two regimes and what characteristics of markets and activities suggest that one or the other is more suitable? Also, if there is just a partial transition from one regime to the other, how are relations between the regulated parts and the unregulated parts, between the sector-specific regulator and the competition authority going to work out? In addition, the process of regime change raises a question of procedure: how is one to deter-mine which markets and activities belong to one domain or the other? Are such regime changes to be irrevocable, or should we allow for the possibility of a 'yo-yo process', a market going from sector-specific regulation to a competi-tion policy regime *and back*?

In the following, I will try to assess these different sets of issues one after the other. I begin with an assessment of the comparative advantages and disadvan-tages of the two policy regimes. Following that, I will discuss the dynamics of (partial) transition between a regime of sector-specific regulation and a compe-tition policy regime. Finally, I will consider some of the issues that are raised by the possible coexistence of both regimes in the same industry. In much of the discussion, I will draw on observations from Germany, partly because this is the case with which I am most familiar and partly because this case is particularly instructive: Germany was the one country in the European Union that initially tried to have the energy sector subjected to competition policy only, without sector-specific regulation. The experiment failed, and the failure contains a lesson for the general issue of how to assess the respective roles of competition policy and sector-specific regulation in network industries.

8.2. Comparative Advantages and Disadvantages of Competition Policy and Sector-specific Regulation

8.2.1. *Article 19, Section 4, Nr. 4 of the German Law Against Restraint of Competition*

To set the scene for a more systematic discussion, I can do no better than to cite the German Law Against Restraint of Competition (Gesetz gegen Wettbe-werbsbeschränkungen—GWB). Under Art. 19, Section 4, Nr. 4 of this law, introduced in 1998, it is an 'abuse of dominance to deny access to a network or another essential infrastructure at an appropriate price to a downstream competitor without showing material reason for the denial'. This rule is based on the notion that access provision itself can be handled as a matter of competition policy. This notion underlay the German resistance to sector-specific regulation in the energy industry, which was only ended by the Energy Law of 2005, which implemented the European Directives of 2003. Promoters of the notion that access provision can be handled as a matter of competition policy pointed to the experience of the United States where the so-called *essential facilities doctrine* was said to have been an integral part of competition policy since the *Terminal Railroad* case of 1912.[16]

The Federal Cartel Office's experiences with this clause have been miserable. The main reason is that, in the present context, the notion of 'appropriate price' does not lend itself to court proceedings in which the burden of proof lies with the cartel office. The legal rule requires the owner of the infrastructure to give proof as to why it would be unconscionable to require him to provide others with access; for everything else, including the assessment of the access price, the burden of proof is with the cartel office. As far as I know, every injunction that the Federal Cartel Office has issued under this provision of the law has been contested in court, and the Federal Cartel Office has lost every single case, at least in the first instance, at the Court of Appeal (Oberlandesgericht—OLG) in Düsseldorf, in whose jurisdiction the Federal Cartel office is located.

Typical responses of this court have been:

- Mandating the granting of access without indicating what the price should be runs counter to the principle that mandates from an administrative authority should be sufficiently specific for the addressees to know what they have to do.[17]

- It is not enough to show that revenues on a distribution grid are significantly higher than the relevant measure of costs; the authority must indicate precisely which individual price it deems to be excessive.[18]

- It is not enough to show that, in a cost-plus system of price determination, some cost components are unduly inflated (like attribution of electricity marketing costs to the grid); the cartel office must also provide proof that no other cost components are understated so that the inflation of some components is outweighed.[19]

8.2.2. *What can competition policy do?*

The difficulties encountered by the Federal Cartel Office reflect the fact that the enforcement of access provision is *not* a suitable object for competition policy.[20] Competition policy consists, by and large, of a set of rules and measures which are designed to *forbid* certain types of behaviour. Competition policy is *not* designed to tell market participants what they should do. Cartel agreements are forbidden. Abuses of dominance are forbidden. Mergers that create or strengthen a dominant position, or, under the new Regulation, mergers that create a significant impediment to effective competition are forbidden. In none of these legal provisions is there any notion that the competition authority should tell companies what to do. Sometimes, the competition authorities do so anyway—for example, when they approve a merger subject to certain obligations on the parties in question.[21] However, these instances are taken to be the exception, sometimes even running counter to the very spirit of competition policy.

The stance of competition policy as a regime of prohibitions is a source of strength as well as weakness. It is a source of strength because the competition authority does not have to evaluate alternative course of actions that it might mandate to the companies. It is therefore not dependent on the information that would be needed for such an evaluation. Even more importantly, the stance of competition policy as a system of prohibitions plays a major role in the submission of competition policy to a rule of law and its insulation from at least the most blatant pressures of political wilfulness. Evaluations of alternative mandates for positive course of actions would involve significant elements of subjective judgement. They would hardly be adjudicable in a court of law—and would for that very reason provide a wonderful playground for interest politics.

From this perspective, Art. 19, Section 4, Nr. 4 of the German Law Against Restraint of Competition is an abuse of language. A rule that forbids the denial of access is not really a prohibition. The objective of this rule is to induce the granting of access, that is, to prescribe a specific behaviour. It is hardly possible to mandate this behaviour without addressing the question of what are to be the price and the quality of access. The rulings of the Düsseldorf court that I have cited indicate some of the difficulties that this question poses for competition policy. Competition policy is not well placed to mandate a price and quality of access.

The US experience with the so-called 'essential facilities doctrine' confirms this assessment. The term 'essential facilities doctrine' refers to a collection of court decisions, beginning with *Terminal Railroad* in 1912. It is not clear whether this collection of court decisions amounts to a general principle along the lines of Art. 19, Section 4, Nr. 4 of the German Law Against Restraint of Competition.[22] What is clear, however, is that in all cases, the courts have refrained from determining the prices at which access had to be granted. They were able to do so because in some cases, it was enough to ask for prices to be non-discriminatory, that is, to grant access to the plaintiff on the same terms as everybody else; in others, they referred the plaintiffs to an existing sector-specific regulator who could deal with the problem.[23]

In a regime of competition policy aiming at prohibitions of certain modes of behaviour, interventions of the competition authority as well as the judicial review of such interventions tend to occur piecemeal, focusing on one or several actions in isolation, without regard to their overall significance in the system of governance of the network and the network industry. However, as I shall explain below, it is hardly possible to deal appropriately with access prices in isolation, without considering their systemic implications, be it for other access prices or for market conditions downstream.

Competition policy interventions occur not only piecemeal; they also occur *ex post*, after the disputed behaviour has been implemented by the company and after the competition authority has had the time to obtain a grip on what is going on. Trying to get the requisite information is a daunting and time-consuming task of its own—the more so, because a network owner who wants to foreclose a downstream market has every incentive to delay the proceedings by withholding information and by exhausting all procedural possibilities that the legal system provides. As long as no final judgment has been pronounced, he can continue with the behaviour in question, presumably foreclosing the downstream markets to competition.

In the case of the German electricity industry, the Federal Cartel Office had begun to investigate grid access pricing in 2001. It issued the first injunctions in 2003. The Court of Appeals refused to grant immediate enforcement and in fact overturned the injunctions in 2004. The Court of Appeals' decision in turn was overturned by the Federal Supreme Court in 2005, which sent the matter back to the Court of Appeal. By this time, the matter had become moot because the system of access provision under general competition policy had been replaced by a system of sector-specific regulation. Between 2001 and 2005, market structure had drastically changed because the large electricity providers acquired more than 200 participations in local and regional distributors, thereby assuring themselves of these distributors' business and foreclosing this business to outside generators. The willingness of local distributors to let themselves be taken into the folds of the large generators was partly motivated by a concern that high prices on transmission grids (including high prices for balancing energy, which were attributed to the grids) provided the large generators with significant margins so that they could threaten the local distributors' business with industrial clients by offering electricity at prices close to or even below short-run marginal costs.[24]

One could argue that competition policy might be more powerful if the position of the competition authority was strengthened. Thus, one might consider giving the authority the right systematically to collect information, for example, on costs on an ongoing basis. One might also consider strengthening the authority's position in legal procedures—for example, by changing the rules concerning the burden of proof. However, such changes would move the authority out of the traditional domain of competition policy and provide it with a kind of ongoing authority over the network in question, in short a kind of sector-specific regulation. Even though it might still be a competition authority for most of its activity, in practice, it would take on some roles of a sector-specific regulator.

8.2.3. *The monopoly problem in network industries*

As mentioned in the introduction, the traditional approach to statutory oversight of network monopolies had focused on customer protection through direct oversight of output prices and quality. The opening of downstream markets for competition provides hope that, at this level, such oversight can, at least eventually, be done away with.

However, the paradigm change that has occurred should not lead to a belief that the 'old' problem of controlling monopoly power has altogether disappeared. In those industries where networks serve as essential facilities for downstream activities, the monopoly problem has merely been shifted to the treatment of these facilities themselves. In part, this is a problem of enforcing access to make sure that control over the network is not used to foreclose downstream competition. Even if access is granted freely, on a non-discriminatory basis, access prices can be used to earn monopoly rents. They can also be used to foreclose competition. The German electricity industry provides examples for both—local distributors using their distribution grids as a source of monopoly profits and large generators using access fees for transmission grids to foreclose other generators competing for industrial clients.

To prevent such uses of monopoly power, it is not enough to impose legal unbundling of networks and to require access provision to be non-discriminatory. To be sure, with legal unbundling, high access prices that are charged on a non-discriminatory basis hit the mother company's downstream subsidiary just as they hit any competing company. However, from the perspective of the mother company, the access fee that the downstream subsidiary pays to the network subsidiary is simply an internal transfer price that has no effect on the mother company's aggregate profit.[25] The same high fee paid by a downstream competitor is a nice source of revenues for the corporation and of costs for the competitor.[26]

At this point, it is useful to recall that the prevention of excessive prices is not one of the success stories of competition policy. In Europe, by contrast to the United States, excessive pricing is prohibited as an exploitative abuse under Article 82 EC (or under Art. 19, Section 4, Nr. 2 of the German Law Against Restraint of Competition). However, attempts to enforce this prohibition have by and large been unsuccessful. At the EU level, the Commission has only been successful in cases involving statutory monopolies; in *United Brands*, the European Court of Justice asked for evidence on the relation of prices and costs and imposed such a standard of proof that, subsequently, the Commission desisted from bringing such cases. At the national level, in Germany, the *Librium/Valium* and *Valium II* cases of the seventies showed all the difficulties of assessing prices on the basis of price–cost comparisons when fixed-cost and common-cost components are large. In these drug cases, the court was unwilling to reject the companies' defence that high margins above variable costs were needed to cover the costs of research, including all the research attempts that fail. Given this past experience, the outcomes of the access pricing cases mentioned above could not really have come as a surprise.

8.2.4. *The need for a systemic approach to access regulation*

Fixed and common costs are important for network infrastructures just as for medical drugs. Networks typically involve significant fixed and common costs. Moreover, they typically serve as infrastructure for multiple services. Cost attribution therefore is central to all decisions about network pricing. Thus, the problem of assessing access prices for these infrastructures is at least as difficult as the problem of assessing drug prices.

The problem of cost attribution is inherently a systemic one. From management science and from economics, we know that there is no one method of attribution which can be considered to be unambiguously 'appropriate', be it as a management tool or as a criterion of welfare economics. From the perspective of welfare economics, some version of Ramsey pricing seems desirable, taking account of differences in demand elasticities in order to minimize the welfare impact of price distortions. However, in practice, Ramsey pricing is problematic because it requires a lot of information and is vulnerable to sabotage from the company in question. In practice, therefore, one tends to work with less informationally demanding, more robust procedures such as cost-plus regulation, efficient-component pricing, price cap regulation with different baskets, or benchmarking regulation. The different approaches have different advantages and disadvantages, which can only be assessed in terms of their implications for the entire system of regulated prices.[27]

Given that the problem of cost attribution is central to network pricing and given that this problem has no one 'appropriate' solution, judicial review of any one individual price will hinge on who has authority to choose the cost attribution method. Under the competition policy tradition of assigning the burden of proof to the cartel authority, the authority will find it all but impossible to prevent the use of access pricing as a device to foreclose competition in downstream markets.

Even if one approach is accepted as unambiguously 'appropriate', within this approach, any one price will have to be assessed as part of a *system* of prices. To determine whether regulated prices permit the network owner to recover his costs or whether these prices provide proper incentives for network investments, it is not enough to look at a single price in isolation; one must consider the whole system of prices.

Other aspects of access regulation also raise systemic concerns. At a very fundamental level, there is a trade-off between the promotion of competition in downstream activities through access regulation upstream and the promotion of competition in upstream activities themselves. The stricter the access regulation is, the smaller are companies' incentives to invest upstream on their own. Assessments of this trade-off are likely to differ across industries, with more weight given to the promotion of upstream competition in telecommunications and less weight in the electricity sector.

Further, for at least some industries, the picture of a well-defined essential facility upstream and a well-defined set of services downstream is misleading because it neglects the complexity of the vertical chain of value creation. In these industries, a key question concerns the definition of bottlenecks to which access needs to be granted. In practice, this question is not at all easy to answer, and different answers tend to involve conflicting visions of where the industry is going.

As an example, consider interconnection-based network access versus pure resale models in telecommunications. Interconnection means that access is granted only to a predefined part of the infrastructure and that the entrant has to invest into an own infrastructure (though that may be slim). With pure resale, the entrant could offer the service to customers by renting everything from the incumbent. A model of interconnection-based access is based on the notion that competitive infrastructure investments are beneficial. A model of pure resale is based on the notion that competition in services is to be preferred, either because competitive infrastructure investments are unlikely to be forthcoming or because such investments involve duplication of existing infrastructures and are therefore wasteful.

Thus, in the German discussion about the introduction of mandatory access regulation to permit resale, opposition has come not only from Deutsche Telekom, but also from those companies who had entered the market on the basis of the first model, getting access to the bare wire from Deutsche Telekom

215

and providing basic service to customers. These companies see resale regulation as a threat to their own investments. The important point is that, in this case, one model of competition in downstream markets is at odds with another. Whoever intervenes has to take a choice and should be aware of this.[28]

8.2.5. *Is sector-specific regulation always preferable?*

Given the observation that access regulation requires a systemic approach and competition policy intervenes piecemeal, one might be tempted to see sector-specific regulation as the appropriate answer to all the challenges that have been formulated in the preceding subsections. Sector-specific regulation certainly is able to articulate an intervention policy in systemic terms. With a suitable basis in the underlying legal norms, it should also be able to overcome the procedural difficulties that arise in the framework of competition policy—for example, determine basic principles for cost accounting and cost attribution, collect the requisite information on an ongoing basis, intervene in a timely manner, with little delay from court proceedings.

However, before one jumps to the conclusion that every network or other essential facility should be subject to sector-specific regulation, one should take a step back and reflect on possible drawbacks. Objections must be raised at three levels. First, it is not clear that a regulatory authority is as effective in practice as these theoretical reflections would seem to suggest. For instance, collecting information on an ongoing basis may be better than doing so *ad hoc*, when a problem is perceived, and one first has to fight before one gets the information. However, even if the information is collected on an ongoing basis, the company in question may have plenty of scope to manipulate it. The regulatory authority may also have a hard time processing the information (especially if it is understaffed).

Second, experience suggests that sector-specific regulation is more likely to be captured than competition policy. The examples I gave in the introduction about the relation between Deutsche Telekom and Deutsche Post, the Regulatory Authority, and the competition authorities over the past decade probably have to do with the fact that the German government is a major shareholder in both companies, and, even though the Regulatory Authority is in the domain of the economics, rather than finance ministry, it is more subject to political pressure from the government than the Federal Cartel Office.

There are two reasons for the difference. First, competition policy concerns all industries alike. In any one case, therefore, the competition authority can invoke equal-treatment arguments—and by forcing these arguments to mobilize allies—to resist political pressure. Second, interventions of a sector-specific regulator cut to the core of the company's business and are of central importance to its profit line. With so much more at stake, the company itself has stronger incentives to try and mobilize pressure against the regulator.

Third, and perhaps most importantly, the very strength of sector-specific regulation is also its weakness. The ability to intervene and mandate a certain course of action involves the risk that this may just be the wrong thing to do. Where competition policy just prohibits companies from doing something, sector-specific regulation imposes a course of action upon them. A caricature of what this could mean was provided by the California electricity crisis in 2000 where the incompatibility between the development of market-determined wholesale prices upstream and regulated retail prices downstream caused the distributors to become insolvent and in the process imposed blackouts on households as well as firms.

Whereas the deleterious effect of regulation in the California crisis was easy to recognize and should have been easy to correct, many issues are more subtle so that it is not easy to recognize and correct errors, let alone to do so in a timely fashion. What investment policies are the network companies going to follow under sector-specific regulation? What cost of capital is the regulator assessing? How is risk taken into account in assessing capital costs? What about regulatory risk—for example, the risk that, under a standard based on the costs of efficient service provision, technical change leads to a reduction of regulated access prices for a long-lived facility that does not yet embody tomorrow's technology?

For each of these questions, we may feel that, in a given case, the regulator should be able to come up with a reasonable answer. However, in thinking along such lines, we leave the paradigm of the market system being wiser than any one participant or any one regulator. There may be good reasons for this; in some network industries, the monopoly problem may be important enough to warrant regulatory intervention. However, we need to be aware that this very intervention blunts the market processes. The main justification for intervening anyway is probably that incumbent monopolists in such industries themselves do not leave much room for market processes, and that the imposition of access regulation upstream may induce some market dynamics downstream. However, this requires an assessment that the benefits of invigorating competition in downstream markets outweigh the costs of statutory intervention upstream.

8.2.6. *An example*

The electricity sector provides a case in point. The increases in electricity prices since 2005 have raised a lot of popular discontent. This discontent has fuelled activities of politicians and authorities alike, from the European Commission's Sector Enquiry and subsequent proposals for structural intervention to the German government's proposal to provide the Federal Cartel Office with increased powers to prosecute exploitative abuses in the energy sector. Yet, there is little empirical evidence that electricity pricing actually does involve an exploitative abuse, that is, that the competition authorities' inability to intervene is based on a lack of powers, rather than a lack of a case. An empirical study by London Economics (2007) for the European Commission has found that, in Germany in 2003–5, wholesale electricity prices involved margins of some 27 per cent above marginal costs (more precisely, the average variable costs of the marginal power plant). However, such a number is meaningless unless they are put into some relation to fixed costs.

London Economics did provide a comparison to fixed costs, but the results of this comparison seem highly dependent on the specification they chose. They argued that investment in a new CCGT power plant with a generating capacity of 400 MW and a lifetime of fifteen years would be worthwhile if surpluses above variable costs came to some €67,000 per year. Under marginal cost pricing, the four large suppliers in Germany would have earned some €76,000 per MW of capacity on average per year in 2003–5, some 13 per cent above the amount required to provide for the hypothetical new power plant. Prices above marginal costs could therefore be deemed to be excessive.

However, this assessment depends on the rate of return on capital that is used. If, instead of the rate of 6.5 per cent used by London Economics, one were to use a rate of 10 per cent or higher (as is common, for example, in telecommunications regulation), the required surplus per year would rise from €67,000 to over €80,000, which would not have been covered under marginal-cost pricing as assessed by London Economics.

More importantly, I have doubts whether it makes sense to compare the surplus above variable costs that is required for an investment in the marginal power plant to be worthwhile with the average surplus above variable costs that is achieved on *all* power plants. The latter presumably is bloated by surpluses from water and nuclear energy, which have very low, sometimes even negative, variable costs, and rather higher fixed costs. For a proper assessment of the surpluses that were earned, one would need to assess investment costs for the entire portfolio of power plants. Implicitly, this also raises the question of what is an appropriate portfolio of power plants.

At this point, however, we are in the middle of a systemic problem. The various types of power plants differ in the degree of flexibility with which they can be run up or down in response to foreseen and unforeseen changes in demand. Some power plants will always be running, others only at times of peak demand. Any assessment of the costs of the portfolio of power plants has to take these differences into account. Any such assessment also has to take into account that residual supply elasticities are lower, and market power is higher, at peak times when all available capacity is being used, than at off-peak times when some excess capacity is available. Surpluses of revenues over variable costs are therefore easier to obtain at peak times than at off-peak times, and most probably the surpluses that are earned at peak times make an above-average contribution to covering capital costs—for the power plants that provide base-load electricity as well as the power plants that provide peak-load electricity.[29]

Given the systemic character of the problem, competition policy is not well-placed to establish whether electricity pricing is excessive or not. Most likely, the attempt by a competition authority to establish an exploitative abuse will fail even if such an abuse is there. However, before one jumps to the conclusion that one needs sector-specific regulation in order to control electricity prices, one must take account of the risks inherent in such control. As indicated, the assessment of electricity prices is a delicate matter which can be highly sensitive to the details of the analysis that one undertakes. A regulatory authority is no more immune to error than a competition authority; it only has more powers to impose its view of the matter through regulation. However, if it errs in the direction of restraining prices too much, this affects investment incentives. Given that environmental concerns and the coming exhaustion of important primary-energy sources call for innovations and new investments, the costs of such errors can be quite substantial. It may therefore be preferable to leave the generation and the sale of electricity in the domain of competition policy, rather than subjecting them to sector-specific regulation; the weakening of present-day consumer protection that is thereby entailed is probably less important than the risk of blunting innovation and investment incentives in electricity production.

The very same concern also calls for ensuring that electricity markets are open to competition by outsiders. If we are searching for new and improved technologies to generate electricity from available primary energy sources, we should not be satisfied to leave this search just to the former monopolists. The dictum of Sir John Hicks, according to which the nicest monopoly rent is a quiet life, suggests that monopolists who are not threatened by competition are not likely to be very active innovators. In this context, one should recall the experience of the United States where the market opening provided by the Public Utilities Regulatory Policy Act (PURPA) of 1978 induced a remarkable amount of entry by new firms with new techniques for electricity generation and showed that the incumbent monopolists had missed the train on technical progress. There may also be a risk that large incumbents, in particular, the former statutory monopolists, may have a bias towards techniques which reinforce their market position, in political markets as well as electricity markets, that is, techniques where minimum efficient scale is large so that they can claim that generation is a natural monopoly after all.

Given the importance of searching for new and improved technologies for electricity generation and given the notion that this search should not just be left to the former monopolists, I infer that it is crucial to have a well-functioning access regime for electricity grids. Past experience with different approaches suggests that this calls for sector-specific regulation of access pro-vision. The very same concern which makes for caution with respect to a sector-specific regulation of electricity prices thus also militates for the impos-ition of sector-specific regulation of grid access as a precondition for effective competition in electricity generation and sales.

8.3. How Should the Line be Drawn between the Regulated and Unregulated Parts of a Network Industry?

8.3.1. *Naive versus sophisticated approaches*

Given the assessment that there are certain activities where competition pol-icy is unlikely to be effective on an ongoing basis and where the benefits of sector-specific regulation—in particular, for enhancing competition in down-stream markets—are deemed to outweigh the costs, the question arises how large the domain of sector-specific regulation should be and how relations of regulated and unregulated domains, of sector-specific regulation, and com-petition policy are to be organized. In some sectors, this question has been approached somewhat naively. Thus, the European Electricity and Gas Direct-ives provide for a sector-specific regulation of the networks, but *not* for a sector-specific regulation of production or trading of electricity and gas. Presumably, the distinction was based on the view that networks continue to be natural monopolies, and network access is a precondition for competition in down-stream markets, but, once this precondition is met, competition will set off on its own.

By contrast, the European Telecommunications Directives of 2002 introduce a more sophisticated system for determining which activities are subject to sector-specific regulation and which ones are not. Activities are classified by 'markets'. The basic principle is that sector-specific regulation should be im-posed in those markets and *only* in those markets of the industry where workable competition does not exist and is unlikely to arise in the near future and that in all other markets the industry should be subject to general com-petition rules.

To determine which markets are to be subjected to sector-specific regulation, the Telecommunications Directives specify a two-step procedure. In a first step, called 'market definition', the regulatory authority, following a recom-mendation from the European Commission, draws up a list of markets to be analysed. In a second step, called 'market analysis', the regulatory authority, in consultation with the European Commission and with the other regulatory authorities in the EU, determines for each market on the list whether there is 'effective competition' in this market. Effective competition is said to be present if and only if no firm in the market has 'significant market power'.

The wording of the legal norms and of the Commission's guidelines suggests that 'significant market power' is similar to, but—in view of the different purposes of the different legal norms—not quite the same as 'dominance' in Article 82 EC.

The sophisticated approach differs from the naive approach in two respects. First, the division of the industry into the parts that are subject to sector-specific regulation and the parts that are subject to general competition policy is not fixed in the law, but is left to be decided by the authorities in a well-specified procedure, presumably subject to judicial review. Second, the division of the industry into the parts that are subject to sector-specific regulation and the parts that are subject to general competition policy is based on considerations of competition and market power rather than the distinction between network infrastructures and downstream activities.

This means, that, in principle, one can have downstream activities that are subject to sector-specific regulation, and one can have network infrastructures that are partly or entirely *not* subject to sector-specific regulation. An example for the former is given by final consumer prices for basic fixed-line analogue or ISDN service. An example for the latter could be the markets for rentals of long-distance fixed lines at the highest level of the geographic network hierarchy in Germany where a significant number of alternative suppliers have built their own infrastructures and could in principle offer alternatives to the regulated offerings of Deutsche Telekom.[30]

I have serious doubts whether the sophisticated approach for determining which parts of the industry should be regulated is really superior to the naive approach. In particular, I am not convinced that the 'market' is an appropriate unit of analysis for this question. Recognition of the difficulties that are involved in fact induces the practitioners to use the term 'market' in a somewhat different sense from the way it is used in competition policy. I consider this differentiation of legal terminology according to which legal norm is being applied to be problematic, the more so, since the Telecommunications Directives and national Telecommunications Laws themselves contain explicit references to origins of the terms in competition law. In the following, I will substantiate this criticism.

8.3.2. Is the 'market' the proper unit of reference? The problem of 'cross-border' systemic effects

The above discussion of the comparative advantages and disadvantages of sector-specific regulation and competition policy named systemic interdependence of different activities as a major reason for failures of competition policy, the point being that competition policy intervention tends to be piecemeal and *ad hoc*, with little scope for embedding the analysis of the presumed abuse in a wider systemic context. Unfortunately, such concerns play no role on the sophisticated approach of the Telecommunications Directives. Under this approach, therefore, we must reckon with the possibility that, because of systemic interdependence, different activities should be analysed jointly but are in fact in different domains, one in the domain of competition policy, the other in the domain of sector-specific regulation.

As an example, consider the treatment of termination charges in mobile telephony. The European Commission has named network specific termination services as one of the set of markets to be analysed, much against the resistance of the industry and some national governments who would have preferred termination services of all networks to be put in one 'market'. Given the definition of network-specific markets for termination services, the outcome of 'market analysis' is a foregone conclusion—for obviously every network operator is dominant for access provision in his own network. The question then becomes what regulation the network operators will be subjected to. The recurrence of complaints about termination charges suggests that some regulation of these charges might be called for.

However, by what standard should regulated termination charges be set? The mobile network operators claim that they need high termination charges in order to finance their overall networks. The problem of attributing fixed and common costs here cuts across the boundary between regulated and unregulated activities. To assess the appropriateness of proposed termination charges, the regulator needs to have some notion of what is—or what should be—the contributions of unregulated, competitive activities to covering fixed and common costs. However, how would he get the information that he would need to assess these contributions? Wouldn't the very imposition of an information requirement for these activities contradict their status as being 'unregulated'?

In mobile telephony, markets for basic service and for the initiation of communications are, for the most part, highly competitive and have therefore not been subjected to sector-specific regulation. Before the European Directives of 2002 were implemented, this unregulated regime was also applied to call terminations. Member State governments saw mobile telecommunications as a success story with which they did not want to interfere. The substantive reason given was that this sector was engaged in intense *systems competition*, which made it unnecessary to worry about each individual component of these systems.

As a matter of economics, it is not clear that the systems competition argument carries very far. The person who calls the client of a mobile phone company does not generally profit from that particular company's offerings himself. Moreover, if he urgently needs to reach that person, he has no way of substituting this company's termination service by some other service. The companies argue that their exploiting the market power which this structure gives them is actually welfare-enhancing because it corresponds to the Ramsey–

Boiteux rule of having margins that are highest where demand elasticities are lowest, but in these arguments, they forget that the Ramsey–Boiteux rule applies to market demands, not the demands faced by any one company.[31] As an assessment of distortions induced by market power, the Commission's judgment therefore seems to be correct.[32]

However, we should appreciate that there are many other markets in which firms have market power, which we do not subject to sector-specific regulation. Airlines have extraordinary market power on certain routes from or to airports where they hold rights to most of the slots. Even so, this is not deemed to be a reason for subjecting them to sector-specific regulation. Presumably, the argument is that, if we wanted to imposed sector-specific regulation in every market in which a firm has and uses market power, then we should find ourselves with a bigger job than we could handle. There are just too many such markets and too many such firms.

In the given example, the main objection is that, because of the systemic interdependence, it is impossible to do the regulatory job properly if terminations alone are subjected to it. One should subject either the entire spectrum of markets to it or none. Given the overall degree of satisfaction with the performance of this industry, the former seems hardly appropriate. I therefore wonder whether it would not be better to forego a sector-specific regulation of mobile telecommunications altogether. On the one hand, this means accepting monopoly pricing and ensuing distortions for terminations; on the other hand it avoids getting into a mode where regulation is imposed, but cannot really be handled properly.

The very same logic suggests that, perhaps, it is not so sensible to exempt the markets for rentals of fixed-line capacity at the highest level of the geographic network hierarchy from sector-specific regulation. Here, too, the existence of significant common costs of different parts of the fixed-line network throws doubt on the workability of piecemeal exemptions.

The overriding message of these remarks is *not* that we should have more regulation or less regulation than the Telecommunications Directives are providing for. The message is, rather, that the imposition of sector-specific regulation should be conditioned on system effects, in particular, in relation to the networks, rather than market power. If we are willing to admit the existence and exploitation of market power in a standard competition policy regime for other industries, then, for network industries, the mere existence of market power in part of the industry is not a good reason for imposing regulation. If, instead, we are worried about systemic aspects of the industry, for example, with respect to cost attribution for services important for access provision, then we should focus on those systemic aspects, rather than market power. In this case, the mere absence of market power in a given market may not be a good reason for exempting the activity in question from regulation.

8.3.3. Is the 'market' the proper unit of reference?
The problem of market definition

Scepticism about the use of the market as the proper unit of reference is also warranted on procedural grounds. Experiences that we have had with the 'old' Telecommunications Law in Germany, 1998–2004, provide a few lessons. Under the old Telecommunications Law, the imposition of various kinds of sector-specific regulation was conditioned on the company's being dominant in the sense of competition law. This is somewhat akin to the prevailing European framework condition regulation on the company being found to have significant market power. Under this regime, for example, Deutsche Telekom was subject to an *ex ante* regulation of final-customer prices in those markets where it was held to be dominant.

At some point, the company tried to use the dominance requirement as a lever to get out of regulation. As one might expect, this gave rise to the usual game of what is the relevant market. However, in contrast to what we would expect from merger control cases, they went for narrow rather than wide definitions of relevant markets. Given the weight of incumbency, a wide definition would easily have supported a finding of dominance. However, they could make a case that such a finding was not justified for a suitably picked narrowly defined 'market'. So they first applied for deregulation in the market for foreign calls from Germany to Turkey, from Germany to Denmark, and from Germany to the United States. Subsequently, they proposed to look at the market for business calls between Frankfurt and Berlin and the market for foreign calls to Uzbekhistan.

In dealing with these applications, the regulatory authority initially accepted Deutsche Telekom's market definitions and then, on the basis of further analyses of these markets, deregulated the phone calls to Turkey, but not to Denmark and the United States. Subsequently, however, they rejected Deutsche Telekom's market definitions for business calls between Frankfurt and Berlin and for calls to Uzbekhistan. In the latter decision, they argued that any provider of telecommunications services to some foreign country was a potential provider of telecommunications services to any other foreign country as well, and so on the basis of considering potential competition, all foreign calls should be treated as belonging to the same market.

The regulatory authority's first reaction to Deutsche Telekom's applications reflected a straightforward application of the competition policy practice of market definition to the matter on hand. Their subsequent change of stance was motivated, first, by their coming to understand the difficulties that the deregulation of excessively differentiated 'markets' would pose for the viability of the system, and, second, by their realizing that the need to go through these applications market by market, doing a proper analysis of dominance for each 'market', would impose an enormous administrative cost.

These experiences are relevant for the handling of 'market analysis' under the new European regime. To be sure, 'market analyses' are preceded by the stage of 'market definition'. However, the term 'market definition' in telecommunications law does not mean the same thing as in general competition law. Whereas in general competition law the term 'market definition' refers to the specification of the 'market' that is relevant for demand, supply, and pricing decisions of the various participants, the term 'market definition' in telecommunications law is much broader. Thus, geographic aspects of market definition play no role in the recommendations of the European Commission; yet they are a key element in competition analysis. Moreover, the 'markets' that the European Commission has recommended for 'market definition' represent *aggregates* of market in the competition-policy sense. For instance, in basic service, the Commission's Recommendation lumps analogue, ISDN, and ISDN multiplex services all together under the category of 'Access to the public telephone network at a fixed location for residential customers'. Similarly, the German Regulatory Authority continues to follow its previous 'anti-Uzbekhistan' line and does not differentiate by geographic origin or destination.

From a policy perspective, I consider this way of proceeding to be reasonable as a way of dealing with the fact that, as explained in the preceding subsection, a decision about regulation market by market in the competition policy sense of the term is unlikely to yield satisfactory results. Given the systemic concerns that underlie the use of sector-specific regulation in the first place, I am sceptical about narrow market definitions in this context. Apart from the administrative burdens involved in doing separate analyses for lots of narrowly defined 'markets', I see the problem that the regulatory authority or the competition authority will find it hard to deal with cost attribution problems and cross-subsidization problems if regulation is conditioned on dominance in narrowly defined markets. If we decide to have calls to Uzbekhistan and calls to Denmark in different regimes when both types of calls require some of the same infrastructures, we may be undermining the viability of either regime.

I also see an issue of stability of the regulatory environment if 'yoyo effects' in narrowly defined markets lead to repeated changes in the assessment of significant market power. Because of these concerns, the German Monopolies Commission, which initially had recommended applying the concept of market dominance in exactly the same way as under competition law had subsequently recommended that the regulatory authority make extensive use of the 'prognostic element' in its assessments of dominance and that it take account of relations to 'neighbouring markets'.[33]

However, from a legal perspective, such recommendations are problematic. After all, the procedures used in market analysis will be subject to court control. If the legal norms use competition law terminology, why should market participants—or the courts!—accept any use of this terminology which deviates from traditional procedures? In this respect, the European framework is perhaps more flexible than the old German law; after all, relations to neighbouring markets are explicitly mentioned as a matter for consideration. Moreover, the Commission's guidelines stress that 'significant market power' is similar to, but in view of the different context, not quite the same as, 'market dominance'. Whatever the regulators and the courts are going to make of this, I feel uneasy on account of the fact that, at best, we are subject to significant legal uncertainty. At worst, we may end up with a dysfunctional scheme for determining the incidence of regulation.

The broadness of 'market definitions' recommended by the Commission and implemented by the national regulators should be seen as evidence that the 'market' in the competition policy sense is not a natural unit of reference for determining the incidence of sector-specific regulation. It simply pays too little attention to systemic structures and their implications for the viability of competition policy. For legal hygiene, however, it would be better if the legal norm was geared to the systemic effects rather than the presence or absence of significant market power, and the procedure for 'market definition' and 'market analysis' did not involve any departure from standard competition policy procedures.

From the experience of competition policy, we know that the precise definition of the market always involves a certain element of arbitrariness. If products are differentiated, the notion of relevant market itself is problematic because boundaries between sub-markets are hardly discernible. In competition policy, this arbitrariness of market definition makes for the livelihood of lawyers and economic experts, with some haphazardness of results. However, these cases typically involve a once-for-all decision. A merger is prohibited or allowed, an abuse of dominance is proscribed or not, and then the case is closed. In contrast, in the telecommunications sector, market definitions are the basis for investigating significant market power, the finding of which is the basis for instituting an *ongoing system* of regulation. Here the arbitrariness of precise definitions and the haphazardness of legal outcomes pose a more serious problem. Criteria that yield haphazard outcomes are not a good basis for institutional arrangements that provide the requisite combination of continuity, legal certainty, and substantive appropriateness.

8.3.4. *Is the 'market' the proper unit of reference?* *'market definition' as a political act*

Given the preceding criticisms, the naive approach practised in the energy sector begins to look better. If networks are subjected to regulation and downstream activities are not, one has a clear distinction along systemic lines, which may not be the same as a distinction according to market power. Something like this naive approach was in fact suggested by the German Monopolies Commission, which, under the 'old' telecommunications law of

1996, had reported once every two years on the development of competition in telecommunications and made recommendations on whether to change the list of markets in the law. The Monopolies Commission recommended considering functionally separate groups of relatively homogenous markets with a view to deregulating all or none of them, regardless of concerns about dominance. Thus, in 2003 and 2005, it recommended taking *all* long-distance and foreign voice telecommunications out of the domain of sector-specific regulation even though, in some of the markets that were involved, Deutsche Telekom still held a clearly dominant position. Neglect of such dominance was justified by the observation that many markets with dominant firms are subject to competition policy without any idea for sector-specific regulation, that is, that dominance cannot be the appropriate distinguishing criterion.

Such assessments are at bottom political in nature. The Monopolies Commission's recommendations under the old telecommunications law in fact were addressed to the German Parliament, as recommendations to change the law. I believe that the step of 'market definition' under the European Telecommunications Directives is similarly political in nature. The Directives and national laws merely dress it up as an administrative act which implements the law and which is itself subject to judicial review.

To be sure, the legal norms list substantive criteria for the inclusion of a market in the list that is drawn up under the heading of 'market definition'. However, these criteria are soft and do not lend themselves to judicial review. More importantly, these criteria cannot be seriously applied unless one has already done the market analysis, which, however, only comes afterwards. The list of markets drawn up under the heading of market definition should include those markets which exhibit a significant and durable structure of legal barriers to entry, which do not exhibit a tendency towards a development of effective competition, even in the long run, and for which competition policy is insufficient to counteract the market failures that result from market power. I fail to see how these criteria can be reliably assessed when the market analysis has not yet been done. Moreover, the third criterion, whether competition policy is deemed to be able to counteract market failures or not involves subjective judgement and is hardly compatible with a serious judicial review of administrative decisions.

I would prefer it if the political nature of the first step of the procedure was made more explicit, perhaps under a different name, without any pretence that this is comparable to what competition economists understand by 'market definition'. I would also prefer it if the detailed analysis of the second step paid more attention to the systemic aspects of the problem because these aspects are central to the distinction between the two policy modes. Bringing in such concerns at a later stage, by reinterpreting the terms that are used in the legal norms to make them fit the problem seems inappropriate. Such reinterpretations of terms may provide a pragmatic way to deal with the inappropriateness of the approach. However, it undermines the status of competition policy and sector-specific regulation as being carried out under a rule of law. It also reduces transparency and immunizes the authorities from political and judicial controls. It is perhaps not a coincidence that, in the implementation of the European Telecommunications Directives, there have been hardly any instances of deregulation. In what was ostensibly introduced as a system for organizing the transition from sector-specific regulation to competition policy wherever possible, we have mainly seen the imposition of additional sector-specific regulation.

8.4. On the Coexistence of Competition Policy and Sector-specific Regulation

In this final section of the chapter, I will discuss some issues that arise from the simultaneous application of competition policy and sector-specific regulation in the same industry. As discussed in the introduction, there are several dimensions to this simultaneity—substantive, legal, institutional. I first consider some substantive issues and will then move on to a discussion of legal and institutional arrangements.

8.4.1. *Substantive issues*

Two sets of substantive issues arise. The first set involves issues that arise because competition policy and sector-specific regulation rely on legal norms that use the same terminology. The second set involves issues that arise because competition policy and sector-specific regulation are applied to the same industries.

When legal norms for competition policy and sector-specific regulation involve the same terminology the challenge is to preserve the viability of this terminology as a basis for administrative and legal practice. There is a tension here between, on the one hand, the need for legal precision and, on the other hand, the need for appropriateness in different applications. The former calls for inflexibility, the latter for flexibility in one's use of the terms. The above discussion of the use of the term 'market' in current telecommunications provides a case in point. Although I applaud the pragmatism with which the matter has been approached, I am uneasy about the fact that, because of the difference in purposes, we now have different uses of this term in the application of telecommunications law and in the application of competition law.

Other examples concern the standards and procedures that authorities and courts use in practice to fill the legal terms with content. An example is given by cost standards that are used to assess prices. For instance, in its discussions with electricity producers, the Federal Cartel Office in Germany has pointed to the fact that existing power plants have been built a long time ago and have long been written off. Therefore, the Federal Cartel Office argues, capital costs for these power plants should not play a role in assessing current electricity prices. Implicitly, this argument takes historically realized costs as the appropriate standard for assessing prices. By contrast, legal norms guiding sector-specific regulation tend to impose standards that involve forward-looking, long-run incremental costs, sometimes with a proviso that cost is to be assessed on the basis of the most efficient technology available. Given the well-known incentive effects of cost-plus pricing rules, I consider the latter standard to be more appropriate. More importantly, I consider the difference between these standards to be problematic. For an integrated electricity company, such differences can provide room for regulatory arbitrage. Moreover, in a dynamic setting, where activities are moved from one domain to the other as the need for sector-specific regulation decreases, such differences mean that, when this move occurs, not only the institutional arrangements, but also the substantive standards for statutory oversight are changed.

Differences can also arise in the assessment of defences that the companies give for certain practices. An example is provided by the German Regulatory Authority's assessment of Deutsche Telekom's pricing of DSL connections in 2000. The text of decision explains at length why the authority considers the price that Deutsche Telekom charged for DSL connections to be predatory. Then, at the very end, the authority explains that it is not going to proscribe Deutsche Telekom's pricing policy after all because cheap pricing for fast internet connections is going to promote the declared policy objective of the German government of enhancing the use of the internet in German society. With this reasoning, the Regulatory Authority departed from the legal tradition of German competition law which had long held that substantive defences for presumed abuses had to be based on the objective of the very law that was involved, that is, the Law Against Restraint of Competition and that an appeal to any arbitrarily chosen objective of public policy was not compatible with the requirements of a stable rule of law in competition policy. Leaving aside the question whether Deutsche Telekom's pricing in the particular case was indeed predatory, I consider it problematic if sector-specific regulation has different standards in assessing the abusiveness of a disputed practice when the legal norm actually uses the same terms as the Law Against Restraint of Competition.

Whereas these examples raise questions of consistency in the application of competition-policy concepts in different legal norms and across different industries, a second set of issues raises questions of consistency in the treatment of a given industry. If a network industry is subject to sector-specific regulation and competition policy at the same time, one needs to have some mechanism to ensure that the different regimes do not work at cross-purposes.

Thus, if there are common costs that concern activities in the domain of sector-specific regulation as well as activities in the domain of competition policy, standards and procedures for dealing with them should be consistent. If there is an interdependence between, say, the definition of the relevant markets in the assessment of a merger of electricity producers and the viability of the regulatory regime for grid access, this interdependence should be taken into account (as was not sufficiently done in the VEBA-VIAG (E.ON) and RWE-VEW merger approvals in 2000).

In thinking about these different issues, we see that they involve two different notions of policy coherence. On the one hand, we want competition policy to be coherent across sectors. Competition policy gains its legitimacy from the fact that it applies the same rules to all industries and all market participants. Discrimination would undermine this legitimacy. On the other hand, we also want a certain consistency of statutory policy towards a given industry. Moreover, the policy should be appropriate for the industry in question. In the case of a network industry which, after all, has specific features which are the reason for subjecting this industry to sector-specific regulation, we wouldn't want, for example, abuse-of-dominance proceedings under competition policy to be at odds with what the sector regulator is doing in his domain. As yet, we have little understanding of how to resolve the conflict between these two notions of policy coherence.

8.4.2. *Institutional issues*

Policy coherence is to some extent a matter of institutional arrangements. However, the tension between the two notions of coherence poses a major challenge for institution design. The challenge is all the greater because the different authorities are subject to different kinds of influences. Experience seems to show that sector-specific regulation is rather more susceptible to regulatory capture than competition policy. In some instances where sector-specific regulators have departed from traditions of competition policy in the application of competition policy norms, it seems clear that pressure from the political system has played a significant role. The difference reflects the fact that companies under sector-specific regulation, unlike companies under competition policy, have a strong and persistent interest in lobbying the political authorities as well as the regulators. The fact that Member State governments continue to hold significant shares in some of the former monopolists has also played a role.

At a very basic level, one would like to ensure that the different institutions cooperate where such cooperation is needed. As far as I can tell, legal norms already provide for such cooperation, at least in the form of statutory consultation on decisions of mutual interest. Rules for mutual access to relevant information seem rather weaker and should probably be strengthened.

However, when there are separate authorities, or even just separate units within a given authority, exchanges of information and views will not be sufficient for policy coherence. One possibility to go further might be to follow an example set by banking supervision in Germany: the supervisors are employees of the Bundesbank working on behalf of (and under orders from) the supervisory authority. By this device, the Bundesbank has the information it needs for its role in monetary policy—in particular, the soft information which is not contained in published numbers—and yet there is a separation of responsibilities. A similar arrangement, with employees of the regulator applying competition law on behalf of the competition authority might improve the coherence of competition policy across sectors while ensuring that the regulator has the information about the unregulated part of the industry that he needs.

Whereas the discussion so far has focused on concerns that arise when different parts of the same industry, with well-defined boundaries, are subject to different policy regimes, existing arrangements in the European Union also raise concerns about the possibility that the very same activities might be subject to both regimes simultaneously. As mentioned in the introduction, European competition law—in particular, Articles 81 and 82 EC—cannot be overruled by national law. The legal norms that provide the basis for sector-specific regulation are based on European Directives, but are strictly speaking national laws and can therefore not pre-empt the application of European competition law, although they can—and in the case of Germany do—pre-empt the application of national competition law. Thus, in the cases of Deutsche Telekom and, more recently, Telefónica, the Commission has relied on Article 82 EC to condemn pricing policies that had previously been approved by the national regulators. The Commission's decision in the case of Deutsche Telekom has by now been confirmed by the CFI. In the case *Konsolidierer/Deutsche Post*, the Federal Cartel Office, acting under the auspices of Regulation 01/2003, used Article 82 EC to force the company to grant access to competitors where the regulator had failed to act.[34]

In these cases, the simultaneous applicability of European competition law and national regulatory law has led to healthy rivalry of authorities, which has helped to counteract the effects of regulatory capture at the national level. This rivalry of authorities worked the way it did because, under existing case law, the Treaty (and therefore European competition law as part of the Treaty) is directly applicable in the Member States of the European Union. In each case, actually, the competition authorities held that they were not contravening any explicit mandates of the regulatory authorities, but merely objecting to the companies' uses of the leeway left to them by the regulatory authorities—for example, the leeway for setting individual prices under a price-cap regime. If, in the Deutsche Telekom and Telefónica cases, the prices in question had actually been mandated by the regulators, the Commission would have had to initiate Treaty violation proceedings against the Member States in question, which probably would have taken much more time and would therefore have been less effective.

From the perspective of the companies that are concerned, the coexistence of different legal regimes is a source of legal uncertainty and of costs. It would, in principle, be desirable to have a more streamlined system.[35] Given the relative standing of European law and national law, however, such a system would require a European competence for sector-specific regulation. Even then, there would be a question of how to mark the boundaries between the two regimes.

A discussion of policy coherence in sector-specific regulation and competition policy would not be complete without a mention of the courts. Given that some of the legal norms in sector-specific regulation and competition law are ostensibly the same, I consider it important that judicial review should, at least ultimately, rest with the same courts, and that these courts should be aware of the underlying unity of the legal norms. In the case of antitrust law, ultimate authority rests with the European Court of Justice. The decentralization of European antitrust enforcement under Regulation 01/2003 involves a risk that the practices of national competition authorities and national courts may diverge, but then this divergence can be eliminated by the European Commission taking over important cases or by the national courts asking for guidance from the European Court of Justice.

By contrast, in the area of sector-specific regulation, the role of the European Court of Justice is weaker because the law that is being applied is national, subject to European Directives. The ultimate arbiters of this law are the highest courts of the different Member States. There is thus a danger that the underlying unity of certain legal norms may be lost as the highest courts of the different Member States may interpret these norms differently, or as their interpretation in cases involving sector-specific regulation under national law may diverge from their interpretation by the European Court of Justice in cases involving competition policy under European law. In the interest of the unity of the law, it is to be hoped that, in matters of legal norms that are common to both areas, the authority of the European Court of Justice as the ultimate source of jurisdiction on competition law will be extended to the law of sector-specific regulation.

Notes

[1] For helpful comments I am grateful to Petros Alexiadis, Christoph Engel, Amelia Fletcher, Richard Gilbert, Felix Höffler, and Xavier Vives. I am also grateful to the German Monopolies Commission and its staff, whose work in 1998–2006 contributed greatly to my understanding of the issues.

[2] For a discussion of how precisely to define the notion of natural monopoly, see Baumol, et al. (1982).

[3] For overviews, see Newbery (2000); Organisation for Economic Co-operation and Development (2001a).

[4] For an account of past approaches, see Viscusi, et al. (2001).

[5] For details, see Monopolkommission (2002; 2004a; 2006).

[6] As of 2001, a study commissioned by the German Monopolies Commission showed that mobile networks imposed hardly any competitive pressure on fixed-line networks; the study also suggested that, for large-scale data communication, substitutability would never be perfect (Monopolkommission 2002, paras 88–98). Beginning in 2005, relations between mobile and fixed-line telecommunications markets have drastically changed so that by now the wholesale loss of customers to mobile networks is a major worry of the fixed-line incumbent (Monopolkommission 2006, paras 60–7).

[7] Thus, Deutsche Bundespost in the 1980s was still insisting that anything but a wire-attached grey phone with a traditional dial would pose a risk to the safety of its network—at a time when wireless touchtone phones were becoming the norm in the rest of the world.

[8] Whereas the state-owned Deutsche Bundespost had been a perennial loss-maker, with losses in the mail system exceeding profits from telecommunications by far, today, after the separation from telecommunications, and after privatization, the traditional mail activities of Deutsche Post are highly profitable, with profits-to-sales ratios in the letters segment lying significantly above 10 per cent in each of the past ten years.

[9] References to directives are given at the end of this volume.

[10] Having the network industries come into the domain of European integration has vastly expanded the Commission's domain of activity. Sometimes the Commission gives the impression that it treats the factual, as opposed to legal, integration of markets as a policy objective in its own right, on a par with the objectives of competition policy. Thus, the Commission's DG Competition Report on Energy Sector Inquiry of 10 Jan. 2007 has subheadings 'Concentration', 'Vertical Foreclosure', 'Market Integration', 'Transparency', 'Price Issues', without any acknowledgement of the fact that market integration as such is a political aim that may have little to do with competition and with economic performance. The Commission's attitude to the proposed takeover of the Spanish energy provider Endesa by the German company E.ON, like its 2000 decision in the VEBA/VIAG merger case, gives the impression that, when a proposed merger holds a prospect of promoting market integration at the expense of competition, the competition concerns take second place.

[11] By contrast, the *Trinko* and *Crédit Suisse* decisions of the United States Supreme Court have made clear that, in the United States, the existence of sector-specific regulation rules out the application of the corresponding provisions of antitrust law.

[12] References to decisions in individual cases are given at the end of this volume.

[13] In this context, it is worth noting that, under Regulation 01/2003, European antitrust law can also be invoked by the national competition authority. Thus, in a more recent case involving *Deutsche Post*, the Federal Cartel Office proscribed an exclusionary abuse that the Regulatory Authority had refused to deal with. The German Postal Law, under which the Regulatory Authority was acting, had a wider specification than the Postal Directive permitted of the domain where the incumbent retained his statutory monopoly. Whereas the Treaty infringement proceedings initiated by the European Commission would have taken a few years, the Cartel Office's intervention led to an immediate termination of the abuse.

[14] The Commission has used this line of argument again in the more recent *Telefonica* case. In Apr. 2008, the CFI confirmed the validity of the argument in the *Deutsche Telekom* case.

[15] The Regulatory Authority asserted that, under the price-cap regime, the anti-exclusionary and anti-discriminatory provisions of the law were to be applied to the basket, rather than the individual components of the basket. In fact, as was pointed out by the Federal Cartel Office as well as the Monopolies Commission, this assertion in fact was in conflict with the law, which stipulated a price-cap basket approach only for the anti-exploitative provisions of the law.

[16] For a systematic discussion of the essential facilities doctrine and practice, see Lipsky and Sidak (1999); Géradin and Sidak (2005).

[17] This Judgment of the OLG Düsseldorf in the case *Fährhafen Puttgarden*, which concerned access to the port of Puttgarden, was subsequently voided by the Bundesgerichtshof [BGH] (Federal Supreme Court). The BGH suggested that, at least in a first go, it was reasonable to expect the parties in question to bargain about the access price. However, if the bargaining did not lead to a satisfactory conclusion, the Federal Cartel Office might be required to set and justify the access price yet.

[18] This Judgment of the OLG Düsseldorf in the matter of grid pricing of *Stadtwerke Mainz*, a municipal electricity distributor, was also voided by the BGH, and the case was sent back to the OLG. However, even as it voided the lower court's judgment, the Federal Supreme Court stressed the need to allow for a significant margin of error in assessing excessive pricing. On the case, see Monopolkommission (2005: paras 563–77) (165* in the Engl. summary).

[19] This Judgment of the OLG Düsseldorf in the case of *TEAG*, a distribution company of E.ON, was not appealed. On the case, see Monopolkommission (2005: paras 558–62) (164* in the Engl. summary).

[20] The German Monopolies Commission argued this point even before the Federal Cartel Office had tried to interfere with the electricity companies' access pricing practices. Its 2002 report Monopolkommission (2003: paras 726–869) (115*–146* in the Engl. summary) provides a systematic treatment of the pros and cons of sector-specific regulation and competition policy for regulating network access and recommends a move to sector-specific regulation for the energy sectors. The discussion here follows the same line of argument. A similar treatment of these issues is provided by Newbery 2006.

[21] Thus, in the German energy mergers of 2000 *VEBA/VIAG* and *RWE/VEW*, the European Commission and the Federal Cartel Office enjoined the companies to increase cross-border interconnector capacities and to award these capacities by auctions that would be open to competitors. The insignificance of the market opening that was thereby achieved provides a serious warning against overconfidence in the effects of behavioural remedies.

[22] In *Trinko*, the Supreme Court remarked that, as yet, no such general principle had as yet been established, but, given the existence of sector-specific regulation, the matter did not need to be considered.

[23] Lipsky and Sidak (1999); Monopolkommission (2003: paras 746–53).

[24] Newbery (2002); Becker (2004).

[25] The same argument applies to pricing for balancing energy. If the network subsidiary of an electricity company pays high prices for balancing energy and the balancing energy is produced by another subsidiary of the same company, the price for balancing energy is just an internal transfer price. According to an investigation of the Federal Cartel Office in 2003/2004, for each of the four transmission grids, above 80 per cent of

the balancing energy was supplied by a sister company of the grid operator; the difference between the price for balancing energy and the ordinary spot price was attributed to the grid and incorporated into grid transmission fees. Markets for balancing energy were, in principle competitive, but strict 'prequalification requirements' imposed by the network operators made entry of outsiders all but impossible (see Monopolkommission 2005: paras 1196–206 (254*–5* in the Engl. summary)).

[26] This problem would be eliminated or at least reduced if, as proposed by the European Commission, there was ownership unbundling, i.e. vertical disintegration, as well as legal unbundling. However, until now, ownership unbundling has been politically infeasible in large parts of the European Union. Höffler and Kranz (2007) argue that ownership unbundling would come at a cost in terms of insufficient co-ordination of investments in generation and in transmission; they suggest that it might be sufficient to have legal unbundling with incentives of network managers tied to the profits of the network company, rather than the mother company.

[27] For overviews, see Armstrong (2001); Laffont and Tirole (2000); Armstrong and Sappington (2007).

[28] For a discussion of trade-offs that are involved and of the implications of these trade-offs for competition policy and regulation, see Cave and Crowther (2004).

[29] Attempts to infer power abuses from the mere observation that margins are highest when residual supply elasticities are lowest are therefore futile. Nevertheless, this observation is presented by London Economics (2007) and by von Hirschhausen, Weigt, and Zachmann (2007) as if it permitted an inference concerning the abusiveness of electricity pricing.

[30] Monopolkommission (2004: para. 74; 2006: para. 72).

[31] Equivalently, the Ramsey–Boiteux analysis requires some taking account of the business which very low-base prices to one's own customers take away from one's competitors (Höffler 2006).

[32] For a systematic discussion, see Monopolkommission (2004: paras 210–23).

[33] Monopolkommission (2002: paras 140–59, in particular para. 153).

[34] The extent to which national regulatory law actually pre-empts the application of competition law is a matter of dispute. In Germany, most scholars hold that, as a *lex specialis*, the law establishing sector-specific regulation pre-empts the Law against Restraint of Competition (see e.g. Möschel 1999; 2001). However, in assessing the Federal Cartel Office's injunction against Deutsche Post in 2005, the Düsseldorf Court of Appeal suggested that even without appealing to European law there might be a dual authority of the two laws and the two institutions.

[35] This concern seems to be a reason why, in the United States, the Supreme Court, in *Crédit Suisse* even more than in *Trinko*, went rather far in asserting that sector-specific regulation pre-empts the application of antitrust law. One may wonder whether the Supreme Court's stance in *Crédit Suisse* is not apt to leave some aspects of firm behaviour out of the domains of both antitrust law and regulation—the latter because the legal norms underlying the sector-specific regulation do not provide enough of a basis for intervention, the former, because the existence of sector-specific regulation is deemed to pre-empt the application of antitrust law. Would something like the antitrust prosecution of exclusionary in the AT&T case in the seventies still be possible after Crédit Suisse?

9

European Telecoms Regulation: Past Performance and Prospects[1]

Jordi Gual and Sandra Jódar-Rosell

9.1. Introduction

The liberalization of telecommunications services is one of the most ambitious reforms implemented by the European Commission as part of its goal of ensuring competition in the internal market. It aims at the reform of an industry which represents around 2.6 per cent of EU-15 value added. Moreover, if the reform succeeds in improving the telecommunications' infrastructure it is likely to spur productivity gains for the whole economy.

Liberalization is not an easy task. The strong technological changes that motivated the reforms in the first place pose some challenging issues regarding the proper regulatory framework that should govern the transition to competition. The success or failure of the liberalization strategy is very important for future policy, since the telecommunications approach has been replicated, with minor differences, in the liberalization of other network industries.

In the present chapter we review this liberalization strategy and provide an analysis of its performance. We argue that, in the design of the liberalization process, the Commission had to determine the scope of the necessary *ex ante* intervention and to ensure market integration while at the same time creating a framework flexible enough to accommodate the convergence of communication technologies. Section 9.2 reviews the first set of measures adopted by the Commission, which formed the '1998 framework' and dealt mainly with the first two requirements: the degree of *ex ante* intervention and market integration. The outcome of this first framework varied significantly between Member States, reflecting the numerous implementation choices that were left at their consideration.

Section 9.3 discusses the revision and amendment of the '1998 framework', which gave birth to the 'New Electronic Communications Framework' in

2003. The major amendments were motivated by the growing convergence of communication technologies, which suggested the need for a more technology-neutral approach to regulation. The new framework was also used to tackle with new instruments the main goals already considered in 1998. First, the introduction of criteria that would determine, as competition developed in the industry, the gradual move from *ex ante* intervention towards *ex post* control by means of competition policy. Secondly, the objective of market integration reinforced by the introduction of provisions pushing towards more harmonized rules. Nevertheless, the concern remains that the old technology-specific regulation will linger through the definition of relevant product markets that are too narrow or through the geographical markets that are too wide in scope. The higher level of harmonization sought by the Commission also risks losing the benefits of regulatory experimentation, which may not be negligible at a time when new generation networks are being deployed.

9.2. The Liberalization Process up to 2003: Introducing Competition

The need for a set of regulations to control the liberalization of telecoms is explained by the particular characteristics defining the industry. The most relevant of these are the existence of significant scale and scope economies within and between the different segments, as well as vertical economies and network effects (Armstrong 1997). In this context, effective competition cannot be achieved by merely removing any exclusive right in those segments in which competition is considered possible. At least in the early stages of liberalization, some *ex ante* regulation is needed to open the market while ensuring that entrants are not penalized by any legacy or first-mover advantage of incumbents.

The European Union's Telecommunications Policy starts in 1984, with the necessary harmonization of technical standards across Member States and the agreement on a common position in the international telecommunications arena. Nevertheless, it is not until 1987 when the main provisions governing the liberalization process began to be discussed. From 1987 to 1998, the Commission set the rules that ought to be transposed to national legislation (or to be directly applied by Member States) before 1998, the year in which all the telecommunication markets were officially liberalized. This set of Directives and Regulations, which we name 'the 1998 framework', was intended gradually to move the sector from monopoly to competition and was in place until 2003, when it was amended to cope with the convergence of technologies.

Nevertheless, increased competition was not the sole objective behind the '1998 framework'. As it is common to other network industries that were liberalized during the same period, the liberalization process is characterized by the additional requirement of market integration. The European Commission chose its market integration strategy so as to satisfy the need for some *ex ante* regulation (to ensure effective entry) and the requirement of a 'level playing field'. This strategy can be termed, after Gual (2008), 'host country rules within limits'. Essentially, it amounted to identifying the minimal set of conduct and structure regulations for competition to emerge and impose it to Member States. These defined the 'limits' in the integration strategy. The specific implementation of those regulations was left to Member States, hence the qualification of 'host country rules'.

The approach taken by the Commission, though well targeted to address all the sources of concern, left too much scope for discretion to Member States. As a result of this, it will be shown at the end of this section that the outcome of the '1998 framework' is mixed and varies significantly between countries.

9.2.1. *The Commission's concerns and measures to protect nascent competition*

In any network industry, the transition to competition cannot be achieved just by allowing for free entry to the market. The initial market structure is often characterized by the existence of a vertically integrated multiproduct monopoly. In this setting, the incumbent enjoys a first-mover advantage over potential entrants and its pricing structure usually involves cross-subsidies across the different services. Hence, the liberalization strategy must take into account the effects of these two issues on emerging competition. First, it should minimize the effect of any first-mover advantage on the entrants' ability to compete. And second, it also needs to make sure that prices charged by the incumbent truly reflect the expected profitability for the entry decision. Moreover, there is the need to address the competition problems that are likely to appear in the form of abuses of dominant position. Although the latter can be subject to *ex post* regulation by competition authorities, the European Commission believes that *ex post* intervention would not prevent irremediable damage to entrants.

The directives and regulations of the '1998 framework' can thus be grouped according to the type of concern they intend to address.

ENSURING EFFICIENT ENTRY

Exclusive and special rights were clearly the main barriers to entry into the industry. For competition to emerge, it was necessary to remove these rights and to implement, instead, a system of general authorizations with minimum compliance requirements. Of course, these requirements can always be used strategically by governments, especially if they (partially) own the incumbent or if they have strong preferences for national champions. Transparent and objective rules may minimize this risk. The harmonization of these rules across Member States is thus essential to satisfy the objective of market integration.

A second concern is to ensure that entry occurs where it is efficient. For this to happen, entrants must be able correctly to assess, for each of the business segments, their expected profits in case of entry. Unfortunately, the regulated prices of the monopoly period convey little information on expected profitability under competition. Relative prices between business segments are usually distorted either by direct regulation or by the universal service regulations imposed to the incumbent. Allowing entry under such conditions may trigger excessive entry in some segments (Crandall 2005) while potentially efficient competitors are kept out of the market in others.

The European Commission addressed both issues by gradually abolishing exclusive rights in those segments less subject to tariff distortions[2] and encouraging tariff rebalancing in the public voice telephony segment. Member States were also encouraged to establish national schemes to share the cost of Universal Service Obligations (USOs) among all the players in the market.[3] The date for the final liberalization of the public voice telephony segment was established in the so-called 'Full Competition Directive',[4] which set it for January 1998 (with some extensions for small and less-developed networks requiring further structural adjustments). Finally, to ensure the objectiveness, harmonization, and transparency of the requirements imposed to potential entrants in the provision of voice services, the Commission issued the 'Liberalization Directive'[5] limiting the scope of possible requirements and the procedure to be followed in the granting of licences.

MINIMIZING THE RISK OF MARKET TIPPING

Telecommunication markets are subject to high switching costs and network effects that create an important degree of inertia in the consumers' decision on which network to join.[6] First of all, bigger networks are more valuable to consumers and this penalizes entrant providers that have to build customer bases from scratch. Second, this difficulty is reinforced by the switching costs that would be faced by a consumer willing to change provider (a new phone number, discontinuances, and delays in the availability of the service, etc.). The incumbent enjoys thus an enormous first-mover advantage and can easily price its products in such a way that prevents new entrants from reaching the critical network size to remain in the market.

The risk of tipping the market substantially decreases if interconnection between all the networks is made mandatory. This was done by the European Commission in its 'Interconnection Directive',[7] which regulated the obligation to interconnect at non-discriminatory and cost-oriented prices. In particular, incumbents were required to publish reference offers and to 'provide interconnection facilities and information to others under the same conditions and of the same quality as they provide for their own services'. Moreover, in order to decrease switching costs, number portability—that is, the possibility to keep the phone number when changing provider—and carrier pre-selection were mandated shortly after.[8]

PREVENTING THE ABUSE OF THE INCUMBENT'S DOMINANT POSITION

While competition is not sufficiently developed, incumbents can abuse their dominant position in several ways. First, incumbents control an essential input for entrants—namely, the subscriber's access. In the absence of *ex ante* regulation, the incumbent could squeeze the entrants' margins by distorting retail prices and interconnection rates. Secondly, interconnection prices could also be used to leverage his dominant position to adjacent markets and prevent firms in those markets to offer bundles of both products. Finally, if regulated and liberalized activities coexist, profits from the regulated activities can be used to cross-subsidize prices in the competitive ones in order to drive entrants out of the market. Given the strong network effects and switching costs, a successful foreclosure of the markets to new entrants may be difficult to overturn by an *ex post* intervention.

Price regulations on undertakings with significant market power (SMP) have thus been implemented by the Commission both at the retail and interconnection levels. Interconnection prices must be cost-oriented and accounting separation was imposed to facilitate monitoring.[9] The Commission also encouraged the creation of national regulatory authorities (NRAs), legally separated from telecommunications' providers and the government, with the power to fix tariffs and monitor the entire telecommunications sector.

Besides all these provisions, a very significant step in European telecoms regulation was the introduction of local loop unbundling (LLU) in order further to increase competition in local access.[10] According to this regulation, undertakings with SMP are obliged to provide access at a regulated price to the physical copper pair that connects the network termination point at the subscriber's premises to the main distribution frame or equivalent facility. This is considered the least replicable facility and, hence, the main bottleneck for the emergence of competition.

9.2.2. *Scope left to Member States and its effects*

The approach taken by the Commission, as it has been said, consisted in imposing a minimal set of regulations while leaving to Member States the implementation details and the freedom to impose additional measures. In particular, the Commission was neutral on issues of public ownership and vertical separation of the incumbent. The Member States' individual position with regards to these two issues, along with differences in the degree of independence of the NRA and in the delays incurred in the adoption of the commission's directives, caused significant differences in the regulation of telecoms at the national level. Moreover, the regulations proposed in the '1998 framework' were sufficiently vague to leave Member States scope for discretion in implementing them. Tables 9.1 and 9.2 list some of the main regulation areas and the implementation options selected by each country as of 2000.

There is substantial variation in the options selected, as well as variation in their potential for promoting competition and constraining the incumbent's behaviour. Regarding entry regulations, Member States can choose among two different methods to grant licences: 'beauty contests' and auctions. The former are less transparent and they may be more suited to satisfy political preferences. On the other hand, auctions identify the more efficient competitors and generate competition *ex ante*, provided they are well designed.

The regulation of access to the infrastructure is another source of divergences and discretionality. Although Commission directives required that interconnection and access rates had to be based on costs, leaving a fair return on investment, they did not specify the methodologies to compute either the costs or the level of fair returns. A number of countries opted for an accounting approach and used fully distributed costs (FDCs), a concept which is not related to marginal cost, since it takes into account all the costs of the firm and not only those incurred in case of expanding output (or services). Moreover, since it is assessed at historic prices, it may yield too high estimates if new technologies are more efficient. A second possibility, based on economic costs, is to use long-run incremental costs (LRICs). LRICs provide the right incentives for entry (Vogelsang 2003) but are very complex to compute and may incentivize non-price forms of exclusion, such as quality degradation, if the fixed economic costs of the service are not taken into account (Laffont and Tirole 2000). Finally, an alternative to cost-based regulation is given by the use of the efficient component-pricing rule (ECPR). A sophisticated ECPR can be close to the Ramsey-optimal price structures that a policymaker should implement in order to encourage efficient entry and network investment, but it is again very information demanding. Hence, a simple version of the ECPR is sometimes used in the form of retail-minus pricing. This approach sets the interconnection or access price at $(1-x)$ per cent the retail price, where the x should account for the marginal cost of retail minus any additional cost directly attributed to the provision of the access or interconnection service.

Line of business restrictions may be required to ensure that the incumbent does not alter interconnection terms to leverage its dominant position to adjacent markets (that is, in mobile communications). They may also be needed to ensure she does not try to protect her dominant position in the relevant market by delaying the deployment of new networks or softening facilities-based competition (that is, competition from cable-TV providers).

Table 9.1. Scope for discretion (1)

	Entry regulations		Pricing methodology Local Loop (b)	Access to infrastructure
	Licensing regime for mobile (IMT-2000) (a)	Cost standard for interconnection by SMP operators (b)		Regulation applied to wholesale prices for bitstream access (2003) (c)
Austria	Auction	FDC	FL-LRAIC	Commercial Neg.
Belgium		FDC	-	Mandatory reference offer
Germany	Auction	LRAIC	LRIC	Not available
Denmark	Auction	FDC	FDHC and best practice	Cost-oriented
Spain	Beauty contest	Multi-standard	-	Retail minus (40%)
Greece		FDC	LRIC	Reasonable, non-discrimination, transparency
France	Beauty contest	FDC	Company specific	NRA sets prices
Finland	Beauty contest	Company specific		Subject to Comp. Law review
Italy	Beauty contest	FDC	FDHC	Retail minus (50%)
Ireland		FDC	-	Cost-oriented + retail pricing obligations
Luxembourg		FDC		Not available
Netherlands	Auction	EDC	EDC	Reasonable, non-discrimination, transparency
Portugal	Beauty contest	FDC	-	Retail minus (40%) for some offers plus mandated discounts for the rest
Sweden	Beauty contest	AIC	FDCC	LRIC proposed
United Kingdom	Auction	LRIC + FDC	FL-LRAIC	Retail minus

Notes: FDC: Fully distributed costs; (FL-) LRAIC: (Forward-looking) long-run average incremental costs; LRIC: Long-run incremental costs; FDHC: Fully distributed historic costs; EDC: Embedded direct costs; AIC: Average incremental costs.

Sources: (a) OECD Regulatory Overview; (b) DG Implementation Report 2000; (c) ERG Common position.

Table 9.2. Scope for discretion (2)

	Line of business restrictions		Market power	
	Fixed/Mobile provision (1998) (d)	Fixed/cable provision (2000) (a)	Exists Cross-ownership of cable and incumbent PTO (e)	Type of regulation of end-user voice telephony tariffs of SMP operators (b)
Austria	Legal separation	No restriction	No	*Ex ante* approval by the NRA under ONP conditions
Belgium	Legal separation	Only if Comp. Law requires it	No	Price cap
Germany	Legal separation	Only if Comp. Law requires it	Yes	Price cap/NRA approval
Denmark	Direct operation by PTO	Divested	Yes	Price cap
Spain	Legal separation	No restriction	No	Price cap
Greece	Legal separation	PTO with SMP not allowed	No	*Ex ante* approval by the NRA under ONP conditions
France	Direct operation by PTO	No restriction	Yes	*Ex ante* approval by the Ministry under ONP conditions
Finland	Direct operation by PTO	No restriction	Yes	Freely set by operator
Italy	Legal separation		No	Price cap/NRA approval
Ireland	Direct operation by PTO		No	Price cap
Luxembourg	Direct operation by PTO		Yes	Freely set by operator
Netherlands	Direct operation by PTO	No restriction	No	Price cap/NRA approval
Portugal	Legal separation	No restriction	Yes	*Ex ante* approval by the Ministry under ONP conditions
Sweden	Legal separation	Only if Comp. Law requires it	Yes	Price cap
United Kingdom	Legal separation	PTO provision not allowed were cable exists	No	Price cap

Notes: PTO: Public Telecommunications Operator; SMP: Significant Market Power; NRA: National Regulatory Authority; ONP: Open Network Provision.

Sources: (a) and (b) see Table 9.1; (d) OECD Cross-ownership and Convergence; (e) OECD Broadband and Telephony Services.

243

Table 9.3. Results at the end of the '1998 framework' (1)

	No of operators actually offering public voice telephony (a)	No of operators with a combined mkt share >90%	Incumbent mkt share in local calls (b)	Local call charge, 3min. (c)	National call charge, 3min. (c)	10 min. call to near EU country (d)	Change in Local call charge, 3min. 2003–TRY	Change in National call charge, 3 min. 2003–TRY	Change in 10 min. call to near EU country 2003–TRY
Austria	27	5	51%	19.13	63.78	2.81	−32.80%	−41.67%	
Belgium	21	5	81%	23.57	64.83	2.24		−53.85%	
Germany	26	5	90%	13.25	46.96	1.39	−0.83%	55.68%	
Denmark	30	7	n.a.	11.87	32.53	0.68	−13.94%		−69.40%
Spain	27	3	80%	11.89	37.93	2.04	−19.09%	−71.88%	
Greece	12	1	91%	13.58	45.30	4.35	−36.11%	−19.84%	
France	14	3	81%	16.99	42.16	2.52	43.64%	−2.00%	−22.00%
Finland	4	3	95%	15.68	22.66	1.84	33.05%	22.70%	
Italy	42	4	70%	12.73	26.97	2.27	−13.77%	−62.16%	
Ireland	8	1	95%	15.17	50.60	1.54			
Luxembourg	9	1	n.a.	9.95	33.07	1.54			
Netherlands	76	2	76%	13.98	35.97	0.92	0.00%	102.44%	
Portugal	11	2	n.a.	20.38	44.04	3.78	0.00%	−22.36%	
Sweden	53	9	56%	12.32	29.75	0.59	50.20%	44.74%	
U. Kingdom	113	9	57%	23.65	78.93	5.68	−14.03%	43.46%	

Notes: (a) National operators only. Figures for Denmark and the Netherlands are not strictly comparable with the others since they refer to the operators that have been allocated geographical numbers and/or access codes.
Germany: Figure for local calls. Local operators: 45 (local calls), 46 (LD/Int); National operators in LD/Int: 46.
Greece: Figure for local calls. 13 national operators for LD/Int.
Spain: Figure for local calls. Local operators: 13 (local calls), 13 (LD/Int); National operators in LD/Int: 25.
France: Figure for local calls. Local operators: 4 (local calls), 4 (LD/Int); National operators in LD/Int: 18.
Ireland: Figure for local calls, 12 national operators for LD/Int.
Finland: Figure for local calls. Local operators: 43 (local calls); National operators in LD/Int: 11.
(b) Market shares based on retail revenues. Data for local calls include calls to the Internet.
Finland: Combined market share of TeliaSonera, Elisa, and Finnet.
(c) USD PPP cents, VAT included.
(d) USD PPP, including VAT.
TRY: Year in which tariff rebalancing was completed.

Table 9.4. Results at the end of the '1998 framework' (2)

	Commercial launch DSL	Incumbent mkt share broadband (2003)	Broadband subscribers per 100 inhab.	Price per mbps (e)	Price per mbps. % change 2003–2001	Access paths per employee (f)	Change in access lines per employee 2003–1997	2003–2000
Austria	Nov 1999	31%	7.6	0.08	−37.02%	605	120.29%	43.99%
Belgium	Oct 1999	51%	11.7	0.02	−154.52%	710	171.22%	54.20%
Germany	Aug 1999	93%	5.6	0.06	−2.69%	527	113.26%	29.09%
Denmark	July 1999	67%	13	0.14	0.07%	412	50.43%	22.57%
Spain	1999	55%	5.4	0.18	−24.33%	867	205.61%	44.97%
Greece	Jun 2003	0%	0.1	0.22		666	137.61%	43.26%
France	Nov 1999	57%	5.9	0.12	19.99%	551	143.59%	33.39%
Finland	May 2000	68%	9.5	0.08	11.02%	424	47.30%	41.55%
Italy	Dec 1999	60%	4.1	0.12	−74.72%	1,020	152.73%	40.58%
Ireland	May 2002	45%	0.8	0.22		366	112.98%	91.45%
Luxembourg	2001	84%	3.5	0.17	−2.11%	650	61.87%	53.23%
Netherlands	Jun 2000	34%	11.8	0.06	−82.22%	592	62.99%	32.87%
Portugal	Dec 2000	74%	4.8	0.14	−25.30%	883	234.21%	48.57%
Sweden	Oct 2000	45%	10.7	0.08	45.25%	810	194.08%	87.88%
U. Kingdom	Jul 2000	33%	5.4	0.11	1.94%	362	52.23%	11.14%

Notes: (e) Average across incumbents' offers, USD PPP.
(f) Include mobile and broadband access paths (excluding cable) from 2000 onwards.
Sources: OECD and European Commission's Implementation Reports.

Legal separation is a mild form of achieving this, the most effective way being complete divestiture or ownership restrictions. Nevertheless, this last form of separation can be inefficient if there are significant scope economies. Finally, retail price regulation is commonly done in the form of price caps applied to a basket of services. Differences between countries in this case are confined to the power of the incentives to reduce costs.

9.2.3. Results at the end of this stage

Successful competition is expected to drive prices down, expand the range of products available to consumers, and improve incumbents' efficiency levels, among other benefits. A quick look at some of these performance variables back in 2003 shows that achieving these goals was not an easy task. After sixteen years of directives and recommendations and five years after the official liberalization of the fixed telephony market, the results of the '1998 framework' were somewhat mixed. Tables 9.3 and 9.4 provide a broad summary of the performance of each of the EU-15 countries. In what follows, we review the main conclusions that can be derived from their analysis.

The improvement of the incumbents' overall efficiency levels constitutes the main success of the framework. As data from the OECD reveals (see Figure 9.1), the number of access paths per employee—which includes fixed lines, mobile, and broadband connections—increased significantly in all countries between 2000 and 2003. Nevertheless, the performance of European countries seems to be superior to that of non-EU OECD members. Figure 9.1 depicts each country's efficiency improvement against its level in 2000. In general, European Union countries managed to achieve larger improvements despite their already higher efficiency levels in 2000.

The '1998 framework' had fewer remarkable results in the broadband segment. Most countries experienced important price reductions in monthly fees, but their magnitude seems to depend on specific rules that were not determined by the framework and which differed between Member States. In particular, as Figure 9.2 shows, price reductions were larger (and the incumbents' market shares were lower) in those countries where the incumbent did not own cable assets. Moreover, despite these price cuts, average broadband penetration in the EU-15 was quite low (7.1 per cent) by 2003, compared to those non-EU OECD countries who had launched DSL around the same period or later (Korea, 24.2 per cent; Switzerland, 10.1 per cent; or Norway, 8 per cent).

The role of the '1998 framework' in the introduction of effective competition in conventional telephony was even more disappointing. Although the market had experienced a significant amount of entry by 2003, it still remained highly concentrated in the hands of the incumbent. Certainly, the

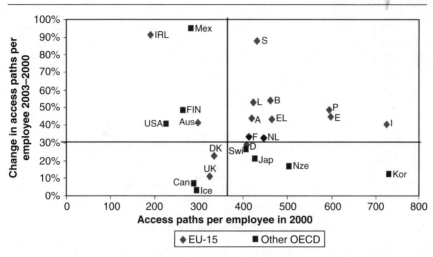

Figure 9.1. The '1998 framework' may have boosted incumbents' efficiency in the EU-15
Source: OECD Communications Outlook 2005.

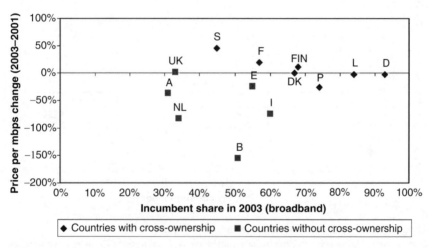

Figure 9.2. Cable and telephony cross-ownership hindered price cuts
Sources: OECD, European Commission, and own calculations.

economics of the telecommunications sector make it prone to concentration but the relatively low market shares of the incumbents in Austria, Sweden, or the United Kingdom suggest that there is room for decreasing concentration in other countries.

Turning to prices, their levels were quite dispersed across countries in 2003—possibly due to differences in cost conditions and demand characteristics—but

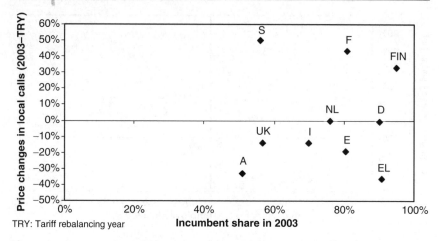

Figure 9.3. No apparent relationship between price cuts and incumbent market share
Source: European Commission's Implementation Reports and own calculations.

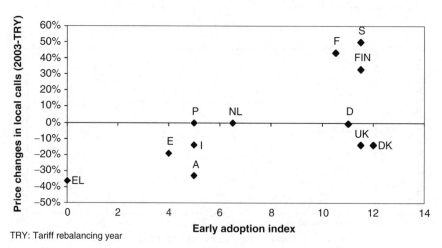

Figure 9.4. Early adoption does not seem to favour price cuts
Sources: European Commission's Implementation Reports and own calculations. The index summarizes the Commission's view on the degree of transposition in May 1997. For each key measure in the directives, countries add one point to the index if main provisions are in place: half point if only some of them are in place or if a derogation is granted; zero points otherwise.

very few countries experienced price decreases in all the segments after the end of the tariff-rebalancing period. Interestingly, the countries that benefited the most from price cuts—Spain, Greece, and Italy—were not the countries with lower incumbent market share or the early adopters of the Commission directives (see Figures 9.3 and 9.4).

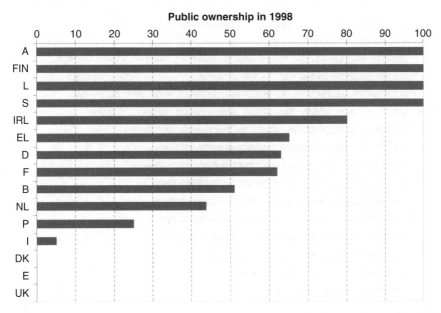

Figure 9.5. Public ownership was the norm when the '1998 framework' was implemented

Source: European Commission's Implementation Reports.

The fact that a common framework leads to these mixed and heterogeneous results across countries could be explained by the great variety of policies that were finally applied in practice. The pattern exhibited by fixed telephony prices and efficiency, for example, seems to be more the result of the price incentive schemes implemented by each national government than the result of competitive pressure arising from new entrants. Similarly, the observed price reductions in the broadband segment suggest that national preferences towards line of business restrictions determine the level of competition that arises in the market.

In addition to these policies, the literature has identified other possible explanations of this heterogeneity in the results. The extension of privatization is among the most commonly analysed features[11] and it certainly varies across Member States (see Figure 9.5). Most studies coincide in its positive effect, especially when it is combined with the introduction of competition in the sector. For example, Li and Xu (2004) find that, on average, full privatization increases investment per capita, penetration in the fixed and mobile segments, labour and total factor productivity, and the volume of network traffic. However, prices also increase. This effect is, nevertheless, reversed when competition is introduced in addition to privatization. The combination of both features also reinforces the positive effect on penetration. Partial privatization, on the contrary, has no significant effects.

249

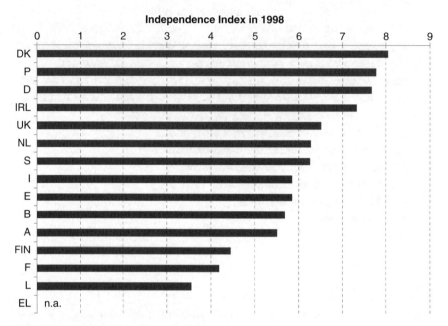

Figure 9.6. NRA's independence could be improved in most Member States
Source: Gual and Trillas (2006).

The establishment of a national regulatory authority is another commonly analysed feature and it is also generally found to yield positive results. Estache, Goicoechea, and Manacorda (2006) finds that a NRA reduces prices (especially in developed countries open to competition), increases the quality of the service, and improves labour productivity. Nevertheless, there is evidence that the characteristics of the NRA also have an influence on performance. On the one hand, Wallsten (2003) finds that the introduction of the NRA prior to the privatization process is associated with higher penetration (in fixed and mobile segments) and telecommunications' investment. In addition, this sequencing also seems to increase the investors' willingness to pay at the privatization stage, which is interpreted as investors giving more value to environments with clearer rules. On the other hand, the degree of independence of the NRA with respect to the government also seems to matter. This finding is of particular relevance for the European case, since the creation of a NRA was mandated for all countries but its degree of independence largely varied from one to another (see Figure 9.6). Edwards and Waverman (2006) finds that a higher regulatory independency, as measured by an index of several institutional features of NRAs, yields lower interconnection rates and mitigates the positive effect of public ownership on those rates. Using a slightly different index, Gual and Trillas (2006) finds a weak negative effect of regulatory independence on labour productivity, while its effect on penetration is not significant.

Line of business restrictions, the extension of privatization, or the independence of NRAs constitute important pieces of regulation that were not contemplated in the '1998 framework'. Nevertheless, the framework considered other rules that could also contribute to the heterogeneity of its success due to differences in their implementation or in the timing of their adoption.

Member States differed, for example, in the year of adoption of policies that favour entrants vis-à-vis incumbents—such as carrier pre-selection, number portability, or LLU. Gual and Trillas (2006) provides some indication on the effects of such policies on penetration and productivity. These policies are all aggregated into an index, with higher values reflecting more favourable entry conditions. Pro-entrant policies are found to increase penetration but to have non-significant effects on labour productivity.

As could be seen in Tables 9.1 and 9.2, Member States also differed on the costing methodology used for interconnection regulation. Chang, Evans, and Schmalensee (2003) finds that most countries using some form of direct cost-based interconnection had telecommunications investments above the EU average in 1997. Similarly, most of the countries not using fully distributed costs had investments above the EU average. No significant results are found for long-run incremental cost methodologies.

Finally, differences in the pricing of access to the infrastructure needed for broadband provision could also explain some of the observed variance in broadband penetration. It is generally accepted[12] that facilities-based competition is more effective than service-based competition in promoting the adoption of broadband technologies (Aron and Burnstein 2003; Distaso, Lupi, and Manenti 2004). Service-based competition can promote the early adoption of the technology, but it may decrease its diffusion speed (Denni and Gruber 2006). The level and relative prices of the different forms of access to the infrastructure—local loop, bitstream, etc.—determine the optimal choice for a broadband provider between a facilities- or service-based provision of the service. Hence, the rulings of NRAs with regards to access prices can influence broadband adoption by favouring one form of service provision over the other. Besides these rules, the dominant form of access provision in a country also depends on the initial coverage of cable networks and the existence of cross-ownership restrictions. Again, these are factors that vary between Member States and which were outside the scope of the framework.

9.3. Regulation in a Converging Environment

When the '1998 framework' was designed, different types of signals (voice, data, or television) were transmitted through different types of specialized networks. Recent technical advances, however, have made possible the transmission of any of these signals over any digital network. Traditional networks specialized in one type of content have been upgraded to become digital and thus are now capable of transmitting voice, data, or television indifferently. The result of this technological progress is a new competitive environment. Firms in the telecommunications industry face an environment with a richer set of possible strategies than was anticipated when the rules for controlling the liberalization process were designed. In this context, maintaining regulations that constrain the behaviour of certain players based on assumptions that are now less likely to hold can be counterproductive. Indeed, one may even question the necessity of *ex ante* regulation at all.

The convergence of technologies implies the entry of new and strong competitors in all markets. Any strong player in the traditional market of voice, data, or video transmission can now become a multiproduct provider. Hence, from three adjacent markets with very few players in each, we move to a single converged market with stronger and more numerous players. Moreover, the scope for product differentiation is also larger than before, through the possibility of offering different combination of services. It seems, thus, that the motivation behind the '1998 framework' regulations—namely, the introduction of competitors with the minimal guarantees to survive, is of less importance in this new environment. On the contrary, new concerns arise. On the one hand, the increasing role of content in the demand for telecommunications services raises issues regarding exclusive vertical relationships and the possible foreclosure of application providers in, for example, the provision of IPTV (television over IP) or VoIP (voice over IP). As opposed to the case of other web content, broadband providers can restrict access to certain providers of these applications without significantly decreasing the value of the connection. Relatedly, new capacity will have to be built eventually to carry all this content, raising the problem of pricing the use of the network and its expansion. Finally, bundling and tying may become more important in the strategic toolkit of telecom providers, suggesting the need for an increased monitoring of their possible anticompetitive use. The role for *ex ante* regulation seems to be confined then to ensure the interconnection of all networks and the fairness of switching costs for the consumers. Indeed, too much *ex ante* regulation is not without risk in this converged environment. First of all, the effects of *ex ante* regulation in one market are easily translated to adjacent product markets. Hence, its overall effects are hard to establish, increasing the risk of regulating related markets. Secondly, asymmetric regulation may put some firms at disadvantage unless the motivations for concern are very well founded. Finally, regulation of access to networks has to be carefully designed since there is the risk of discouraging investment in more efficient networks such as next generation networks (NGNs).

9.3.1. *The new strategy of the European Commission*

Recognizing this converging process, the European Commission made a move towards a more technology-neutral regulation of the telecommunication markets in 2003. The '1998 framework' was abandoned in favour of the 'New Electronic Communications Framework', which extends the harmonized minimal set of regulations to communication networks (and services provided over these networks) irrespective of the type of information they convey.[13] In short, the telecommunications' market now becomes the electronic communications' market (ECM).

The overall approach still follows the 'host country rules within limits' of the '1998 framework', with the difference that competition policy principles and *ex post* regulation take an increased role and there is a higher harmonization effort on the minimal set of rules.

GRADUAL SHIFT TO *EX POST* INTERVENTION

Following the principles of competition law, all NRAs are required to define the relevant markets of the ECM appropriate to their national circumstances and periodically assess the competition conditions in these markets.[14] If operators with SMP (under the principles of either single or joint dominance) are found, then ex ante regulation may be applied to them. Otherwise, if a relevant market is found to be effectively competitive, the obligations imposed to operators in that market should be consequently amended or withdrawn. The Commission initially proposed a minimum list of 18 markets to be analysed by NRAs. The revision of the 'new framework' shortens this list to 7 markets, mostly at the wholesale level.[15]

MEASURES TO INCREASE HARMONIZATION

When operators with SMP are identified in a relevant market, the Commission established a short list of possible regulations to impose in wholesale markets,[16] or in the retail market,[17] if this is not enough to achieve the objectives defined on Article 8 of the Framework Directive (2002/21/EC).[18] NRAs must select at least one of the regulations for wholesale markets and must ask for approval if a non-listed measure is preferred.

Besides listing explicitly the set of measures to be implemented, the Commission took additional steps to ensure that similar regulations were imposed in countries facing similar situations. In particular, NRAs are required to submit their intended regulations to public consultation and to inform the Commission about them. Moreover, in the case of transnational markets, NRAs are required to cooperate. Nevertheless, the most significant measure adopted by the Commission is Article 7 of the Framework Directive, which grants veto power to the Commission on NRAs' decisions with respect to market definition and the designation of undertakings with SMP. Hence, the Commission may overturn any decision of a NRA in these fields if it considers that it is contrary to Community Law or to the objectives set on the above- mentioned Article 8. After the first revision of the 'new framework', the Commission proposes to extend the veto power to the particular regulations applied by NRAs and entrust a common European regulator with the task of assessing these remedies.[19]

MEASURES TO REDUCE THE SCOPE LEFT TO MEMBER STATES

Relative to the '1998 framework', the 'new framework' includes some measures to reduce the scope that was left to Member States with respect to line of business restrictions, structural separation, and entry regulations. To begin with, legal separation of cable TV and other public electronic communications networks is required when these three conditions are met: (a) the undertaking is controlled by a Member State or benefits from special rights; (b) is found to be dominant in some relevant market; and (c) operates a cable TV network established under special or exclusive rights.[20] Secondly, the same directive also requires Member States to ensure that any vertically integrated undertaking with SMP does not (price or non-price) discriminate in favour of their own activities. Since price discrimination is already banned by the Access and Interconnection Directive,[21] this requirement may be a way to introduce some degree of vertical separation. Indeed, the Commission proposes to amend this directive in order to give regulators mandatory powers to impose this form of separation.[22] Finally, the 'new framework' also requires the provision of electronic communication network or services to be subject to a general authorization and not licensed. With the revision of the 'new framework', this would also extend to mobile communications and the possibility of a harmonized secondary market for spectrum would be introduced.

9.3.2. The risks of the new framework

The appearance of the 'new framework' recognizes the increased role that competition policy can play in this converged environment. Nevertheless, when put into practice the concern remains on whether it tackles the risks of *ex ante* regulation in an appropriate manner. Furthermore, the higher level of harmonization sought by the Commission may provide for market integration but only at the expense of experimentation.

With respect to the first issue, the technological neutrality of the 'new framework' and, hence, the symmetry in the *ex ante* regulation hinges on the definition of relevant markets. A good definition is important since obligations imposed to operators with SMP run the risk of becoming equivalent to technology-specific regulation. This is even more determinant if one takes into account that one of the most significant obligations on SMP undertakings is granting access to their network. The list of relevant markets considered for *ex ante* regulation by the Commission does not include any true converged market. Instead, it closely mimics the division according to technologies that was in place during the old framework (Gual 2004). Retail provision of voice and data, for example, is separated into two different markets even though these services are increasingly offered in bundles. The same can be said about the provision of fixed and mobile communications. The Commission justifies this approach by the present demand conditions. Nevertheless, the revised framework will enter into force around 2010 and will be in place for several years. It is very likely that demand conditions will evolve in the meantime.

Certainly, the list of markets proposed by the Commission can be modified by NRAs to include broader or narrower markets. By doing this, the different evolution of demand conditions across countries can be taken into account. Similarly, NRAs can in principle define the geographic scope of a market to be smaller than the whole Member State territory. This is particularly relevant for the identification of SMP operators in wholesale markets for access, since it would allow the NRAs to recognize the competitive constraints placed by facilities-based competitors in those areas in which their networks are already deployed (Cave 2007). Indeed, the UK has just followed this path with the definition of sub-national markets for wholesale broadband access. These markets reflect different competitive conditions—identified mainly by the number of principal operators and the population that can be served—at different local exchanges.[23]

So far, however, most NRAs have only redefined markets in order to narrow them to the specific technology predominant in their country.[24] In any case, should a NRA wish to redefine a proposed relevant market, his decision is subject to the veto power of the Commission by the application of Article 7. Given the preferences of the Commission in favour of the proposed relevant product markets, as well as its cautionary look at sub-national geographical markets, the existence of this veto power could create uncertainty with respect to the rules set by the NRA.

The Commission's definition of relevant markets is also very related to the concern that arises regarding its position with respect to new-generation networks (NGNs). In the revision of the 'new framework', the Commission states: 'The use of more efficient technology to provide existing regulated services does not alter the justification for that regulation; the move to NGNs does not provide an opportunity to roll back regulation on existing services if the competitive conditions have not changed.'

NGNs are capable of providing existing as well as new services. By conditioning mandatory access to the ability of these new networks to provide existing services, the Commission may be distorting the investment incentives of operators with SMP in some regulated market. The deployment of a NGN can be done in several manners, using different combinations of technologies. Each of these combinations is associated with a particular building cost and a certain range of products and services that can be provided at a given quality of service. The optimal deployment is likely to imply the use of different combinations for locations differing in the type of services demanded and in the willingness to pay for them. Imposing mandatory access to the new network conditions the expected profits arising from the provision of these services and, as a consequence, may distort the combination of technologies finally deployed. The deployment of NGNs could even be delayed if the revised framework, which is going to be implemented in the years to come, generates significant regulatory uncertainty in the meantime.

In addition to this, the effect of LLU regulations over the old, well-known copper infrastructure is still unclear. Recent studies (Gual and Jódar-Rosell 2007) suggest that unbundling may entail a higher level of investment but the effect in terms of broadband adoption is more modest. Moreover, this effect is likely to depend on getting the relative access prices right, which is not an easy task. In any case, unbundling regulations have almost accomplished their goal of enabling new entrants to achieve a solid position, so that they may undertake further network investments. In this sense, extending mandatory access to NGNs seems more difficult to justify.

A final concern about the new framework arises from the level of harmonization sought by the Commission. Harmonization implies a trade-off between market integration and the benefits of regulatory experimentation. Given the risks previously identified, one should not dismiss the potential magnitude of these benefits.

9.4. Conclusion

To the eyes of the European consumer, the prospects for telecommunications services look promising. Part of this optimism is due to the successes of the Commission's telecommunications policy. Ensuring efficient entry in the industry, through the enforcement of tariff rebalancing, has been the first of them. The rate rebalancing policy enabled potential entrants to assess properly expected profits, something that was not possible under the old system of regulated tariffs with its cross-subsidization between business segments. The second success has been the minimization of the risk of market tipping. This was achieved through the mandatory interconnection of networks in non-discriminatory terms and the implementation of regulations aimed at the reduction of switching costs. These measures had the effect of considerably reducing network effects, thereby minimizing the critical network size needed by the entrants to remain in the market. Finally, the third success has been the modernization of price regulation through the use of incentives. This has prevented the abuse of the incumbents' dominant position and it seems also to have boosted their efficiency levels.

However, the assessment of these successes in terms of industry performance variables calls for a more moderate evaluation and shows a wide dispersion across Member States. Overall, the regulatory framework that ended in 2003 was not very successful at decreasing the dominance of incumbents or promoting broadband penetration. Moreover, very few countries experienced price decreases in all the business segments after the end of the tariff rebalancing period. Several factors are behind these facts. First, Member States have differed in their policy stance on public ownership or vertical separation of the incumbent operator, issues on which the Commission has remained silent, except very recently on the separation issue. Second, the independence of NRAs and the timing of implementation of European directives and regulations also vary considerably across Member States. Finally, the regulations proposed by the Commission left Member States a significant scope for discretion.

In view of the mixed results at the end of the first regulatory framework, the ultimate reasons behind the increased level of competition have to be found in the intense innovation process that has led to the convergence of communication technologies. Since early 2000, broadband has evolved to become a vehicle which will enable real competition in the industry, through the entry of strong players from adjacent markets. In this respect, one should worry about any policy that may compromise convergence and, as a consequence, broadband development.

Indeed, competition policy is now placed at the heart of the new regulatory framework, whose scope has been broadened to include all electronic telecommunications technologies. In so doing, the Commission intends to implement an evolving framework, in line with the convergence process, and a consistent application of rules across countries. Hence, NRAs are required periodically to define relevant markets and assess their level of competition, lifting unnecessary *ex ante* regulation once an acceptable level of rivalry is reached. Nevertheless, the practice so far has been the definition of relevant (product and geographic) markets in the traditional way, with few signals that the framework is moving towards a more dynamic assessment of market boundaries. Thus, the status quo has changed little and we risk ending up with players constrained by different regulations according to the technology they use.

In addition to this, there are still some regulatory features outside the scope of the new framework—such as public ownership of the incumbent and its ownership of cable assets—that hinder broadband development. It is true that mandatory unbundling of the local loop seems to matter more than these features. However, the positive effect of mandatory unbundling should not imply that we can disregard the risks posed by the present regulatory framework with respect to new generation networks. The present unbundling rules apply to an already deployed network whose functioning and potential are quite well understood. Contrary to the simple upgrade of the existing network, the deployment of a NGN comes along with significant changes in the management of the network and the need to redefine business models and pricing structures, and to coordinate in new standards. In this respect, the identification of successful competitive strategies will be an evolutionary process that will benefit considerably from experimentation. This entails substantial risks for the operators and requires a predictable regulatory framework that does not impose the extension and harmonization of unbundling rules. The mandatory unbundling of a network which still has to be deployed and whose properties are not well understood is, in our view, one of the largest risks posed by the new regulatory framework (see Table 9.3).

Notes

[1] This chapter is a revised and partial version of a paper prepared for the IESE conference 'Fifty Years of the Treaty: Assessment and Perspectives of Competition Policy in Europe', held in Barcelona, 19–20 Nov. 2007. We are grateful to Mireia Raluy for her excellent research assistance. The opinions expressed here are solely those of the authors and do not necessarily reflect the views of 'la Caixa' (Caja de Ahorros y Pensiones de Barcelona).

[2] Voice and data services for corporate networks and closed user groups Commission Directive 90/388/EEC, satellite communications Commission Directive 94/46/EC, the use of cable networks for the provision of already liberalized telecommunications services Commission Directive 95/51/EC and, finally, mobile and personal communications Commission Directive 96/2/EC.

[3] Communication COM 96 608 on the 'Assessment Criteria for National Schemes for the Costing and Financing of Universal Service in Telecommunications and Guidelines for the Member States on Operation of such Schemes'; Commission Directive 97/33/EC and Commission Directive 98/10/EC.

[4] Commission Directive 96/19/EC.

[5] Commission Directive 97/13/EC.

[6] For a comprehensive review of the sources and consequences of switching costs and network effects, see Farrell and Klemperer (2006).

[7] Commission Directive 97/33/EC.

[8] Commission Directive 98/61/EC.

[9] Commission Directive 97/33/EC.

[10] Regulation No. 2887/2000.

[11] See Estache, Goicoechea, and Manacorda (2006) for a survey.

[12] See Gual and Jódar-Rosell (2007) for a brief review.

[13] Commission Directive 2002/21/EC.

[14] Ibid.

[15] Commission Recommendation 2007/879/EC.

[16] Commission Directive 2002/19/EC.

[17] Commission Directive 2002/22/EC.

[18] Among these objectives, those of 'ensuring that users, including disabled users, derive maximum benefit in terms of choice, price, and quality' stand out.

[19] Directive Proposal, COM2007 697 final.

[20] Commission Directive 2002/77/EC.

[21] Commission Directive 2002/19/EC.

[22] Directive Proposal, COM2007 697 final.

[23] Case UK/2007/0733: Wholesale Broadband Access in the UK. Comments pursuant to Art. 73 of Commission Directive 2002/21/EC. 'Principal Operators' are those whose coverage is above the 10 per cent threshold set by Ofcom, BT, the cable operator, and six LLU operators.

[24] This is the case for broadcasting transmission services. See the Commission staff working document SEC 2006 837 ('On Relevant Product and Service Markets within the Electronic Communications Sector Susceptible to ex ante Regulation'): 13.

10

Regulation and Competition Policy in the Banking Sector

Elena Carletti and Xavier Vives

10.1. Introduction

The banking sector, and the whole financial sector more generally, is one of the most regulated sectors of the economy because of reasons linked to systemic risk and consumer protection. In most countries its regulation dates back to well before the introduction of competition policy. Given this peculiarity and the idea that competition is detrimental to stability, competition in the banking sector was basically suppressed until financial market liberalization started in the United States in the 1970s and continued later on in Europe. Since the beginning of the liberalization process, several important banking crises have occurred (in diverse places like the United States (S&Ls), Scandinavia, Spain, and the recent one derived from the subprime crisis).

Special provisions in the application of competition policy to the banking sector remained also long after the start of the liberalization process. For example, until December 2005, competition policy was applied in Italy by the central bank rather than by the competition authority. Similarly, in the Netherlands the banking sector was exempted by competition policy until 2000, two years later than the other sectors. In contrast, neither the European Treaty nor the merger regulation includes special provisions for banking, with the only exception of the provision of Article 21 of the merger regulation that leaves Member States the possibility to protect legitimate interests such as prudential control. The important question—which we address in this chapter—is to which extent competition policy has been applied in practice, and how competition policy has affected the development of regulation and the stability of the sector.

Several aspects can make competition policy prominent in banking. Indeed, the banking sector is important because of its weight in the economy and because it is crucial to provide finance to firms. Financial firms often need to collaborate (for example, in payment systems) and this may raise competition issues. Finally, there are concerns that the implementation of the single financial market in the European Union is being slow and that this may hinder competition.[1]

The chapter starts with a brief review of the academic literature on competition and stability in banking, discussing the rationale for regulating the banking sector in 10.2, the competitive mechanisms specific to the sector in 10.3, and the potential trade-off between competition and stability in 10.4. The discussion highlights how the literature is moving away from the traditional view that competition hurts stability. However, results are still too inconclusive to generate clear policy implications except for the need to enforce competition policy in banking.

After doing that, the chapter describes the normative arrangements of competition policy in the banking sector in Europe in 10.5; and in 10.6 it reviews the most important cases analysed by the Commission in the financial sector. Given the structure of the financial sector across Europe, mergers and cartels have played so far a much greater role. We first describe the evolution of the concentration process in 10.6.1 and then look in 10.6.2 at cases which involved conflicts between the Commission and the Member States. Concerning cartels we review in 10.6.3 the so-called 'Lombard Club' in Austria, various cases involving Visa International, and the recent examination against the Groupement des Cartes Bancaires. Then, in 10.6.4, we move to the description of the case of abuse of dominance position investigated by the Commission against Clearstream. Finally in 10.6.5 we turn to state aid, and describe the two important cases of Credit Lyonnais and of the capital transfers to the German Landesbanken in the early 1980s. It is in the area of state aid that stability and competition considerations come directly into play and restructuring of banks in financial difficulties assumes a special connotation. Before concluding we turn in 10.7 to the issues of financial integration and current developments in financial regulation and supervision, and describe the main results of the enquiries that the Commission conducted in the financial sector.

Several messages are derived in 10.8. In line with the developments in the academic literature, it emerges that competition policy is now taken seriously in the financial sector. The European Commission has by now examined cases in all areas of antitrust and has adopted important, landmark decisions. It has opposed anticompetitive mergers and has contrasted the attempt to pursue national protectionism by certain Member States as well as forms of cooperation in pricing schemes and in credit card systems. Also, the Commission has underlined how regulatory measures, imposing, for example, minimum capital requirements, cannot justify the granting of state aid to financial institutions if they entail distortions of competition. In this sense, the Commission has opposed both anticompetitive behaviour and protectionism that in many cases is encouraged directly by national regulators or governmental authorities.

Still, much remains to be understood in terms of the relation and balance between competition and stability. The concern that regulation can act as a barrier to competition and the difficulty of understanding the working of competition in a highly regulated environment where economic aspects like asymmetric information, switching costs, and network externalities are present needs both further research and special attention in the application of competition policy.

10.2. Regulation in the Banking Sector: Rationale and Instruments

It is well known that banks are special because they are more vulnerable to instability than firms in other sectors, and because people hold a non-negligible share of their wealth in bank deposits.[2] Instability can originate from the liability side or the asset side of banks. The former is related to runs and systemic crises; the latter to the excessive risk that banks can take in their investment decisions because of the high leverage and opaque assets. This is particularly the case when deposits are insured, because deposit rates are insensitive to banks' risk exposure.

Runs can be related to panics or arise from fundamentals. As shown by Diamond and Dybvig (1983), panic bank runs are random events linked to self-fulfilling prophecies. Given the assumption of first-come-first-served and the low liquidation value of the long-term assets, there are multiple equilibria. If all depositors believe that a panic will not occur, only the consumers in need of early consumption withdraw their funds and their demands are satisfied. In contrast, if depositors believe a crisis will occur, all of them rush to avoid being last in the line. Which of these two equilibria occurs depends on extraneous variables or 'sunspots'. Although sunspots have no effect on the real data of the economy, they affect depositors' beliefs in a way that turns out to be self-fulfilling.

The key issue in the panic approach is the equilibrium selection. There is no real account of what triggers a crisis. This is particularly a problem for policy analysis. Ways to get around the multiplicity of equilibria are suggested by Postlewaite and Vives (1987), and, more recently, by Rochet and Vives (2004) and Goldstein and Pauzner (2005), who use the techniques of global games to generate a unique equilibrium.

The fundamental view of bank runs asserts that crises are linked to the business cycle (for example, Gorton 1988). When the economy goes into recession, the returns on bank assets will be low. If depositors receive information about the impending downturn, they anticipate banks' financial difficulties and try to withdraw their funds early. Given their liabilities are fixed, banks may be unable to remain solvent. Thus, crises are a response to unfolding economic circumstances.

Runs may trigger a systemic crisis. The propagation, or contagion, can occur through the interbank market, the payment system, or through asset prices. The latter may lead to contagion also across different sectors, as shown in Allen and Carletti (2006; 2008) in a context where markets are incomplete and asset prices are determined by the available liquidity or in other words by the 'cash in the market'.

Systemic risk and consumer protection are the main rationales for the introduction of safety-net arrangements in the form of deposit insurance and 'lender of last resort' (LOLR). Deposit insurance prevents the occurrence of panic runs while maintaining banks' ability to provide liquidity insurance (Diamond and Dybvig 1983).

The issue of the optimal form of central bank intervention has long been debated. According to the 'classic' view (Bagehot 1873), central banks should lend freely at a penalty rate and against good collateral. This should guarantee that the LOLR is only used for illiquid banks and in emergency circumstances. In practice, however, it is difficult, even for central banks, to distinguish illiquidity from insolvency. Banks in need of a LOLR are under a suspicion of insolvency since they could otherwise raise funds from the market. As long as markets are sufficient to deal with systemic liquidity crises there should be no need for central bank loans to individual banks. However, the interbank market may fail, as has happened in the recent subprime crisis and then help to individual banks makes sense (as explained in Rochet and Vives 2004).

A related aspect in this debate concerns the potential negative effects of the safety-net arrangements. The main argument is that they worsen the problem of excessive risk taking and call for further regulatory measures in the form, for example, of minimum capital requirements. Moreover, the form of central bank intervention is important for competition policy. Direct subsidies or bailouts of financial institutions fall into the category of state aid and have a direct impact on the application of competition policy to the banking sector.

10.3. Competition in the Banking Sector

Analysing competition in the banking sector is quite complicated. On the one hand, the standard competitive paradigm does not work because of features like asymmetric information in corporate relationships, switching costs and networks in retail banking. On the other hand, some banks' specificities, like the fact that they compete for loans and deposits, can lead to departures from the competitive outcome as banks may want to corner one market to achieve monopoly in the other.

Broecker 1990 analyses how competition in the credit market affects the screening of borrowers by banks when borrowers are of heterogeneous quality and screening tests are imperfect. The main result is that competition worsens the 'winner's curse' problem as a higher loan rate tends to worsen the quality of firms accepting the loan. Increasing the number of banks reduces firms' average credit-worthiness and raises the probability that a bank does not grant any loans. In the limit, the equilibrium maintains some degree of oligopolistic competition. The lower quality of borrowers as competition increases implies also an increase of loan rates to compensate for the higher portfolio risk (Marquez 2002); but not when information acquisition is endogenous, since in this case banks acquire information to soften competition and more competition reduces the winner's curse problem (Hauswald and Marquez 2006). The presence of adverse selection affects also the structure of the industry, as it generates endogenous entry barriers and leads to equilibria with blockaded entry, where only a finite number of banks is active (Dell'Ariccia, Friedman, and Marquez 1999; Dell'Ariccia 2001).

Switching costs are an important source of market power in retail banking. In moving from one bank to another consumers incur costs associated with the physical change of accounts, bill payments, or lack of information (Vives 2001a). The competitive effects of switching costs are twofold. On the one hand, they lead to the exercise of market power once banks have established a customer base which remains locked in. On the other hand, they induce fierce competition to enlarge the customer base. Thus, switching costs may lead banks to offer high deposit rates initially to attract customers and subsequently to reduce them, when consumers are locked in. Different results may, however, be obtained when switching costs are combined with asymmetric information about borrowers' credit-worthiness (Bouckaert and Degryse 2004).

Finally, the presence of networks also affects the degree of competition as it introduces elements of non-price competition in the interaction among banks. For example, the possibility for banks of sharing Automatic Teller Machine (ATM) networks can be used as a strategic variable to affect price competition on the deposit market and foreclose any potential entrant (Matutes and Padilla 1994). A similar conclusion can be reached in frameworks where banks decide to offer remote access to their customers, such as postal or telephone services, in order to introduce vertical differentiation between banks and reduce the degree of horizontal differentiation (Degryse 1996).

One important final note is that competition in networks can also be analysed in two-sided markets. Rochet and Tirole (2002) analyses this issue in the context of credit card associations, where customers' banks and merchants have market power, and consumers and merchants decide rationally whether to buy or accept credit cards. As in the ATM literature, merchants can use card acceptance to increase customer base and relax price competition. Differently from the ATM literature, however, the system has to attract two sides of the market—that is, issuers and acquirers, merchants and consumers. Thus, changes in interchange fees and prices affect the relative price structure of the two sides with important consequences on the equilibrium outcome.

In summary, competition in banking is imperfect and there are many frictions and barriers to entry which may generate rents.[3] In retail banking, switching costs for customers are very important; and reputation and branch networks act as entry barriers. In corporate banking established relationships and asymmetric information are relevant frictions that explain why the market for small and medium-sized firms remains local. Electronic banking pushes in the direction of contestability, but it is also subject to exogenous and endogenous switching costs. In other segments of banking, like wholesale and investment banking, competition is at the international level and may be fierce.[4]

10.4. Competition and Stability: A Real Trade-off?

The analysis of the potential trade-off between competition and stability has gained significant importance in the academic literature in the last decade. Despite this, the results are still not completely conclusive.

Some studies have shown that coordination failures and panic runs can occur independently of the degree of competition in the market. In a model with elements of product differentiation, network externalities, and possibility of bank failures, Matutes and Vives (1996) shows that depositors have self-fulfilling perceptions of banks' success probabilities that lead to multiple equilibria. One equilibrium sees no banks being active. This is due to a coordination problem among depositors, which occurs irrespectively of the degree of competition in the deposit market. However, by raising deposit rates, more competition may exacerbate the coordination problem among depositors. As in Diamond and Dybvig (1983), deposit insurance eliminates the non-banking equilibrium and stabilizes the system, but it is not always welfare-enhancing.

Following the empirical findings in Keeley (1990) of a negative effect of higher charter values on risk taking, the theoretical literature has initially stressed how competition worsens banks' incentives to take risk (for example, Allen and Gale 2004) and how regulation can help in mitigating this perverse link (for example, Hellmann, Murdock, and Stiglitz 2000; Matutes and Vives 2000). The general idea is that greater competition reduces banks' charter values (or rents available to shareholders and/or managers). This increases the attractiveness of the gains from taking risks, and therefore the incentives to exploit the non-convexity in banks' pay-off functions.

This result implies the need of regulating the banking system to limit the adverse consequences of intense competition and achieve stability. One possibility is to limit competition directly through ceilings on interest rates or limits on entry. Another possibility is to design regulation so to 'correct' the negative effects of competition on banks' risk taking. Risk-adjusted deposit insurance premiums or appropriate capital requirements may be sufficient for this purpose, even though, depending on the circumstances, they may need to be complemented by interest rate ceilings or entry restrictions (Matutes and Vives 2000).

Although the view of a detrimental relationship between competition and stability remains pervasive, some recent studies have suggested that such a relationship needs not be robust. For example, when entrepreneurs—and not banks—choose the risk of the investment project, greater competition in the loan market reduces entrepreneurs' incentives to take risks—thus implying also safer portfolios for banks (Boyd and De Nicoló 2005; and also Caminal and Matutes 2002). If competition has an ambiguous effect on stability, the role of regulation needs rethinking. Boot and Marinc (2007) analyses the impact of capital regulation on entry and bank monitoring. The main insight of the analysis is that when banks are heterogeneous in quality and compete for market share, increasing capital requirements leads to more entry into banking. Competition improves the monitoring incentives of better-quality banks and deteriorates the incentives for lower-quality banks.

All in all it seems plausible to expect that, once a certain threshold is reached, an increase in the level of competition will tend to increase risk-taking incentives and the probability of bank failure. This tendency may be contained by reputational concerns, by the presence of private costs of failure of managers, or by regulation. Constraining regulation may be particularly important for institutions that have run into trouble, their margins being severely eroded, and develop an incentive to use 'gambling for resurrection' strategies. In any case the question remains open as to what degree of market power should be allowed in banking. Competition policy should be enforced in banking as the exercise of market power may be very important in the sector—despite electronic banking. The question is whether the application of competition policy should be modulated because of the stability concern.

10.5. Competition Policy in the Banking Sector in the European Union

We now turn to the institutional design of competition policy for the banking sector. Before the liberalization process the status quo was far away from the optimal balance between the benefits of competition (in terms of efficiency, quality provision, innovation, and international competitiveness) and the potential increase in instability. Regulation was tight and central banks in Europe were too complacent, with collusive agreements among banks, sometimes even fostering them. The costs of tight regulation should be apparent.

For example, rate regulation induces overinvestment in services, excess entry, and introduces the possibility of regulatory capture. The situation has now changed and currently the three main areas of competition policy: mergers, cartels, and abuse of a dominant position, as well as the rules concerning state aid, apply fully to the banking sector.

Several points concerning the development and the current design of competition policy are worth being stressed. In the United States the *de facto* antitrust exemption for banking ended with the Supreme Court decisions in 1944, 1963, and 1964; but the criteria for the evaluation of mergers are still somewhat more lax than those used in other sectors. The safe haven thresholds for the Herfindahl index below which a merger is not challenged are higher for banking than for other industries.[5] Furthermore, mergers are analysed and decided upon by the relevant regulator (the Office of the Comptroller of the Currency, the Federal Deposit Insurance Corporation, or The Federal Reserve), with the DoJ conducting a parallel review which may result in an appeal against the decision of the regulator. This arrangement created several problems in the past as the DoJ appealed against the decision of the Fed three times between 1990 and 1992, and required from the merging parties more divestitures than the Fed in seven cases between 1997 and 1999.[6]

The European Commission did not apply the old articles 85 and 86 of the Rome Treaty till the Zuechner case in the early 1980s. This was because banking was seen as a special sector, where business was heavily influenced by the monetary and financial policies of Member State authorities, in particular central banks and supervisors, rather than by market forces (Ghezzi and Magnani 1998).

In line with the evolution at the European level the design of competition policy in banking has been substantially strengthened also at the national level and many exceptions have been removed over the last two decades. For example, since December 2005 competition policy in Italy is enforced also in the banking sector by the general competition authority rather than by the Bank of Italy. In the Netherlands, the Competition Act of 1998 applies to the banking sector, but only since 2000. Similarly, in Portugal, the banking system is subject to merger control since 2003, although with a delay of five years relative to the other sectors. Finally a decision of the French Supreme Court in 2003 concerning the merger between Crédit Agricole and Crédit Lyonnais made it clear that the banking sector was subject to merger control in France (see Carletti, Hartmann, and Ongena 2006; 2007).

Despite these changes, some important specificity concerning the relationship between competition and stability remains in the institutional design of competition policy in banking. As stated in Article 21(3) of the European merger regulation, 'Member States may take appropriate measures to protect legitimate interests other than those taken into consideration by the EC Merger Regulation ... Public security, plurality of the media and prudential rules shall be regarded as legitimate interests.' Taking it literally, this provision implies that, at least in merger control, stability considerations may override competition concerns. In Canada, a merger of financial institutions may be exempted from merger control if the Minister of Finance certifies that it is in the best interest of the Canadian financial system. In the Netherlands, the Minister for Economic Affairs can overturn a merger decision of the competition authority if this conflicts with the one of the supervisory authority. In Switzerland, the supervisor may replace the competition authority and approve a bank merger, if that is necessary to protect the interest of creditors (see again Carletti, Hartmann, and Ongena 2006; 2007).

Whereas it is plausible to assume a more lenient approach towards market power in banking, it remains unclear whether the presumption that stability considerations should override competition concerns is warranted. The question is rather to which extent stability considerations should influence the design of competition policy. Relatively to the European framework, one wonders also whether, given the level of integration of financial markets and the supranational effects of mergers examined by the Commission, the stability exception should rather be implemented by some kind of supranational authority. This issue is related to the current debate of whether a European banking regulator is needed (see, for example, Vives 2001b), also in light of the attempt of some Member States to use the stability exception to put obstacles to financial integration.

10.6. The Application of Competition Policy to the Banking Sector in the European Union

Given the market structure of the banking sector, mergers and cartels have played so far a much greater role in the application of competition policy in Europe. Concerning the former, we distinguish between cases leading to competitive considerations and cross-border cases in which factors other than competitive considerations played an important role.

10.6.1. *Mergers*

The banking industry has experienced an important process of consolidation in the last two decades. The number and the size of mergers and acquisitions (M&A) have increased substantially in most European countries. This process has taken place mostly at the domestic level, increasing substantially the levels of concentration in most countries such as Belgium, France, Greece, Portugal, Spain, and the UK (see Table 10.1 and Figure 10.1).[7]

Cross-border M&A have also increased significantly in the last decade despite remaining inferior in number and size relative to domestic transactions.

Table 10.1. Banking concentration in European markets (CR5 in assets)

Country	CR% in total assets		
	1997	2003	2006
Belgium	54.0	83.5	84.4
Denmark	70.0	66.6	64.7
Germany	17.0	21.6	22.0
Ireland	41.0	44.0	45.0
Greece	56.0	66.9	66.3
Spain	32.0	43.1	40.4
France	40.0	46.7	52.3
Italy	25.0	27.5	26.3
Luxembourg	23.0	31.8	29.1
Netherlands	79.0	84.2	85.1
Austria	44.0	44.2	43.8
Portugal	46.0	62.7	67.9
Finland	88.0	81.2	82.3
Sweden	58.0	53.8	57.8
United Kingdom	24.0	32.8	35.9

Source: ECB (2004, 2005, 2007a).

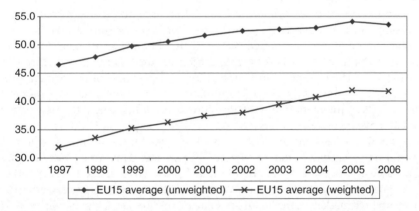

Figure 10.1. Share of CR5 in % of total assets
Source: ECB (2006, 2007).

Whereas during the period 2000–4, cross-border deals accounted on average for only 14 per cent of the total value of M&A in the euro area, this percentage increased to 38 per cent between 2005 and 2006 (European Central Bank 2007a); and it is expected to grow further also in light of the high levels of domestic concentration reached in some countries.

Few domestic mergers have led so far to significant competitive concerns and have been blocked by the competition authority, withdrawn, or subject to remedies. This contrasts with the United States, where typically mergers have been approved subject to some branch divestiture to limit concentration in the local markets.[8] This may reflect different worries of the competition authorities. In the United States, as well as in the United Kingdom, there is a concern about the effect of consolidation on retail banking and, in particular, on lending to small and medium enterprises.[9] In contrast, in continental Europe market power at the local level does not seem to be always perceived as a big problem by national authorities. In Spain, for example, mergers of large domestic banks (like Santander with Central Hispano in October 1999, or Bilbao-Vizcaya with Argentaria in January 1999) raised concerns only in terms of the potential softening of competition in the product market deriving from concentrated equity participations in industries like energy or telecommunications. In Belgium, no remedies have been imposed to bank mergers so far despite the high sector concentration. In general, national regulatory authorities in Europe, with the acquiescence sometimes of competition authorities, have worried more about protecting and enlarging their national champions than about the possible consequences of consolidation for customers. Nevertheless, mergers among large national banks (like UBS and SBC in Switzerland)[10] do seem to have a potentially large impact at the retail level which needs to be carefully examined.

Two important cases where the United Kingdom and the European Commission took a tougher stance were the attempt of Lloyds TSB Group to acquire Abbey National and the merger between the Swedish SE Banken and FöreningsSparbanken in 2001. Following the British procedure, the first case was analysed by the Competition Commission upon request of the Secretary of State for Trade and Industry. The examination showed potential anticompetitive effects in the market for personal current accounts, where the new entity would have increased its market share up to 27 per cent, and in the market for the supply of banking services to small and medium enterprises, where it would have reached a market share of 17 per cent. This would have further increased the dominance of the big four banks active in the British market (Barclays, Royal Bank of Scotland/NatWest, HSBC, and Lloyds itself) leading to a combined market share of 77 per cent in the market for personal current accounts and of 86 per cent in the one for small and medium enterprises. Tacit collusion concerns loomed large since Abbey was perceived to be a maverick. Based on these elements, the merger was found to lead to severe anticompetitive effects that could have not been addressed even with remedies. The decision of blocking this merger indicated that domestic consolidation in the UK was no longer possible thus opening up the system to foreign takeovers such as the acquisition of the same Abbey National by Santander later in 2004.

Around the same time, in June 2001, SE Banken and FöreningsSparbanken notified the European Commission of their plans to merge. The two parties were the third and fourth largest financial institutions in Sweden and their merger would have allowed them to become the leading institution with market shares of 43 per cent in deposits, 41 per cent in total lending, and 50 per cent in the mutual funds market. The analysis led the Commission to conclude in its Statement of Objections that the merger had anticompetitive effects on several markets and in particular on the market for services offered to households and small and medium enterprises. As a result of these objections the parties decided to withdraw their merger proposal. The anticipation of concessions in the magnitude of 1 million forced offloads out of the 5 million customer base made the deal unattractive. As Jacob Wallenberg, SEB chairman put it, this case 'shows that in a small country you can become dominant so quickly that it's very difficult to create strong entities with the efficiencies that allow you to take steps into a larger market place' (*Financial Times*, 20 Sept. 2001). This raises the need to look towards cross-border mergers to realize economies of scale once competition policy in banking is taken seriously by either domestic or European Union authorities. In this sense competition authorities become a major player in the restructuring of the sector in the European Union (see Vives 2005).

10.6.2. *The interaction between the EU competition authority and Member States in cross-border bank mergers*

Differently from domestic mergers, cross-border mergers do not entail substantial anticompetitive effects. However, they can—and have been—subject to regulatory and supervisory obstacles through the provisions of Article 21 of the merger regulation.

The 'seminal' case in this respect was the attempt by Banco Santander Central Hispano (BSCH) to acquire joint control of the Portuguese Champalimaud group in 1999. The Portuguese authorities immediately opposed the operation, even before the parties notified it to the European Commission. Upon request by the Commission, the Minister explained that the concentration raised prudential concerns because of the lack of clarity and transparency of the resulting group, as well as other concerns related to the infringement of procedural rules and the protection of national interests. It was made clear in the press that

a restructuring of the Portuguese banking system will be necessary and it appears...of good sense that, in a first phase...this is made among national groups. Foreign groups, including BSCH, will have to compete on their own and should not perturb such a restructuring. It would be totally false to arrange the system by suddenly transferring the control of large national institutions to foreign owners.[11]

The Commission objected to these motivations by arguing that neither the procedural infringement of the parties nor the protection of national interest could be considered legitimate interests in the sense of Article 21(3) and lead to an opposing decision. In particular, the attempt of a Member State to protect national interest was clearly against financial integration and the principle of non discrimination by reason of nationality embodied in Article 12 of the Treaty. The only legitimate interest which could have been used without prior approval of the Commission was the one linked to prudential considerations, but the proposed merger was not raising any credible prudential concern. The dispute between the Commission and the Portuguese authorities went on until November 1999, when BSCH notified the Commission of its intention to acquire Banco Totta & Acored and Credito Predial Portogues, two commercial banks belonging to the Champalimaud Group. The new operation cancelled the previous proposal, and it was approved by both the Commission and the Portuguese Government without conditions.

Two other important examples of the attempt of Member States to hinder the process of European integration under the provision of Article 21(3) were the planned takeovers of the Italian Banca Nazionale del Lavoro (BNL) and Banca Antoniana Popolare Veneta (Antonveneta) by the Spanish Banco Bilbao Vizcaya Argentaria (BBVA) and the Dutch ABN AMRO, respectively, in 2005. Both takeovers were approved by the Commission under the simplified procedure in April 2005. As normal praxis, they were also notified to the Bank of Italy for supervisory approval. The supervisory process, however, did not run smoothly. Shortly after the approval by the Commission, both BBVA and ABN AMRO complained that the Bank of Italy was creating obstacles to their respective bids in infringement of Article 21 of the European Commission Merger Regulation. ABN AMRO argued that the Bank of Italy favoured the counter-bid by the Italian bank BPI, thus applying discriminatory treatment towards foreign acquirers; whereas BBVA claimed that the Bank of Italy had conditioned the approval of the bid upon the acquisition of more than 50 per cent shares in BNL. The Commission intervened at first only in favour of BBVA indicating to the Bank of Italy that it was operating in violation of Article 21(4) of European Commission merger regulation. The Bank of Italy removed the condition imposed on the approval of the bid, but BBVA abandoned the bid given its limited success after the offering period.

Differently, the battle between ABN AMRO and BPI became much more complex. ABN AMRO lodged complaints for violations of national law before the Italian Stock Market Authority, Consob, the Bank of Italy, and national courts. This helped revive the case and bring it back to the attention of the Italian government and other competent authorities. The Commission also intervened with the Commissioner McCreevy sending a formal letter to Mr Fazio threatening to sue Italy. The turning point came in July 2005 when the Court confiscated the shares of BPI and its allies and the Consob froze the BPI's offer, just two weeks after the Bank of Italy had approved the request of BPI to acquire control of Antonveneta. Following this, the Bank of Italy itself suspended its approval and calls asking for the resignation of Fazio mounted inside the Italian government and by public opinion. The whole episode led to a dramatic change in the Italian financial sector. After Fazio resigned in

December 2005, the Government approved quickly a new law which reformed the mandate of the Italian governor and transferred the competence over competition policy from the Bank of Italy to the Italian Antitrust Authority.

Another important case of conflicts between the European Commission and the Member States was the merger between Unicredito Italiano and Bayerische Hypo-und Vereinsbank AG (HVB) in 2005. According to the examination conducted by the Commission, the merger had its greatest effects in Poland, where the parties would become the leading market player with 21 per cent of the assets through the undertakings Pekao owned by Unicredito and BPH controlled by HVB. More specifically, the parties would obtain the leadership in the market for the custody accounts and the distribution of mutual funds and the second position in the market for services to household customers with market shares around 35–45 per cent and 15–25 per cent, respectively. However, given the structure of the Polish market and the presence of other important competitors, the Commission considered the anticompetitive effects not to be significant enough and cleared the proposed merger in October 2005. The Polish government opposed the clearance decision by filing a formal complaint with the European Court of Justice, and by requiring Unicredito to sell its entire holding in BPH. The claim was that, according to the Privatization Agreement signed at the time of the acquisition of Pekao in 1999, Unicredito could not acquire any bank in Poland for the subsequent ten years without ministerial authorization.[12] This clause was meant to protect competition on the Polish banking market. The Commission regarded the attempt to enforce the 'non-competition clause' of the Pekao privatization as being incompatible with the European Commission rules on the freedom of establishment and the free movement of capital, and it launched an official procedure against Poland for misuse of Article 21 of the European Commission merger regulation. The conflict ended in April 2006 with an agreement between Poland and Unicredito. According to this, Unicredito was allowed to merge Pekao and BPH under the condition that it would sell 200 of the 480 branches of BPH and the brand BPH itself, and that it would preserve employment at both Pekao and BPH for two years.

A different example of cross-border merger was represented recently by the tripartite takeover of ABN AMRO by the consortium formed by RBS, Santander, and Fortis. The Commission imposed remedies consisting in the upfront divestiture of ABN AMRO's Dutch factoring subsidiary and part of its commercial banking business in the Netherlands because of overlap with Fortis (which was perceived to be an aggressive competitor in those markets). In this case it is notable that the Dutch supervisor did not put obstacles to a cross-border acquisition that has as objective to partition the local bank and integration by pieces in the three acquirers.

The cases described above show how Member States can abuse the provision of Article 21(3) so to protect and strengthen national interests. This is further worsened by the potential discretion embedded in the supervisory control. Until recently, the national supervisory regulations for the prudential assessment of mergers and acquisitions lacked specificities in terms of the evaluation criteria, procedural rules, and—in most cases—transparency; and, according to a survey conducted by the Commission in April 2005, the 'misuse of supervisory powers' represented one of the main obstacles to cross-border consolidation. Competition policy can therefore play a crucial role not only in watching and preventing excessive market power, but also in limiting the discretion and power of national supervisors. This claim is also supported by the empirical results in Carletti, Hartmann, and Ongena (2007) that the opaqueness of the supervisory control of M&A leads to inefficiencies in the supervisory process that can be at least partly removed by strengthening merger control. The need to ensure more transparency and legal certainty in the supervisory control led recently to the adoption of Directive 2007/44/EC of the European Parliament and of the Council of 5 September 2007 (the 'Qualifying Holdings Directive'). The new Directive, which must be implemented by March 2009 and is based on the approach of maximum harmonization, specifies evaluation criteria and uniform procedural rules for the prudential assessment of acquisitions of qualified holdings, and it requires supervisors to justify their negative decisions. The reasons behind a negative decision are to be made public at the request of the proposed acquirer or at discretion of the Member States. Although this directive represents an important step in addressing the problems embedded in the supervisory control, it fails to ensure sufficient transparency. The approach concerning the disclosure of the negative decisions still leaves much to the discretion of the supervisory authorities and has the potential of reintroducing supervisory obstacles in the consolidation process (Kerjean 2008). Only if these obstacles are removed, the natural pecking order of consolidation first via national mergers, then regional (geographically nor by cultural affinity), and finally fully international can proceed (see Vives 2005).

10.6.3. *Cartels*

The most important cartel in the banking sector examined by the Commission is the so-called 'Lombard Club' which took place among the eight biggest Austrian banks between 1994 and June 1998. The cartel consisted of a highly institutionalized price-fixing scheme covering the whole Austrian territory in a 'down to the smallest village' approach. The agreement included the fixing of interest rates for loans and savings for households and for commercial customers and of fees charged on consumers for certain services. The Commission discovered the cartel following reports in the Austrian press. On the basis of the overwhelming evidence found during numerous investigations, the Commission declared the cartel represented a serious infringement of Article 81 of the European Union Treaty. Fines were imposed for a total of

€124.26 million on eight Austrian banks. These were then reduced by 10 per cent under the so-called Leniency Notice of 1996 given the high cooperation that the banks offered during the investigation and their lack of objections. Overall, the 'Lombard Club' cartel was one of the most shocking cartels ever discovered, and it showed that price fixing is clearly pursued in banking as in any other sector.

Another important area where the Commission intervened under Article 81 of the Treaty relates to card and payment systems. The first case concerned various rules and regulations that Visa International notified to the Commission in January 1977 applying for negative clearance under Article 81(1) or an exemption under Article 81(3). The Commission sent initially a comfort letter in 1992, but reopened the case in 1997 after a complaint filled by a British association of retailers. The case turned out to be quite complicated and lasted for several years. The Commission issued several decisions pertaining to different aspects of the proposed agreement. The most-disputed aspect concerned the EU intra-regional Multilateral Interchange Fee (MIF)— that is, the interchange reimbursement fee that the acquiring bank has to pay to the issuing bank for each intra-regional transaction with a Visa card where issuer and acquirer are different. The initial point of dispute was the possibility for the Visa Board to set the MIF at whatever level and to keep it secret. At the end of a long and complicated negotiation process, Visa proposed a package of reforms and the Commission granted an exemption under Article 81(3). The reformed proposal contained a reduction of both the level of the intra-regional MFI to a fixed rate per transaction of €0.28 for direct debit cards and the level of the ad valorem per transaction fee applicable to certain types of credit and deferred cards till an average level of 0.7 per cent by 2007. These modifications represented a reduction of more than 50 per cent of the costs for an average direct debit card transaction and of more than 20 per cent for the other category. Visa proposed also to fix the fees in a transparent way on the basis of cost studies carried out by Visa and audited by an independent accounting firm. The MIF would not exceed a cap based on three categories of costs: the cost of processing transactions, the cost of free funding for cardholders, and the cost of providing the payment guarantee. The imposition of a cap on the MIF was meant to prevent the association of issuers from setting excessively high interchange fees. According to Rochet 2007, however, such cap has no economic basis since there is no clear evidence of a market failure and pricing distortions may go either way.

The Commission intervened again against Visa under Article 81 in October 2007 when it imposed a fine of €10.2 million. The infringement concerned the refusal of Visa to accept Morgan Stanley as a member in the United Kingdom from March 2000 till September 2006. Visa motivated its refusal with the argument that Morgan Stanley was a competitor and that as such, according to an internal rule, it could have not been accepted as a member. The

Commission objected that at the time of the infringement Morgan Stanley was not present in the EU market. Moreover, the exclusion of Morgan Stanley from Visa membership was found to hinder significantly the competitiveness of Morgan Stanley on the market for providing merchants with credit card capabilities in the United Kingdom (as retailers expect banks to offer card acceptance contracts as a package including both Visa and MasterCard). The case ended with an unusual settlement. In August 2004, the Commission sent a Statement of Objections to Visa, which then concluded a settlement agreement with Morgan Stanley in September 2006 and admitted the latter as a member. As a consequence, Morgan Stanley withdrew its complaint but the Commission still went ahead and fined Visa.

In October 2007, the Commission intervened against the Groupement des Cartes Bancaires under Article 81 of the Treaty. The Groupement managed the system of payments by 'CB' card which accounts for over 70 per cent of card payments in France. The examination concerned some price measures adopted by the Groupement which hindered the issuing of cards in France at competitive rates by certain member banks. In particular, banks that were not 'sufficiently' active in terms of acquisition of merchants or installation of ATM had to pay a fee of up to €11 on each card issued. These measures were motivated by the need to combat free-riding on the investments made by the main incumbent banks and to encourage new competitors to be fully active on both sides of the market. The Commission found, however, that these measures, although applicable in principle to all members, had been applied only against certain, smaller members thus restricting competition in the French payment card market. Since the Groupement had voluntarily notified the measures to obtain a decision of compatibility with the competition rules, the Commission ordered the annulment of the current measures and the prohibition to impose similar ones in the future without imposing any fine. It can be argued, however, whether the Commission in its analysis took proper account of the two-sided nature of the credit card market (issuing cards and acquiring merchants). Indeed, in a two-sided market for a practice to be anticompetitive it has to be shown that it constitutes a barrier to entry to the system and not only to one side of the market (since a barrier on one side may encourage entry on the other side).[13]

All these cases make clear the determination of the Commission to pursue price-fixing and exclusion agreements in the banking sector, in particular when they go against the creation and functioning of the Single Euro Payments Area (SEPA). Such behaviour contrasts with the previous approach of some national regulators that supported and even encouraged collusion and rent creation among banks with the aim of avoiding disruptions and preserving a stable system. But what is the best approach? Should competition rules be applied fully to the banking sector or should the persecution of cartels be more lenient in the banking sector? Does price fixing enhance stability? Most of the academic literature suggests that some market power is beneficial for stability, but most probably there are more efficient ways of preserving stability than price fixing. Competition should be fostered and stability should be maintained with an efficient prudential framework and adequate arrangements for crises resolution.

10.6.4. *Abuse of dominant position*

The Commission examined only one case of abuse in the financial system so far in relation to the clearing and settlement of securities. The examination originated from an ex-officio investigation into clearing and settlement services launched by the Commission in March 2001. After collecting information from a number of operators, the Commission focused its examination on Clearstream Banking AG and its parent company Clearstream International SA for potential abuse against Euroclear Bank in the market for the provision of cross-border clearing and settlement services for securities issued according to German law to intermediaries situated in other Member States. Clearstream operated in a clear dominant position in that market being the only Central Securities Depositories (CSDs) conducting the 'primary' clearing and settlement services (that is, Germany's only *Wertpapiersammelbank*), and therefore being an unavoidable trading partner. Despite numerous requests, Clearbank denied Euroclear the access to the CASCADE RS, an IT platform through which it provides clearing and settlement services for registered shares issued in Germany, for more than two years until November 2001. Also, between January 1997 and January 2004, Clearstream charged a higher per transaction price to Euroclear Bank than to other security depositories outside Germany. The Commission recognized that both behaviours constituted an abuse of dominant position in terms of refusal to supply and price discrimination, which impaired Euroclear Bank's ability to provide a comprehensive and innovative pan-European service in the downstream market for cross-border clearing and settlement of EU securities. The negative decision was adopted although the infringements had already come to an end in order to clarify the legal situation in an evolving and important market for European integration like clearing and settlement services.

10.6.5. *State aid*

State aid includes all forms of guarantees granted directly by the state—that is, by central, regional, or local authorities, and by undertakings under the dominant influence of public authorities. It is in this area that stability and competition considerations come directly into play. State intervention typically takes the form of public ownership or financial support in the form of LOLR, taxpayers' money, or transfer of assets. This is particularly likely in countries where the state is used to intervene in the banking sector as in France, Germany, and Italy.

A central case of state aid in the banking sector analysed by the Commission was the rescue through a series of complicated bailouts of the state-owned Crédit Lyonnais—the largest French bank at the time—by the French authorities in the years 1994–7. The problems of Crédit Lyonnais originated from an accumulation of bad projects that eventually threatened the company's solvency, with losses of French Francs (FRF) 1.8 and 6.9 billion in 1992 and 1993, respectively. Examples of such projects were a 'major office block development in the northern French town of Lille that helped local politicians to regenerate the town but then proved difficult to let' [ERisk.com], and the purchase of the US insurance company Executive Life, which, according to US authorities, was in violation of regulations. A further dubious operation was the financing of the purchase of two film-production studios—including the MGM studios. The French State provided the first aid in 1994 in the form of a capital increase of FRF 4.9 billion and the underwriting by the state of the risks attached to about FRF 42.7 billion of non-performing property assets transferred to a special hiving-off company. Only one year later, the state intervened again by creating another hive-off vehicle, the 'Consortium de Réalisation' (CDR), which took about FRF 190 billion of Crédit Lyonnais' troubled assets. These interventions were approved by the Commission in 1995 provided that the net cost to the state would not exceed FRF 45 billion. Important conditions attached to the approval were the separation of the ownership of CDR from Crédit Lyonnais and the future privatization of Crédit Lyonnais. However, in September 1996, the French authorities submitted to the Commission a new plan to grant emergency aid amounting to nearly FRF 4 billion together with a restructuring aid. The Commission approved the emergency aid but at the same time initiated the at-the-time Article 93(2) procedure (now Article 88(2)). In July 1997, the French authorities submitted a new restructuring plan for Crédit Lyonnais as requested by the Commission. The plan, which constituted an additional aid of value between FRF 53 and 98 billion, was subject to a series of modifications and finally received a conditional approval in May 1998 under the derogation of the at-the-time Article 92(3) (c). Crédit Lyonnais was fully privatized in 1999 and was finally acquired by Credit Agricole in 2003.

The episode of Crédit Lyonnais, which led to estimated costs for the French taxpayers of between €20 and €30 billion (up to 2.5 per cent of GDP at that time), illustrates several pitfalls. First, it shows that state ownership did not prevent bad transactions from taking place. Political interference and government guarantees blurred any notion of risk/return management and market discipline thus leading to an accumulation of projects that eventually threatened the company's solvency. Second, the case showed the difficulty for the

Commission to judge the compatibility of large aids with the Treaty, especially on short notice. Moreover, as noted by some commentators (for example, Tsakatoura 2008), the Crédit Lyonnais case showed that, despite not being clearly stated in the regulation, the Commission considered banking as a special sector with respect to state aid. Considerations linked to stability concerns presumably played an important role in the Commission's final decision.

Another important case of state aid concerned the capital transfer in the early 1990s to seven German regional public banks (Landesbanken) and the consequent abolition of the so-called state guarantees. The investigation originated from a complaint of the Association of German private banks stating that various Landesbanken received capital transfers in the form of public housing and other assets from the local governments, which partly or fully owned the banks, in order to satisfy increased minimum capital requirements. The allegation was that the transfers constituted state aid as they were remunerated below market rate and created a distortion of competition in favour of the Landesbanken. The investigation was long and complicated, economically as well as politically. In 1999, the Commission adopted the first negative decision concerning the transfer to WestLB and it ordered a recovery of some €800 million. In 2003, the CFI, however, annulled the decision on the basis of lack of clarity in the calculations of the Commission. The Commission reopened the investigation, showed that the remuneration agreed by the local governments in return for the transfer of the assets was very low (less than 1 per cent) and below the market rate, and ordered Germany to recover the appropriate amounts from the Landesbanken. The amounts to be recovered differed in size ranging from €6 million plus interest for Landesbank Hessen-Thüringen to €979 million plus interest for WestLB. The investigation also led to the gradual abandonment of the state guarantees for both Landesbanken and Saving Banks. This raised the question of whether the Landesbanken would change their asset investment strategies. According to some commentators,[14] the Landesbanken would increasingly abandon arbitrage trading in securities with very low profit margins. The failure of Sachsen LB in August 2007 and its subsequent bailout for €17 billion may have indeed been a result of the aggressive strategy pursued by the bank after the removal of the state guarantees.[15]

The two landmark cases examined show the commitment of the Commission not to let uncontrolled aid to the banking sector proceed without check. The aim is to reach an appropriate balance with the legitimate objective to preserve financial stability. The doubt remains, however, whether the granted aids were the least costly methods of preserving the receiving institutions. In this respect, it is important to evaluate also the future effects of state aid in terms of risk taking and moral hazard problems for the institution receiving the subsidy as well as for its competitors for which, as found by Gropp,

Hakenes, and Schnabel (2006), this negative potential effect seems to be even more severe.

10.7. Integration and Liberalization in the Financial Industry in Europe: Recent Developments

Much has happened in the European financial landscape since the creation of a single market in 1992 and the introduction of the euro in 2002. Numerous regulatory measures have been adopted by the European Union in order to create broad and deep capital markets through financial liberalization and integration. One important measure was the launching through the Lamfalussy process of the Financial Services Action Plan (FSAP), which aimed at creating a single and integrated financial market in Europe by 2005, in particular in retail banking.

The integration of European banking markets has proceeded through minimal harmonization and home-country regulation. Since the implementation of the Second Banking Directive in 1989, banks have been free to establish branches in other European countries and remain under the regulation of their home supervisor. Mutual recognition has been complemented with increasing harmonization of the standards for prudential regulation through several financial sector directives and the work of the Lamfalussy committees. The goal is to establish an institutional infrastructure to facilitate supervisory convergence, cooperation, and information sharing. In particular, the Committee of European Banking Supervisors is mandated to develop common standards, guidelines, and interpretative recommendations. A notable work of the Committee relates to the implementation of the Capital Requirements Directive (CRD) for banks and investment firms. Other important legislative steps for the integration of financial markets are the forthcoming Solvency II Directive for insurance companies, and the Markets in Financial Instruments Directive for financial markets. Work is under way to integrate securities clearing and settlement systems. According to the EU regulation 2560/2001 on cross-border transfers and cash withdrawals since 1 July 2003 consumers are charged the same for cross-border transfers and for domestic transfers, and can withdraw cash in the 15 euro countries at the same cost as in their own country.

None the less, the existing framework does not provide yet a level playing field for financial institutions across Europe and financial integration is not yet fully achieved. Considerable cross-country differences persist in the legal and regulatory framework for financial institutions' operations mainly because of remaining national discretion. Apart from stability concerns, the lack of convergence implies a high regulatory burden for cross-border financial institutions.

Financial integration has progressed slowly and unevenly across different activities and segments. It is high in wholesale banking and in certain areas of corporate finance (especially in public corporate bond issuance and private equity markets), modest in some relationship aspects of banking, and low in retail banking, particularly in loans to consumers (Barros, et al. 2005 and European Central Bank 2007b). Retail banking is the most important sub-sector of banking, representing over 50 per cent of the total EU gross income and approximately 2 per cent of total European Union GDP in 2004 (European Central Bank 2007b). Despite technological progress and innovation, retail banking remains regional, since proximity to clients, access to information, and long-term relationships are still the key competitive drivers. Cross-border banking is especially performed via foreign establishments—branches or sub-sidiaries—in the target jurisdiction. Foreign establishments have recently expanded their role although they still account only for approximately 15 per cent of the total banking assets. Most of those assets are held by foreign subsidiaries (European Central Bank 2007b).

The concern for the low integration and competition in retail banking led the Commission to open a sector inquiry in 2005. The inquiry, which was concluded in January 2007, highlighted several major barriers for cross-border competition. The Commission found high concentration levels in several markets for payment cards and payment systems, large variations in merchant fees and in interchange fees between banks, high and sustained profitability (in particular in card issuing), and divergent technical standards. According to the Commission all these elements contribute to restrict entry, charge higher fees, put obstacles to passing over lower fees or costs to cardholders, sustain market power, and prevent efficient operations.

Concerning the retail banking product markets, the Commission stressed how the conjunction of sustained high profitability, high market concentra-tion, and evidence of entry barriers raises concerns about banks' ability to influence the level of prices for consumers and small firms in some Member States. The presence of credit registers, holding confidential data that lenders use to set loan rates, may be used to exclude new entrants to retail banking markets. Some forms of cooperation among banks, as those taking place among savings and cooperative banks, can reduce competition and deter market entry. The widespread practice of product tying can reduce customer choice and increase banks' power in influencing prices. Finally, the presence of high switching costs can lead to high profit margins for banks.

Some of the concerns expressed in the Commission's inquiry are certainly legitimate although it has to be stressed that the existence of high profits is not per se the symptom of lack of competition. The analysis should centre on the sources of market power like exogenous and endogenous switching costs and practices such as tying. Furthermore, in two-sided markets, such as payment cards, care must be taken to conduct a proper analysis that deals with their specificities.

10.8. Concluding Remarks

Banking is no longer an exception in the enforcement of competition policy rules. This is as it should be, since the provision of a competitive 'financial input' in the production process is crucial for the competitiveness of an economy. Given the fragility of the financial system, however, there may be a potential trade-off between competition and stability. Although recent theories have questioned such a trade-off, it remains unclear whether competition policy should be more lenient with market power in the banking industry. This applies, for example, to the evaluation of mergers. The reason is that market power may have a moderating effect on the incentives to take risk. The question of whether a certain, implicit or explicit, 'banking exception' in competition policy will remain is therefore still open.

Two other reasons explain the attention of antitrust authorities to the sector. The first is that financial institutions tend to enter into collaborative agreements (this is the case for example, in credit cards or clearing and settlement systems). The second is that, as we have seen, many financial markets remain segmented in Europe and competition is perceived to be weak. Although, clearly, competition policy should aim at improving consumer welfare rather than forcing integration per se, it has a crucial role in keeping markets open. The lifting of artificial impediments to cross-border mergers will permit there to be large, well-diversified institutions without having excessive market power in any market. This is the area where regulatory changes should concentrate most, and where competition policy has and should be used to prevent artificial and unjustified barriers to financial integration based on a misuse of supervisory powers. In this respect, it is also questionable that in an integrated financial market and monetary area prudential matters stay in national hands, particularly for European Union-wide institutions (see Vives 2001b). This undermines the rationale for the prudential exception to protect a legitimate national interest. However, care should be taken since cross-border mergers may be a substitute for direct entry and could end up with large institutions meeting in different European markets raising tacit collusion concerns because of this multi-market contact.

Notes

[1] Competition problems may also arise in trading, securities services, and the organization of exchanges. Those, however, are out of the scope of the present chapter.

[2] See Carletti (2008) and Carletti and Hartmann (2002) for a review of the issues discussed in sects 2–4.

[3] Degryse and Ongena (2008) provide evidence of those rents.

[4] See Vives (2001a; 2001b).

[5] Bank mergers are not challenged if the HHI does not increase by more than 200 above 1,800 or if its parties' market share is below 35 per cent.

[6] The appeals concerned the cases *First Interstate of Hawaii/First Hawaiian* and *Fleet/ Norstar* in 1991 and *Society Corporation/Ameristrust Corporation* in 1992.

[7] It is worth emphasizing that the appropriate concentration measures in banking as a multiproduct industry are in relation to the relevant product and geographic market. Aggregate measures provide an imperfect indication of the concentration in the relevant market.

[8] Prager and Hannan (1998) provide evidence that horizontal mergers of US banks in the period 1991–4 increased market power.

[9] In the UK, concerns about market power in the payments' system have also lead to its regulation by the OFT.

[10] See Neven and von Ungern-Sternberg (1998).

[11] *Visão*, 24 June 1999.

[12] It is interesting to note how the market was positive towards the proposed concentration. Analysts quoted by Reuters envisaged that the merger would be favourable to the Polish economy as it would encourage consolidation and efficiency in the banking system.

[13] See Rochet and Tirole (2003) for an analysis of two-sided markets and Wright (2004) for the dangers of using one-sided logic to two-sided markets.

[14] e.g. *Herald Tribune*, 21 Oct. 2004.

[15] *Financial Times*, 22 Aug. 2007.

11

European Union Regulation and Competition Policy among the Energy Utilities[1]

Richard Green

11.1. Introduction

Energy was at the heart of the European Union's first precursor, the European Coal and Steel Community. As the European Union's competition policy developed, however, the energy utilities—gas and electricity companies—were rarely affected. The utilities were believed to be natural monopolies, because of the cost of duplicating the networks of pipes or wires used to deliver the product. If the industry was fated always to be a monopoly, competition policy would be an inappropriate tool for dealing with it. Regulation, which promised consumers reasonable prices and companies reasonable profits, was seen as a much better model. In some countries (such as the United States and Spain), there was a formal system of regulation covering privately owned utilities. In many others, it was more a matter of self-regulation, often combined with public ownership.

The structure of the industries varied between countries. At one extreme, Electricité de France dominated its industry, responsible for generation, high-voltage transmission, and most local distribution. In contrast, Germany's electricity sector had nine interconnected utilities, forty-six regional utilities, and around 800 local distributors (Schulz 1995). Most of the country's generation was owned by the interconnected utilities, which sold bulk power to the smaller bodies, as well as selling directly to their own customers. These customers were those connected to the distribution systems owned by the interconnected utilities—sales were almost never separated from ownership of the distribution assets. England and Wales had the Central Electricity Generating Board, responsible for generation and transmission, and twelve Area Electricity

Boards, responsible for distribution and sales. Northern Ireland, however, had a vertically integrated Board, and Scotland had two. In Spain, most utilities owned both generation and distribution, but there was an independent transmission company, Red Electrica de Espana. The largest group, Endesa, was a net generator, while the second largest company, Iberdrola, was a net buyer of power.

The structure of the gas industry was similarly diverse. Once again, France had a dominant national firm, Gaz de France, with an import monopoly and 80 per cent of final sales, while Germany had a three-tier structure, with local and regional companies and a top tier of importers and producers (Lohmann 2006). ENI of Italy dominated production, importing, and transmission, but there were more than 700 independent distribution companies. In Great Britain, twelve publicly owned Area Boards were formed into British Gas in 1972, allowing the latter to develop a national pipeline network and replace gas made locally from coal with natural gas from the North Sea. British Gas owned some of these gas fields itself, and was a monopsony buyer for other producers. The gas industry in Spain was very small for much of the 1970s and 80s, but when it started to grow rapidly, consolidation occurred. Catalana de Gas and Gas Madrid merged in 1991 to form Gas Natural, with an import monopoly and 90 per cent of distribution (International Energy Agency 1996).

This chapter will start by outlining the reasons why it was (and is) hard to create competition in the energy utilities. Some countries started to do so in the 1980s and early 1990s, however, in another example of the process of decentralized experimentation described by William Kovacic in Chapter 12 of this volume. Their perceived successes were important in persuading the European Commission to pursue a similar course. The Commission was able to pursue a two-pronged approach, first by agreeing liberalization directives that had to be transposed into national law, changing the rules under which the energy utilities operated, and second in the normal course of its competition policy, deciding on mergers and on agreements between firms. The Commission added a third prong in 2005, when it opened a sector inquiry into the gas and electricity industries. This reported in January 2007, and the chapter will consider this report and its implications.

11.2. Obstacles to Competition in the Energy Sector

Electricity and gas both depend upon networks—the product cannot be economically delivered to consumers without a direct connection to the power station or the source of the gas. The network is a natural monopoly—it would normally be too expensive to duplicate—and so the industry's costs will be minimized if there is only one network operator within a given area. There are also significant economies of scale in transmission—moving gas or electricity in large quantities over long distances—and so it is generally best to organize this activity on a regional, or national, scale. Economies of scale in distribution exist, but are less important, and so distribution companies can be quite small without incurring an excessive cost penalty. This means that while in some countries the distribution companies have millions of customers each, in others, there are many distribution companies with only a few thousand customers each.

In both gas and electricity, the physical limits on the networks must be respected, and so every company using the network must respect the instructions of the system operator. Because generation and demand for electricity must be kept continually in balance if the system is not to suffer a catastrophic black-out, the system operator has to keep plant running part-loaded as insurance against failures, and other stations must be in reserve, ready to replace these if they are called upon. Electricity will always flow along every available path on a network, in inverse proportion to the resistance (strictly speaking, impedance) on each path, and the flows will instantly reallocate themselves if part of the network fails. This means that every part of the network must be operated sufficiently far within its limits that if there was a failure elsewhere, that part of the network would still be in a stable condition. This complicates the task of defining the maximum capacity on any part of the network, as it depends on what is happening elsewhere, and how many contingencies the system operator wishes to protect against. There are other ancillary services, such as reactive power, which are essential to control the voltage level on the system, and the system operator has to procure these.

Gas networks are easier to control—the gas must actually be pushed down the routes chosen by the system operator, and minor imbalances between supply and demand can be met by varying the pressure in the system. The gas industry faces an issue that the electricity industry does not, in that it needs storage. The demand for gas is much higher in winter than in summer, but to maximize production from a gas field, it is important to keep the flow steady. Furthermore, long-distance pipelines, or Liquefied Natural Gas (LNG) facilities, that were built to meet the winter peak demand, would be seriously over-sized for the rest of the year. The answer is to have storage available near demand, in the form of depleted fields, salt caverns, or (most expensively) LNG stores. Gas is put into storage over the summer, and taken out during the winter. Storage facilities have significant economies of scale, but need not be considered a natural monopoly, if the principle of allowing multiple companies to use a network is conceded.

The deregulation process in the European Union and elsewhere, described below, took that principle as a given, and experience has shown that it is generally possible to have many companies following the orders of a system operator, without compromising the integrity of the system. However, the structure of the European Union's utilities has presented other obstacles to the growth of competition. First, the networks were primarily built for national use. Cross-border interconnectors usually have much lower capacity than the lines within a country, particularly in the electricity industry. In the gas industry, many European countries depend upon imports, and so they necessarily have strong cross-border pipelines.

The gas industry's traditional import contracts, however, acted as an obstacle to competition. Their heavy investment needs meant that producers were keen to minimize their risks by signing long-term contracts, often for the entire output of a gas field, and often giving the producer a high degree of control over how the field was operated. These contracts often banned the buyer from selling the gas on to another user, if it found itself unable to use the gas, and some contracts were 'take or pay', with high minimum volumes.

If electricity trade across European borders was limited by the low levels of interconnection, and gas trade by the terms of import contracts, this meant that most EU energy markets were national in scope, rather than international. As we have already seen, in many EU countries, the gas and electricity sectors were dominated by a few large companies. When competition was regarded as impossible, or at least inappropriate, this had no downside to offset the possibility of economies of scale. The downside only emerged once competition was seen as desirable, and the liberalization process began.

Effective liberalization requires that any competent company can have equal access to the facilities it needs to buy or sell electricity or gas, whether competing to sell to final customers or to deliver energy to the network. In the case of electricity, that means access to the transmission and distribution networks at the same price (for a given pattern of usage) as incumbent companies. A generator must have a fair opportunity to sell ancillary services, such as reserve power, and a retailer must be able to deal with unanticipated surpluses or shortages between its contracted purchases and its customers' demand. In gas, the conditions are similar, with equal access to storage as another essential requirement. Integrated network operators will naturally have an incentive to favour their own affiliated companies, and there need to be measures to reduce the impact of these incentives. One approach is to impose strict behavioural rules, although monitoring these can be a complex process. A second, which avoids the need for such monitoring, is to separate the networks from the rest of the industry. We will see, however, that the political consensus required for this more radical solution to be imposed throughout the European Union does not yet exist.

11.3. Moves towards Deregulation

During the 1980s, things started to change for the energy utilities. A long period during which prices in many countries had been falling in real terms had ended with the oil shocks of 1973 and 1979. Once prices were rising, the perceived performance of the utilities was less favourable, and governments were more open to alternative policies (Gilbert, Kahn, and Newbery 1996).

Two approaches to policy formation can be distinguished.[2] In the public-interest approach, disinterested policymakers attempt to implement the policies that will maximize welfare across society. For most of the post-war period, they sincerely believed that regulation, and often state ownership, was the best approach to the energy utilities. The utilities' poor perceived performance in the 1970s challenged this view, and policymakers became willing to try a new approach, that of liberalization. Successful experiments in some countries and in some industries act as a spur to extend the approach to other countries and industries, in a process of learning.

In the private-interest approach, policymakers, firms, and consumer groups promote policies that they believe will further their own interests. Once again, there can be a learning effect as new information makes participants re-appraise the likely impact of a policy. The focus of decision-making, however, is no longer on overall social welfare, but on the benefits to whichever group can assemble the most powerful coalition. The kinds of policies favoured can thus differ between countries, owing to the relative bargaining strength of the key groups. For example, Ando and Palmer (1998) finds that electricity liber-alization in the United States was more likely to occur in States with above-average prices and stranded cost burdens, in which consumers had more to gain from changing the status quo. In Europe, in contrast, Damsgaard (2003) finds that liberalization was more likely in low-price countries. This would accord with the view that producer interests had more influence here, and that the countries that liberalized were mostly those in which producers believed they had little to lose, and perhaps something to gain.[3] Eising (2002) argues that Electricité de France originally argued for EU measures to improve its access to export markets, and then discovered that the Commission favoured measures that would require it to open up its domestic market, going beyond the company's original objective. Similarly, the large German utilities, which had originally opposed liberalization, came to believe that liberalization at the EU level would allow them access to the customers of municipal utilities, something that the latter's political connections would make impossible in a purely German reform. In both cases, the companies' beliefs changed over time in response to a shifting set of policy options, and growing experience of liberalization in practice. That experience started in the Anglo-Saxon coun-tries, the United States and the United Kingdom.

In the United States, access to interstate gas pipelines was gradually liberal-ized from the 1980s, and the pipeline operators evolved into companies that shipped gas, at regulated rates, over their network, but could not own it (Makholm 2007). Gas was traded on wholesale markets with published prices linked to supply and demand, and shipped by companies that held contracts with the pipelines. This was thus an early example of a utility opening up to competition, even though Makholm argues that it took around fifteen years for the system to reach maturity. An earlier law, the Public Utility Regulatory Policies Act of 1978, did not try to create a competitive market, but did require electric utilities to buy power from certain 'qualifying facilities' (particularly combined heat and power plants) at the utility's avoided cost of generation. A similar law, brought in by the Thatcher government in the United Kingdom, allowed new entrants to generate electricity as their principal line of business (rather than simply selling excess power from a station mostly used to power an industrial site) and required the Area Boards to buy this power at their avoided cost. That cost depended on the Bulk Supply Tariff set by the Central Electricity Generating Board, which promptly rebalanced it, adding a fixed fee and lowering the marginal charges. This cut the price that the Area Boards would offer to entrants, and, unsurprisingly, practically no entry took place (Hammond, Helm, and Thompson 1986).

Soon afterwards, however, the government turned its attention from reforming nationalized industries to privatizing them. British Telecommunications (BT) was privatized in 1984, mainly to free it from the self-imposed constraint of a limit on government borrowing, followed by British Gas in 1986. BT was to experience competition from one entrant, while the gas market for large consumers was, in theory, opened up to any company that wished to compete with British Gas. In practice, any competitor would have needed to inform British Gas of its plans when it applied to use its network, and, since the incumbent could then have undercut their offer with a confidential, individualized contract, no entry took place. Scarcely a year after its privatization, British Gas was referred to the Monopolies and Mergers Commission, which required the company to publish both its network charges and its prices to large customers (Monopolies and Mergers Commission 1988). British Gas was also required to leave at least 10 per cent of the output of any new North Sea gas fields for other companies. With access to gas, the network, and customers, entrants finally had a chance to compete with British Gas. A few years later, the company was given a formal price control for its network charges, but in a dispute over their level, asked to be referred to the Monopolies and Mergers Commission once more. The end result of the process was that the government decided to open up the entire retail market to competition by 1998, and British Gas decided to separate its pipelines from its sales to consumers. While Centrica (the company trading as British Gas) is still the largest gas retailer, the overall market is now competitive, with many participants.

The initial failure of competition in the gas industry motivated the Energy Secretary, Cecil Parkinson, to restructure the electricity industry in England and Wales for competition when he was asked to privatize it. In March 1990, the Central Electricity Generating Board was divided into a transmission company and three generating companies. Three companies turned out to be too few for effective competition, but entry to the industry, and later pressure (from the industry's regulator) for divestitures, eventually delivered a competitive structure. Retail supply was also opened to competition, starting with the largest customers, and, after the first year, fewer than half of these (by volume) were buying from their local incumbent. Domestic consumers, able to choose their supplier from 1998 or 1999 onwards, took longer to switch, but more than half have now done so. A series of mergers has transformed the industry's structure. The fourteen regional networks are now owned by seven companies, three of which have no interests in generation or retailing in the United Kingdom. Six integrated groups dominate retailing, particularly to domestic customers, who commonly take both gas and electricity from the same company, making Centrica one of the largest power companies, at least as measured by sales to domestic customers. About one-third of the industry's output comes from generators without a mass-market retail business, but these have faced a rocky financial ride over the first years of this century, as wholesale prices fell and then rose again. Retail prices have been less volatile, reducing risks for the vertically integrated companies.

Norway was the second country to liberalize its electricity industry—in 1991—when its cooperative power pool was changed into a wholesale spot market, Statnett Marked (*sic*). Norway, which is a member of the European Economic Area but not of the European Union, has a large number of electric utilities of different sizes. Practically all of the country's generation is hydroelectric, and the utilities traded power amongst themselves in order to make best use of the available water, and because many utilities had more or less generation than retail demand. Unlike Britain, Norway allowed all its customers to choose their retailer from the start of liberalization.

New Zealand and the Australian state of Victoria were two other pioneers, starting their liberalizations in 1993 and 1994, respectively. Finland opened its market to large consumers in 1995, and Sweden in 1996. Sweden and Norway created the world's first international electricity market, Nord Pool, in part because a purely Swedish market would have been unacceptably concentrated, with Vattenfall producing half of the country's output. Spain started a process of liberalization with a law to encourage more competitive wholesale procurement in 1994, and a 1996 agreement on retail competition (Kahn 1998). By this time, however, the European Commission had adopted its own policy on electricity liberalization.

11.4. The First Directives

The European Commission first produced a draft directive on electricity liberalization in 1991 (Eising 2002), but it was not until December 1996 that

Directive 96/92/EC was adopted. This Directive was a compromise between countries that were already in the course of liberalization, or were planning to start soon, and those that had been content with their existing systems. At all stages in the liberalization debate, the Commission has had to reconcile a range of views on the best structure for the industry. Some countries, such as the United Kingdom, have favoured liberalization throughout the process, and have gone further with most aspects of their domestic policies than the Commission has (so far) attempted to impose at an EU level. Other countries have opposed liberalization, for a range of reasons. These can include the desire to maintain a high level of social obligations, such as common tariffs throughout a country, fears for security of supply if investment is 'left to the market', and the wish to maintain 'strong' national companies. The Commission has always had to find a consensus between these different views. In the negotiations over the first Directive, one way of doing this was to allow countries several choices in how they implemented the Directive, setting minimum standards that the leaders already comfortably exceeded. The aim of the Directive was to create competition in generation, and in supply to the largest consumers.

While the Directive was being negotiated, it looked as if the choice with the largest impact on the industry would be over how competition in generation was organized. France, in particular, had wanted to keep a planned system, rather than one based on free competition. It had therefore argued for the creation of a 'single-buyer model', with an organization responsible for buying generation in an orderly manner, and then selling it on to retailers and consumers. The Commission did want to create competition for generators, however, and in this model, a tendering procedure would be adopted when the single buyer wanted more capacity. The alternative was a system of authorization, through which any qualified generator could take its own decision on when to enter the market. In order to sell their power, on the wholesale market or to final consumers, these generators would need 'third party access' to the grid. To meet the concerns of some Member States, there were two variants: negotiated third-party access, in which the companies involved would decide the network charges, and regulated third-party access, in which this would be the task of the government, or a government-appointed body.

In the event, when the Commission wrote the detailed rules for the single-buyer model, they were designed to ensure that the two systems would 'lead to equivalent economic results and hence to a directly comparable level of opening-up of markets and to a directly comparable degree of access to electricity markets' (European Commission 1996, Article 3.1). Member States could ensure this by giving eligible customers—those large enough to be granted a choice of supplier—third-party access to the grid, on either negotiated or regulated terms. Alternatively, a customer could contract with a generator, and the single buyer might be required to purchase this power on behalf of the customer, but at a price equal to its own selling price to them, less a published tariff for transmission and distribution. This was intended to be equivalent to the generator selling directly to the customer at a price exactly matching the single buyer's offer, and paying the transmission and distribution charge itself. We do not know how this system would have worked in practice, because, once these rules were announced, the French government declared that the single-buyer model would no longer achieve their aims for it, and opted for third-party access, along with every other Member State.

Member States had to establish transmission system operators and distribution system operators, which would run their grids and dispatch generators according to transparent, objective, criteria. Transmission, but not distribution, system operators had to have managerial independence from the other activities of an integrated electricity company. Integrated companies had to keep separate accounts for generation, transmission, and distribution.

Large customers were to be allowed to choose their electricity retailer, and distribution companies their wholesale supplier. Every customer taking more than 100 GWh a year had to be declared eligible to choose its retailer, and each Member State had to designate enough other eligible customers to open a percentage of its market equal to the EU average share of customers taking 40 GWh a year or more. This was a slightly cumbersome way of saying that 27 per cent of each national market had to be opened. In February 2000, three years after the entry into force of the Directive, the threshold fell to 20 GWh, or 30 per cent of each national market, and, in February 2003, it would fall to 9 GWh, or 35 per cent of each national market. Member States could exceed these thresholds, and 66 per cent of the overall European market was declared to be open by 2000 (European Commission 2001a). There was an option for Member States to refuse to allow their eligible customers to be supplied by a company from another country, if an identical customer in that country would not be eligible to receive a competitive supply. Member States could also decide not to apply some (specified) parts of the Directive, to promote public service obligations, as long as this did not significantly affect the development of trade or competition for eligible consumers.

A directive on gas followed eighteen months later (European Commission 1998). It copied much of the electricity Directive, but did not go as far. Gas undertakings had to keep separate accounts for transmission, distribution, and storage activities, but there was no requirement for managerial separation between them, or to establish a formal system operator role. Third-party access to the system could be negotiated or allowed on the basis of regulated tariffs, as with electricity—there was no suggestion of a single-buyer role.

Member States should designate enough eligible customers to open 20 per cent of their consumption to competition from July 2000. From July 2003, this should rise to 28 per cent, and to 33 per cent from July 2008. From the start, this should include all gas-fired electricity generators and those customers taking at least 25 million cubic metres of gas a year, although a more restrictive definition could be imposed if this would open more than 30 per cent of a Member State's market. After 2003, the minimum threshold should fall to 15 million cubic metres a year (unless this exceeded 38 per cent of the market), and, after 2008, to 5 million cubic metres (or 43 per cent of the market).

Member States could grant a temporary derogation from third-party access, subject to Commission approval, if take-or-pay gas contracts would present an undertaking with 'serious economic and financial difficulties.' This depended on the undertaking finding itself selling less gas than the minimum take in its contract, and being unable to find an alternative way of disposing of the gas. Derogations were also available for Member States that were not connected to the rest of the EU, and had a single supplier with a market share of more than 75 per cent (where competition would be impractical, and the rest of the European Union would not be significantly affected), and for those where gas had been supplied for less than ten years.

11.5. The Second Directives

Most Member States complied with these Directives on time, and the Commission was able to report reductions in prices to eligible consumers—furthermore, the reductions appeared greatest in countries with the highest degree of market opening (European Commission 2001b). None the less, the Commission also reported some problems with the markets, particularly where integrated companies could impede access to transmission and distribution, and determined that a new energy directive would be needed. The Commission wanted this to lead to market opening for all non-domestic electricity consumers from 1 January 2003, for all non-domestic gas consumers from 1 January 2004, and for all consumers from 1 January 2005.

During negotiations, this timetable slipped, so that all non-household customers were to become eligible from 1 July 2004, and all consumers from 1 July 2007. The importance of public service obligations was increased, with an annex spelling out the measures on consumer protection that Member States were expected to implement. Member States were also required to monitor and report on security of supply, and, in the electricity industry, could conduct tenders for new capacity if this was necessary to secure adequate supplies. Tenders were also allowed to promote renewable generation, or energy efficiency measures. The two Directives issued on 26 June 2003 did take substantial steps towards liberalization, however, and in aligning the frameworks for electricity and gas. The (unused) single-buyer model was discontinued, as was tendering as the normal way of procuring generation capacity—authorization was expected to provide enough conventional capacity in most circumstances.

System operators were created for gas transmission, LNG facilities, storage, and distribution, with similar duties to those in electricity. All of these operators had to be unbundled from other parts of vertically integrated undertakings, in both their legal form and their management. Member States were allowed to exempt distribution operators with fewer than 100,000 customers from this requirement, however. Separate accounts were required for transmission and distribution, and, until full market opening, for supply to eligible and non-eligible consumers.

Third-party access to the networks had to be on the basis of regulated tariffs, and each Member State had to appoint a regulator able to approve these tariffs, or at least the methodologies used to set them, in advance. Companies investing in significant new gas infrastructure (interconnectors between countries, LNG terminals, or storage facilities) were able to request exemption from third-party access if this was necessary to make their investments economic. The regulators would also approve the tariffs, or rules, used to set charges for balancing the system.

Member States were slower to implement these Directives in national law than the first liberalization Directives, and the Commission had to issue warning notices to eighteen of them in October 2004, pointing out that they had not notified it of the measures they had taken. In September 2005, it referred Estonia, Ireland, Greece, Spain, and Luxembourg to the Court of Justice, obtaining judgments against Luxembourg and Spain because they had not transposed the Directive into their national law, showing the limitations of this instrument. In other areas, the Commission can take direct action, although even in these, the interaction with Member States can be an important constraint. It is to these areas that we now turn.

11.6. Agreements between Firms

The European Commission has long had the power to police agreements between firms for their impact on competition, and has used this power to further liberalization in the energy utilities. In the run-up to liberalization, a number of companies signed long-term contracts that had the impact of foreclosing entry to the market, and the Commission has taken action against some of these.

For example, in Spain, Gas Natural and Endesa had agreed a long-term contract for gas which covered all of Endesa's foreseeable needs for power generation.[4] Since generators are particularly attractive clients for entrants to the gas industry, having large, steady, demands, this contract went a significant way towards foreclosing entry to that industry. Furthermore, Endesa was not allowed to resell the gas in this contract, but had a second contract, with a higher price, covering its needs as a gas retailer. This amounted to market segmentation, giving Endesa a better price where its demand was potentially more elastic, and driving up the price in the normal wholesale market. When the Commission investigated, the parties agreed to modify the contract. The contract length was cut by one-third, and the volumes involved by one-quarter, while Endesa was allowed to resell any gas it did not use itself. In northern Europe, the Norwegian company Statkraft had two long-term contracts covering the interconnector between Norway and western Denmark.[5] Between them, they reserved the whole of the cable's capacity. The Danish incumbent, Elsam, would have 60 per cent of the capacity for twenty years, while E.ON of Germany would have 40 per cent for twenty-five years, together with a matching contract for transit through Denmark and capacity on the Danish–German interconnector. The Commission warned the parties of its 'doubts about the compatibility with competition law of [these] agreements' during 2000, and they were abandoned, freeing up the entire capacity of the cable from January 2001 (European Commission 2001a: 156).

Sometimes, the problem blocking cross-border trade may not be access to the interconnector itself, but access to the national grids. When the English and French transmission system operators sought the Commission's views on arrangements for access to the cross-Channel interconnector, they were encouraged to choose a full open tender for this, while RTE, the French system operator, reviewed the way it managed internal transit rights and made them compatible with the arrangements for using the interconnector.

Contracts in the gas sector seem to have been particularly prone to contain anticompetitive clauses. The use of destination clauses, requiring that the gas be used in a particular country, was one common feature that limited the extent of cross-border trading, and hence inhibited the growth of a European gas market. In a series of cases, the European Commission was able to enforce changes to contracts between Gazprom of Russia and gas importers from Austria, France, Germany, Italy, and the Netherlands.[6] For any one importer, a contract with territorial restrictions will be less valuable than one without, *ceteris paribus*, because it is less flexible. If a number of importers all agree contracts with territorial restrictions, however, and know of the restrictions in the other contracts, each will be aware that it faces less competition from the other importers, and will be willing to pay a higher price for the gas. Imposing destination clauses can therefore be a profit-maximizing strategy for an exporting company, if it has sufficient market power to make these the norm, a condition which Gazprom might meet.

Anticompetitive gas contracts did not only come from outside the EU, however. Gaz de France had sold gas to ENI and ENEL of Italy, with territorial clauses requiring ENI to use the gas outside France, and ENEL to use it inside Italy, clauses that the Commission found to be incompatible with the Common Market in 2004.[7] In an earlier case, EdF Trading had sold gas from the United Kingdom to the German company Wingas,[8] with a contract that specified a reduction in volume if EdF started selling gas in Wingas' home market (except to certain incumbent firms). In other words, if EdF started to compete with Wingas, it would be at the expense of its wholesale profits. Following a Commission investigation in 2002, the contract was changed, allowing EdF to sell to any wholesaler without penalty.

11.7. Merger Policy

The Commission's powers over mergers are more recent than those over other aspects of competition policy, but cross-border mergers in the utility sector were very unusual before liberalization started. After liberalization, however, there has been a steady stream of cases which qualify for Commission review, as described by Codognet, et al. (2002), which shows how the utilities were attempting to improve their position in the new multinational markets. In many of these cases, the Commission has been able to negotiate pro-competitive changes to the companies' structures or operations in return for allowing the mergers. The Commission must strike a balance between measures that improve the workings of the market, so that the merger does not harm competition, despite the generally higher level of concentration that it will bring about, and leaving the firms with the belief that the amended merger is still in their own interests.

We will start the discussion with one of the later cases considered by the Commission, however, and one that it blocked, as it shows the competition concerns that utility mergers can raise. Gas de Portugal was the subject of a takeover bid from Energias de Portugal, the local electricity incumbent, and ENI, the Italian oil and gas firm.[9] The Commission blocked the merger because it believed that it would strengthen the dominance of the two firms in the Portuguese markets for gas and electricity, respectively. The Commission believed that the relevant markets were national in scope, given the weak interconnectors between Portugal and Spain, and the fact that plans for an Iberian electricity market had been repeatedly delayed. Both companies were dominant in their sector, for Energias de Portugal had 70 per cent of the generation capacity and almost all the electricity distribution in the country. Gas de Portugal remained a legal monopoly until the derogation from the second gas directive, given to Portugal as an emerging market, expired in 2007.

Energias de Portugal would be the most likely entrant to the gas industry once this was opened to competition, selling gas to its electricity customers; it was also a significant potential customer for any other gas company, given the possibility of building gas-fired power stations. Combining the two companies would have the impact of foreclosing the gas market. Similarly, Gas de Portugal was a likely entrant to the electricity industry, both in retailing power to its gas customers, and in building gas-fired power stations. While the companies proposed some divestitures to ameliorate the adverse effects on competition, the Commission believed that these were insufficient, and blocked the bid.

When Energias de Portugal appealed,[10] the CFI pointed out that the Commission had made an error in law, in assessing the state of competition in the gas market while this was still subject to a derogation that allowed Gas de Portugal to remain a monopoly. The Court ruled that 'in the total absence of competition, there was no competition that could be significantly impeded' by the merger (European Commission 2005: 113). In fact, the parties had offered remedies that would have improved competition in the short term, and the Commission was wrong to concentrate on the future detriments without taking these into account. However, even though the Court held that the Commission's analysis of the gas market had been legally incorrect, it upheld the decision to block the merger, since the detrimental effects in the electricity sector were sufficient justification for this.

The first significant merger in the electricity sector that the Commission reviewed was that between Veba and Viag of Germany, which created E.ON in 2000.[11] This merger qualified for Commission review, because of the companies' turnover outside Germany, while a simultaneous merger between RWE and VEW was reviewed by the Bundeskartellamt. The two authorities coordinated their responses, requiring the companies to divest their stakes in VEAG, the utility serving the eastern part of Germany, and to improve their network access rules. This allowed VEAG to become a fully independent competitor (of the German companies—it was soon bought by Vattenfall of Sweden), partially offsetting the increase in concentration brought about by the mergers. Veba and Viag had imposed a fee for transmitting power between northern and southern Germany, even if the flows might be netted off against other (simultaneous) transactions in the opposite direction, and this rule was abandoned, making it easier for other companies to move power around the country.

The following year, 2001, EdF took a large stake in Energie Baden-Wurtemburg (EnBW).[12] EdF was the dominant electricity company in France, and while there were many potential entrants to this market, EnBW had an adjoining service territory across the Rhine, making it a particularly strong candidate. The merger thus eliminated a potential competitor, and also made it much easier for EdF to retaliate against any German firm that entered its home market by expanding sales in that entrant's territory. The Commission's chosen remedy was to improve the level of competition in the French wholesale market by requiring EdF to auction Virtual Power Plants. These are contracts that effectively give the buyers the right to the output from a power station, which they can dispatch and either use themselves or sell on to other retailers. EdF was required to sell contracts for 5 GW of nuclear capacity and 1 GW of cogeneration capacity, lasting for five years. EdF was also required to give up its voting rights in Compagnie Nationale du Rhone, a smaller French utility.

Soon after its acquisition, EnBW was involved in the takeover of the Spanish firm Hidroelectrica del Cantabrico, acting in a consortium with Grupo Villar Mir.[13] Once again, the merger eliminated a potential entrant to the French market and gave EdF more ability to retaliate against any other entrant from the same country. In this case, the Commission decided that the low level of interconnection between France and Spain was the priority issue to tackle, and obtained commitments from EdF to build additional interconnectors that would raise the capacity from 1.1 GW to 4 GW.

The Commission has also used a merger that threatened to create horizontal market power to eliminate vertical integration. In 2005, E.ON of Germany was cleared to acquire the gas trading and storage activities of MOL of Hungary.[14] MOL would remain active in gas production and transmission, but E.ON would acquire its import contracts. E.ON also owned distribution companies in Hungary, and the combination of these with a dominant position in storage and wholesaling raised competition concerns. The companies' proposed remedies were for MOL to divest its remaining share of its trading and storage subsidiaries (thus achieving a complete separation between production and transmission, and trading and storage) and to offer a large-scale gas release programme, accounting for 14 per cent of national demand. The Commission cleared the merger on the basis that the benefits of separating trading and transmission, and the size of the gas release programme, made up for any anticompetitive concerns from combining the remaining import contracts with E.ON's retail businesses.

While this case shows the Commission's ability to get concessions from merging companies, two other cases involving E.ON reveal the limits to its power. In 2001, E.ON merged with Ruhrgas of Germany and acquired PowerGen of the United Kingdom. At the time when the Ruhrgas merger was notified to the Commission, the PowerGen deal had been agreed, but not completed. For the Commission's purposes, both E.ON and Ruhrgas had two-thirds of their EU turnover in one Member State, and so the merger was referred to the German authorities. The Bundeskartellamt recommended that the merger should be blocked, but the German government approved it. It is interesting to speculate whether the Commission would have taken a different line, had the PowerGen deal been completed more quickly and the Ruhrgas decision fallen to it.

In 2005, Gas Natural of Spain launched a takeover bid for Endesa. The dominant firm in the gas industry was attempting to acquire one of the two largest electricity companies in Spain, and had proposed divesting some of Endesa's power stations to Iberdrola, the other large power company. Once again, two-thirds of the firms' EU turnover was within the same Member State, and the Spanish authorities decided to allow the merger to go ahead. For a number of governments, the attractions of creating a national champion appear to outweigh the disadvantages of a less-competitive home market, and the Commission is unable to intervene. In the case of Endesa, however,

Gas Natural's bid was thwarted when E.ON of Germany launched a counter-offer, offering a price that Gas Natural was not willing (or able) to match. Assessing the cross-border bid was the task of the Commission, which cleared it.[15] There was very little overlap between E.ON and Endesa—E.ON had not previously been active in Spain and Endesa had little activity in most of E.ON's markets. The only potential competition concern could be whether, by increasing E.ON's reach and hence the overall level of multimarket contact within Europe, the merger increased the likelihood of tacit collusion. E.ON's bid in turn was to fail, however, when the Spanish construction firm Acciona built up a blocking stake in Endesa, and then launched its own counter-bid with Enel of Italy. E.ON bought Enel's existing assets in Spain, and as the level of concentration in the Spanish market did not increase, the transaction was cleared by the Commission.[16] The case clearly shows the ability of Member States to take actions that conflict with the Commission's desire for a competitive European energy market.

11.8. The Impact of Liberalization

What impact has liberalization actually had on the European energy utilities and their customers? We start with the level of prices, as the most prominent indicator of what is happening in the market. However, while it is a prominent indicator, it is also an ambiguous one. Prices can fall, or rise, for reasons unconnected with liberalization. Sometimes, pre-liberalization prices are too low, and so a rise is highly desirable. Figures 11.1 and 11.2 show electricity and gas prices since 1991, averaged across the EU-15. (Most of the data presented in this section will be for the EU-15, as this allows for a longer run of consistent figures.) Electricity prices have generally fallen over most of the period, before rising in recent years, driven by higher fuel costs, and particularly gas costs. Gas prices fluctuated in the 1990s, before rising strongly in 2000–1 and after 2004.

These figures show average prices, and there can be substantial variation between countries. One aim of liberalization is to reduce these price differences. If one country has access to cheaper energy sources, companies in that country should be able to export to places where prices had been higher, making prices converge. Prices will not necessarily equalize, for network costs may well differ, and different consumption patterns may imply that some customers take a higher proportion of their demand at peak times, and rightly pay a higher average price, even if their price within each hour is identical. Table 11.1 presents figures for the coefficient of variation of annual energy prices across the EU-15, and shows that they do indeed fall slightly in the post-liberalization period. Thus far, liberalization is working as its sponsors presumably hoped.

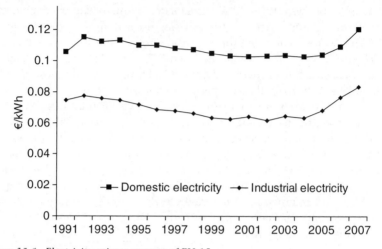

Figure 11.1. Electricity prices: average of EU-15

Source: Eurostat. Prices are for domestic customers Dc (3.5 MWh/year) and industrial customers Ie (2GWh/year).

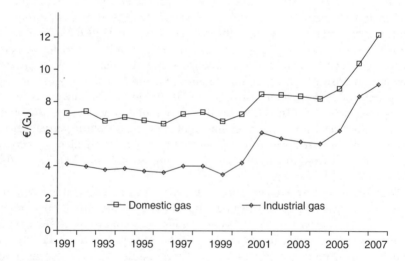

Figure 11.2. Gas prices: average of EU-15

Source: Eurostat. Prices are for domestic customers D3 (84 GJ/year) and industrial customers I3-1 (42 TJ/year).

300

Table 11.1. Price volatility within and across countries

	Variation across countries		Volatility within countries over time	
	1991–1998	2000–2007	1991–1998	2000–2007
Electricity: EU-15 domestic	0.280	0.234	0.057	0.094
Electricity: EU-15 industrial	0.182	0.151	0.070	0.131
Gas: EU-15 domestic	0.188	0.151	0.056	0.190
Gas: EU-15 industrial	0.170	0.160	0.092	0.238
Electricity: US regulated States: domestic			0.034	0.081
Electricity: US regulated States: industrial			0.053	0.110
Electricity: US liberalized States: domestic			0.045	0.126
Electricity: US liberalized States: industrial			0.079	0.240

Source: author's calculations from Eurostat and Energy Information Administration data.
US data are for 1995–2002 and 2000–7.

An allied aspect of price convergence is the ratio of prices within a country for different consumer types. In some regulated systems, particular customer classes might be favoured with relatively low prices, but these would be unsustainable in a liberalized industry—no other consumer group in a competitive market would be willing to pay above the odds to subsidize the favoured group. During the 1990s, Greece appears to have favoured domestic electricity customers, who paid little more for their power than industrial customers (within the two classes shown in Figure 11.1), whereas domestic customers in Italy paid twice as much as their more-favoured industrial customers. In the 1990s, the average annual coefficient of variation for this ratio across the EU-15 was 0.201, whereas 2000–7 it had fallen to 0.165. A similar convergence occurred with the ratio of domestic to industrial gas prices, with the coefficient of variation falling from 0.295 in 1991–8 to 0.214 in 2000–7. Liberalization therefore seems to be bringing a more equal treatment of different customer types across countries, although a wide variation still exists.

We should also consider price variations over time. We should expect that in a liberalized market prices will fluctuate over time more than in a regulated system where they are based on average costs. In a fully competitive market, the cost of the marginal supply should set the price for all customers, and this will be more volatile than average costs. If customers dislike price volatility, this will reduce welfare, although that cost should be offset against the benefits of a more accurate signal of the marginal cost of consumption. Furthermore, tariffs with prices fixed for several years are now available, even to domestic customers, and increasingly popular, in several countries with liberalized markets, including Sweden and the United Kingdom.

Table 11.1 shows that the volatility of gas and electricity prices within each country over time did increase between our two periods. The figures given are the average, across the EU-15, of the country-by-country coefficients of variation of annual electricity prices for each eight-year period. The question is the extent to which this was due to liberalization, however. As the overall level of energy prices was rising in the second period, this would naturally create a higher coefficient of variation than in the first period. The EU data, on their own, do not allow us to disentangle these two causes. However, we can compare the electricity price data with those from US States which remained regulated throughout the period, and saw very similar increases in volatility. This would imply that liberalization in the European Union did not lead to an increase in price volatility over time, in contrast to the position in the States that were liberalized in the United States.[17]

While prices can be seen as the outcome of liberalization (and of other factors), what has happened inside the various markets? Figure 11.3 shows how the structure of the generation market within each Member State has changed since 1999, as proxied by the share of the largest generator. For the less-concentrated markets, the three-firm concentration ratio or the Herfindahl index might give a better measure, but Eurostat publishes only the share of the largest firm. The market share in 1999 is measured along the horizontal axis, and that in 2006 (or 2005, if 2006 data are not available) is measured along the vertical axis. Countries near the bottom of the graph have the most competitive generation markets (at least by this proxy), while those that are furthest from the 45-degree line have improved the most. Two features immediately stand out. First, there is a wide variation between Member States, from the complete monopolies in Cyprus and Malta, to Finland, the United Kingdom and Poland, where the largest generator has only one-fifth of the market. Second, while a few markets have become far more competitive

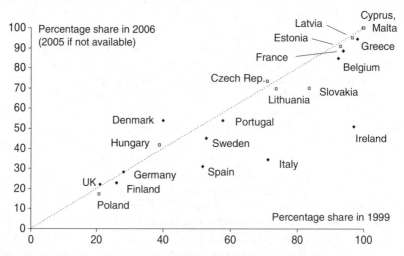

Figure 11.3. Share of the largest electricity generator in EU Member States
Source: Eurostat. New Member States have hollow markers.

(particularly Ireland, Italy, and Spain), in many of the less competitive markets, the share of the largest generator has hardly changed over the seven-year period. There is no significant increase in concentration, however. There is one apparent increase, in Denmark, but that country consists of two separate systems, connected to Norway and Sweden (and part of Nord Pool) and to Germany, but not connected to each other. There was a dominant generator in each system, with potential market power at times when the interconnectors were congested (which was often the case for West Denmark). In 2006, the Danish gas company DONG merged with these generators (and with two distribution companies), but sold some of their assets to Vattenfall. Within each half of Denmark, the asset sales meant that concentration was lower, but the common ownership of the remaining stations increased the national figure. At the level of the whole Nordic market, concentration will have increased somewhat, but from a low level that is unlikely to cause problems.[18]

Can the picture of concentration within national markets be seen as a success for the Commission? The problem is that it does not have powers to intervene within a Member State unless trade between Member States is affected. Concentration has not got worse, but in many Member States it is high and has not got significantly better. Where there have been dramatic falls in concentration, this is the result of national initiatives, not those of the Commission. The Commission has achieved some asset sales and other reductions in concentration in exchange for approving mergers, but, overall, its impact has been limited.

If competition within a country is too weak, international trade may provide an effective remedy. Figure 11.4 shows gross trade in electricity by the EU-15

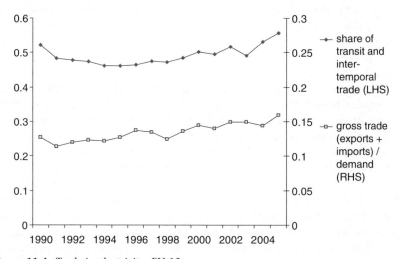

Figure 11.4. Trade in electricity: EU-15

Table 11.2. Market shares in gas, end 2004

	Share of top 3 shippers		Share of top 3 shippers
Austria	80%	Italy	62%
Belgium	n/a	Luxembourg	n/a
Denmark	97%	Netherlands	85%
Finland	n/a	Portugal	n/a
France	98%	Spain	73%
Germany	80%	Sweden	78%
Greece	n/a	UK	36%
Ireland	84%		

Source: European Commission (2005).

(the sum of national exports and imports) as a proportion of electricity consumption, which has risen slightly over the period. These flows can be broken down into three categories: transit flows, as when some of the power exported from France to Italy actually flows through Germany, being treated as an import and an export by that country; inter-temporal trades, as when Sweden receives thermal power from Denmark overnight and exports hydro power at peak times, and net trades with no counter-flow. If the market develops in ways that promote short-term arbitrage, we might expect the inter-temporal trades to rise, relative to the total. This is consistent with the upper line in Figure 11.4, which shows that transit and inter-temporal trades together have been rising slightly as a total of the gross trade.

Data on the gas industry are more limited. Table 11.2 presents a snapshot of the market shares of the top three shippers in most countries of the EU-15 at the end of 2004. As with electricity, there is a range of concentration levels, although only the United Kingdom, and perhaps Italy, could be considered as unconcentrated. The earlier benchmarking reports do not contain comparable data, and so it is not possible to make comparisons over time, as in Figure 11.3. Similarly, the analysis of electricity trade in Figure 11.4 is not possible for gas. Eurostat data for gas trade are based on the country of ultimate production, and cannot be used to show whether any gas originally destined for one country has been delivered to a second. Total trade volumes, defined in the Eurostat manner, are based on the difference between national production and consumption, and hence do not show changes linked to liberalization.

It is possible to compare the level of competition for end-users, however, for both electricity and gas. Figure 11.5 shows that many countries have effective competition for large business users of electricity, with six Member States reporting switching of more than 50 per cent since liberalization. These include the three that opened their markets before 1999 (Finland, Sweden, and the United Kingdom), and experience in the United Kingdom and elsewhere shows that switching tends to grow over time. (The United Kingdom is one of

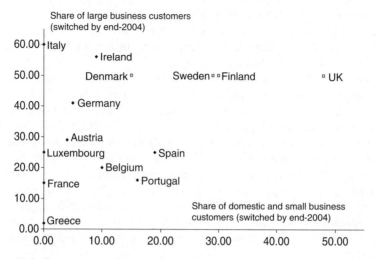

Figure 11.5. Customer switching in EU Member States: electricity

Source: European Commission (2005). The hollow markers represent figures of '>50%' for business switching.

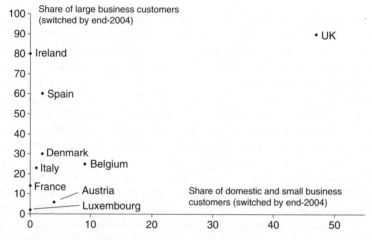

Figure 11.6. Customer switching in EU Member States: gas

Source: European Commission (2005).

four Member States that reports its switching as 'over 50 per cent'. In practice, almost every large customer will have switched its retailer since 1990.) In other countries, the share of large customer switching is much lower, and well below the 50 per cent observed in the United Kingdom in its first year of liberalization. The level of switching by small business and domestic electricity customers is lower in almost every Member State, and three (France, Greece, and Italy) had not opened their markets to domestic customers by 2004. Once again, the countries with the highest level of switching tend to be those where the markets have been open for longest.

In the gas market, Figure 11.6 shows that switching has been much lower in most Member States, reflecting the generally shorter time that the markets have been open. The United Kingdom, where the market has been open for longest, is the clearest exception to this. Ireland has seen high levels of switching among industrial customers,[19] having a high proportion of gas-fired power stations, which are particularly likely to seek a competitive supply. In Spain (which also has a high proportion of gas consumption by power stations), a large-scale gas release programme by the incumbent in 2001 allowed strong competition to sell to business users. Elsewhere, these levels of switching are disappointing, and suggest that most of the EU's gas markets are not yet open to effective competition, a suggestion that the Commission acted on during 2005.

11.9. The Sector Inquiry of 2005–7

The European Treaties allow the Commission to take action against firms with a dominant position, and, on 13 June 2005, the Commission launched its first sector-wide inquiries, covering banking and energy. The energy sector inquiry had been triggered by a period of rising energy prices, in which consumers had complained to the Commission that they had been unable to get acceptable offers from energy companies. In electricity, the focus of the inquiry was on wholesale price formation, as affected by generators' dispatching and bidding strategies, and on barriers to entry and to cross-border trade. In gas, the focus was on long-term import agreements, agreements between incumbent firms to swap gas, and barriers to cross-border trade.

The inquiry started by collecting an impressive amount of data from the firms in the industry, and released its preliminary analysis in February 2006, stating that the level of competition was unsatisfactory. A public consultation and further analysis followed, before the final conclusions were announced in January 2007. These confirmed the Commission's view that further action would be needed to create properly competitive energy markets in Europe. The Commission listed eight main concerns:

Market concentration

At the wholesale level, gas and electricity markets remain national in scope, and generally maintain the high level of concentration of the pre-liberalization period. This gives scope for exercising market power.

Vertical foreclosure

The current level of unbundling of network and supply interests has negative repercussions on market functioning and on incentives to invest in networks. This constitutes a major obstacle to new entry and also threatens security of supply.

Market integration

Cross-border sales do not currently impose any significant competitive constraint. Incumbents rarely enter other national markets as competitors. Insufficient or unavailable cross-border capacity and different market designs hamper market integration.

Transparency

There is a lack of reliable and timely information on the markets.

Price formation

More effective and transparent price formation is needed in order to deliver the full advantages of market opening to consumers. Many users have limited trust in the price formation mechanisms, while regulated supply tariffs below market prices discourage new entry.

Downstream markets

Competition at the retail level is often limited. The duration of retail contracts for industrial customers and local distribution companies can have a substantial impact on the opportunities for alternative suppliers to successfully enter the market.

Balancing markets

Currently, balancing markets often favour incumbents and create obstacles for newcomers. The size of the current balancing zones is too small, which leads to increased costs and protects the market power of incumbents.

LNG markets

LNG supplies widen Europe's upstream supplier base and are therefore important for both security of supply and competition between upstream suppliers. The potential for LNG supplies to favour less-concentrated downstream markets still needs to be realized.[20]

Many of these problems were interrelated—if markets can be made international, they will usually be less concentrated. Increasing the physical capacity between countries requires investment and takes time (although, in some cases, surprisingly small investments can release a large amount of transmission capacity), but changes to market rules should, in principle, be easy to achieve. In practice, of course, many such changes create winners and losers, and the latter will try to block or delay the change, but this opposition can be overcome if there is enough political will. Significant amounts of political will would be required to break down vertical integration in the energy utilities, but doing so would allow entrants better access to infrastructure, and remove fears that balancing was being manipulated in favour of incumbents. With more market participants, it is likely that wholesale markets would become more transparent, and prices more acceptable to consumers.

However, dealing with long-term contracts that may be preventing entry to retailing does present a problem. Governments interfere with the freedom to contract at their peril, and customers can have good reason for committing to a retailer willing to offer a stable price for a long period. Banning such contracts might thus be inappropriate, although the first British regulator did require retailers to allow all domestic consumers to change company with twenty-eight days' notice—and later argued for the rule to be relaxed.[21]

The Commission argued that a two-pronged approach would be needed to deal with these problems. First, the Commission would use its competition powers to the full, paying particular attention to cases of high market concentration, vertical foreclosure within markets, and barriers to cross-border trade. Two formal investigations of suspected abuse of a dominant position were launched during 2007, following dawn raids to discover evidence in May 2006. ENI has been accused of capacity hoarding and strategic underinvestment to reduce imports to the Italian gas market.[22] RWE has been accused of foreclosing access to the gas market in its territory by charging high prices for access to infrastructure, fragmenting its network into an excessive number of zones (which also raises rivals' costs), and failing to release capacity to allow customer switching.[23] Second, the Commission needed to address a number of structural and regulatory issues. These centred on the problems caused by vertical integration, and the need to eliminate gaps in regulation covering cross-border trade.

In January 2007, the Commission proposed two approaches for dealing with vertical integration (European Commission 2007d). The more comprehensive would be to insist on full ownership unbundling of transmission system owners. This would be an enduring solution that would not require any special regulation or on-going monitoring, but subsequent events have shown that it would be unacceptable to a number of Member States. The problem is that it forces large companies to dispose of assets, something that many of them are unwilling to do, and they can call on the support of those governments that believe in the benefits of having national champions. The alternative is to create independent system operators, fully unbundled from the rest of the industry, which would operate transmission assets but would not necessarily own them. An independent system operator should not suffer from any conflicts of interest that would lead it to favour particular users, but the contractual arrangements to set it up will be complicated, and will need continual monitoring. It is therefore a second-best solution, but may be the best politically feasible outcome.

Where regulation is concerned, the Commission wants to strengthen the role of national regulators, as well as improving coordination between them. The Commission will propose a directive to ensure that regulators have strong ex-ante powers over the following areas: (i) all aspects of third party access to networks; (ii) access to gas storage; (iii) balancing mechanisms; (iv) market surveillance of e.g. power exchanges; (v) compliance with functional and account unbundling for distribution system operators; (vi) all cross border issues; (vii) consumer protection including any end-user price controls; (viii) information gathering; (ix) sanctions for non-compliance.[24]

The Commission had considered an evolutionary approach for strengthening coordination between national regulators by requiring Member States to give them an objective to further the Community's interests, and believes that it will be insufficient. Two remaining alternatives were to strengthen the existing European Regulators Group for Electricity and Gas (ERGEG), giving it a formal role in harmonizing some technical decisions, and to create a new, pan-European, body to deal with cross-border issues. Once again, this second approach may meet political resistance from Member States.

The Commission unveiled its Third Energy Package in September 2007 (European Commission 2007b). The Commission is not insisting on ownership unbundling, allowing Member States to appoint an independent system operator instead. This decision reflects the political realities of the situation. In the area of regulatory reform, however, the Commission has chosen the more ambitious proposal, and announced plans to establish an Agency for the Cooperation of Energy Regulators. This would set out a framework for cooperation by national regulators and oversee transmission system operators' cross-border operations. It would decide which infrastructure projects to exempt from third-party access, and make decisions on specific technical issues assigned to it.

The Commission is also concerned about the potential for companies based outside the European Union to act in an anticompetitive manner. The draft directives make it clear that the unbundling requirements would apply throughout the European Union to a company active in generation, gas production, or retailing anywhere in the European Union, even if the company comes from a third country. Furthermore, the draft directives prohibit companies from outside the European Union from acquiring networks inside the European Union, unless an agreement between the European Union and the company's home government specifically allows it. The aim of such an agreement would be to ensure that the company faced the same rules as a European firm, and in particular has to unbundle any transmission network it might own.

This proposal has attracted strong criticism from Gazprom of Russia, which is a vertically integrated company believed to have ambitions to expand in the European Union and no desire to unbundle at home. Gazprom's legal monopoly over Russian gas exports already gives it a strong position in the European Union, but the 'Chicago' argument that vertical integration by a monopoly does no (additional) harm should not apply, as the company faces competition from other exporting countries. There is thus a danger that it might seek to use control of a transmission company to discriminate against a company importing gas from another source, and the Commission's policy is an appropriate precaution against this. There would be little point in creating a strictly separated structure inside the European Union, only for companies from elsewhere to be able to discriminate in favour of vertically integrated affiliates located just across the European Union's borders.

11.10. Conclusions

The Commission appears to have a clear vision of its aim for the energy utilities—to create markets in which as many firms as possible have access to the transmission grids in order to sell electricity and gas to consumers across Europe. This vision has evolved over time, and the more ambitious parts of it—ensuring that every consumer can choose their retailer, and enforcing separate ownership of the transmission grids—have been added after the process had already been underway for some time. None the less, the Commission's actions, in legislating and in using its competition policy powers, have been consistent with a policy of promoting this vision by any means at its command.

At the same time, many of the utilities have been attempting to strengthen their positions, by merging to create pan-European companies that will be strong in a number of markets. Quite apart from any belief that bigger is better, the theory of multimarket contact implies that creating a foothold in the home market of a rival company reduces that rival's incentive to compete strongly in the firm's own home market. In some cases, national governments have seen a strong (or at least large) utility as an objective worth supporting, through actions ranging from taking a lenient view on competition concerns to actively brokering deals. Many of the merger cases considered in this chapter have come about through the interplay of these different aims.

Has European energy liberalization improved welfare? To answer this question, it is necessary to consider what would have happened in its absence, and that requires detailed country-by-country studies that are beyond the scope of this chapter. Newbery and Pollitt (1997) and Domah and Pollitt (2001) assess the privatization of the Central Electricity Generating Board and of the Regional Electricity Companies in England and Wales, finding that both policies improved welfare (although inadequate competition in the former case meant that most of the benefits went to the companies' shareholders rather than to consumers). Damsgaard and Green (2005) assesses the liberalization of the Swedish electricity industry, estimating that welfare rose by 11 billion kroner over the first eight years after liberalization, or by between 2 per cent and 4 per cent of the annual spending on electricity. We need more studies of the same kind, to assess the results of liberalization in other Member States.

We should also recognize that liberalization in the European Union is still a work in progress. The Commission's report on Prospects for the Internal Market (2007d) lists a number of other steps that need to be taken to improve its workings, including steps to make markets more transparent, a review of long-term gas contracts, better access to gas storage, more coordination of investment in transmission, and enforcement of the rules on unbundling distribution system operators. Much has been achieved in designing a framework for effective competition, but it is not yet fully in place across Europe.

Is the glass half-full or half-empty? Consumers in one Member State can benefit from a competitive market in that country, even if those in neighbouring countries do not have real choices. Some energy markets are becoming more liquid, and steps are being taken to improve cross-border flows, such as the scheme to link the Belgian, Dutch, and French power markets, creating an implicit auction for the transmission capacity between the countries. At the same time, several Member States have been attempting to create (or at least facilitate) national champion companies, which would have a dominant position in at least part of the European market. If the market does become pan-European, then this local strength would become irrelevant, except in so far as it created a company able to compete aggressively in other areas. The danger, however, is that the market will remain fragmented, and that large companies that meet in a number of separate, but asymmetric, markets will be unwilling to compete too strongly in any of them. Security of supply has to remain a concern, as well—does Europe have access to enough different sources of gas that it can afford to give up the prospect of buyer power to offset the actions of large exporters, particularly Russia?

As always, a lot depends upon political will. If we want to create an energy sector without significant market power, the policies required are clear, and have been applied successfully in a number of countries.[25] The key actions are to separate transmission from the rest of the industry and to deal with horizontal market power within a country. Increasing cross-border transmission capacity is certainly possible, by investment and by better coordination, and, if the will exists, that will help to create markets that, if not quite pan-European, certainly encompass several Member States. Transmission is expensive, however, and this means that relying on imports to increase competition within a national market, rather than on more competitive local production, will usually be a second-best policy.

The Commission is also in the world of the second-best when it uses merger policy to improve the structure of national markets. The constraints are that the Commission can only react to the mergers that are actually proposed, and that the remedies imposed have to appear better to the parties than the status quo. The first constraint means that the Commission may never get the chance to affect conditions in some national markets, if no eligible merger is proposed. The second limits the extent of the concessions that the Commission can win. Unless there are significant efficiency gains, or other companies will be worse off after the merger, it will be hard for the Commission to amend a merger in such a way that consumers will be better off after it, while the merging companies still believe that the merger is going to lead to an increase in their profits. Otherwise, the Commission may only be engaged in damage limitation, approving mergers that will still make consumers worse off, even after amendment.

The Commission can only use the tools that are available to it, however. If Member States are unwilling to take action, or to agree a new Directive, the Commission is limited to the tools of competition policy rather than regulatory reform. The problem is that these may not be enough to make the markets properly competitive. The worst of all possible worlds would be if a company could have a position that is sufficiently dominant for the energy markets to work badly, without ever actually abusing a dominant position and triggering action from the authorities. The Commission has been investigating some cases of alleged abuse, however, and shortly before this chapter was revised, was able to use this investigation to reach an agreement with Europe's largest energy utility, E.ON of Germany. E.ON has agreed to divest its transmission activities in exchange for the Commission's agreement to end the investigation into its alleged market abuse.

Could E.ON's change of position trigger a shift in the policymaking equilibrium? So far, both France and Germany have been opposed to ownership unbundling of transmission, preventing the Commission from making this a compulsory policy. E.ON may now want its domestic competitors to face the same constraint that it has just accepted, and may attempt to change the German government's position. If this leaves France isolated among the larger Member States, the Commission could have the opportunity it needs to bring in full ownership unbundling.

Ownership unbundling is not a panacea. Many national markets remain concentrated, and cross-border shareholdings may reduce competitive pressure from companies in neighbouring markets. None the less, it would be an important step towards full liberalization of the EU energy markets.

Notes

[1] This chapter was commissioned by the IESE Business School for the IESE conference 'Fifty Years of the Treaty: Assessment and Perspectives of Competition Policy in Europe', held in Barcelona, 19–20 Nov. 2007. I would like to thank Xavier Vives, Nils-Henrik von der Fehr, and participants at the conference for helpful comments.

[2] These paragraphs draw heavily on a part of Damsgaard and Green (2005) for which Niclas Damsgaard was the lead author.

[3] This answer does not necessarily fit every case, given that the first electricity liberalization in Europe—in England and Wales—involved the break-up of the incumbent utility against the strong opposition of its senior management.

[4] Case COMP/37.542 Gas Natural + Endesa.

[5] Case COMP/37.125 Statkraft + I/S Elsam + 18.

[6] Cases COMP/38.085 PO/Territorial restrictions Austria, COMP/38.307 PO/Territorial restrictions Germany Gasprom, COMP/38.307 PO/Territorial restrictions Netherlands.

[7] Case COMP/38.662 GDF–ENEL, GDF–ENI.

[8] Case COMP/36.559 British Gas + Wingas + 1.

[9] Case COMP/M.3440 ENI/EDP/GDP.

[10] Case T–87/05 *EDP-Energias de Portugal SA* v. *Commission*.

[11] Case COMP/M.1673 VEBA/VIAG.

[12] Case COMP/M.1853 EDF/EnBW.

[13] Case COMP/M.2434 Grupo Villar Mir/EnBW/Hidroelectrica del Cantabrico.

[14] Case COMP/M.3696 E.ON/MOL.

[15] M.4110 E.ON/ENDESA.

[16] M.4685 ENEL/ACCIONA/ENDESA.

[17] States that started to liberalize and then abandoned the experiment, such as California, are excluded.

[18] The Commission was concerned at the merger's effects on the Danish gas market, and required DONG to release gas amounting to about 10 per cent of Danish demand to potential competitors for six years and to dispose of the larger of its two storage facilities. M.3868 DONG/ELSAM/ENERGI E2.

[19] The Benchmarking Report (European Union 2005) gives a figure of 100 per cent for large business switching, but the country review states that customers taking 64 per cent of total consumption have switched, and that 80 per cent of the market is eligible, implying 80 per cent switching within this segment.

[20] European Commission (2007a: 7–11).

[21] This was some years after leaving his post, and after the market had become far more competitive. By that time, he believed that the restriction was inhibiting the development of long-term fixed-price offers, or of 'energy service' offers that helped customers invest in energy efficiency (Littlechild 2006).

[22] Case COMP 39.315 ENI.

[23] Case COMP 39.402 RWE.

[24] European Commission (2007d: 13).

[25] Several of the points in this paragraph were made by Nils-Henrik von der Fehr when he discussed this chapter, although he may not agree with my reformulation of them.

12

Competition Policy in the European Union and the United States: Convergence or Divergence?[1]

William E. Kovacic

12.1. Introduction

From the late nineteenth century through to the first half of the twentieth century, the enforcement of statutes forbidding anticompetitive practices was an endeavour unique to the United States. In this period, a handful of other jurisdictions—for example, Canada in 1899—had adopted competition laws, but none applied these commands in a manner that compelled domestic or foreign firms to take notice. To come ahead a quarter-century to 1975, the few jurisdictions with actively enforced competition laws included the European Union, Germany, and the United States. Even at this time, questions of cross-border enforcement dealt mainly with skirmishes over the imposition of treble damages in private US antitrust suits upon foreign firms.

I doubt that in 1975 even the most ardent enthusiast for competition law imagined what would transpire in the coming decades. Who foresaw in 1975 that by 2007 the Soviet Union would dissolve, China would pursue far-reaching market-oriented reforms, and the European Union would include several former Soviet Republics and nations that once were known in the West as members of the Warsaw Pact? And who anticipated in 1975 that by 2007 most nations would turn to market-based systems to promote economic growth, or that the number of jurisdictions with competition laws would exceed 100?

The transformation of economic policy and the regulatory framework in individual states has coincided with advances in communications, finance, and transport that have intensified cross-border integration in the production and sale of goods and services. These developments have increased the interdependence of national or regional regulatory regimes. Decisions taken in one jurisdiction about a cartel, a merger, or an abuse of dominance can have substantial cross-border spill overs.

As a group, the world's competition systems feature noteworthy substantive and institutional similarities. Only an observer unfamiliar with the larger history of the evolution of national legal systems would find this shocking. At the same time, in an environment of ever greater economic and regulatory interdependence, there is broad awareness of how the substantial multiplicity of competition systems with dissimilar substantive standards, procedures, institutional arrangements, and capabilities can discourage business transactions that spur economic growth and can needlessly increase the cost of controlling anticompetitive conduct.

Recognition of the potential costs associated with the multiplicity of competition systems has inspired various measures to promote international convergence upon superior norms.[2] Many initiatives principally involve public authorities. These include voluntary multinational networks such as the International Competition Network (ICN) and the competition committee of the Organization for Economic Cooperation and Development (OECD); regional collaborations (for example, the Andean Pact, CARICOM, and COMESA), and bilateral discussions between individual competition agencies. These largely public activities coexist with projects in various non-government networks such as professional associations and academic organizations. Non-government advisors have played a vital role in the work of some of the public agency networks, such as the ICN.

Amid abundant convergence-related activity within all of these institutions, why should the level of convergence between the competition systems of the European Union and the United States be a specific focus of attention? More than any other single force, the interaction of the competition policy systems of the European Union and United States deeply influences the convergence process within all of the multinational and regional networks. This is a function of domestic expenditures (the European Union and the United States spend more money on public enforcement than other jurisdictions), outlays for international projects (the European Union and the United States spend the most on international networking and have the largest foreign technical assistance programmes related to competition policy), experience (the European Union and the United States have a larger base of current and older cases and engage in substantial non-litigation policymaking activity), and economic significance (the European Union and the United States are the largest economic markets on the planet). This gives the European Union and the United States unequalled capacity to project their competition policy preferences beyond their own borders. What happens in the European Union and the United States does not stay there.

This chapter examines the state of the relationship between the competition policy systems of the European Union and the United States.[3] The second part of the chapter begins by discussing, as a normative matter, what type of convergence on competition policy norms we should hope to see between the European Union and the United States—or among all of the world's competition authorities. The third part then offers a positive description of existing similarities and differences between the EU and US competition policy systems. The fourth part reviews centrifugal and centripetal forces that promise to affect the extent to which the two systems converge or diverge in the future and the fifth part discusses possible paths for improvement in the relationship and for the attainment of better practices in competition policy.

To foreshadow my overall assessment, I regard progress towards greater cooperation in the implementation of competition policy and the mutual adoption of superior norms between the European Union and the United States to be a genuine success story in the modern transatlantic relationship. Despite differences in philosophy, procedure, analytical technique, and, occasionally, substantive outcomes, the past decade has featured important enhancements in measures by public and non-government bodies in both jurisdictions to improve cooperation in the formulation and implementation of competition-policy standards governing transatlantic commerce. Moreover, the EU/US cooperation has provided important insights for building a framework of global and regional cooperation through multinational networks such as the ICN and the OECD. These efforts can foster widespread convergence upon superior analytical concepts and implementation techniques.

Progress to date has not been inevitable or automatic. Nor will it be so in the years to come. Past achievements have required a substantial commitment of resources to institution building that does not show up in the usual roster of accomplishments—notably, case counts—by which public agencies most often are judged. Future improvements will depend on the willingness of agency leaders to provide these resources, and more. Good relationships in this area do not come on the cheap.

Resources will not be the only challenge for the EU and US competition agency leadership. The public agencies in the European Union and the United States cooperate extensively, yet they also compete for influence and recognition. The drive to be seen as the global leader in competition policy is an underlying source of tension that can sharpen the edge of disagreement about specific matters or larger policy issues. Despite these tensions, an interjurisdictional rivalry channelled in constructive directions can have useful consequences. A competition to attain superior substantive approaches and implementation techniques is a competition worth having.

12.2. Why does Convergence or Divergence between the EU and US Systems Matter?

The interest in mapping out the EU and US competition policy systems stems from more than curiosity about comparative study. For at least three reasons, the differences today can have considerable practical, economic significance. First, there is a high and increasing degree of interdependence between the regulatory regimes of individual jurisdictions. In many areas of regulatory policy, the jurisdiction with the most intervention-minded policy has power to set a global standard. It is the rare multinational enterprise that does not operate in the European Union and in the United States. For matters such as abuse of dominance or mergers, firms generally must conform their behaviour to the practice of the most restrictive major jurisdiction with competition laws. By any measure, the European Union and the United States are major jurisdictions—'major' in the sense of having the nominal authority and enforcement capability to compel fidelity to their demands.

The second reason concerns the process of enforcement. Even when the European Union and United States apply the same substantive standards and ordinarily reach the same assessment of the same commercial practice, differences in the procedure for investigations and agency decision-making can impose costs on affected enterprises. In the case of merger reviews, these costs include the time and out-of-pocket expense of complying with varied filing requirements and accounting for differences in the timing of government reviews. Where it is possible to achieve simpler, more-common procedures, the EU and US agencies can reduce the cost of executing routine transactions without any reduction in the quality of their substantive analysis.

The third reason involves the development of new competition systems around the world. The European Union and the United States spend substantial resources for technical assistance for new competition policy systems and for countries considering the adoption of new competition laws. By far, most of the eighty or so jurisdictions that have adopted new competition laws in the past thirty years have civil law systems. Their competition systems usually rely on an administrative enforcement model that resembles the EU regime. By comparison, few civil law countries have established competition systems that use the adversarial prosecution model employed by the US Department of Justice. Because the EU institutional platform is more compatible with the institutional arrangements in most civil law countries, many transition economies have an inclination to look first to EU models in designing and implementing their competition systems. This condition means that EU norms, more than US norms, tend to be more readily absorbed into the newer competition policy regimes.

12.2.1. *The operating systems and applications of competition law*

Experience with technical assistance programmes and the adoption of competition-policy systems permits us to derive a more general observation about the global development of competition policy. To use a computer technology metaphor, the operating system of a jurisdiction's competition laws consists of the institutional framework through which legal commands are formulated and applied. As noted above, most jurisdictions are civil law systems. This ensures that the EU institutional framework which relies (compared to the US) upon more highly specified legal commands and emphasizes policy development through an expert administrative body will be the most popular institutional model among the world's competition authorities. The US competition law framework is grounded mainly in a common law methodology. The United States relies substantially upon open-ended statutory commands and the elaboration of doctrine through case-by-case litigation in the courts. By reason of history and modern practice, relatively few jurisdictions will embrace this model.

With respect to the operating systems of the world's competition laws, the EU's institutional arrangements were destined to attain a dominant share. That dominance is likely to continue. An interesting issue for global competition norms is the choice by individual jurisdictions of substantive analytical 'applications' and related investigative techniques to run upon a chosen operating system. Where will countries look to obtain the basic applications that they will run through their institutional operating systems? In areas such as the treatment of cartels and horizontal mergers, the United States has provided the analytical applications that most of the world's competition law systems use today. The United States also has designed implementation applications, such as the use of leniency to detect cartels, that enjoy broad popularity around the world. Moreover, US applications such as the use of private rights of action and the use of criminal sanctions to punish cartels are receiving a close look in many civil law countries, although the adoption of these applications will require civil law countries to make some important adjustments to their existing institutional arrangements.

Thus, the European Union enjoys a dominant share concerning the operating system for competition law, and the market for applications remains highly competitive. The European Union and the United States account for the leading share of applications concerning substantive analysis and investigative methods, but a number of jurisdictions have produced important refinements of EU or US applications for their own use. The applications have an open-source element to the extent that individual countries often retain freedom to make adaptations suited to their own needs. The level of adaptation sometimes is constrained by the obligation that individual states owe to superior legal authorities. For example, accession to the European Union has required candidates to conform their laws to those of the Community. This might be seen, in rough terms, as a form of tying analytical applications to an institutional framework. Even so, the European Union's own analytical applications often draw upon concepts and experience from the United States. Individual jurisdictions, large or small, have considerable capacity to shape the development of substantive applications by their own success in advancing the state of the analytical art.

12.2.2. Diversification and convergence: normative principles

From a normative perspective, how should we regard the simple existence of differences between the European Union and the United States with regard to substantive principles, analytical approaches, and implementation techniques? Two normative principles strike me as appropriate. First, some degree of difference is not only inevitable but healthy. Complete homogeneity across individual systems—a harmonization that unified jurisdictions by doctrine and process—'drives out experimentation and diversity of our regulatory levers'.[4] The history of competition policy has featured a continuing search for optimal substantive rules and implementation methods. This search has benefited from continuous, decentralized experimentation with respect to analytical principles (for example, the DoJ's adoption of revised merger guidelines in 1982), enforcement procedures (for example, the creation in the 1970s of the US system for mandatory pre-merger notification and waiting periods), investigation techniques (for example, the DoJ's leniency reforms of the 1990s), and organizational innovation (for example, the UK Office of Fair Trading's recent restructuring to integrate competition and consumer protection operations).

Insistence on uniformity across systems, or a requirement that innovations within individual jurisdictions proceed only after a broad consensus among the global community of competition authorities has been achieved would stymie these and other valuable measures. Competition policy has a strong experimental aspect. Improvements in substantive standards are likely to be achieved by an incremental process of adjusting enforcement boundaries inward and outward, and by assessing the consequences of pressing for more or less intervention. Refinements in organizational structures and investigational techniques likewise require experimentation (should an agency's economists be located in a separate division that reports directly to the head of the agency, or should they reside in teams of case handlers?) and the observation of results. The only way to answer basic questions about substantive policy and implementation is to test alternatives, and that testing benefits from decentralization that does not require consensus-building across jurisdictions for every adjustment from the status quo.

319

The second normative principle is that there should be mechanisms to promote adoption of superior norms. In a series of speeches presented during his chairmanship of the Federal Trade Commission, Timothy Muris presented a three-stage framework by which independent jurisdictions could realize the benefits of decentralized experimentation and promote the broad adoption of superior norms.[5] By 'superior norms' I mean norms that (a) promote the accurate diagnosis of the actual or likely competitive significance of observed behaviour and (b) promote the design of government intervention (by initiating a case, by performing a study, or by acting as an advocate before other public institutions) that corrects the problem at issue.

The first stage of the Muris framework consists of decentralized experimentation within individual jurisdictions. The second involves the identification of superior substantive standards and implementation methods. In the third stage, individual jurisdictions voluntarily opt in to superior norms. This framework anticipates and welcomes experiments that depart from the status quo and supplies the means for promoting the widespread adoption of superior approaches. I will have more to say below about what the European Union and the United States can do with regard to the vital second stage of this process.

To the Muris framework I would add a fourth element. Notwithstanding differences that might exist at any one moment between the European Union and the United States or across other systems, individual jurisdictions should build institutional mechanisms that increase interoperability. This entails careful attention to enhancing channels of communication and discussion that link related functional units across agencies (that is, between DG Comp and the DoJ and the FTC) and connect related institutions outside the competition agencies. A useful approach to achieving the fourth element is suggested in the New Transatlantic Agenda,[6] which was established in 1995. The NTA sought to improve the quality of regulatory policy and to reduce the cost of the regulatory framework governing transatlantic commerce by improving EU/US cooperation. As Professors Mark Pollack and Gregory Shaffer characterize its approach,[7] the NTA seeks to strengthen EU/US regulatory coordination by enhancing:

- *Intergovernmental contacts* among the chiefs of government and other high-level public officials (such as agency or department heads);
- *Transgovernmental contacts* on a day-to-day basis among lower-level officials; and
- *Transnational contacts* among non-government institutions and individuals, including academics and the business community.

Beyond providing a way to structure the routine interaction between the EU and US competition policy systems, the NTA's three-level approach provides a useful means for identifying superior norms—the second element of the Muris framework. Without a conscious process to identify and adopt superior ideas, decentralization cannot fulfil its promise as a source of useful policy innovations. By promoting improved interoperability in routine operations and helping identify superior norms, this approach also can provide the foundation on which EU and US policymakers choose to opt in to such norms.

As sketched out here, the process that generates transatlantic competition norms would be adaptable and evolutionary. In the field of competition law and in other areas of public policy there is a tendency to speak of convergence upon 'best' practices. I believe it is more accurate and informative to say that the objective is convergence upon 'better' practices.[8] The development of competition policy in any jurisdiction is a work in progress. This stems from the inherently dynamic nature of the discipline. Lest they be frozen in time, good competition policy systems consciously evolve through their capacity to adapt analytical concepts over time to reflect new learning.[9] To speak of 'best' practices suggests the existence of fixed objectives that, once attained, mark the end of the task. Envisioning problems of substance or process as having well-defined, immutable solutions may neglect the imperfect state of our knowledge and obscure how competition authorities must work continuously to adapt to a fluid environment that features industrial dynamism, new transactional phenomena, and continuing change in collateral institutions vital to the implementation of competition policy.

Perceiving the proper role of EU and US competition agency officials to be the continuing pursuit of *better* practices can focus attention on the need for the continuing reassessment and improvement of competition policy institutions. A common commitment by EU and US competition officials to make the cycle of reassessment and refinement a core element of their operations should be a central element of future cooperation. The routine process of evaluation should focus on the adequacy of the existing legislative framework, the effectiveness of existing institutions for implementation, and the quality of substantive outcomes from previous litigation and non-litigation interventions. This type of inquiry would help ensure that each competition agency consider how it can upgrade its substantive standards and operational methods. For each agency, the upgrade could take the form of increasing activity with respect to some practices and doing less with respect to others.

12.3. Similarities and Dissimilarities in the Substance of EU and US Competition Policy

I share the often-expressed view of EU and US competition officials that the general trend of competition policy in the two jurisdictions has been towards common acceptance of substantive standards and the analytical concepts that support the implementation of those standards. An overview of overall goals and specific areas of activity verifies that proposition and also underscores noteworthy differences.

12.3.1. *The objectives of competition policy*

It is nearly thirty years since Robert Bork's *Antitrust Paradox* underscored the importance of objectives to the operation of a competition policy system. 'Antitrust policy', Bork wrote, 'cannot be made rational until we are able to give a firm answer to one question: What is the point of the law—what are its goals? Everything else follows from the answer we give.'[10]

Modern discourse between EU and US government officials has featured many statements about the proper aims of competition law. The speeches of top agency leaders in both jurisdictions indicate broad agreement on the question of goals. Each jurisdiction accepts the broad proposition that the central aim of competition law is 'the objective of benefitting consumers'.[11] Consistent with the single-minded focus on 'consumer welfare', EU and US antitrust officials routinely disavow any purpose of applying competition laws to safeguard individual competitors as an end in itself. EU officials also have grown accustomed to hearing, by direct quotation or paraphrase, the US Supreme Court's admonition that the proper aim of antitrust law is 'the protection of *competition*, not *competitors*'.[12]

At one level, the apparent agreement on overall objectives would seem to be, and is, an important step towards achieving convergence between the two systems. A commitment to apply competition policy commands to improve consumer well-being forces the agency to consider to some extent how a proposed form of intervention will deliver benefits to consumers. This can be at least a mild discipline upon the exercise of agency discretion and a means to develop an internal norm that focuses on effects upon end users. At the same time, however, the concept of 'consumer welfare' and the principle of protecting 'competition, not competitors' are so open-ended that their true meaning in practice depends on how they are applied. It is a relatively barren exercise for EU and US officials to invoke these phrases without taking the further difficult step of achieving agreement on what these phrases mean.

I regard the habit of EU and US officials to invoke consumer welfare and related expressions as a useful start to a larger and continuing discussion about the objectives of competition law. I do not think that these phrases alone tell us much about the deeper levels of meaning that each jurisdiction attaches to them. Nor do I think that the phrases deny each jurisdiction considerable discretion to achieve varied policy ends through the process of interpretation and application.

12.3.2. *Substantive competition policy*

The general trend of EU and US competition policy in the past two decades has been in the direction of greater convergence with regard to the appropriate focus of government enforcement and the application of litigation and non-litigation policy instruments. This part of the chapter discusses similarities and dissimilarities. Section 12.4 below examines the reasons for these developments. It describes centripetal forces that have tended to pull the EU and US systems together and centrifugal forces that draw the two systems apart.

SUBSTANTIVE SIMILARITIES

'Cartels'. Both the European Union and the United States treat cartels harshly. Speeches of EU and DoJ officials today depict cartels as the most serious form of anticompetitive behaviour, and both institutions have devoted substantial effort to prosecuting offenders and to devising new techniques for detecting covert arrangements. Recoveries in the high nine figures occur today with some regularity. The modern trend in sanctions in both jurisdictions has been to increase punishments for violators, and two EU Member States (Ireland and the United Kingdom) have adopted policies, like that of the DoJ, of seeking incarceration for individual offenders. There is a continuing debate within the European Commission and in the Member States about the desirability of relying to a greater degree on criminal sanctions.

This is an area in which EU practice in the past decade has converged substantially upon US norms by a process of voluntarily opting in. Cartel enforcement is a major example in which the European Union embraced techniques—most notably, leniency—that had been tested extensively in the United States. More broadly, global acceptance of a powerful anti-cartel norm is a vivid illustration of the operation of the Muris framework for convergence: an initial period of decentralized experimentation (that is, the US leniency enhancements of the early and mid-1990s), the identification of superior practices (for example, through the deliberations of the OECD competition committee), and voluntary opting in (dozens of jurisdictions have adopted leniency programmes).

'Horizontal mergers'. Horizontal-merger policy in the European Union and the United States reflects a substantial degree of similarity. The elaboration and revision of merger guidelines in both jurisdictions in the past twenty years has yielded extensive convergence on the analytical framework. Merger decisions by the courts of both jurisdictions—notably, *AirTours*[13] in the European Union and *Arch Coal*,[14] *Giant/Western*,[15] *SunGard*,[16] and *Whole Foods*[17] in the United States—have tended to press EU and US enforcement authorities to satisfy more demanding evidentiary standards and withstand closer judicial scrutiny of proof offered to demonstrate likely anticompetitive effects. *AirTours* and *Arch Coal* are both similar in their insistence that prosecutors show how the collaboration among firms in a coordinated effects case will unfold after the merger is completed.

'State intervention in the economy'. Competition policy in the European Union and the United States reflects a growing awareness of how various forms of government intervention can harm competition as severely as private restraints. Statements by the leadership of the enforcement agencies in both jurisdictions indicate that the European Union and the United States treat government-imposed barriers to rivalry as serious obstacles to competition. The common concern about anticompetitive government intervention has been manifest by the prosecution of cases, the performance of sector studies, and the initiation of advocacy projects.

Although EU and US enforcement officials have a shared suspicion of government restraints on competition, the EU system provides a more powerful platform to address such restrictions. The United States has no counterpart to the state aids portfolio of the European Union. Moreover, the European Union has no exemption for decisions taken by Member State public authorities that matches the breadth of state action immunity available under the Parker[18] doctrine. Owing to the mutual distrust of EU and US officials about anticompetitive state intervention, I have classified this category of activity as an area of substantive similarity. Due to the stronger legal platform available to the European Union to challenge such restraints, and the breadth of the Parker immunity in the United States, this area also could have been included in the substantive dissimilarities section below.

SUBSTANTIVE DISSIMILARITIES

'Abuse of dominance'. In some respects, the formative statutory texts of the European Union and the United States create a basis for differences in the treatment of dominant firm conduct. By their own terms and by judicial interpretation, the US antitrust statutes have no equivalent to the excessive pricing prohibition in Article 82. The Commission has not used its excessive pricing authority expansively, but the EU Members States have shown a greater willingness to apply this measure under their own competition laws. The bare terms of Article 82 also provide a less-certain basis for determining that the prosecutor must show that denominated forms of abuse (for example, tying) had actual or likely anticompetitive effects.

The interpretations of Article 82 by the CFI and the CoJ have tended to create a wider zone of liability for dominant firms than the decisions of the US courts under Section 2 of the Sherman Act. At the margin, US courts have tended to say that courts and enforcement agencies commit greater errors by intervening too much rather than too little. This perspective does not appear in EU jurisprudence or in speeches by EU enforcement officials.

In their technical findings and in their attitude, modern US Supreme Court decisions in cases such as *Brooke Group*,[19] *Trinko*,[20] and *Weyerhaeuser*[21] have demonstrated greater scepticism about abuse of dominance claims than judicial decisions in matters such as *France Telecom/Wanadoo*,[22] *Michelin II*,[23] and *British Airways*.[24] EU decisions in *IMS Health*[25] and *Microsoft*[26] show a greater inclination to condemn refusals to deal than modern US rulings such as *Trinko*. Unlike *Brooke Group* and *Weyerhaeuser*, the *France Telecom/Wanadoo* decision rejects the need to apply a recoupment test to resolve allegations of exclusionary pricing. A finding of dominance can occur in the European Union at or somewhat below a 40 per cent market share, while the US offence of attempted monopolization usually treats shares below 50 per cent as being inadequate to establish substantial market power.

A major question for the two jurisdictions is how much an effects-oriented standard will become the common core of analysis in abuse of dominance matters. The EU white paper on dominance[27] and speeches by EU officials indicate receptivity to greater express reliance on an effects test and to reduced emphasis on the category-based assessment sometimes evident in cases such as *British Airways*. If there were broad EU/US agreement in concept on the value of an effects test, there still will remain the question of application. For example, the CFI decision in *Microsoft* on tying issues stated that the court was focusing on the actual or likely competitive effects of the challenged conduct. Yet the CFI's analysis of tying claims superficially resembles the treatment of tying allegations in the decision of the US Court of Appeals for the District of Columbia Circuit in 2001[28] on the DoJ complaint against Microsoft.[29] Even in the context of what is called an effects test, outcomes often will hinge upon the quantum and quality of evidence that a court demands before it is willing to find actual anticompetitive effects or to infer likely adverse effects.

VERTICAL CONTRACTUAL RESTRAINTS

EU and US vertical restraints policy has displayed an important degree of convergence over the past two decades, particularly in the current EU vertical restraints guidelines, which moved towards more tolerant treatment of such restrictions. Notably, dissimilarities remain. Particularly after the Supreme Court's abandonment in the *Leegin*[30] case of the per se prohibition on minimum resale price maintenance, US doctrine now evaluates vertical contractual restraints under a rule of reason analysis. Tying arrangements nominally remain subject to categorical prohibition, but what the Supreme Court still calls a per se rule increasingly has come to resemble a variant of a reasonableness inquiry. By contrast, European Union law relies more heavily on per se condemnation, with minimum resale price maintenance being one noteworthy example.

'Non-horizontal mergers'. Compared to US competition law and policy, EU policy creates more conceptual possibilities for intervention in conglomerate and vertical transactions. Looking forward, there are questions about how expansively these possibilities will be exercised. The CFI decisions in *Tetra Laval*[31] and *GE/Honeywell*,[32] while they recognized the legitimacy of the European Commission's portfolio effects theories in principle, found that the Commission had failed to supply adequate proof to establish a violation. At

325

a minimum, these decisions suggest that the Commission will be required to satisfy relatively demanding standards of proof when challenging a conglomerate merger. One also expects the perspective of the CFI in *Tetra* and *Honeywell* to be absorbed into the Commission's newest formulation of enforcement guidelines for non-horizontal mergers.

12.4. Centrifugal and Centripetal Forces

This part of the chapter seeks to do two things. The first is to offer some explanations for how the trends in policy came to pass. The second is to identify institutional and other forces that promise to foster a greater degree of convergence in the future and to highlight forces that are likely to retard convergence. In 12.5 I will discuss means to reinforce processes that promote convergence.

12.4.1. *Divergence: The centrifugal forces*

Discussions about EU and US competition law often default to a collection of familiar hypotheses to explain differences between the two jurisdictions. Thus, it is often said that the European Union protects competitors, the United States protects competition; the United States is beholden to the stale, backward-looking 'Chicago School' of economics, the European Union embraces the progressive, forward-looking post-'Chicago School'; the United States gave up on bringing abuse of dominance cases after 2000, the European Union is pressing ahead to keep this and other areas of competition law alive.

I do not deny the appeal of these propositions to those of us who periodically must construct an easily grasped narrative to organize academic papers, write newspaper articles, or script speeches. I do dispute their accuracy. I am convinced that the conventional explanations divert our attention away from an examination of deeper, more-persuasive explanations—many of them rooted in the institutional arrangements of the two systems—for why the two systems diverge. To see the underlying conditions more clearly is the first, necessary step to considering how and where the two systems might converge more completely on common standards. Below, I describe four considerations that tend to be overlooked in conventional discussions about why the European Union and the United States diverge.

DELEGATION OF THE DECISION TO PROSECUTE:
THE ROLE OF PRIVATE RIGHTS

In roughly the past thirty years, judicial fears that the US style of private rights of action—with mandatory treble damages, asymmetric shifting of costs, broad rights of discovery, class actions, and jury trials—excessively deters legitimate conduct having spurred a dramatic retrenchment of antitrust liability standards.[33] This is most evident in the progression towards more lenient treatment of dominant firm conduct. The intellectual roots of this development are as much (or more) rooted in the work of modern Harvard School scholars such as Phillip Areeda, Stephen Breyer, and Donald Turner as they are in the scholarship of 'Chicago School' academics such as Robert Bork and Richard Posner.

EU competition law has evolved without the tempering force of these concerns. For most of the history of the Treaty of Rome, the decision to prosecute in competition cases has been dedicated to public authorities. Had the United States private rights of action been more constrained (for example, by making treble damages discretionary rather than mandatory), my prediction is that US doctrine for abuse of dominance would more closely resemble existing EU standards. The persistent inclination of US courts to raise liability standards to offset perceived excesses of private rights creates what could turn out to be a permanent fissure between the EU and US approaches to dominant firm conduct and other forms of business behaviour.

The major variable on this point is the possible future enhancement of private rights in the European Union. An interesting question for the future is whether and how much the EU's modernization programme (which dilutes the policy-making powers of DG Comp) and its efforts to encourage Member States to augment private rights will affect the evolution of substantive doctrine. EU policymakers generally have disavowed the adoption of measures (such as mandatory trebling) that are associated with overreaching in the US system. None the less, any expansion of private rights necessarily denies public authorities the gatekeeping function—in determining the type and ordering of cases to be prosecuted—that they have enjoyed in the past. And it is possible that the courts of the Member States will regard private litigants as being, in at least some sense, less trustworthy custodians of the public interest than the public agencies.

DISSIMILAR PROCEDURES: ADMINISTRATIVE
V. ADVERSARIAL MODELS

The EU model of policymaking relies chiefly on elaboration by an administrative body whose decisions are subject to judicial review. To some degree, the operations of the US FTC use the same model. For the US system as a whole (including the operations of the FTC), the bulk of key decisions, such as measures to prevent the consummation of a merger, cannot be taken without judicial approval. In other words, where decisions to intervene have relatively powerful consequences, the US system gives the courts an earlier, more significant role in determining whether the prosecutors' preferences will be fulfilled.

In some respects, the US reliance on the adversarial model imbues the US public enforcement system with greater caution in deciding to intervene. DoJ and FTC investigative techniques, for example, rely less heavily than the European Union on responses to questionnaires and places greater weight on investigational hearings and depositions to gather and test evidence. Judicial control in the European Union is hardly absent (witness the CFI decisions in 2002 in *AirTours*, *Tetra*, and *Schneider*[34]), but it is generally less intrusive and immediate than it is in the United States. On the whole, this inclines the US agencies to demand, perhaps, a greater quantum and quality of evidence before deciding to prosecute.

By the same measure, the administrative model has made the European Union more cautious in some instances about deciding not to intervene. Administrative practice in many civil law systems, and in the European Union, compels public authorities to give reasons why they have declined to act upon complaints lodged by citizens or juristic persons. As the CFI decision in *Sony/Impala*[35] demonstrates, third parties can obtain judicial review of certain decisions by the Commission to close a file in a merger case. Thus, if the Commission were to decide that positive efficiency effects dictated that a merger be allowed to proceed, Commission officials would need to be prepared to document the expected efficiency consequences. Although the Tunney Act procedures in the United States somewhat encumber the DoJ's capacity to settle cases, the US public agencies generally have much greater freedom to ignore third-party complaints and decide not to prosecute.

ASSUMPTIONS ABOUT UNDERLYING ECONOMIC CONDITIONS

Decisions of courts and enforcement agencies in the US system to relax antitrust prohibitions may stem from assumptions about the operation of the US economic system. Important characteristics of the US system include relatively strong capital markets, comparatively few impediments to the formation of new business enterprises, and an effective mechanism for recycling the assets and personnel of failed firms back into the economy. These features give the US system a substantial degree of adaptability and flexibility.

These conditions may help account for the assumption, reflected in decisions by courts and enforcement agencies, to disfavour intervention in a wide range of disputes. US abuse of dominance doctrine and policy, for example, assumes a considerable capacity on the part of rivals, suppliers, and consumers to adapt, reposition, and otherwise protect themselves in the face of apparent overreaching by specific firms. The same assumptions probably help explain the trend since the 1970s to disfavour intervention concerning vertical restraints—particularly in light of the expectation that distribution channels will be highly resilient and adaptable. By contrast, it is possible that, because EU officials perceive the economy of the community and its Member

States to be less flexible and adaptable, there is less confidence that market processes alone will provide a sufficient antidote, in the absence of public intervention, to offset seemingly anticompetitive business practices. The many measures underway in the European Union to liberalize markets—to facilitate capital formation, to promote broad acceptance of a competition culture, and to realize the Treaty's longstanding aims for community-wide economic integration—gradually could change assumptions about the robustness and resilience of markets and induce a relaxation of restrictions on business conduct.

THE SOURCES OF AGENCY HUMAN CAPITAL

In the aggregate, the backgrounds of the personnel of the EU and US public agencies differ in an important respect. In the leadership, management, and case-handling positions, a larger percentage of personnel in the US agencies have experience outside the civil service. The revolving door in the United States creates a circulatory process that routinely brings academics and private-sector practitioners into the competition agencies to a greater degree than one sees in the European Union.

I do not claim that this circumstance has immense effects. It does mean that the US agencies have a larger group of officials, from top management to relatively junior case-handlers, who have worked in private firms. This element of experience can provide a stronger basis with which to make confident judgements about which arguments advanced by private firms have merit and which do not. A lack of this practical perspective can increase an institution's general wariness about the motives for business behaviour and the significance of specific business tactics.

The mix of personnel in the Commission and in the Member State competition authorities has been changing over time. One sees somewhat more acceptance of a revolving-door process which, although it does not spin with the speed of the US system, has brought a larger number of personnel with academic and private practice experience into the EU agencies. In slow and almost imperceptible ways, this can change the culture of enforcement inside the agency, as well as altering the perceptions and attitudes of private-sector bodies which absorb personnel who have departed the public competition agencies.

12.4.2. Convergence: the centripetal forces

Various existing phenomena tend to press the EU and US competition policy systems together in their treatment of substantive antitrust issues. Some of these phenomena take place inside the competition agencies; some take place in interactions between the agencies; and some take place outside the government enforcement bodies. Many of the phenomena described here are interdependent, such that developments outside the competition authorities can have major effects on the agencies themselves.

CONSULTATION BETWEEN THE EU AND US COMPETITION AUTHORITIES

Using the three-level NTA framework of intergovernmental, transgovernmental, and transnational contacts introduced in 12.2 above, modern experience reveals considerable interaction between the EU and US competition agencies and an intensification of activity in this decade. To some extent, the intensification of cooperative activity has stemmed from the highly visible disputes between the two jurisdictions in the Boeing/McDonnell Douglas[36] and GE/Honeywell mergers and the perceived need to explore ways to avoid similar policy disagreements in the future. Based on past experience, it is possible—even likely—that publicly voiced disagreements over the disposition of the Microsoft matters in the two jurisdictions will inspire deeper contacts and discussions concerning abuse of dominance cases. Fuller mutual discussion about these and other matters would be valuable enhancements to the EU/US relationship.

Intergovernmental contacts have continued at the highest levels between the Commission and the US federal antitrust agencies. These include regular, formal EU/US bilateral consultations and a variety of other interactions. The EC Commissioner for Competition, the DG Comp Director-General, DoJ's Assistant Attorney General for Antitrust, and the FTC's Chairman played pivotal roles in the formation of the ICN in 2001 and have cooperated extensively in the past six years in the design and implementation of ICN work plans. Contact among high-level EU and US officials is also commonplace at conferences and in discussions about specific policy matters. Measured by the sheer volume of contacts or the breadth and depth of discussions, the intergovernmental level of discourse in competition policy is more expansive today than at any period of the EU/US relationship.

A recent, important dimension of the intergovernmental relationship that goes beyond competition policy alone deserves emphasis. In this decade, the FTC has undertaken extensive discussions with DG Comp, DG Sanco, and DG Internal Market to explore policy connections between competition policy and intellectual property and competition policy and consumer protection policy. This has been identified as an increasingly important concern in matters such as healthcare and nutrition, where decisions taken on issues such as advertising have significant competition and consumer protection implications. What we are seeing is the beginning of a new framework of regulatory relationships that recognizes the interdependency of what may have been conceived of as largely independent policy regimes. At the same time, the

FTC has expanded cooperation with EU Member States, such as the United Kingdom, that, like the FTC, combine the competition and consumer-protection portfolios in one agency and have expressed an interest in promoting the integration of policymaking between these two disciplines.

The same expansion of EU/US interaction has taken place for what the NTA framework refers to as *transgovernmental* contacts. In recent years, the EU and US competition authorities have expanded the work plan of the existing staff-level merger working group and have established new working groups dealing with such matters as antitrust/intellectual property issues. The frequency of staff-level meetings, by teleconference or face-to-face meetings, also has increased to address a variety of matters within and outside the context of the formal working groups. For the DoJ and the DG Comp, there has been a noteworthy expansion of interaction as DG Comp has implemented its own variant of the DoJ's leniency programme for the prosecution of supplier cartels. Regular staff-to-staff contacts also have increased dramatically in the context of joint work on ICN and OECD projects.

A similar intensification of activity can be documented for *transnational contacts*. Measured by the agenda of conferences and non-conference activities, the major professional legal societies—among them, the American Bar Association and the International Bar Association—have expanded the energy they devote to EU/US competition policy. Beyond activities sponsored by these bodies, there has been a noteworthy increase in the number of conferences and continuing legal education programmes with a large transatlantic component that attracts a substantial transnational audience of academics, practitioners, and government officials. The same can be said for trade associations, such as the International Chamber of Commerce (ICC), and academic bodies, including institutions such as the Association of Competition Economics (ACE), based in Europe. Collectively, these non-government networks have played a crucial role in educating the academics, the business community, and the legal profession about the foundations of competition policy in both jurisdictions and about current policy developments. By engaging government policymakers and participants from non-government constituencies in formal public debate and informal discussion, these bodies help formulate a consensus about competition policy norms and provide a key source of relational glue for the competition policy community. Their significance can be observed in the growing tendency of government-based networks, such as ICN and OECD, to include non-government parties in their work.

It is possible to trace a number of specific policy outcomes to the three levels of contacts (intergovernment, transgovernment, and transnational) sketched above. Though not a complete accounting, the following list includes noteworthy measures rooted in the expanded interaction between government and non-government parties across the two jurisdictions.

- Enhancements in formal EU/US protocols involving merger review, including the coordination of pre-merger inquiries in both jursidictions.
- New EU guidelines on merger policy and intellectual property licensing that featured significant discussion with US competition authorities and non-government bodies (such as the internationally oriented legal societies and business associations) and reflected, in a number of respects, in contributions by the US agencies and by the non-government groups.
- Continuing augmentation and implementation of the EU leniency programme in ways that reflected substantial consultation and interaction with the DoJ's anti-cartel unit.
- Greater transparency in US practice for merger and non-merger matters, including emulation in a growing number of instances of the EU practice of providing explanations for a decision not to prosecute where the enforcement agency has undertaken a substantial investigation.
- The successful launch of a new multinational competition policy network (the ICN) and the healthy invigoration of the work plans of existing networks such as the OECD.

The continuation of EU/US cooperation through these channels—high-level agency contacts, operational unit contacts within the competition agencies, and contacts involving non-governmental bodies—will continue to operate as forces that tend to promote convergence over time. There also is reason to expect that such contacts will intensify. For example, the implementation of the 2006 SAFEWEB legislation will enable the FTC to engage in a regular programme of staff exchanges and internships with DG Comp, the competition authorities of the EU Member States, and with other competition agencies globally. I am convinced that a programme that has a DG Comp attorney or economist resident in the FTC at all times and has an FTC attorney or economist resident at all times in DG Comp will improve each agency's understanding of the other institution and will help supply the 'human glue' that binds the two bodies together.

ABSORPTION OF A COMMON BODY OF INDUSTRIAL ORGANIZATION KNOWLEDGE

With some variation, the world's elite graduate programmes in economics offer a roughly similar curriculum in industrial organization economics. Students in these graduate programmes become familiar with the same body of industrial organization literature. Owing to personal tastes and philosophies, instructors inevitably differ in the emphasis they give to specific topics and with respect to the policy preferences they articulate in class. Despite these differences, students emerge from these graduate programmes with a generally common intellectual framework and a roughly similar set of analytical norms. Above all, recipients of advanced degrees in economics are likely to share the belief that sound microeconomic analysis is an essential foundation for sensible competition policy.

In recent years, a number of competition authorities have adopted organizational reforms that elevate the role of economic analysis in the decision to prosecute. The Commission is one of these agencies. Earlier in the decade, DG Comp created the office of the Chief Economist and gave the holder of that office a direct reporting line to DG Comp's top leadership. The Chief Economist (initially Lars-Hendrik Röller and now Damien Neven) has a staff that now exceeds twenty economists. In the European Union and in other jurisdictions, the establishment of a separate economics unit can become the instrument by which economic analysis exerts more influence in guiding the selection and prosecution of cases.

As this institutional reform takes root, economic analysis and the preferences of economists are likely to assume increasing importance in the Commission's investigation of proposed cases, the formulation of complaints, and the prosecution of alleged infringements. The economic learning of economists in the office of the Chief Economist will closely resemble the learning of economists in the DoJ's Economic Analysis Group and the FTC's Bureau of Economics. To the extent that economists' perspectives become reflected more expansively in the work of DG Comp, as one predicts they will over time, the analytical approach that the Commission takes in deciding whether to bring cases probably will converge more closely upon the approach that the DoJ and the FTC take.

CRITICAL JUDICIAL OVERSIGHT

At a conference in Brussels early in 2001, I watched a panel of EU practitioners offer the view that DG Comp enjoyed virtually unbounded freedom to set merger policy without the prospect of effective judicial review. One panelist called the CFI a 'lapdog'. Another likened Luxembourg to a 'door mat'. Two members of the the lapdog/door mat tribunal were sitting in the audience, and I wondered what was going through their minds.

Commentators would not make the same assertions about judicial review in the European Union today. The CFI decisions in *AirTours*, *Tetra*, *Schneider* (including the recent CFI ruling on costs[37]), and *GE/Honeywell* inspired a basic rethink of merger policy and, more generally, organization and process within the Commission. These decisions have had the effect of pressing EU merger policy closer to US merger policy, whose reach recently has been questioned severely in the *Oracle*,[38] *SunGard*, *Arch Coal*, *Giant/Western*, and *Whole Foods* decisions.

12.5. A Suggested Agenda for the Future: Concepts and Means

There is a variety of ways to build upon existing forms of EU/US cooperation in competition policy to identify and promote convergence upon superior norms. The discussion below describes conceptual focal points for further cooperation and describes specific means that the EU and US competition policy communities might take to address these points.

12.5.1. Concepts

For all of the progress in cooperation achieved to date, there is considerable room for learning about basic forces that shape policy in the European Union and United States and therefore influence the transatlantic relationship. Discussions among government officials and within non-government networks tend to focus on specific enforcement developments (for example, the resolution in the European Union and the United States of each jurisdiction's Microsoft cases) or matters of practical technique and not to ask basic questions about the origins and institutional foundations of the systems. The discussion below suggests that the agenda for discourse inevitably must expand to incorporate examination of these considerations if cooperation is to be enriched and common progress towards better practices is to be achieved.

TOWARDS A DEEPER UNDERSTANDING OF THE ORIGINS
AND EVOLUTION OF BOTH SYSTEMS

The many recurring discussions about transatlantic competition policy often rest upon a terribly incomplete awareness about how the EU and US systems originated and have evolved over time. A relatively small subset of the US competition policy community engaged in transatlantic issues is familiar with the distinctive path by which competition policy concepts developed within the EU Member States and supplied the foundation for the EU competition policy regime itself.[39] European specialists in competition policy likewise often display a fractured conception of the origins and evolution of the US system—a conception often derived from the works of US scholars whose grasp of the actual path of US policy evolution is itself infirm. An accurate sense of where the policies originated and how they have unfolded is essential to understanding the influences that have shaped modern results in specific cases. To move ahead, discourse at all three levels embodied in the NTA must look back for a richer understanding of competition policy history.

SCRUTINIZING THE ANALYTICAL AND POLICY
ASSUMPTIONS IN SPECIFIC CASES

The modern EU/US relationship has featured important instances of disagreement and will do so again in the future. Amid the many discussions of cases such as *Boeing/McDonnell Douglas*, *GE/Honeywell*, and *Microsoft*, two things seem to have received inadequate attention. The first, which only the competition agencies can perform, is a careful, confidential examination of the specific theories of intervention and an examination of the evidence upon which each jurisdiction relied in deciding how to proceed. The side-by-side, behind-closed-doors deconstruction of the decision to prosecute (or not to prosecute) would seem to be a valuable way to identify alternative interpretations and test them in an uninhibited debate involving agency insiders (and, perhaps, experts retained by each agency to assist in the review of the case). Yet discussions of this type generally do not take place.

Even more general discussions of cases that occupy considerable attention at conferences and seminars infrequently come to grips with what appear to be differences in assumptions about the operation of markets and the efficacy of government intervention as a tool to correct market failure. Embedded in EU and US agency evaluations of the highly visible matters mentioned earlier are differing assumptions about the adroitness of rivals and purchasers to reposition themselves in the face of exclusionary conduct by a dominant rival, the appropriate trade-off between short-term benefits of a challenged practice and long-term effects, and the robustness of future entry as a means for disciplining firms that presently enjoy dominance. Putting these and other critical assumptions front and centre in the discussion, along with the bases for the assumptions, would advance the transatlantic relationship in the future.

FOCUSING ON HOW INSTITUTIONAL DESIGN AFFECTS DOCTRINE

In discussing competition law, there is a tendency for academics, enforcement officials, and practitioners to focus on developments in doctrine and policy and to assign secondary significance to the institutional arrangements by which doctrine and policy take shape. As I have suggested above, this tendency can cause one to overlook the important role that the design of institutions can play in influencing substantive results. It is impossible to understand the development of EU and US competition law without considering the impact of:

- Private rights of action and mandatory treble damage liability in shaping the views of US courts and enforcement agencies about the appropriate boundaries of substantive doctrine concerning antitrust liability.
- The experience gained by European competition authorities in carrying out responsibilities for policing excessive pricing as an abuse of dominance in informing their views about the wisdom and administrability of measures that mandate access to specific assets.
- The nature and timing of judicial oversight in merger control.
- The internal organization of competition agencies, including the placement of economists within the agency organization chart and the procedure for their participation in the decision to prosecute.
- The decision to accept a revolving door in recruitment—the manner in which the competition agency recruits professional personnel and the

backgrounds of the agency's professionals who work for the agencies and the parties who appear before the agencies.

Consider, again, the possible impact of creating robust private rights of action in the American style—with mandatory treble damages, with relatively permissive standards for the aggregation of class claims, and asymmetric fee-shifting in which only a prevailing plaintiff recovers its fees.[40] In establishing this variant of a private right of action, the jurisdiction must keep in mind the possible interaction between the operation of private rights of action and public law enforcement. If courts fear that the private party incentives to sue are misaligned with the larger interests of the public (put another way, when the courts do not trust the private plaintiff as much as they trust a public prosecutor) or they fear that the remedial scheme (for example, mandatory treble damages for all offences) deters legitimate business conduct excessively, the courts will use measures within their control to correct the perceived imbalance. The courts may 'equilibrate' the antitrust system by constructing doctrinal tests under the rubric of 'standing' or 'injury' that make it harder for the private party to pursue its case; adjust evidentiary requirements that must be satisfied to prove violations; or alter substantive liability rules in ways that make it more difficult for the plaintiff to establish the defendant's liability.

The first of these methods only governs suits by private plaintiffs. Of particular significance to public enforcement authorities is the possibility that the courts, in using the second and third measures listed above, will endorse principles that apply to the resolution of all antitrust disputes, regardless of the plaintiff's identity. In the course of making adjustments in evidentiary tests or substantive standards to correct for perceived infirmities in private rights of action, courts may create rules of general applicability that encumber public prosecutors as much as private litigants.

This hypothesis helps explain the modern evolution of US antitrust doctrine. Since the mid-1970s, the US courts have established relatively demanding standards that private plaintiffs must satisfy to demonstrate that they have standing to press antitrust claims and have suffered 'antitrust injury'.[41] In this period, the courts have endorsed evidentiary tests that make it more difficult for plaintiffs to prove concerted action involving allegations of unlawful horizontal and vertical contractual restraints. With some variation, courts also have given dominant firms comparatively greater freedom to choose pricing and product development strategies.

Collectively, these developments have narrowed the scope of the US antitrust system. Most of the critical judicial decisions in this evolution of doctrine have involved private plaintiffs pressing treble damage claims. Perhaps the most interesting area in which to consider the possible interaction between the private right of action and the development of doctrine involves the fields of monopolization and attempted monopolization law. Litigation involving exclusionary conduct by IBM provides a useful illustration.[42] In the late 1960s, the DoJ initiated an abuse of dominance case that sought, among other ends, to break up IBM into several new companies. By 1975, roughly forty-five private suits had been filed against IBM alleging unlawful exclusionary conduct and seeking treble damages. The sum of all damage claims in the private cases exceeded €4 billion—a considerable amount at the time.

My intuition is that the courts reacted to the private cases with apprehension and were ill at ease with the possibility that a finding of illegal monopolization would trigger the imposition of massive damage awards against IBM. The courts in these matters could not refuse to treble damages if they found liability, but they could interpret the law in ways that resulted in a finding of no liability. IBM paid settlements to a small number of the private claimants, but it achieved vindication in most of the cases. The results in the private damage cases against IBM and several other leading US industrial firms in this period imbued US monopolization doctrine with analytical approaches and conceptual perspectives that viewed intervention sceptically.

My hypothesis about the American competition policy experience is that US antitrust doctrine would have taken a somewhat different path had there been no private rights of action, or if the damage remedy in private actions had been less potent—for example, limiting recovery to actual damages, or permitting trebling only for violations of per se offences such as horizontal price-fixing. Specifically, US antitrust doctrine would have assumed a more intervention-oriented character if the power to enforce the American competition statutes were vested exclusively in public enforcement authorities, or if the private right of action had been circumscribed in one or more of the ways indicated above.

This raises the question of what will happen in the European Union and its Member States if private rights of action grow more robust. My tentative prediction is that an expansion of private rights could lead judicial tribunals to adjust doctrine in ways that shrink the zone of liability. For example, an expansion in private rights of action could cause EU abuse of dominance doctrine to converge more closely upon US liability standards governing monopolization.

DEVOTING ATTENTION TO INTER- AND INTRAJURISDICTIONAL MULTIPLICITY AND INTERDEPENDENCY

Efforts to formulate effective competition policy increasingly will require EU and US competition agencies to study more closely how other government institutions affect the competitive process. To an important degree, both jurisdictions resemble a policymaking archipelago in which various government bodies other than the competition agency deeply influence the state of competition.[43] Too often each policy island in the archipelago acts in relative isolation, with a terribly incomplete awareness of how its behaviour affects the entire archipelago. It is ever more apparent that competition agencies must use non-litigation policy instruments to build the intellectual and policy infrastructure that connects the islands and engenders a government-wide ethic that promotes competition.

To build this infrastructure requires competition authorities to make efforts to identify and understand the relevant interdependencies and to build relationships with other public instrumentalities. This is particularly evident in the relationship between competition policy and intellectual property.[44] Better coordination could limit inconsistencies between the two systems and ensure that both can more effectively encourage innovation and competition. While cooperation and convergence activities involving competition policy and intellectual property policy have grown more intense in recent years, to date they have tended to be intra-disciplinary. Few cooperation and convergence activities account for the interdependency of the competition policy and intellectual property regimes.

12.5.2. Means

Members of the EU and US competition policy community could use several means to address the conceptual issues outlined above. Most means involve a reorientation of bilateral activity to invest more expansively in a knowledge base that would inform routine discussions at all three levels of the NTA framework. Possible specific techniques are summarized below.

PERIODIC COMPREHENSIVE REVIEWS OF INSTITUTIONAL ARRANGEMENTS

Both jurisdictions at regular intervals should undertake a basic evaluation of the effectiveness of their competition policy institutions. In many respects, the European Union stands far ahead of the United States in carrying out this type of assessment. The major institutional reforms introduced in the past year—modernization, reorganization of DG Comp, and the introduction of a new position of economic advisor—indicate the European Union's close attention to these issues.

Key focal points for a parallel inquiry in the United States ought to include the scope of coverage of the competition policy system, the adequacy of existing substantive rules and remedies, the type and consequences of public enforcement, the role of private rights of action, and the design and administration of public enforcement bodies. Such an assessment ought to involve participation of government officials, private parties, consumer groups, and academics. Given the continuing changes that confront competition agencies, the two systems should undertake this comprehensive assessment less than once per decade.

EX POST EVALUATION

The European Union and the United States routinely should evaluate its past policy interventions and the quality of its administrative processes.[45] In every budget cycle, each authority should allocate some resources to the *ex post* study of law enforcement and advocacy outcomes. Beyond studying what it has achieved, a competition authority should choose selected elements of its enforcement process and methodology for assessment. Rather than treating *ex post* evaluation as a purely optional, luxury component of policymaking, we must regard the analysis of past outcomes and practices as a natural and necessary element of responsible public administration. Even if definitive measurements are unattainable, there is considerable room for progress in determining whether actual experience bears out the assumptions that guide our acts. One element of the process of examining past decisions would be the type of detailed case study mentioned earlier in this paper. An elaborate deconstruction of specific cases would provide an informative basis for analysing differences in philosophy and substantive perspective and for identifying variations in procedure.[46]

ENHANCEMENT AND DISCLOSURE OF DATABASES

The European Union and the United States should prepare and provide a full statistical profile of their enforcement activity. The maintenance and public disclosure of comprehensive, informative databases on enforcement are distressingly uncommon in our field. Every authority should take the seemingly pedestrian but often neglected step of developing and making publicly available a database that (a) reports each case initiated; (b) provides the subsequent procedural and decisional history of the case; and (c) assembles aggregate statistics each year by type of case. Each agency should develop and apply a classification scheme that permits its own staff and external observers to see how many matters of a given type the agency has initiated and to know the identity of specific matters included in category of enforcement activity. Among other ends, a current and historically complete enforcement database would promote better understanding and analysis, inside and outside the agency, of trends in enforcement activity.[47] For example, access to such databases would give competition agencies greater ability to benchmark their operations with their peers.

ASSESSMENT AND ENHANCEMENT OF HUMAN CAPITAL

Continuous institutional improvement will require the EU and US competition agencies regularly to evaluate their human capital. The capacity of an agency's staff deeply influences what it can accomplish. The agencies routinely must examine the fit between their activities and the expertise of their professionals. The agencies could share views about developing a systematic training regimen for upgrading the skills of their professionals. For example, where the agencies are active in areas such as intellectual property that require special expertise, the agencies could explore whether they have acquired the requisite specialized skills—for example, by hiring some patent attorneys. The experiences of the agencies with entry and lateral recruitment—including the costs and benefits of the revolving door—would be useful focal points for discussion. A fuller programme of staff exchanges also might supply an effective means for improving the discussion at the staff level and educating each agency about how the other builds capability.

INVESTMENTS IN COMPETITION POLICY
R&D AND POLICY PLANNING

An essential element of continuous institutional improvement is the enhancement of the competition agency's knowledge base. In many activities, particularly in conducting advocacy, the effectiveness of competition agencies depends on establishing intellectual leadership. To generate good ideas and demonstrate the empirical soundness of specific policy recommendations, competition authorities must invest resources in what former FTC Chairman Timothy Muris has called 'competition policy research and development'.[48] Regular outlays for research and analysis serve to address the recurring criticism that competition policy lags unacceptably in understanding the commercial phenomena it seeks to address.

Examining the R&D function is one element of exploring larger questions about how the competition agencies should set priorities and, within the larger competition policy community, about what competition agencies should do. The question of setting priorities is likely to assume greater importance in the European Union as certain functions that once occupied considerable EU attention devolve to the Member States, freeing resources for the Commission to design new programmes. The consideration of how we measure agency performance, and assess the mix of its activities, is a topic for a larger discussion within the competition community. For example, on the scorecard by which we measure competition agencies, there is continuing awareness that we should count the suppression of harmful public intervention just as heavily as the prosecution of a case that forestalls a private restraint.[49]

12.6. Conclusion: Future International Relationships

The *best* practice in competition policy is the relentless pursuit of *better* practices. A basic implication of past work and the future programme I have suggested here is that the competition authorities (and non-government bodies) must be willing to invest significant resources in the development and maintenance of the relationships as a dedicated objective even though such investments do not immediately generate the outputs—most notably, cases—by which competition authorities traditionally are measured. The success of the relationships requires investments in the type of overhead and network building that commentators, practitioners, and, perhaps, legislative appropriations bodies often view with some scepticism. Thus, one challenge is for the competition authorities to develop acceptance of a norm that regards these investments as valuable and necessary.

Competition agencies also must confront the question of how many resources, even in the best of circumstances, they can devote to the construction and maintenance of networks that provide the framework for international relations in this field. The European Union and the United States are engaged not only in their own bilateral arrangements, but also bilateral agreements with other jurisdictions, participation in regional initiatives, and work in multinational networks such as ICN and the OECD. The European Union and United States are major partners in all of these overlapping ventures, and each year each agency must decide, through its commitment of personnel, to 'buy', 'sell', or 'hold' its position in each venture. Each agency is aware that the participation in these activities cannot be carried out effectively—namely, with good substantive results—except through the allocation of first-rate personnel. There is no point in trying to do this work on the cheap.

The hazard is that the European Union, the United States, and other jurisdictions may experience, or may now be encountering, some measure of international network or relationship fatigue. Thus, a further focus for consideration by the two jurisdictions, individually and jointly, is how best to devote their resources. In this decision, both agencies are likely to regard the transatlantic relationship as a top priority. This is true because of the importance of the relationship to the regulation of transatlantic commerce and because the European Union and the United States always will have distinctive interests and common issues owing to their comparatively larger base of experience. Moreover, the EU/US relationship has served, in effect, as a bilateral testbed for substantive concepts and processes that can be rolled out in a larger multinational setting. Experience within the bilateral relationship has usefully informed EU and US decisions about what might be accomplished in the larger spheres. As the European Union and the United States approach perceived limits on how much they can dedicate to this growing collection of international initiatives, the larger competition policy community will need to abandon a case-centric vision of what agencies should do and accept the need for institution building, at home and abroad, as a vital ingredient of sound competition policy for the future.

Notes

[1] This chapter was prepared for the IESE conference 'Fifty Years of the Treaty: Assessment and Perspectives of Competition Policy in Europe', held in Barcelona, 19–20 Nov. 2007. The views presented here are the author's alone and not necessarily those of the US FTC or any of its members. The author is grateful to William Kolasky, Mario Monti, and Wouter Wils for very helpful comments and suggestions.

[2] By 'norms' I mean consensus views within a group about how members of the group—such as jurisdictions with competition laws—ought to behave. See Kovacic (2003).

[3] This chapter develops themes presented in two of my earlier papers: Kovacic (2002; 2005a).

[4] Cukier (2007: 50) quoting Viktor Mayer-Schoenberger.

[5] See Muris (2002; 2001).

[6] The New Transatlantic Agenda 1995. <http://ec.europa.eu/external_relations/us/new_transatlantic_agenda/text.htm>.

[7] Pollack and Shaffer (2001).

[8] Kovacic (2005b).

[9] In part, this is an inevitable consequence of drawing upon the discipline of economics, which itself evolves over time, to formulate substantive rules and analytical techniques (Kovacic and Shapiro 2000).

[10] Bork (1978: 50).

[11] Kroes (2007: 1).

[12] The much-quoted aphorism appears in *Brunswick Corp.* v. *Pueblo Bowl-O-Mat, Inc.*, 429 US 477, 488 1977 quoting *Brown Shoe Co.* v. *United States*, 370 US 294, 320 1962 (emphasis in orig.).

[13] Case T–342/99, *Airtours plc* v. *Commission* [2002] ECR II–2585, 5 CMLR 7.

[14] *FTC* v. *Arch Coal*, 329 F. Supp. 2d 109 D.DC 2004.

[15] *FTC* v. *Foster*, No. 07–352, 2007 WL 1793441 D.NM 29 May 2007.

[16] *United States* v. *SunGard Data Sys.*, 172 F. Supp. 2d 172 D.DC 2001.

[17] *FTC* v. *Whole Food Market, Inc.*, 502 F. Supp. 2d 1 D.DC 2007.

[18] *Parker* v. *Brown*, 317 US 341 1943.

[19] *Brooke Group Ltd.* v. *Brown & Williamson Tobacco Corp.*, 509 US 209 1993.

[20] *Verizon Communications Inc.* v. *Law Offices of Curtis* v. *Trinko, LLP*, 540 US 398 2004.

[21] *Weyerhaeuser Co.* v. *Ross-Simmons Hard-Wood Lumber Co., Inc.*, 127 S.Ct. 1069 2007.

[22] Case T–340/03, *France Telecom SA* v. *Commission* [2007] ECR II–107.

[23] Case T–203/01, *Manufacture Francaise des Pneumatiques Michelin* v. *Commission* [2003] ECR II–4071.

[24] Case T–219/99, *British Airways PLC* v. *Commission* [2003] ECR II–5917.

[25] Case C-418/01, *IMS Health GmbH* v. *NDC Health GmbH* [2004] ECR I–5039.

[26] Case T–201/04, *Microsoft* v. *Commission* [2007] OJ C 269 of 10.11.2007: 45 <http://eur-lex.europa.eu/LexUriServ/LexUriServ.do?uri=OJ:C:2007:269:0045:0046:EN:PDF>.

[27] 'DC Competition Discussion Paper in the Application of Article 82 of the Treaty to Exclusionary Abuses', 2005 <http://ec.europa.eu/comm/competition/antitrust/art82/discpaper2005.pdf>.

[28] *United States* v. *Microsoft Corp.*, 253 F.3d 34 DC Cir. 2001.

[29] *United States* v. *Microsoft Corp.*, Civil Action No. 98–1232 D.DC filed 18 May, 1998. Complaint <http://www.usdoj.gov/atr/cases/f1700/1763.htm>.

[30] *Leegin Creative Leather Products, Inc.* v. *PSKS, Inc.*, 127 S.Ct. 2705 2007.

[31] Case T–5/02, *Tetra Laval BV* v. *Commission* [2002] ECR II–4381.

[32] Case T–210/01, *General Electric* v. *Commission* [2005] ECR II–5575.

[33] This view is elaborated in Kovacic (2007).

[34] Case T–310/01, *Schneider Electric* v. *Commission* [2002] ECR II–4071.

[35] Case T–464/04, *Independent Music Publishers and Labels Association Impala* [2006] ECR II–02289.

[36] *Boeing/McDonnell Douglas*, Case IV/M.877 [1997], OJ L/336.

[37] Case T–351/03, *Schneider Electric* v. *Commission* [2007] ECR II–02237.

[38] *United States* v. *Oracle Corp.*, 331 F. Supp. 2d 1098 ND Cal. 2004.

[39] The pre-eminent account of this history is Gerber (1998) (repr. 2001).

[40] The discussion here is based in part on Kovacic (2004a).

[41] These requirements are described at American Bar Association (2003: 838–69).

[42] For a discussion of the government and private suits against IBM in the late 1960s and in the 1970s, see Kovacic (1999: 1285).

[43] The dimensions and consequences of policymaking fragmentation within individual jurisdictions are analysed in Gavil, Kovacic, and Baker (2002). See also Kovacic (2004b: 316) describing fragmentation of policymaking affecting competition in the United States.

[44] See Kovacic and Reindl (2005), 'An Interdisciplinary Approach to Improving Competition Policy and Intellectual Policy', *Fordham International Law Journal*, 28: 1062.

[45] The potential contributions of *ex post* analysis of completed government interventions to the development of competition policy are examined at Kovacic (2006: 503).

[46] For a suggestion of the content of such a case study, see Kovacic (2001: 805).

[47] For a formative treatment of the value of good statistical records for the analysis of competition policy, see Posner (1970: 365).

[48] The concept of 'competition policy research and development' and its role in determining institutional capability are analysed at Muris (2003a: 359).

[49] Competition agencies must confront government restrictions on competition with the same commitment and determination with which they challenge private restraints. See Muris (2003b).

Bibliography

Books and Articles

Aghion, P., and P. Bolton (1987), 'Contracts as a Barrier to Entry', *American Economic Review*, 77: 388–401.

—— N. Bloom, R. Blundell, R. Griffith, and P. Howitt (2005), 'Competition and Innovation: An Inverted U-Relationship', *Quarterly Journal of Economics*, 120(2): 701–28.

Agrawal, A., I. Cockburn, and J. McHale (2006), 'Gone but not Forgotten: Knowledge Flows, Labor Mobility, and Enduring Social Relationships', *Journal of Economic Geography*, 6(5): 593–617.

Ahlborn, C., D. S. Evans, and A. J. Padilla (2005), 'The Logic and Limits of the "Exceptional Circumstances Test" in Magill and IMS Health', *Fordham International Law Journal*.

—— and A. J. Padilla (2008), 'From Fairness to Welfare: Implications for the Assessment of Unilateral Conduct under EC Competition Law', in C. D. Ehlermann and M. Marquis (eds), *European Competition Law Annual 2007: A Reformed Approach to Article 82 EC* (Oxford: Hart Publishing).

Aktas, N., E. de Bodt, and R. Roll (2004), 'Market Response to European Regulation of Business Combinations', *Journal of Financial and Quantitative Analysis*, 39(4): 731–58.

—— —— —— (2007), 'Is European M&A Regulation Protectionist?', *Economic Journal*, 117: 1096–121.

American Bar Association (2003), Section of Antitrust Law, *Antitrust Fundamentals* (5th edn, Chicago).

Allen, F., and E. Carletti (2006), 'Credit Risk Transfer and Contagion', *Journal of Monetary Economics*, 53: 89–111.

—— —— (2008), 'Mark-to-market Accounting and Liquidity Pricing', *Journal of Accounting and Economics*, 45(2/3): 358–78.

—— and D. Gale (2004), 'Financial Intermediaries and Markets', *Econometrica*, 72(4): 1023–61.

Ando, A. W., and K. L. Palmer (1998), *Getting on the Map: The Political Economy of State-level Electricity Restructuring*, Discussion Paper, 98–19 (Washington, DC: Resources for the Future).

Areeda, P., and D. Turner (1975), 'Predatory Pricing and Related Practices under Section 2 of the Sherman Act', *Harvard Law Review*, 88: 697–733.

Armstrong, M. (1997), 'Competition in Telecommunications', *Oxford Review of Economic Policy*, 13: 64–82.

—— (2001), 'The Theory of Access Pricing and Interconnection', in M. Cave, S. Majumdar, and I. Vogelsang (eds), *Handbook of Telecommunications Economics*, i (Amsterdam: Elsevier Science), 295–337.

Armstrong, M., and D. E. M. Sappington (2007), 'Recent Developments in the Theory of Regulation', in M. Armstrong and R. Porter (eds), *Handbook of Industrial Organization*, iii (Amsterdam: Elsevier Science), 1557–700.

Aron, D. J., and D. E. Burnstein (2003), 'Broadband Adoption in the United States: An Empirical Analysis', paper presented before the Thirty-first Research Conference on Communication, Information, and Internet Policy, Arlington, VA, Sept. 2003.

Ashenfelter, O., et al. (2006), 'Empirical Methods in Merger Analysis: Econometric Analysis of Pricing in FTC vs Staples', *International Journal of the Economics of Business*, 13: 265–79.

Athey, S., and K. Bagwell (2001), 'Optimal Collusion with Private Information', *RAND Journal of Economics*, 32: 428–65.

Audretsch, D. B., and M. Feldman (1996), 'R&D Spillovers and the Geography of Innovation and Production', *American Economic Review*, 86(4): 253–73.

Auerbach, A. J. (2005), *Taxation and Capital Spending* (University of California, Berkeley and National Bureau of Economic Research).

Bagehot, G. (1873), *London Street: A Description of the Money Market* (London: H. S. King).

Bain, J. (1956), *Barriers to New Competition: Their Character and Consequences in Manufacturing Industries* (Cambridge, MA: Harvard University Press).

—— (1959), *Industrial Organization* (New York: Wiley).

Ballard, C., J. Shoven, and J. Whalley (1985), 'General Equilibrium Computations of the Marginal Welfare Costs of Taxes in the United States', *American Economic Review*, 75(1): 128–38.

Barros, P., et al. (2005), 'Integration of European Banking: The Way Forward', Monitoring European Deregulation, 3 (London: Center for Economic Policy Research).

Baumol, W. J., J. C. Panzar, and R. D. Willig (1982), *Contestable Markets and the Theory of Industry Structure* (New York: Harcourt Brace Jovanovich).

Beard, T. R., G. S. Ford, and T. M. Koutsky (2005), 'Mandated Access and the Make-or-Buy Decision: The Case of Local Telecommunications Competition', *Quarterly Review of Economics and Finance*, 45: 28–47.

Becker, P. (2004), 'Pro und Kontra einer Regulierung aus Sicht der Stadtwerke', in U. Leprich, H. Georgi, and E. Evers (eds), *Strommarktliberalisierung durch Netzregulierung* (Berlin: Berliner Wissenschafts-Verlag), 121–30.

Benini, F., and C. Bermig (2007), 'Milestones in Maritime Transport: EU Ends Exemptions', *EC Competition Policy Newsletter*, 1: 20–2.

Bergman, M., M. Jakobsson, and C. Razo (2005), 'An Econometric Analysis of the European Commission's Merger Decisions', *International Journal of Industrial Organization*, 23: 717–37.

Bernheim, D., and M. Whinston (1998), 'Exclusive Dealing', *Journal of Political Economy*, 106: 64–103.

Berry, S., J. Levinshon, and A. Pakes (1995), 'Automobile Prices in Market Equilibrium', *Econometrica*, 63(4): 841–90.

Besley, T., and P. Seabright (1999), 'The Effects and Policy Implications of State Aids to Industry: An Economic Analysis', *Economic Policy*, 14(28): 13–53.

Beverley, L. (2008), 'Stock Market Event Studies and Competition Commission Inquiries', Centre for Competition Policy Working Paper, 08–16 (Norwich: University of East Anglia Centre for Competition Policy).

Block, K. B., F. C. Nold, and J. G. Sidak (1981), 'The Deterrent Effect of Antitrust Enforcement', *Journal of Political Economy*, 89: 429–45.

Bolton, P., and D. Scharfstein (1990), 'A Theory of Predation Based on Agency Problems in Financial Contracting', *American Economic Review*, 80: 93–106.

—— J. Brodley, and M. Riordan (2000), 'Predatory Pricing: Strategic Theory and Legal Policy', *Georgetown Law Journal*, 88: 2239–330.

Boot, A. W. A., and M. Marinc (2007), 'Competition and Entry in Banking: Implications for Capital Regulation', University of Amsterdam Working Paper.

Borenstein, S. (1999), 'Rapid Price Communication and Coordination: The Airline Tariff Publishing Case (1994)', in J. E. Kwoka and L. J. White (eds), *The Antitrust Revolution* (3rd edn, Oxford: Oxford University Press).

Bork, R. H. (1966), 'The Rule of Reason and the Per Se Concept: Price Fixing and Market Division', *Yale Law Journal*, 75(3): 373–475.

—— (1978), *The Antitrust Paradox* (New York: Free Press).

Bottazzi, L., and G. Peri (2004), 'Innovation and Spillovers in Regions: Evidence from European Patent Data', *European Economic Review*, 47(4): 687–710.

Bouckaert, J., and H. Degryse (2004), 'Softening Competition by Inducing Switching in Credit Markets', *Journal of Industrial Economics*, 52: 27–52.

Boyd, J. H., and G. De Nicoló (2005), 'The Theory of Bank Risk-taking and Competition Revisited', *Journal of Finance*, 60(3): 1329–43.

Brander, J., and B. Spencer (1985), 'Export Subsidies and International Market Share Rivalry', *Journal of International Economics*, 18: 83–100.

Bris, A., N. Brisley, and C. Cabolis (2008), 'Adopting Better Corporate Governance: Evidence from Cross-border Mergers', *Journal of Corporate Finance*, 14(3): 224–40.

Broecker, T. (1990), 'Creditworthiness Tests and Interbank Competition', *Econometrica*, 58: 429–52.

Brueckner, J. K. (2001), 'The Economics of International Codesharing: An Analysis of Airline Alliances', *International Journal of Industrial Organisation*, 19: 1475–98.

Burkhart, M., and E. Berglof (2003), 'European Takeover Regulation', *Economic Policy*, 18(1): 171–213.

Caballero, R., E. M. R. A. Engel, and J. C. Haltiwanger (1995), 'Plant-level Adjustment and Aggregate Investment Dynamics', *Brookings Papers on Economic Activity*, Economic Studies Program, Brookings Institution, 26: 1–54.

—— and A. Jaffe (1993), 'How High are the Giants' Shoulders: An Empirical Assessment of Knowledge Spillovers and Creative Destruction in a Model of Economic Growth', *NBER Macroeconomics Annual*, 8: 15–74.

Caminal, R., and C. Matutes (2002), 'Market Power and Banking Failures', *International Journal of Industrial Organization*, 20(9): 1341–61.

Campa, J. M., and I. Hernando (2004), 'Shareholder Value Creation in European M&As' *European Financial Management*, 10(1): 47–81.

Carletti E. (2008), 'Competition and Regulation in Banking', in A. Thakor and A. Boot (eds), *Handbook of Financial Intermediation and Banking* (Amsterdam: Elsevier Science).

—— and P. Hartmann (2002), 'Competition and Stability: What's Special about Banking?', in P. Mizen (ed.), *Monetary History, Exchange Rates and Financial Markets: Essays in Honour of Charles Goodhart*, ii (Cheltenham: Edward Elgar), 202–29.

Carletti, E., P. Hartmann, and S. Ongena (2006), 'Cross-border Banking and Competition Policy', *European Central Bank Research Bulletin*, 4: 7–10.

—— —— —— (2007), *The Economic Impact of Merger Control* (Frankfurt: Center for Financial Studies).

Carlton, D. W., and M. Waldman (2001), 'Competition, Monopoly, and Aftermarkets', NBER Working Papers, 8086 (Cambridge, MA: National Bureau of Economic Research).

—— —— (2002), 'The Strategic Use of Tying to Create and Preserve Market Power in Evolving Industries', *RAND Journal of Economics*, 33: 194–220.

Cave, M. (2003), 'The Economics of Wholesale Broadband Access', *Multimedia und Recht-Beilage*, 10: 15–19.

—— (2007), 'The Regulation of Access in Telecommunications: A European Perspective', mimeo (Coventry: Warwick Business School).

—— and P. Crowther (2004), 'Co-ordinating Regulation and Competition Law? *Ex ante* and *ex post*', in *The Pros and Cons of Antitrust in Deregulated Markets* (Stockholm: Konkurrensverket [The Swedish Competition Authority]), 11–28.

Chang, H. H., D. S. Evans, and R. Schmalensee (2003), 'Has the Consumer Harm Standard Lost its Teeth?', AEI–Brookings Joint Center Working Paper; MIT Sloan Working Paper (Washington, DC) <http://ssrn.com/abstract=332021>.

—— H. Koski, and S. Majumdar (2003), 'Regulation and Investment Behaviour in the Telecommunications Sector: Policies and Patterns in US and Europe', *Telecommunications Policy*, 27: 677–99.

Chi, K. S., and D. Leatherby (1997), *State Business Incentives: Trends and Options for the Future* (Lexington, KY: Council of State Governments).

Choi, J. P., and C. Stefanadis (2001), 'Tying, Investment, and the Dynamic Leverage Theory', *RAND Journal of Economics*, 32: 52–71.

Codognet, M.-K., J.-M. Glachant, F. Lévêque, and M.-A. Plagnet (2002), *Mergers and Acquisitions in the European Electricity Sector: Cases and Patterns* (Paris: Cerna, Centre d'économie industrielle, École nationale supérieure des mines de Paris).

Collie, D. R., (1998), 'State Aid in the European Union: The Prohibition of Subsidies in an Integrated Market', *International Journal of Industrial Organization*, 18: 867–84.

—— 'Prohibiting State Aid in an Integrated Market' (2002), *Journal of Industry, Competition and Trade*, 2(3): 215–31.

—— (2005), 'State Aid to Investment and R&D', *European Economy, Economic Chapters*, 231: 1.

Compte, O. (1998), 'Communication in Repeated Games with Imperfect Private Monitoring', *Econometrica*, 66: 597–626.

—— F. Jenny, and P. Rey (2002), 'Capacity Constraints, Mergers and Collusion', *European Economic Review*, 46(1): 1–29.

Connor, J. M. (2005), 'Price-fixing Overcharges: Legal and Economic Evidence', Staff Paper, 04–17 (West Lafayette, IN: Purdue University).

Cooper, R., D. V. DeJong, R. Forsythe, and T.W. Ross (1992), 'Communication in Coordination Games', *Quarterly Journal of Economics*, 107: 739–71.

Cournot, A. A. (1938), *Researches into the Mathematical Principles of the Theory of Wealth* (New York: Macmillan).

Cramton, P., and J. A. Schwartz (2001), 'Collusive Bidding: Lessons from the FCC Spectrum Auctions', *Journal of Regulatory Economics*, 17: 229–52.

Crandall, R. (2005), ' "The Remedy for the Bottleneck Monopoly" in Telecom: Isolate it, Share it or Ignore it', *University of Chicago Law Review*, 72: 3.

Craycraft, C., J. Craycraft, and J. Gallo (1999), 'Antitrust Sanctions and a Firm's Ability to Pay', *Review of Industrial Organization*, 12: 171–83.

Crocker, K. J., and T. P. Lyon (1994), 'What do Facilitating Practices Facilitate? An Empirical Investigation on Most-favored-nation Clauses in Natural Gas Contracts', *Journal of Law and Economics*, 37: 297–322.

Cukier, K. N. (2007), *Governance as Gardening: A Report of the 2007 Rueschlikon Conference on Information Policy* <http://www.cukier.com/writings/Rueschlikon2007-infogov-cukier.pdf>.

Damsgaard, N. (2003), *Deregulation and Regulation of Electricity Markets* (Stockholm: EFI [Economic Research Institute]).

—— and R. J. Green (2005), 'Regulatory Reform in the Swedish Electricity Industry: Good or Bad?', SNS Occasional Paper, 95 (Stockholm, Studieförbundet Näringsliv och Samhälle Forlag).

David, P., B. Hall, and A. Toole (2000), 'Is Public R&D a Complement or Substitute for Private R&D? A Review of the Econometric Evidence', *Research Policy*, 29(4–5): 497–529.

Davies, S., and B. Lyons (2007), *Mergers and Merger Remedies in the EU: Assessing the Consequences for Competition* (Cheltenham: Edward Elgar).

—— M. Olczak, and H. Coles (2007), 'Tacit Collusion, Firm Asymmetries and Numbers: Evidence from EC Merger Cases', Centre for Competition Policy Working Paper, 07–7 (Norwich: University of East Anglia Centre for Competition Policy).

de Broca, Hubert (2006), 'The Commission Revises its Guidelines for Setting Fines in Antitrust Cases', *EC Competition Policy Newsletter*, 3: 1–6.

Degryse H. (1996), 'On the Interaction between Vertical and Horizontal Product Differentiation: An Application to Banking', *Journal of Industrial Economics*, 44(2): 169–82.

—— and A. Irmen (2001), 'Attribute Dependence and the Provision of Quality', *Regional Science and Urban Economics*, 31: 547–69.

—— and S. Ongena (2008), 'Competition and Regulation in the Banking Sector: A Review of the Empirical Evidence on the Sources of Bank Rents', in A. Thakor and A. Boot (eds), *Handbook of Financial Intermediation and Banking* (Amsterdam: Elsevier Science).

Dell'Ariccia, G. (2001), 'Asymmetric Information and the Structure of the Banking Industry', *European Economic Review*, 45: 1957–80.

—— E. Friedman, and R. Marquez (1999), 'Adverse Selection as Barrier to Entry in the Banking Industry', *RAND Journal of Economics*, 30: 515–34.

Deloitte (2007), 'The Deterrent Effect of Competition Enforcement by the OFT', OFT Report 962 (London: Office of Fair Trading).

Denni, M., and H. Gruber (2006), 'The Diffusion of Broadband Telecommunications: The Role of Competition', Departmental Working Papers of Economics, 60 (Rome: University Roma Tre).

Department of Trade and Industry (2007), 'Peer Review of Competition Policy' (London: Department for Business Enterprise and Regulatory Reform) <http://www.berr.gov.uk/files/file39863.pdf>.

Dewatripont M., and P. Seabright (2006), ' "Wasteful" Public Spending and State Aid Control', *Journal of the European Economic Association*, 4(2–3): 513–22.

Diamond, D. W., and P. H. Dybvig (1983), 'Bank Runs, Deposit Insurance and Liquidity', *Journal of Political Economy*, 91: 401–19.

Distaso, W., P. Lupi, and F. Manenti (2004), 'Platform Competition and Broadband Adoption in Europe: Theory and Empirical Evidence from the European Union', paper presented to the European Association for Research in Industrial Economics, Brussels.

Domah, P., and M. G. Pollitt (2001), 'The Restructuring and Privatisation of Electricity Distribution and Supply Businesses in England and Wales: A Social Cost–Benefit Analysis', *Fiscal Studies*, 22(1): 107–46.

Duso, T., D. Neven, and L.-H. Röller (2007), 'The Political Economy of European Merger Control: Evidence Using Stock Market Data', *Journal of Law and Economics*, 50(3): 455–89.

—— K. P. Gugler, and B. B. Yurtoglu (2006a), 'EU Merger Remedies: An Empirical Assessment', in J. Stennek and V. Ghosal (eds), *The Political Economy of Antitrust: Contributions to Economic Analysis* (Amsterdam: Elsevier Science).

—— —— —— (2006b), 'How Effective is European Merger Control?', Markets and Politics Working Paper, SP II 2006–12 (Berlin: Wissenschaftszentrum).

Easterbrook, F. (1984), 'The Limits of Antitrust', *Texas Law Review*, 63: 1–40.

Eckbo, E. (1983), 'Horizontal Mergers, Collusion and Stockholder Wealth', *Journal of Financial Economics*, 11: 241–73.

Economic Advisory Group on Competition Policy (2005), 'An Economic Approach to Article 82' (Brussels: Europa/European Union Documents).

—— (2006), 'Non-Horizontal Mergers Guidelines: Ten Principles', Note by the EAGCP Merger Subgroup: M. Ivaldi, B. Lyons, M. Schnitzer, J. van Reenen, F. Verboven, N. Vettas, and X. Vives (Brussels: Europa/European Union Documents) <http://ec.europa.eu/comm/competition/mergers/legislation/non_horizontal_guidelines.pdf>.

Edwards, G., and L. Waverman (2006), 'The Effects of Public Ownership and Regulatory Independence on Regulatory Outcomes: A Study of Interconnect Rates in EU Telecommunications', *Journal of Regulatory Economics*, 29(1): 23–67.

Eising, R. (2002), 'Policy Learning in Embedded Negotiations: Explaining EU Electricity Liberalization', *International Organization*, 56(1): 85–120.

Enrich, P. (1996), 'Saving the States from Themselves: Commerce Clause Constraints on State Tax Incentives for Business', *Harvard Law Review*, 110(2): 377–468.

Epstein, R. A., and M. S. Greve (eds), *Competition Laws in Conflict: Antitrust Jurisdiction in the Global Economy* (Washington, DC: AEI Press).

Estache, A., A. Goicoechea, and M. Manacorda (2006), 'Telecommunications Performance, Reforms, and Governance', Policy Research Working Paper, 3822 (Washington, DC: World Bank).

European Central Bank (2004), 'Report on EU Banking Structures' (Frankfurt: European Central Bank).

—— (2005), 'Report on EU Banking Structures' (Frankfurt: European Central Bank).

—— (2006), 'Report on EU Banking Structures' (Frankfurt: European Central Bank).

—— (2007a), 'Report on EU Banking Structures' (Frankfurt: European Central Bank).

—— (2007b), 'Financial Integration in Europe' (Frankfurt: European Central Bank).

—— (2001a), 'Competition Report 2000' (Brussels, Commission of the European Communities).

—— (2001b), 'Completing the Internal Energy Market', CES (2001) 438 (Brussels, Commission of the European Communities).

—— (2005), 'Report on Progress in Creating the Internal Gas and Electricity Market: Technical Annex' (Brussels, Commission of the European Communities).

—— (2007a), 'DG Competition Report on Energy Sector Inquiry', SEC (2006) 1724 (Brussels: Europa/European Union Documents) <http://ec.europa.eu/comm/competition/sectors/energy/inquiry/index.html#final>.

—— (2007b) 'Explanatory Memorandum of the Third Energy Package' (Brussels, Commission of the European Communities).

—— (2007c), 'Guidelines on the Assessment of Non-horizontal Mergers' (Brussels, Commission of the European Communities).

—— (2007d) 'Prospects for the Internal Gas and Electricity Market', SEC (2007) 12 (Brussels, Commission of the European Communities).

—— (2007e), 'Report on Competition Policy 2006', 25 June 2007 (Brussels, Commission of the European Communities).

—— (2008), 'Guidance on the Commission's Enforcement Priorities in Applying Article 82 EC Treaty to Abusive Exclusionary Conduct by Dominant Undertakings' (Brussels, Commission of the European Communities).

—— (var. years) 'Report on the Implementation of the Telecommunications Regulatory Package' (Brussels, Directorate-General Information Society).

European Commission, Directorate-General for Competition (2005), 'Staff Discussion Paper on the Application of Article 82 of the Treaty to Exclusionary Abuses' (Brussels, Commission of the European Communities).

European Community Green Paper (2001), 'Review of Council Regulation (EEC) No 4064/89' (Brussels: Europa/European Union Documents).

European Parliament (1996), 'Directive 96/92/EC of the European Parliament and of the Council of 19 December 1996 Concerning Common Rules for the Internal Market in Electricity' (Brussels, Commission of the European Communities).

—— (1998), 'Directive 98/30/EC of the European Parliament and of the Council of 22 June 1998 Concerning Common Rules for the Internal Market in Natural Gas' (Brussels, Commission of the European Communities).

—— (2003a), 'Directive 2003/54/EC of the European Parliament and of the Council of 26 June 2003 Concerning Common Rules for the Internal Market in Electricity and Repealing Directive 96/92/EC' (Brussels, Commission of the European Communities).

—— (2003b), 'Directive 2003/55/EC of the European Parliament and of the Council of 26 June 2003 Concerning Common Rules for the Internal Market in Natural Gas and Repealing Directive 98/30/EC' (Brussels, Commission of the European Communities).

European Regulators Group (2003), 'ERG Revised Common Position on Wholesale Bitstream Access' <http://www.erg.eu.int/documents/docs/index_en.htm>.

Farrell, J. (1987), 'Cheap Talk, Coordination and Entry', *RAND Journal of Economics*, 18: 34–9.

—— (2003), 'Negotiation and Merger Remedies: Some Problems', in F. Leveque and H. Shelanski (eds), *Merger Remedies in American and European Union Competition Law* (Cheltenham: Edward Elgar), chap. 6.

—— and M. Katz (2006), 'The Economics of Welfare Standards in Antitrust', *Competition Policy International*, 2(2): 3–28.

—— and P. Klemperer (2006), 'Coordination and Lock-in: Competition with Switching Costs and Network Effects' (1 May 2006), Competition Policy Center Paper, CPC06–

058 (Berkeley, CA: Institute of Business and Economic Research, Competition Policy Center, University of California, Berkeley).

—— and M. Rabin (1996), 'Cheap Talk', *Journal of Economic Perspectives*, 10: 103–18.

Farrell, J. and C. Shapiro (1990), 'Horizontal Mergers: An Equilibrium Analysis', *American Economic Review*, 80(1): 107–26.

Fingleton, J., F. Ruane, and V. Ryan (1999), 'Market Definition and State Aid Control', *European Economy*, 3: 65–88.

Friedman, J. (1971), 'A Noncooperative Equilibrium for Supergames', *Review of Economic Studies*, 28: 1–12.

Fumagalli, C., and M. Motta (2001), 'Advertising Restrictions in Professional Services', in G. Amato and L. Laudati (eds), *The Anticompetitive Impact of Regulation* (Cheltenham: Edward Elgar).

—— —— (2006), 'Exclusive Dealing and Entry, When Buyers Compete', *American Economic Review*, 96: 785–95.

Garces, E., D. Neven, and P. Seabright (2009), 'The Ups and Downs of the Doctrine of Collective Dominance: Using Game Theory for Merger Policy' in B. Lyons (2009), *Cases in European Competition Policy: The Economic Analysis* (Cambridge: Cambridge University Press), chap. 14.

Garcia, J.-A., and D. Neven (2005), 'State Aid and Distortion of Competition, a Benchmark Model', HEI Working Paper, 06 (Geneva: Graduate Institute of International Studies).

Garcia-Murillo, M., and D. Gabel (2003), 'International Broadband Deployment: The Impact of Unbundling', paper presented before the Thirty-first Research Conference on Communication, Information, and Internet Policy, Arlington, VA, Sept. 2003.

Garrod, L., B. Lyons, and A. Medvedev (2008), 'Empirical Identification of Error Type in EC Merger Settlement', Centre for Competition Policy Working Paper, 08–00 (Norwich: University of East Anglia Centre for Competition Policy).

Gavil, A. I., W. E. Kovacic, and J. B. Baker (2002), *Antitrust Law in Perspective: Cases, Concepts and Problems in Competition Policy* (Eagan, MN: West Group).

Genesove, D., and W. P. Mullin (2001), 'Rules, Communication, and Collusion: Narrative Evidence from the Sugar Institute Case', *American Economic Review*, 91: 379–98.

Géradin, D., C. Ahlborn, V. Denicolò, and A. J. Padilla (2006), 'DG Comp's Discussion Paper on Article 82: Implications of the Proposed Framework and Antitrust Rules for Dynamically Competitive Industries' <http://ssrn.com/abstract=894466>.

—— and D. Henry (2005), 'The EC Fining Policy for Violations of Competition Law: An Empirical Review of the Commission Decisional Practice and the Community Courts' Judgments', Working Paper, 03/05 (Brussels: Global Competition Law Centre).

—— and J. G. Sidak (2005), 'European and American Approaches to Antitrust Remedies and the Institutional Design of Regulation in Telecommunications', in M. Cave, S. Majumdar, and I. Vogelsang (eds), *Handbook of Telecommunications Economics*, ii (Amsterdam: Elsevier Science).

Gerber, D. J. (1998), *Law and Competition in Twentieth-century Europe: Protecting Prometheus* (Oxford: Clarendon Press).

Ghezzi, F., and P. Magnani (1998), 'L'applicazione della disciplina antitrust comunitaria al settore bancario', in M. Polo (ed.), *Industria Bancaria e Concorrenza* (Bologna: Il Mulino), 259–328.

Gifford, D., and R. Kudrle (2005), 'Rhetoric and Reality in the Merger Standards of the United States, Canada and the European Union', *Antitrust Law Journal*, 72: 423–69.

Gilbert, R. J., E. P. Kahn, and D. M. Newbery (1996), 'Introduction: International Comparisons of Electricity Regulation', in R. J. Gilbert and E. P. Kahn (eds), *International Comparisons of Electricity Regulation* (Cambridge: Cambridge University Press).

Goergen, M., and L. Renneboog (2004), 'Shareholder Wealth Effects of European Domestic and Cross-border Takeover Bids', *European Financial Management*, 10(1): 9–45.

Goldberg, P., and G. Maggi (1999), 'Protection for Sale: An Empirical Investigation', *American Economic Review*, 89(5): 1135–55.

Goldstein, I., and A. Pauzner (2005), 'Demand Deposit Contracts and the Probability of Bank Runs', *Journal of Finance*, 60: 1293–328.

Goolsbee, A. (2004), 'The Impact and Inefficiency of the Corporate Income Tax: Evidence from State Organizational Form Data', *Journal of Public Economics*, 88(11): 283–9.

Gorton G. (1988), 'Banking Panics and Business Cycles', *Oxford Economic Papers*, 40: 751–81.

Goyder, D. G. (1993), *EC Competition Law* (2nd edn, Oxford: Clarendon Press).

—— (2003), *EC Competition Law* (4th edn, Oxford: Clarendon Press).

Green, E. J., and R. H. Porter (1984), 'Noncooperative Collusion under Imperfect Competition', *Econometrica*, 52: 87–100.

Gregg, B. J. (2006), 'A Survey of Unbundled Network Element Prices in the United States' (Columbus, OH: National Regulatory Research Institute, Ohio State University).

Gropp, R., H. Hakenes, and I. Schnabel (2006), 'Competition, Risk Shifting, and Public Bail-out Policies', Working Paper (University of Frankfurt).

Gruber, H., and F. Verboven (2001), 'The Evolution of Markets under Entry and Standards Regulation—The Case of Global Mobile Telecommunication', *International Journal of Industrial Organization*, 19(7): 1189–212.

Gual, J. (2004), 'Market Definition in the Telecoms Industry', in P. Rey and P. Buigues (eds), *The Economics of Antitrust and Regulation in Telecommunications* (Cheltenham: Edward Elgar).

—— (2008), 'Integrating Regulated Network Markets in Europe', in G. Gelauff, I. Grilo, and A. Lejour (eds), *Subsidiarity and Economic Reform in Europe* (Berlin: Springer-Verlag), 157–76.

Gual, J., and F. Trillas (2006), 'Telecommunications Policies: Measurement and Determinants', *Review of Network Economics*, 5(2): 249–72.

—— and S. Jódar-Rosell (2007), 'Broadband Regulation: An Empirical Assessment', Working Paper Series, 05/2007 (Barcelona: 'la Caixa').

Hammond, E., D. Helm, and D. Thompson (1986), 'Competition in Electricity Supply: Has the Energy Act Failed', *Fiscal Studies*, 7(1): 11–33.

Hannah, L., and J. Kay (1981), 'The Contribution of Mergers to Industrial Concentration: A Reply to Professor Prais', *Journal of Industrial Economics*, 29(3): 331–2.

Harrington, J. (2008), 'Optimal Corporate Leniency Programs', *Journal of Industrial Economics*, 56(2): 215–46 <http://www.econ.jhu.edu/People/Harrington/amnesty11–05.pdf>.

Hausman, J., and G. K. Leonard (2005), 'Using Merger Simulation Models: Testing the Underlying Assumptions', *International Journal of Industrial Organization*, 23: 693–8.

—— and J. G. Sidak (2005), 'Did Mandatory Unbundling Achieve its Purpose? Empirical Evidence from Five Countries', *Journal of Competition Law and Economics*, 1(1): 173–245.

Hauswald, R., and R. Marquez (2006), 'Competition and Strategic Information Acquisition in Credit Markets', *Review of Financial Studies*, 19(3): 967–1000.

Hay, G. A. (1999), 'Facilitating Practices: The Ethyl Case (1984)', in J. E. Kwoka, Jr. and L. J. White (eds), *The Antitrust Revolution* (3rd edn, Oxford: Oxford University Press).

Hellman, T. F., K. Murdock, and J. Stiglitz (2000), 'Liberalization, Moral Hazard in Banking and Prudential Regulation: Are Capital Requirements Enough?', *American Economic Review*, 90(1): 147–65.

Höffler, F. (2006), 'Monopoly Prices versus Ramsey Prices: Are they "Similar" and does it Matter?', *Journal of Industry, Competition and Trade*, 6: 27–43.

—— and S. Kranz (2007), 'Legal Unbundling can be a Golden Mean between Vertical Integration and Separation', Economics Discussion Paper, bgse15_2007 (Bonn: University of Bonn) <http://www.whu.edu/cms/fileadmin/redaktion/LS-RegOek/unbundling_071115.pdf>.

Huck, S., K. Konrad, W. Mueller, and H.-T. Norman (2007), 'The Merger Paradox and Why Aspiration Levels Let it Fail in the Laboratory', *Economic Journal*, 117: 1073–95.

Hufbauer, G., D. Berliner, and K. Elliot (1986), *Trade Protection in the United States: 31 Case Studies* (Washington, DC: Institute for International Economics).

—— and H. Rosen (1986), *Trade Policy for Troubled Industries*, Policy Analyses in International Economics, 15 (Washington, DC: Institute for International Economics).

Hylton, K. N. (2003), *Antitrust Law: Economic Theory and Common Law Evolution* (Cambridge: Cambridge University Press).

Ilzkovitz, F., and R. Meiklejohn (2006), *European Merger Control: Do we Need an Efficiency Defence?* (Cheltenham: Edward Elgar).

International Energy Agency (1996), *Energy Policies of IEA Countries*, Spain, 1996 Review (Paris, Organisation for Economic Cooperation and Development).

Ivaldi, M., et al. (2003a), 'The Economics of Unilateral Effects', DG Competition Report (Brussels: Europa/European Union Documents) <http://ec.europa.eu/comm/competition/mergers/studies_reports/studies_reports.html>.

—— et al. (2003b), 'The Economics of Tacit Collusion', DG Competition Report (Brussels: Europa/European Union Documents) <http://ec.europa.eu/comm/competition/mergers/studies_reports/studies_reports.html>.

—— and F. Verboven (2005a), 'Quantifying the Effects from Horizontal Mergers in European Competition Policy', *International Journal of Industrial Organization*, 23: 669–91.

—— —— (2005b), 'Quantifying the Effects from Horizontal Mergers: Comments on the Underlying Assumptions', *International Journal of Industrial Organization*, 23: 669–702.

Jones, A., and B. Sufrin (2004), *EC Competition Law* (2nd edn, Oxford: Oxford University Press).

Jorgenson, D. W., and K.-Y. Yun (1990), 'Tax Reform and US Economic Growth', *Journal of Political Economy*, 98(5): 151–93.

—— —— (1991), 'The Excess Burden of Taxation in the United States', *Journal of Accounting and Finance*, 6(4): 509–11.

Jullien, B., and P. Rey (2007), 'Resale Price Maintenance and Collusion', *RAND Journal of Economics*, 38: 983–1001.

Kahn, E. (1998), 'Introducing Competition to the Electricity Industry in Spain: The Role of Initial Conditions', *Utilities Policy*, 7(1): 15–22.

Kandori, M. (1992), 'The Use of Information in Repeated Games with Imperfect Monitoring', *Review of Economic Studies*, 59: 581–93.

—— and H. Matsushima (1998), 'Private Observation, Communication and Collusion', *Econometrica*, 66: 627–52.

Kaplow, L., and C. Shapiro (2007), 'Antitrust', in A. M. Polinsky and S. Shavell (eds), *Handbook of Law and Economics* (Amsterdam: Elsevier Science).

Keeley, M. (1990), 'Deposit Insurance, Risk and Market Power in Banking', *American Economic Review*, 80: 1183–200.

Kerjean, S. (2008), 'The Legal Implications of the Prudential Supervisory Assessment of Bank Mergers and Acquisitions under EU Law', Legal Working Paper, 6 (European Central Bank, Frankfurt).

Kleiner, T., and A. Alexis (2005), 'Politique des aides d'Etat: une analyse économique plus fine au service de l'intérêt commun', *Concurrences*, 4: 45–52.

Klemperer, P. (2002), 'What Really Matters in Auction Design', *Journal of Economic Perspectives*, 16: 169–89.

Kornai, J. (1986), 'The Soft Budget Constraint', *Kyklos*, 39(1): 3–30.

—— E. Maskin, and G. Roland (2003), 'Understanding the Soft Budget Constraint', *Journal of Economic Literature*, 41(4): 1095–136.

Kovacic, W. E. (1999), 'Designing Antitrust Remedies for Dominant Firm Misconduct', *Connecticut Law Review*, 31: 1289–90.

—— (2001), 'Transatlantic Turbulence: The Boeing–McDonnell Douglas Merger and International Competition Policy', *Antitrust Law Journal*, 68: 805–73.

—— (2002), 'Extraterritoriality, Institutions, and Convergence in International Competition Policy', *American Society of International Law Proceedings*, 97: 309.

—— (2003), 'The Modern Evolution of US Competition Policy Enforcement Norms', *Antitrust Law Journal*, 377: 448–52.

—— (2004a), 'Private Participation in the Enforcement of Public Competition Laws', in G. Canivet, M. Andenas, and D. Fairgrieve (eds), *Comparative Law before the Courts* (London: British Institute of International and Comparative Law).

—— (2005a), 'Competition Policy Cooperation and the Pursuit of Better Practices', in D. M. Andrews, M. Pollack, G. Schaffer, and H. Wallace (eds), *The Future of Transatlantic Relations—Continuity Amid Discord* (Florence: European University Institute, Robert Schuman Centre for Advanced Studies).

—— (2005b), 'Achieving Better Practices in the Design of Competition Policy Institutions', in P. Lugard and L. Hancher (eds), *On the Merits—Current Issues in Competition Law and Policy 195* (Oxford : Intersentia).

—— (2006), 'Using Ex Post Assessments to Improve the Performance of Competition Policy Authorities', *Journal of Corporate Law*, 31.

—— (2007), 'The Intellectual DNA of Modern US Competition Law for Dominant Firm Conduct: The Chicago/Harvard Double Helix', *Columbia Business Law Review*, 1: 1–81.

—— and A. Reindl (2005), 'An Interdisciplinary Approach to Improving Competition Policy and Intellectual Policy', *Fordham International Law Journal*, 28.

—— and C. Shapiro (2000), 'Antitrust Policy: A Century of Economic and Legal Thinking', *Journal of Economic Perspectives*, 14(1): 43–60.

Kroes, N. (2007) (European Commissioner for Competition Policy), 'Antitrust in the EU and the US—Our Common Objectives', Brussels, 26 Sept.

Kühn, K.-U. (2001), 'Fighting Collusion by Regulating Communication between Firms', *Economic Policy*, 16(32): 167–204.

—— (2005), 'Collusion Theory in Search of Robust Themes: A Comment on Switgard Feuerstein's Survey', *Journal of Industry, Competition and Trade*, 5(3): 207–15.

Kühn, K.-U. and X. Vives (1995), 'Information Exchanges among Firms and their Impact on Competition' (Luxembourg: Office for Official Publications of the European Communities).

—— and J. van Reenen (2007), 'Some Economics of European Commission vs. Microsoft' <http://cep.lse.ac.uk/pubs/download/cp223.pdf>. Also at B. Lyons (2009), *Cases in European Competition Policy: The Economic Analysis* (Cambridge: Cambridge University Press), chap. 3.

Laband, D., and J. Sophocleus (1992), 'An Estimate of Expenditures on Transfer Activity in the United States', *Quarterly Journal of Economics*, 107(3): 959–83.

Laffont, J.-J., and J. Tirole (2000), *Competition in Telecommunications: Munich Lectures in Economics* (Cambridge, MA: MIT Press).

Langus, G., and M. Motta (2007), 'The Effect of EU Antitrust Investigations and Fines on a Firm's Valuation', Center for Economic Policy Research Discussion Paper, 6176.

Li, W., and L. C. Xu (2004), 'The Impact of Privatization and Competition in the Telecommunications Sector around the World', *Journal of Law and Economics*, 47(2): 395–430.

Lindsay, A., E. Lecchi, and G. Williams (2003), 'Econometric Study into European Merger Decisions since 2000', *European Competition Law Review*, 24: 673–82.

Lipsky, A. B., and J. G. Sidak (1999), 'Essential Facilities', *Stanford Law Review*, 51: 1187–248.

Littlechild, S. C. (2006), 'Residential Energy Contracts and the 28-Day Rule', *Utilities Policy*, 14(1): 44–62.

Lohmann, H. (2006), *The German Path to Natural Gas Liberalisation* (Oxford: Oxford Institute for Energy Studies).

London Economics (2007), 'Structure and Performance of Six European Wholesale Electricity Markets in 2003, 2004, and 2005', DG Competition Report (Brussels: Europa/European Union Documents) <http://ec.europa.eu/comm/competition/sectors/energy/inquiry/index.html#final>.

Luce, R., and H. Raiffa (1957), *Games and Decisions: Introduction and Critical Survey* (New York: Wiley).

Lyons, B. R. (2001), 'What do we Conclude from the Success and Failure of Mergers?', *Journal of Industry, Competition and Trade*, 1(4): 411–22.

—— (2004), 'Reform of European Merger Policy', *Review of International Economics*, 12(2): 246–61.

—— (2009), *Cases in European Competition Policy: The Economic Analysis* (Cambridge: Cambridge University Press).

Magee, S., W. Brock, and L. Young (1989), *Black Hole Tariffs and Endogenous Policy Theory: Political Economy in General Equilibrium* (Cambridge: Cambridge University Press).

Makholm, J. D. (2007), 'Seeking Competition and Supply Security in Natural Gas: US Experience and European Challenge', CESSA Conference, Berlin, May 2007 <http://www.cessa.eu.com/sd-papers/berlin/CeSSA Berlin 102 makholm.pdf>.

Marquez, R. (2002), 'Competition, Adverse Selection and Information Dispersion in the Banking Industry', *Review of Financial Studies*, 15(3): 901–26.

Martin, S. (2006), 'Remembrance of Things Past: Antitrust, Ideology, and the Development of Industrial Economics', in J. Stennek and V. Ghosal (eds), *The Political Economy of Antitrust: Contributions to Economic Analysis* (Amsterdam: Elsevier Science).

—— C. Strasse (2005), 'La Politique communautaire des aides d'État est-elle une politique de la concurrence?', *Concurrences*, 3: 52–9.

Martynova, M., and L. Renneboog (2006a), 'Mergers and Acquisitions in Europe', in L. Renneboog (ed.), *Advances in Corporate Finance and Asset Pricing* (Amsterdam: Elsevier Science), 15–75.

—— —— (2006b), 'The Performance of the European Market for Corporate Control: Evidence from the 5th Takeover Wave', CentER Discussion Paper, No. 2006–118, Tilburg.

—— —— (2008a), 'A Century of Corporate Takeovers: What have we Learned and Where do we Stand?', *Journal of Banking and Finance*, 32(10): 2148–77.

—— —— (2008b), 'Spillover of Corporate Governance Standards in Cross-border Mergers and Acquisitions', *Journal of Corporate Finance*.

Mathewson, F., and R. Winter (1998), 'The Law and Economics of Resale Price Maintenance', *Review of Industrial Organization*, 13: 57–84.

—— —— (1984), 'An Economic Theory of Vertical Restraints', *RAND Journal of Economics*, 15: 27–38.

Matutes, C., and A. J. Padilla (1994), 'Shared ATM Networks and Banking Competition', *European Economic Review*, 38: 1057–69.

—— and X. Vives (1996), 'Competition for Deposits, Fragility, and Insurance', *Journal of Financial Intermediation*, 5: 184–216.

—— —— (2000), 'Imperfect Competition, Risk Taking and Regulation in Banking', *European Economic Review*, 44(1): 1–34.

Midelfart-Knarvik, K.-H., and H.-G. Overman (2002), 'Delocation and European Integration: Is Structural Spending Justified', *Economic Policy*, 35: 322–59.

Monopolies and Mergers Commission (1988), *Gas: A Report on the Matter of the Existence or Possible Existence of a Monopoly Situation in Relation to the Supply of Gas through Pipes to Persons other than Tariff Customers*, Cm 500 (London: HMSO).

Monopolkommission (2002), *Wettbewerbsentwicklung bei Telekommunikation und Post 2001: Unsicherheit und Stillstand*, Sondergutachten, 33 (Baden-Baden: Nomos Verlagsgesellschaft).

—— (2003), *Netzwettbewerb durch Regulierung, Hauptgutachten 2000/2001* (Baden-Baden: Nomos Verlagsgesellschaft) (Eng. summary: 555–90).

—— (2004a), *Telekommunikation und Post 2003: Wettbewerbsintensivierung in der Telekommunikation–Zementierung des Postmonopols*, Sondergutachten, 39 (Baden-Baden: Nomos Verlagsgesellschaft).

—— (2004b), *Zur Reform des Telekommunikationsgesetzes*, Sondergutachten, 40 (Baden-Baden: Nomos Verlagsgesellschaft).

—— (2005), *Wettbewerbspolitik im Schatten 'Nationaler Champions'*, Hauptgutachten 2002/2003 (Baden-Baden: Nomos Verlagsgesellschaft) (Eng. summary: 575–648).

—— (2006), *Wettbewerbsentwicklung bei der Telekommunikation 2005: Dynamik unter neuen Rahmenbedingungen*, Sondergutachten, 43 (Baden-Baden: Nomos Verlagsgesellschaft).

Moretti, E. (2004), 'Workers' Education, Spillovers and Productivity: Evidence from Plant-level Production Functions', *American Economic Review*, 94(3): 656–90.

Möschel, W. (1999), 'Regulierungswirrwarr in der Telekommunikation', *Multimedia und Recht Beilage*, 3: 3–6.

—— (2001), 'Tangled Telecommunications Regulation', in J. G. Sidak, C. Engel, and G. Knieps (eds), *Competition and Regulation in Telecommunications* (Boston, Dordrecht, and London: Kluwer Academic Publishers), 1–13.

Motta, M. (2000), 'EC Merger Policy and the Airtours Case', *European Competition Law Review*, 21(4): 199–207.

—— (2004), *Competition Policy: Theory and Practice* (Cambridge and New York: Cambridge University Press).

—— and M. Polo (1999), 'Leniency Programs and Cartel Prosecution' (Florence: n.p.).

—— —— (2003), 'Leniency Programs and Cartel Prosecution', *International Journal of Industrial Organization*, 21: 347–79.

—— —— and H. Vasconcelos (2003), 'Merger Remedies in the EU: An Overview', in F. Leveque and H. Shelanski (eds), *Merger Remedies in American and European Union Competition Law* (Cheltenham: Edward Elgar).

Muris, T. J. (2001), 'Merger Enforcement in a World of Multiple Arbiters', prepared remarks at the Brookings Institution Roundtable on Trade and Investment Policy, Washington, DC, 21 Dec.

—— (2002), 'Competition Agencies in a Market-based Global Economy', prepared remarks before the Annual Lecture of the European Foreign Affairs Review, Brussels, 23 July <http://www.ftc.gov/speeches/muris/020723/brussels>.

—— (2003a), 'Looking Forward: The Federal Trade Commission and the Future Development of US Competition Policy', *Columbia Business Law Review*, 2.

—— (2003b), 'State Intervention/State Action—A US Perspective', remarks before the Fordham Annual Conference in International Antitrust Law and Policy, New York, 24 Oct. <http://www.ftc.gov/speeches/muris/fordham031024.pdf>.

Murphy, K., A. Shleifer, and R. Vishny (1991), 'The Allocation of Talent: Implications for Growth', *Quarterly Journal of Economics*, 106(2): 503–30.

Nazzini, R. (2006), 'Article 81 EC Between Time Present and Time Past: A Normative Critique of "Restriction of Competition" in EU Law', *Common Market Law Review*, 43(2): 497–536.

Neven, D. J. (2000), 'The Political Economy of State Aids: Econometric Evidence for the Member States', in Neven and L.-H. Röller, *The Political Economy of Industrial Policy: Does Europe have an Industrial Policy?* (Berlin: Sigma).

—— (2006), 'Competition Economics and Antitrust in Europe', *Economic Policy*, 21(48): 741–91.

—— R. Nuttall, and P. Seabright (1993), *Merger in Daylight: The Economics and Politics of European Merger Control* (London: Center for Economic Policy Research).

—— and L.-H. Röller (2002), 'Discrepencies between Markets and Regulators: An Analysis of the First Ten Years of EU Merger Control', in *The Pros and Cons of Merger Control* (Geneva: Graduate Institute of International Studies).

—— and P. Seabright (1995), 'European Industrial Policy: The Airbus Case', *Economic Policy*, 21: 314–44.

—— and T. von Ungern-Sternberg (1998), 'Competition Policy in Switzerland', *Antitrust Bulletin*, 43(2): 467–517.

Newbery, D. M. (2000), *Privatization, Restructuring, and Regulation of Network Utilities* (Cambridge, MA: MIT Press).

—— (2002), 'Problems of Liberalizing the Electricity Industry', *European Economic Review*, 46, 919–27.

—— (2006), 'The Relationship between Regulation and Competition Policy for Network Industries', Cambridge Working Papers in Economics, 0631 and Electricity Policy Research Group Working Paper, 0611 <http://www.electricitypolicy.org.uk/pubs/wp/eprg0611.pdf>.

—— and M. G. Pollitt (1997), 'The Privatisation and Restructuring of the CEGB: Was it Worth it?', *Journal of Industrial Economics*, 45: 269–303.

Nikpay, A., J. Faull, and L. Kjølbye (2007), 'Article 81', in J. Faull and A. Nikpay (eds), *The EC Law of Competition* (2nd edn, Oxford: Oxford University Press).

O'Donoghue, R., and A. J. Padilla (2006), *The Law and Economics of Article 82 EC* (Oxford: Hart Publishing).

Organisation for Economic Co-operation and Development (1998), 'Cross-ownership and Convergence: Policy Issues', DSTI/ICCP/TISP (98)3/FINAL (Nov. 1998) (Paris: OECD).

—— (1998–2000), 'Regulatory Overview of the Telecommunications Sectors', Country Reponses <http://www.oecd.org/document/35/0,3343,en_2649_34223_1912291_1_1_1,00.html>.

—— (2001a), *Restructuring Public Utilities for Competition* (Paris: OECD).

—— (2001b), 'Structural Separation in Regulated Industries', DAFFE/CLP (Apr. 2001) (Paris: OECD).

—— (2002), *Fighting Hard-core Cartels* (Paris: OECD).

—— (2003a), 'Broadband and Telephony Services over Cable Television Networks', DSTI/ICCP/TISP (May 2003) (Paris: OECD).

—— (2003b), 'Developments in Local Loop Unbundling', DSTI/ICCP/TISP (2002) 5/FINAL (Sept. 2003) (Paris: OECD).

Padilla, A. J. (2007), 'Efficiencies in Mergers: Williamson Revisited', in W. D. Collins (ed.), *Issues in Competition Law and Policy* (Chicago: American Bar Association Antitrust Section).

—— and M. Pagano (1997), 'Endogenous Communication among Lenders and Entrepreneurial Incentives', *Review of Financial Studies*, 10: 205–36.

—— —— (2000), 'Sharing Default Information as a Borrower Discipline Device', *European Economic Review*, 44(10): 1951–80.

Persson, T., and G. Tabellini (2000), *Political Economics: Explaining Economic Policy* (Cambridge, MA: MIT Press).

Pitman, R. (2007), 'Consumer Surplus as the Appropriate Standard for Antitrust Enforcement', *Competition Policy International*, 3(2): 205–24.

Pollack, M. A., and G. C. Shaffer (2001), 'Transatlantic Governance in Historical and Theoretical Perspective', in Pollack and Shaffer (eds), *Transatlantic Governance in the Global Economy* (Lanham, MD: Rowland & Littlefield).

Porter, R. (1983), 'Optimal Cartel Trigger Strategies', *Journal of Economic Theory*, 29: 313–38.

Posner R. A. (1970), 'A Statistical Study of Antitrust Enforcement', *Journal of Law and Economics*, 13: 365–419.

—— (1976), *Antitrust Law: An Economic Perspective* (Chicago: University of Chicago Press).

—— (1979), 'The Chicago School of Antitrust Analysis', *University of Pennsylvania Law Review*, 127: 925–48.

Postlewaite, A., and X. Vives (1987), 'Bank Runs as a Equilibrium Phenomenon', *Journal of Political Economy*, 95(3): 487–91.

Prager, R., and T. Hannan (1998), 'Do Substantial Horizontal Mergers Generate Significant Price Effects? Evidence from the Banking Industry', *Journal of Industrial Economics*, 46(4): 433–52.

Prais, S. (1981), 'The Contribution of Mergers to Industrial Concentration: What Do We Know?' *Journal of Industrial Economics*, 29(3): 321–9.

Raith, M. (1996), 'A General Model of Information Sharing in Oligopoly', *Journal of Economic Theory*, 71: 260–88.

Rasmusen, E., M. Ramseyer, and J. Wiley (1991), 'Naked Exclusion', *American Economic Review*, 81: 1137–45.

Reports of the German Monopolies Commission (various years).

Rey, P. (2003), 'Towards a Theory of Competition Policy', in M. Dewatripont, L. P. Hansen, and S. J. Turnovsky (eds), *Advances in Economics and Econometrics: Theory and Applications* (Cambridge: Cambridge University Press).

—— and J. Stiglitz (1995), 'The Role of Exclusive Territories in Producers' Competition', *RAND Journal of Economics*, 26(3): 431–51.

—— and J. Tirole (2007), 'A Primer on Foreclosure', in M. Armstrong and R. Porter (eds), *Handbook of Industrial Organization*, iii (Amsterdam: Elsevier Science).

Rochet, J. C. (2007), 'Interchange Fees in Payment Card Systems: Price Remedies in a Two-sided Market', in B. Lyons (2009), *Cases in European Competition Policy: The Economic Analysis* (Cambridge: Cambridge University Press).

—— and J. Tirole (2002), 'Cooperation among Competitors: The Economics of Credit Card Associations', *RAND Journal of Economics*, 33(4): 1–22.

—— —— (2003), 'Platform Competition in Two-sided Markets', *Journal of the European Economic Association*, 1: 990–1029.

—— and X. Vives (2004), 'Coordination Failures and the Lender of Last Resort: Was Bagehot Right after all?' *Journal of the European Economic Association*, 2(6): 1116–47.

Röller, L.-H., and P. Buigues (2005), 'The Office of the Chief Competition Economist at the European Commission' (Brussels: Europa/European Union Documents) <http://ec.europa.eu/dgs/competition/officechiefecon_ec.pdf>.

—— H. W. Friederiszick, and V. Verouden (2007), 'European State Aid Control: An Economic Framework', in P. Buccirossi (ed.), *Advances in the Economics of Competition Law* (Cambridge, MA: MIT Press).

Rubinfeld, D. (2004), 'Maintenance of Monopoly: US vs Microsoft', in J. E. Kwoka and L. J. White (eds), *The Antitrust Revolution* (4th edn, Oxford: Oxford University Press).

Salop, S. C. (1986), 'Practices that (Credibly) Facilitate Oligopoly Co-ordination', in J. Stiglitz and G. Mathewson (eds), *New Developments in the Analysis of Market Structure* (Basingstoke: Macmillan).

Schelling, T. C. (1960), *The Strategy of Conflict* (Cambridge, MA: Harvard University Press).

Scherer, F. M. (1970), *Industrial Market Structure and Economic Performance* (Chicago, Rand McNally).

Schmalensee, R., and R. Willig (eds) (1989), *Handbook of Industrial Organization*, i–ii (Amsterdam: Elsevier Science).

Schulz, W. (1995), 'Restructuring the Electricity Market: A German View', in O. J. Olsen (ed.), *Competition in the Electricity Supply Industry: Experience from Europe and the United States* (Copenhagen: DJØF Publishing).

Scott Morton, F. (1997), 'Entry and Predation: British Shipping Cartels, 1879–1929', *Journal of Economics & Management Strategy*, 6(4): 679–724.

Segal, I. R., and M. D. Whinston (2000), 'Naked Exclusion: Comment', *American Economic Review*, 90(1): 296–309.

Simpson, J., and A. L. Wickelgren (2007), 'Naked Exclusion, Efficient Breach, and Downstream Competition', *American Economic Review*, 97(4): 1305–20.

Slade, M., and F. Lafontaine (2008), 'Exclusive Contracts and Vertical Restraints: Empirical Evidence and Public Policy', in P. Buccirossi (ed.), *Handbook of Antitrust Economics* (Cambridge, MA: MIT Press).

Spagnolo, G. (2000), 'Optimal Leniency Programs', Note di lavoro 42/2000 (Milan: Fondazione Eni Enrico Mattei).

Sproul, M. F. (1993), 'Antitrust and Prices', *Journal of Political Economy*, 101: 741–54.

Stigler, G. J. (1964), 'A Theory of Oligopoly', *Journal of Political Economy*, 72: 44–61.

—— (1968), *Industrial Organization* (Chicago: Chicago University Press).

Suurnäkki, S., and M. L. Tierno Centella (2007), 'Commission Adopts Revised Leniency Notice to Reward Companies that Report Hard-core Cartels', *EC Competition Policy Newsletter*, 1: 7–15.

Symeonidis, G. (2000), 'Price Competition and Market Structure: The Impact of Cartel Policy on Concentration in the UK', *Journal of Industrial Economics*, 48(1): 1–26.

Tannenwald, R. (2002), 'Are State and Local Revenue Systems Becoming Obsolete?', *National Tax Journal*, 55(3): 467–89.

Telser, L. G. (1960), 'Why Should Manufacturers Want Fair Trade', *Journal of Law and Economics*, 3: 86–105.

Tiebout, W. (1956), 'A Pure Theory of Local Expenditures', *Journal of Political Economy*, 64(5): 416–24.

Tirole, J. (1988), *The Theory of Industrial Organization* (Cambridge, MA: MIT Press).

—— (2005), 'The Analysis of Tying Cases: A Primer', *Competition Policy International*, 1: 1–25.

Tsakatoura, A. (2008), 'State Aid in the EU Banking Industry', Inter-Lawyer, Lay Firms Directories, webpage.

Tullock, G. (1987), 'Rent Seeking', in *The New Palgrave: A Dictionary of Economics*, 4 vols (Basingstoke: Palgrave Macmillan), iv. 147–9.

Ulltveit-Moe, K.-H. (2007), 'Regional Policy Design: An Analysis of Relocation, Efficiency and Equity', *European Economic Review*, 51: 1443–67.

Valletti, T. (2003), 'The Theory of Access Pricing and its Linkage with Investment Incentives', *Telecommunications Policy*, 27: 659–75.

—— and C. Cambini (2005), 'Investments and Network Competition', *RAND Journal of Economics*, 36(2): 446–67.

van Barlingen, B., and M. Barennes (2005), 'The European Commission's 2002 Leniency Notice in Practice', *EC Competition Policy Newsletter*, 3: 6–16.

Vickers, J. (2004), 'Merger Policy in Europe: Retrospect and Prospect', *European Competition Law Review*, 25(7): 455–63.

—— (2005), 'Abuse of Market Power', *Economic Journal*, 115: F244–F261.

—— (2006) 'Market Power in Competition Cases', *European Competition Journal*, 2: 3–14.

—— (2008), 'A Tale of Two Cases: IBM and Microsoft', *Competition Policy International*, 4: 3–23.

Viscusi, K. W., J. Vernon, and J. Harrington (2001), *Economics of Regulation and Antitrust* (3rd edn, Cambridge, MA: MIT Press).

Vives, X. (1999), *Oligopoly Pricing: Old Ideas and New Tools* (Cambridge, MA: MIT Press).

—— (2001a), 'Competition in the Changing World of Banking', *Oxford Review of Economic Policy*, 17(4): 535–47.

—— (2001b), 'Restructuring Financial Regulation in the European Monetary Union', *Journal of Financial Services Research*, 19(1): 57–82.

—— (2005), 'Europe Banks Future on the Urge to Merge', *Wall Street Journal* (Europe) (13 May).

—— (2006), 'Information Sharing: Economics and Antitrust', in *The Pros and Cons of Information Sharing* (Stockholm: Swedish Competition Authority).

—— (2008), 'Globalization and Industrial Policy', mimeo (n.p.).

—— and G. Staffiero (2009), 'The GE–Honeywell Merger in the EU', in B. Lyons (2009), *Cases in European Competition Policy: The Economic Analysis* (Cambridge: Cambridge University Press), chap. 17.

Vogelsang, I. (2003), 'Price Regulation of Access to Telecommunications Networks', *Journal of Economic Literature*, 41(3): 830–62.

von Hirschhausen, C., H. Weigt, and G. Zachmann (2007), 'Preisbildung und Marktmacht auf den Elektrizitätsmärkten in Deutschland: Grundlegende Mechanismen und empirische Evidenz', mimeo (Dresden: Technical University Dresden).

Wallsten, S. (2003), 'Of Carts and Horses: Regulation and Privatization in Telecommunications Reforms', *Journal of Economic Policy Reform*, 6(4): 217–31.

—— (2006), 'Broadband and Unbundling Regulations in OECD Countries', AEI–Brookings Joint Center Working Paper, 06–16 (Washington, DC) <http://ssrn.com/abstract=906865>.

Whinston, M. D. (1990), 'Tying, Foreclosure and Exclusion', *American Economic Review*, 80: 837–59.

—— (2001), 'Exclusivity and Tying in US vs Microsoft: What we Know, and Don't Know', *Journal of Economic Perspectives*, 15: 63–80.

—— (2006), *Lectures on Antitrust Economics* (Cambridge, MA: MIT Press).

Whish, R. (2003), *Competition Law* (5th edn, London: LexisNexis).

Willig, R. D., W. H. Lehr, J. P. Bigelow, and S. B. Levinson (2002), 'Stimulating Investment and the Telecommunications Act of 1996', ex parte presentation by AT&T to the Federal Communications Commission, 11 Oct. 2002 (n.p.).

Wils, W. (2007), 'The European Commission's 2006 Guidelines on Antitrust Fines: A Legal and Economic Analysis', *World Competition*, 30(2): 197–229.

Wright, J. (2004), 'One-sided Logic in Two-sided Markets', *Review of Network Economics*, 3: 44–64.

Zarakas, W. P., et al. (2005), 'Structural Simulation of Facility Sharing: Unbundling Policies and Investment Strategy in Local Exchange Markets' (Washington, DC: Brattle Group).

Cases Cited

United States

Brooke Group Ltd v. *Brown & Williamson Tobacco Corp*, 509 US 209 (1993).
Jefferson Parish Hospital Dist. No. 2 v. *Hyde*, 466 US 2 (1984).
MASSACHUSETTS *V.* MICROSOFT, 373 F.3d 1199, 1243 (DC Cir. 2004).
Schor v. *Abbott Laboratories*, No. 05–3344 (7th Cir. 2006).
United States v. *AMR Corp*, 335 F.3d 1109 (10th Cir. 2003).
United States v. *Microsoft*, 253 F.3d 34 (DC Cir. 2001).
Virgin Atlantic Ltd v. *British Airways PLC*, 257 F.3d 256 (2d Cir. 2001).
VEBA/VIAG: Commission Decision of 13 June 2000, Case COMP/M.1673 VEBA/VIAG, OJ L 188, 10/07/2001.
United States v. *Terminal Railroad Association*, 224 US 383 (1912).
Verizon Communications Inc. v. *Law Offices of Curtis* v. *Trinko Ltd.*, 540 US 398 (2004).
Crédit Suisse Securities (USA) LLC et al. v. *Billing*, 551 US (2007).

European Union

AKZO v. *Commission*, C–62/86 [1991].
British Airways v. *Commission*, C–95/04 P [2007].
France Télécom SA v. *Commission*, T–340/03 [2007].
IMS Health, C–418/01 [2004].
Microsoft v. *Commission*, T–201/04 [2007].
RTE and ITP v. *Commission*, C–241&242/91 P [1995] ('*Magill*').
Tetra Pak v. *Commission*, C–333/94 P [1996].
Deutsche Telekom v. *Commission of the European Communities*: Commission Decision 2003/707/EC of 21 May 2003, Case COMP/C-37.451, OJ L 263, 9–41; Court of First Instance Decision of 10 Apr. 2008, Case T–271/03, OJ C 128, 29, 24/05/2008.
Wanadoo Espana v. *Telefonica*: Commission Decision of 4 July 2007, Case COMP/C-38.784, OJ C 83, 6–9, 02/04/2008.
United Brands v. *Commission of the European Communities*, European Court of Justice Judgment of 14 Feb. 1978, Case 27/76 [1978] ECR 207.

Germany

Decisions of the Federal Cartel Office

Fährhafen Puttgarden (Scandlines Deutschland/Deutsche Bahn): Decision B9–63220–T–199/97, Bp–63220–T–16/98 of 12 Dec. 1999 <http://www.bundeskartellamt.de/wDeutsch/download/pdf/Kartell/Kartell03/B9_199_97_16_98.pdf> (Engl. summary <http://www.bundeskartellamt.de/wEnglisch/News/Archiv/ArchivNews1999/1999_12_23.php>).

RWE/VEW, Decision B8–309/99 of 3 July 2000 <http://www.bundeskartellamt.de/wDeutsch/download/pdf/Fusion/Fusion99/B8_309_99.pdf> (Engl. summary <http://www.bundeskartellamt.de/wEnglisch/News/Archiv/ArchivNews2000/2000_07_04.php>).

TEAG: Decision B11–40–40100–T–45/01 of 14 Feb. 2003 <http://www.bundeskartellamt.de/wDeutsch/download/pdf/Kartell/Kartell03/B11_45_01.pdf> (Engl. summary <http://www.bundeskartellamt.de/wEnglisch/News/Archiv/ArchivNews2003/2003_02_19.php>).

Stadtwerke Mainz: Decision B11–38/01 of the Federal Cartel Office of 17 Apr. 2003 <http://www.bundeskartellamt.de/wDeutsch/download/pdf/Kartell/Kartell03/B11_38_01.pdf> (Engl. summary <http://www.bundeskartellamt.de/wEnglisch/News/Archiv/ArchivNews2003/2003_04_17.php>).

Konsolidierer/Deutsche Post: Decision B9–55/03 of 11 Feb. 2005 <http://www.bundeskartellamt.de/wDeutsch/download/pdf/Kartell/Kartell05/B9–55–03.pdf> (Engl. summary <http://www.bundeskartellamt.de/wEnglisch/News/Archiv/ArchivNews2005/2005_02_14.php>).

Decisions of the Court of Appeal

Fährhafen Puttgarden: OLG Düsseldorf, Decision of 2 Aug. 2000, pub. *Wirtschaft und Wettbewerb (01/2001)/Entscheidungssammlung* DE–R 569–581.

TEAG: OLG Düsseldorf, Decision of 11 Feb. 2004, Kart 4/03 (V), pub. *Wirtschaft und Wettbewerb (05/2004)/Entscheidungssammlung* DE–R 1239–1246.

Stadtwerke Mainz: OLG Düsseldorf, Decision of 30 July 2003, Kart 22/02 (V), pub. *Wirtschaft und Wettbewerb (04/2005)/Entscheidungssammlung* DE–R 1439–1444.

Konsolidierer/Deutsche Post: OLG Düsseldorf, Decision of 13 Apr. 2005, VI–Kart 3/05, pub. *Wirtschaft und Wettbewerb (06/2005)/Entscheidungssammlung* DE–R 1473–1479.

Decisions of the Federal Supreme Court

Valium–Librium: Bundesgerichtshof Decision of 12 Dec. 1976, pub. *Wirtschaft und Wettbewerb/Entscheidungssammlung* BGH 1445 (= BGHZ 68, 23).

Valium II: Bundegerichtshof Decision of 2 Feb. 1980, pub. *Wirtschaft und Wettbewerb (6/1889)/Entscheidungssammlung* BGH 1678–1684 (= BGHZ 76, 142).

Fährhafen Puttgarden: Bundesgerichtshof, Decision KVR 15/01 of 24 Sept. 2002, pub. *Wirtschaft und Wettbewerb (01/2003)/Entscheidungssammlung* DE–R 977–984.

Stadtwerke Mainz: Bundesgerichtshof, Decision KVR 17/04 of 28 June 2005, pub. *Wirtschaft und Wettbewerb (09/2005)/Entscheidungssammlung* DE–R 1513–1519.

European Directives

Initial Directives Providing for Market Liberalization

Commission Directive 90/338/EEC of 28 June 1990 on Competition in the Markets for Telecommunications Services, OJ L 192, 10–16, 25/07/1990.

Directive 96/92/EC of the European Parliament and the Council of 19 Dec. 1996 concerning Common Rules for the Internal Market in Electricity (Electricity Directive), OJ L 27, 20–9, 30/01/1997.

Directive 98/30/EC of the European Parliament and the Council of 22 June 1998 concerning Common Rules for the Internal Market in Natural Gas (Gas Directive), OJ L 204, 1–12, 21/07/1998.

Directive 97/67/EC of the European Parliament and the Council of 15 Dec. 1997 concerning Common Rules for the Development of the Internal Market of Community Postal Services and the Improvement of Quality of Service (Postal Services Directive), OJ L15, 14–25, 21/01/1998.

These initial directives have by now all been amended and replaced by newer directives, available at <http://ec.europa.eu/comm/competition/liberalisation/legislation/legislation.html>.

Regulatory Framework for the Telecommunications Industry: Directives, Guidelines, and Recommendations

Directive 2002/19/EC of the European Parliament and the Council of the European Parliament and the Council of 7 Mar. 2002 on Access to, and Interconnection of, Electronic Communications Networks and Associated Facilities (Access Directive), OJ L 108, 7–20, 24/04/2002.

Directive 2002/20/EC of the European Parliament and the Council of the European Parliament and the Council of 7 Mar. 2002 on the Authorization of Electronic Communications Networks and Services (Authorization Directive), OJ L 108, 21–32, 24/04/2002.

Directive 2002/21/EC of the European Parliament and the Council of the European Parliament and the Council of 7 Mar. 2002 on a Common Regulatory Framework for Electronic Communication Networks and Services (Framework Directive), OJ L 108, 33–50, 24/04/2002.

Directive 2002/22/EC of the European Parliament and the Council of the European Parliament and the Council of 7 Mar. 2002 on Universal Service and Users' Rights Relating to Electronic Communications Networks and Services (Universal Service Directive), OJ L 108, 51–77, 24/04/2002.

Commission Directive 2002/77/EC of 16 Sept. 2002 on Competition in the Markets for Electronic Communication Networks and Services, OJ 249, 21–6, 17/09/2002.

Commission Guidelines on Market Analysis and the Assessment of Significant Market Power under the Community Regulatory Framework for Electronic Communication Networks and Services, 2002/C 165/03, OJ C 165, 6–31, 11/07/2002.

Commission Recommendation of 11 Feb. 2003 on Relevant Product and Service Markets within the Electronic Communications Sector Susceptible to *ex ante* Regulation in Accordance with Directive 2002/21/EC of the European Parliament and the Council of the European Parliament and the Council of 7 Mar. 2002 on a Common Regulatory Framework for Electronic Communication Networks and Services, 2003/311/EC, OJ L114, 45–9, 08/05/2003.

Index

Index

Index

Index